ANYWHERE OR NOT AT ALL

ANYWHERE OR NOT AT ALL

Philosophy of Contemporary Art

PETER OSBORNE

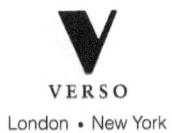

VERSO
London • New York

For Felix

First published by Verso 2013
© Peter Osborne 2013

All rights reserved

The moral rights of the author have been asserted

1 3 5 7 9 10 8 6 4 2

Verso
UK: 6 Meard Street, London W1F 0EG
US: 388 Atlantic Ave, Brooklyn, NY 11217
www.versobooks.com

Verso is the imprint of New Left Books

ISBN-13: 978-1-78168-094-0 (PBK)
ISBN-13: 978-1-78168-113-8 (HBK)

British Library Cataloguing in Publication Data
A catalogue record for this book is available from the British Library

Library of Congress Catologing-in-Publication Data
Osborne, Peter, 1958-
Anywhere or not at all : philosophy of contemporary art / Peter Osborne. – First edition, paperback.
pages cm
Includes bibliographical references and index.
ISBN 978-1-78168-094-0 (pbk. : alk. paper) – ISBN 978-1-78168-113-8 (cloth : alk. paper) 1. Art, Modern–20th century–Philosophy. 2. Art, Modern–21st century–Philosophy. I. Title.
N6490.O733 2013
709.05'101–dc23
2013003012

Typeset in Fournier by Hewer Text UK, Edinburgh
Printed in the United States

Contents

Introduction 1

1 *The fiction of the contemporary* 15
Together in time? – three periodizations of contemporary art – idea, problem, fiction, task – the global transnational, or, the contemporary today – Joseph Bitar – fictionalization of artistic authority/collectivization of artistic fictions: a First Transnational

2 *Art beyond aesthetics* 37
Art versus aesthetics (Jena Romanticism contra Kant) – periodization as historical ontology: postconceptual art – a speculative proposition – an image of romanticism (Benjamin, Schlegel, Lewitt) – fragment and sentence – information and series – process and project

3 *Modernisms and mediations* 71
The double heritage of the modern in art – artistic modernisms: aesthetic, specific, generic – mediations after mediums: nominalism and genre, isms and series – everything, everywhere? Polke and Richter

4 *Transcategoriality: postconceptual art* 99
Smithson and medium (or, against 'sculpture') – the 'interminable avalanche of categories' – ontology of materializations: non-site – conceptual abstraction and 'pure perception'

5 *Photographic ontology, infinite exchange* 117
Distributive unity – the photograph: metonymic model of an imagined unity – digitalization, art and the real (or, anxiety about abstraction) – the visible, the invisible and the multiplication of visualizations

6 *Art space*   133
   Non-places and the textualization of art – architecturalization: three questions – construction and expression – art as displaced urbanism: capitalist constructivism of the exhibition-form – transnationalization: art industry – project space

7 *Art time*   175
   Attention and distraction: boredom as possibility – distracted reception (duration and rhythm) – memory or history? – testimonies: three works – expectation as a historical category (critique of Koselleck) – expecting the unexpected: puncturing the horizon

Acknowledgements   213
Notes   215
Bibliography   255
Image credits   271
Index   273

Introduction

In his joint biography of the French philosophers Gilles Deleuze and Félix Guattari, François Dosse tells the story of the meeting between Deleuze and the painter Francis Bacon, about whom Deleuze had recently written with much enthusiasm in his book *Francis Bacon: Logic of Sensation*. Bacon had apparently responded to the book with equal admiration: 'It's as if this guy were watching over my shoulder while I was painting.' 'What was supposed to be a great meeting', Dosse recounts, 'turned into a disaster.' Deleuze's editor, Joachim Vital, also a great admirer of Bacon, arranged the meeting. He described it as follows:

> The meal was awful, as awful as their discussion . . . They smiled at each other, complimented each other, and smiled again. We were flabbergasted by their platitudes. We tried to salvage the discussion, mentioning Egyptian art, Greek tragedy, Dogen, Shakespeare, Swinburne, Proust, Kafka, Turner, Goya, Manet, Van Gogh's letters to his brother Theo, Artaud, Beckett. Each one tried to take the ball and run with it alone, ignoring the other one.[1]

This often happens when philosophy meets art. When philosophy meets contemporary art, the situation can be even worse. Contemporary art is badly known. To transform our distance from it into that 'unique appearance of a distance, however near it may be',[2] upon which experience of its art character depends, however – to use our ignorance as a spur to knowledge – is more difficult than is suggested by most of the writing that this situation provokes. To make contemporary art the object of some kind of reflective philosophical experience – in an affective engagement with the most fundamental claims made upon us by such art – seems, at times, almost impossible. This is ironic given the well-remarked-upon 'conceptual' character of so much contemporary art. Yet it is precisely this conceptual character that is most often the source of misunderstanding: the idea that such art requires no more than a conceptual interpretation, for example; or that such an understanding is purely or ideally linguistic, in the sense of being reducible to direct propositional expression. 'Straw conceptualism', as this might be called, is one means of sustaining ignorance about contemporary art (which does not mean that there are not some artists whose works are made of such straw). The alternative reduction of art to its aesthetic dimension – pure sensuous particularity – with which the projection of a straw conceptualism is often antithetically associated, is another. The idea that contemporary art is somehow exempt from historical judgement in the present, by virtue of its contemporaneity, is a third.

Perhaps the greatest barrier to a critical knowledge of contemporary art, though, is the common-sense belief that the phrase 'contemporary art' has no *critically* meaningful referent; that it designates no more than the radically heterogeneous empirical totality of artworks produced within the duration of a particular present (our present); that it is, thus, not a proper part of a critical vocabulary at all. Certainly the expression is often used in that way. However, both the conceptual grammar of the phrase – its dependence upon a difference from an art that is not contemporary – and the affirmative inflection of this difference in current usage (contemporary art is more living, more actual, and thus to be valued more highly than other art with which it, paradoxically, shares time) mitigate against such an indifferent empiricism. So what kind of discourse is required to render the idea of contemporary art critically intelligible?

That is the question addressed in this book, in part experimentally, by trying to produce such a discourse. This is a discourse, first, that is neither merely empirical nor temporally inclusive. Not all art that is recently produced, or would call itself or be called by others 'contemporary', can be understood to be contemporary in an art-critically significant sense. 'Contemporary' is, at base, a critical and therefore a selective concept: it promotes and it excludes. To claim something is contemporary is to make a claim for its significance in participating in the actuality of the present – a claim over and against that of other things, some of which themselves may make a similar claim on contemporaneity. So, second, we need a discourse that is responsible to the general critical concept of the contemporary – that is, which engages with the philosophy of time. The notion of the present at stake in art's contemporaneity is not a simple one. Nor does it stand outside of history. This means, third, that such a discourse must be reflexively grounded in the semantic history of 'the contemporary' as a critical category, and attend to the peculiarly privileged role within it of its applications to art. Fourth, such a discourse, though reflexively historically derived, must nonetheless impose certain critical *demands* upon the art that it interprets. The dominant category of modernist art criticism was for many years, up until the 1960s, the category of medium. The subsequent dissolution of the limits of mediums as the ontological bases of art practices, and the establishment of a complex and fluid field of generically artistic practices, has posed new problems of critical judgement to which the concept of the contemporary represents an increasingly powerful response. However, this concept must be *constructed* rather than merely discovered. Finally, in recognition of both the individuality and the contingent historical character of art, a critical discourse of contemporary art can only develop through the interpretative confrontation with individual works. It must participate in the on-going critical history of art, as well as in the revival of a philosophical art criticism. Such, broadly speaking, is the kind of discourse about contemporary art that this book attempts to inhabit and to produce. Its outcome may be polemically condensed into a single and simple, speculative proposition: *contemporary art is postconceptual art*. For reasons of dialectical method, the book as a whole is required to get a sense of precisely what this proposition means in practice and how it functions interpretatively. I shall use the remainder of this introduction to expand upon the intellectual context, method and structure of the book.

Criticism, History, Philosophy

In 1965, as part of his response to a series of 'Charges to the Art Critic' from the directors of a seminar on art education at Pennsylvania State University, and in studied contrast to the growing formalism of the dominant-but-declining modernist criticism of his rival, Clement Greenberg, Harold Rosenberg declared: 'Art criticism today *is* art history, though not necessarily the art history of the art historian.'[3] This assertion appears remarkable today, nearly fifty years later, and not just because of its insistence upon the historical dimension of a practice that has become ever more preoccupied with synchronic relations – in particular, between art and other cultural forms. It is remarkable because, in asserting the independence of the historical dimension of criticism from the discipline of art history, it raises the fundamental but rarely discussed question of precisely what kind of art history art criticism is (or should be), and what its relations to the art history of the art historian might be. This is a question that goes to the heart of thinking about contemporary art, the privileged object of art criticism, not least because it concerns the historical, rather than the merely chronological, determination of contemporaneity. That is to say, it demands a commitment from art criticism to a certain philosophy of time.

Both art criticism and art history have changed since 1965. There are fewer grounds for the condescension of the critic towards the art historian today, and more reasons for a reversal of the relation – in part, because of the historicization of the 1960s itself, with the invention of the burgeoning genre of the history of contemporary art. But the question of the specific character of that art history which art criticism *is*, or might be, has not merely remained unanswered; it has become further obscured from view. Art criticism and art history has each had its own problems to deal with. Intellectually serious criticism of contemporary art remains in the grip of a constantly renewed, self-declared crisis.[4] This crisis is cultural-economic or 'institutional' in origin (contingent upon transformations in the social character of art institutions during the 1980s and 1990s, and their diminishing need for the mediations of a historically oriented criticism), but it is nonetheless intellectual for that. Where it thrives as a cultural force, outside of the academy, art criticism largely concentrates on literary aspects of journalistic presentation and often treats its object as little more than an occasion for communications of a more general kind.[5] Meanwhile, art history has been transformed as a part of broader changes in the disciplines of the arts and humanities in Anglo-American academies. Yet successive widening of the intellectual scope of the discipline – via the new social history of art, feminism, semiotics, psychoanalysis and postcolonial studies, towards the euphoric horizon of studies in 'visual culture' – have not brought it any closer to adequate forms of specifically art-critical judgement, although they have produced a network of discursive affinities between the new art histories and contemporary art itself, at the level of that art's thematic concerns. This is, in part, a result of convergent trends in art-historical and art education. Meanwhile the history of contemporary art – a genre dominated by second-generation *October* art historians – remains largely documentary and reconstructive in character. Its professional formation discourages art-critical judgement, although it often involves a documenting and reconstruction of critical positions held by artists and critics at the time: a kind of criticism by historical proxy. Studies in visual culture often appear closer to art-critical discourse than art-historical ones – indeed, they increasingly occupy institutional spaces of criticism – despite their even greater distance from questions of art judgement. However, this appearance covers over and hence helps to sustain the general absence of historically grounded criticism of contemporary art.

The situation dates back to the failure of the project of a 'critical postmodernism' in the face of the problem of judgement, in the early 1980s. Hal Foster identified the problem early on, but made little headway with it theoretically.[6] Just how blocked it would become can be seen twenty years later in the *October* roundtable discussion, 'The Present Conditions of Art Criticism', in which the very idea of critical judgement caused consternation among the discussants, most of whom still associated it, exclusively, with a late Greenbergian notion of 'quality'.[7] Thierry de Duve attempted to break the impasse with his return to Kant after Duchamp, replacing the former's 'This is beautiful' with the latter's 'This is art', while insisting that the latter continue 'to be read as an aesthetic reflexive judgment with a claim to universality in the strictest Kantian sense', despite the accompanying claim that the term 'art' functions in the judgement as a 'proper name'.[8] Ultimately this foundered on philosophical confusions about both Kant and naming alike. Nonetheless it set a standard for the articulation of art-historical, art-critical and post-Kantian philosophical discourses to which little subsequent work has aspired.

Meanwhile the general theories of representation, both epistemological and political, which predominate in studies of visual culture – usually, if unwittingly, semiotic culturalist variants of the liberal pluralism of US political science – have shown themselves to be singularly ill-suited to grasping the specific and deeply problematic character of the experience of contemporary art. The character and object-domain of the field remain plural and contested, their relations to art unresolved. But the situation is exacerbated, rather than mitigated, by the covert visual essentialism that has inadvertently but inevitably accompanied the formation of the new proto-discipline, in an ironic reprise of the terms of its original adversary, formalist modernism.[9] For the supplement of 'the visual' restores to cultural analysis an aesthetic idealism of vision at the very historical moment in which art's visuality, however pronounced, is its *least* distinguishing trait. Moreover, in so far as 'the visual' is the constituting focus of conceptual interest in visual culture, whether as a given or a construct, it is in principle indifferent to, and hence cuts across, the art/non-art distinction, which cannot be reduced to any particular visual regimes – notwithstanding Michael Fried's generalization of his optical reduction of Greenberg's medium-specific conception of modernist painting.[10] Fried's opticalism is currently enjoying a revival on the back of the popularity of theories of the gaze (which function as one form of theoretical compensation for the aesthetic deficit of the semiotic paradigm), a renewed interest in Greenberg's work, and the resurgence of photographic theory. Yet it remains conceptually removed from the main critical problems posed by the field of contemporary art in general, as Jeff Wall acknowledges in his defence of a Friedian position, by bifurcating the field into two critically discrete domains, the larger of which falls outside the scope of Friedian criticism altogether.[11] Fried's more specifically art-critical contribution to recent debates, alongside those of T.J. Clark, has been historical, in the everyday sense of referring to the art of the past: namely, to develop a criticism through and within conventional art history – a criticism of now 'historical' art – rather than vice versa (that is, to develop the historical aspect of criticism of contemporary art, to which Rosenberg was referring).[12]

Under these conditions, it is useful to approach the questions implicit in Rosenberg's declaration – specifically, *what kind* of art history art criticism (ideally) is and what its relations to 'the art history of the art historian' might be – from a more philosophical standpoint. For, as Rosenberg himself suggested, 'both art criticism and art history need to scan more thoroughly their philosophical substructures' if they are to acquire a more adequate sense of their mutual relations.[13] And in fact, surprisingly in many respects, there has been a resurgence of interest in explicitly philosophical discourses about art over the last two decades as part of the recomposition and diversification of art discourses that has accompanied the industrialization of its institutions. Whether these particular philosophical discourses are adequate to the comprehension and judgement of contemporary art, however, is another matter. While there has been much philosophizing about art, there has been little philosophizing of contemporary art.

The revival of interest in explicitly philosophical discourses about art has taken place against the background of what some have seen as a general 'legitimation crisis' in contemporary art.[14] No doubt, recourse to the established cultural authority of philosophy has played a role here, in association with its relative self-legitimating 'difficulty'. But philosophy's intellectual contribution has been more than ideological. For contrary to the positivistic protestation of Jean-Marie Schaeffer that art itself 'will get along very well on its own' – that is, without critical discourse – this is perhaps less true now than it has ever been. The 'artistic act' may indeed be 'irreducible to the way it legitimates itself', but this means neither that it is non-discursive, nor that the discourses from which it draws its resources are necessarily non-philosophical.[15] Conceptual art, in its canonical sense, surely put paid to any enduring illusions about that – whatever else one may think about it. Indeed, it is precisely the acknowledgement of the immanently philosophical character of contemporary art that led to the revival of the claim, by Arthur Danto among others, that art has ended.[16] Yet this claim could just as easily be read as an inverted (and disavowed) acknowledgement of the inadequacy of the prevailing philosophical discourse on art (namely, 'aesthetics') to the distinctive character of contemporary art: an implicit acknowledgement of inadequacy turned aggressively outwards into a judgement against its cause (namely, the claim of such artworks to the hallowed signifier 'art') and thereby ultimately against contemporaneity itself. Hence Danto's subsequent coinage of the term 'post-historical art'.[17]

Schaeffer returns this claim to its philosophical context when he argues that what he calls 'the speculative tradition' (which runs from Jena Romanticism to Heidegger) misunderstood art from the outset. In this respect, for Schaeffer, the legitimation crisis of contemporary art is the delayed effect of art's philosophical sacralization by Romanticism at the end of the eighteenth century. However, in so far as it derives from a claim for art's autonomy (by virtue of which it is able to *usurp* a certain philosophical function from philosophy itself), this sacralization is actually *constitutive* of 'art' in its modern sense. The aetiology, then, is broadly correct, yet the diagnosis and treatment Schaeffer proposes – a philosophical 'de-sacralization' of art, or what we might call metaphysical disinvestment – are precisely wrong. For, to the extent that there is a legitimation crisis of contemporary art (and one might be excused for believing it oversold, since the market provides sufficient legitimation of its own: 'creative industry'), it is actually a sign of the continuing, if problematic *criticality* of contemporary art – a sign of the fact that art's authority and critical function remain *problems* within contemporary culture, a problem for which art's continuing if uncertain critical and metaphysical dimensions are a conceptual condition.

Danto and Schaeffer represent alternative variants of one primarily negative way in which late analytical philosophy has contributed to recent art-critical discourse. Each is a positivist of a different kind: an analytical-Hegelian positivist and a logical positivist, respectively.[18] However, far more significant has been the affirmative turn towards the conceptual resources of the post-Kantian European philosophical tradition, in the wake of the gradual diffusion of an interest in post-structuralism into Anglo-American art criticism. Heideggerian, Merleau-Pontean and a variety of post-phenomenological approaches – associated with Lyotard and Derrida, and more recently, Deleuze, Jacques Rancière and Alain Badiou – have all enjoyed sustained attention. This has revived interest in the place of art within the German idealist philosophies of the eighteenth and nineteenth centuries: Kant, Schiller, Hegel and the Romantics, but also Schelling, to a lesser degree Schopenhauer, and of course, Nietzsche.

There is little doubt that this return to the post-Kantian European tradition has been, in part, a culturally conservative phenomenon, despite the radicalism associated with its more recent main French proponents. It is 'against Cultural Studies' (in its initial formation, at least) and against certain kinds of *both* 'difficult' and 'popular' contemporary art. But it has also performed a crucial critical function by raising theoretical issues associated with the idea of art in its distinction from other cultural forms of representation – issues that are literally dissolved by the semiotic reductionism and sociologism of most cultural-theoretical approaches. Furthermore, in its recent Rancièrean and (on occasion) Deleuzean guises, it has provided a medium for posing, once again, the now-classical modern question of art's relationship to politics, after a period in which both directly intellectual and political issues were progressively excluded from critical discourse.[19] These are issues that have to be addressed if the dearth of theoretically serious critical writing about contemporary art is to be overcome. However, this turn to the European philosophical tradition as a resource for art-critical discourse has as yet failed to achieve a convincing critical-theoretical purchase on *contemporary* art, because it has failed to come to terms with the decisive historical transformation in the ontology of the artwork that is constitutive of its very contemporaneity. If one considers the works exhibited at the growing number of international biennali, for example, or Documenta – events that in large part constitute the extensive definition of contemporary art – one will find little that most philosophers who write about art are able to engage with concretely in a manner that also engages the discourses and concerns of the art world itself. Although the growing curatorial tendency to aestheticize much recent art, including video work, is one point of convergence.

Thus, while these philosophical discourses on art pose a theoretical challenge to most contemporary art writing, by raising questions about 'aesthetic', about judgement, about subjectivity, about 'nature', and about the ontology of the artwork – which semiotic discourses of cultural theory are unable to ask – they have largely been unable to respond to their own questions other than via discussion of the art of the past. The most they have largely been able to offer – when not declaring art at an end – is thus an artistically conservative recoding of the values of contemporary art. Writings by Heidegger and Merleau-Ponty have played a central role here in the last twenty years, as have the apparently more avant-garde versions of French philosophical theory, which present themselves as philosophies of the new, such as those of Deleuze and Badiou. There has been an inability to grasp contemporary art philosophically in its contemporaneity and hence in its decisive difference from art of the past. The reason for this is two-fold. The first is a continuing conflation of 'art' and 'aesthetic'; the second is an inability to think the concept of art at once philosophically and historically with any kind of futurity.

Art, Aesthetic, Futurity

The first of these reasons, the conflation of art and aesthetic, so thoroughly pervades both philosophical and popular discourses about art that the term 'aesthetics' (*Ästhetik*) has long been used, and continues to be used, as the very name for the philosophical discourse on art – a practice that was already so commonplace in Germany by the 1820s than even Hegel succumbed to it, despite his explicit recognition of its inappropriateness, at the beginning of his *Lectures* on the topic. With the closure of the brief, polemically anti-aesthetic interlude of conceptual art, the slippage has once again largely disappeared from view. In fact, it has recently been actively propounded by Rancière's influential conception of the 'aesthetic regime' of art, by which Rancière appears to believe art is still governed.[20] Badiou's 'inaesthetics', on the other hand, while apparently the opposite of aesthetics, is actually just a paradoxical, alternative formulation of the radically singularizing vision of aesthetic as the philosophical truth of art. As the description of 'the strictly intra-philosophical effects produced by the independent existence of some works of art', inaesthetics is *precisely* what has traditionally been designated by 'aesthetics' as the discourse of the aesthetic conception of art. As Badiou himself puts it, in his third maxim of affirmationist art: 'The truth of which art is the process is always the truth of the sensible *qua* sensible . . .'[21]

The second reason for the failure to grasp art's contemporaneity philosophically – the aforementioned inability to think the concept of art at once philosophically and historically with any kind of futurity – has a more complicated philosophical distribution. It derives, in part, from the aforementioned de-historicizing function of 'aesthetic' in its conceptual distinction from 'art', and in part from a more general refusal of the temporal logic of historical totalization, in its futural, performative or hypothetical dimension, which is inextricable from the *critical* act of *historical* judgements of the present (see Chapter 1, below). Heideggerian ontology of art, for example, whilst philosophically 'anti-aesthetic', is so in the name of a Romanticism of Being, to which 'art' is appended as an 'original' appearing. The history of art is thereby subordinated to an epochal history of Being in which the present's openness to the future functions only as the basis for a 'return to origin'.[22] Ontological in a quite different, but equally unhistorical sense, yet naturalistically futural, Deleuze's proposition that 'the work of art is a being of sensation and nothing else' offers a post-Heideggerian, neo-Nietzschean ontology of art as a diagrammatic construction of forces. Deleuze and Guattari are as insistent on the difference of their ontological concept of 'affect' from 'aesthetic' as they are on that between the concepts of 'percept' and 'perception'. Yet it is precisely the ontological depth of this notion of sensation that makes it only *indifferently* applicable to art, in a principled exclusion of both its conceptual and historical aspects, which parallels the indifference of 'aesthetic' to the art/non-art distinction, while nonetheless functioning meta-critically as the criterion differentiating art from 'philosophy' and 'science'. The problem is that, today, the art/non-art distinction does not primarily concern art's transcendental difference from these other intellectual practices (in a reprise of the neo-Kantian discourse of spheres of validity), but rather its difference from the literality of the everyday.[23]

There is no critically relevant pure 'aesthetics' of contemporary art, because contemporary art is not an aesthetic art in any philosophically significant sense of the term. And there is no critically relevant non-historical ontology of art, because the modern art of which contemporary art remains a distinctive development is irreducibly historical in the temporal structure of its significance. More specifically, it will be argued, *contemporary art* is historically determined as *a postconceptual art*. As such, it actualizes the idea of the work of art to be found in the Jena Romantic philosophy of art, under new historical conditions. The art history that 'art criticism [ideally] *is*' is the art history of a historically reflective (that is, post-Hegelian) Romantic philosophy of art. This was the legacy bequeathed, in an earlier period, to Adorno by Walter Benjamin. It is handed down to us today, developed and transformed (mediated by the subsequent history of modernism) by Adorno's *Aesthetic Theory*.[24]

Aesthetic Theory towers above all other twentieth-century philosophical texts about art. More than any other, it provides us with the philosophical means to clarify the distinction between 'art' and 'aesthetic' in the context of contemporary art. Yet it is itself on occasion not exempt from this terminological confusion, although Adorno is more careful than his English translators.[25] In so far as the present book adopts a systematic philosophical approach to the comprehension and judgement of contemporary art, that approach is thus best described as 'post-Adornian', or at least that of a philosophy of art 'after *Aesthetic Theory*'. But it is a quite specific Adorno that is at stake: not the Kant-orientated Adorno of a recent philosophical aesthetics invested in the recovery of modernist painting,[26] but an Adorno strongly inflected by Benjamin's mediating concept of cultural form, which in Adorno's own work rarely extends beyond the social form of the commodity.[27] Benjamin's writings span the decisive years of early twentieth-century Europe, 1913–40; Adorno's mature work, from *Dialectic of Enlightenment* to *Aesthetic Theory* (1944–69), gave them an afterlife under rather different Euro-American conditions. The 'contemporary art' that still finds its constantly renewed origins in the 1960s begins at the historical point at which Adorno's work breaks off, as a series of new departures, which left behind the impasse of that particular modernism that traced itself back to the latter half of the nineteenth century, within which Adorno himself remained trapped. Writing about such art and its conditions today may set out from what Benjamin and Adorno achieved, but it cannot be restricted merely to extending their work. This threefold *appropriative*, *critical* and *differential* relation to their legacy is marked here, in particular, by the transdisciplinary dynamics of the construction of the book's central concepts: *contemporary, art, aesthetic, modernism, medium (/post-medium/ transmedia), transcategoriality, conceptual art/postconceptual art, distributive unity, art-space* and *art-time*.

This book thus aspires to be philosophical in its interpretative mode, not in a narrowly disciplinary sense, but rather in line with the 'philosophizing beyond philosophy' that Adorno identified as a distinctive feature of Benjamin's thought. This 'beyond philosophy' was, and remains, necessarily at once intellectual and institutional. In Benjamin, its intellectual form was, broadly speaking, that of a modified early German Romantic philosophical model of criticism. Institutionally, it inhabited what critical spaces it could find in the public sphere of intellectual journalism. Adorno mimicked those aspirations, from the safe haven of the university, making occasional sorties into public life (radio), and dealing with academic disciplines negatively, through mutual critique. One task of contemporary criticism is to renew this legacy and develop it further, transforming it again, through critical engagement with the concrete manifestations of an increasingly transnationalized contemporary, postconceptual art. To do so would be to restore to art criticism its central role in constituting the history of art, not simply at the level of its canon, but at the level of the historical temporality of art itself. Today the theoretical register of a more comprehensive intellectual mode of address is less strictly Romantic and more that of a fluid, philosophically reflective transdisciplinarity.[28] The place of philosophy as a discipline within philosophical thought more generally is, one might say, at its best, akin to that of 'laboratory' constructivism within the history of Soviet constructivism: an experimental activity on forms, divorced from life, and the positivities of other knowledges, in the anticipation – or hope, at least – of some subsequent integration into life practice and experience.

It is only possible to grasp the critical issues at stake in contemporary art by moving across (and in the process, reworking the relations between) an array of disciplinary formations, ancient, modern and new: philosophy, art history, art criticism, sociology, psychoanalysis, urban studies, architecture, political theory, literary history and 'theory' per se

– to name but the most prominent. Here, these articulations and crossings are made from the standpoint of a conception of philosophy that recognizes the constitutive role of non-philosophical discourses and experiences in all philosophizing, along with its irreducibility to them. The para-academic, part-public institutions that provided the occasions for the composition of early versions of parts of this book provided the institutional conditions determining their specific transdisciplinarities. I have retained some traces of this trandisciplinary process of construction in the discursive structure of the book, which deliberately exhibits occasional abrupt shifts in discursive register and modes of argumentation, within what I hope is nonetheless an articulated whole.

Loosely Romantic

Chapter 1 deals with the core temporal meaning of 'contemporary art' as the art of contemporaneity. What is 'the contemporary'? Different, often implicit, answers to this question overdetermine the concept of contemporary art. Chapter 2 approaches the postconceptual character of contemporary art, first negatively, through a critique of the conflation of art and aesthetic, and then positively, through the idea of a historical ontology of the artwork. The early Romantic philosophical sources of the structure of postconceptual art are then themselves directly deployed in an interpretation of a work by Sol LeWitt. Chapter 3 provides a critical engagement with some of the philosophical confusions of the literature on modernism. It develops a new philosophical concept of modernism consistent with the idea of the historical ontology of the artwork, and explores the consequences for modernist criticism of the destruction of the ontological significance of 'medium'. Chapter 4 examines the work of the US artist Robert Smithson as an exemplary instance of the transcategorial character of postconceptual art, produced as a consequence of the critical destruction of 'medium'. Chapter 5 explores the necessarily 'distributive' character of the unity of postconceptual works, though an investigation of photographic ontology and the radicalization of its immanent multiplicity of visualizations brought about by digital technology. Chapter 6 outlines the elements for a construction of the concept of art space, within the terms of a historical ontology of urban form. Chapter 7 reflects, correspondingly, on the temporal dimensions of art space – attention, memory, expectation – associated with the idea of the postconceptual work as a 'project', introduced in Chapter 2 and further elaborated through the idea of project space, at the end of Chapter 6.

The structure of the book is, philosophically, loosely Romantic, in the sense that it may be read as a series of seven collections of fragments (hence also as seven fragments), with systematic intent. The radical particularity of the history of art, and the radical nominalism of contemporary art, vitiate any attempt at formally systematic comprehension or presentation, but they demand a constructive systematic intent nonetheless. Whatever unity there is to the book is thus a distributive one, which is carried equally within its parts as across the whole. In order to register the non-conceptual dimension of the historical character of its object ('contemporary art'), I have retained a relationship to the contingencies of the realizations of some particular artistic projects in most chapters. Work by Walid Raad/The Atlas Group provides the artistic bookends that hold the text together. However, the intention is not to construct (or reproduce) a canon, but to develop a critical practice of philosophical interpretation.

1
The fiction of the contemporary

The construction of a critical concept of contemporary art requires, as its premise, the construction of a more general concept of the contemporary. After a brief reflection on the semantics of the contemporary, this chapter outlines such a construction, via the extension of this semantic field to its widest and philosophically most fundamental object: history. The contemporary appears there, first, structurally, as *idea, problem, fiction* and *task*; and second, historically, in its most recent guise as *the time of the globally transnational*. When this conception is transposed onto the artistic field, contemporary art appears, in its strongest critical sense, as the artistic construction and expression of contemporaneity. Two aspects of the artistic articulation of the space-time of the contemporary as a transnational globality are highlighted below, with reference to the work of The Atlas Group, 1999–2005 (to whom I return at the end of the book, in Chapter Seven): the *fictionalization of artistic authority* and the *collectivization of artistic fictions*. Attention to these two constitutive aspects of contemporary art, as an art of contemporaneity in a global context, makes the work of The Atlas Group emblematic of a new kind art, which aspires to articulate the fiction of our incipiently global contemporaneity to its fullest extent.

Together in time?

The root idea of the contemporary as a 'living, existing, or occurring together' in time, specifically, within the periodicity of a human life, has been around a long while. Derived from the medieval Latin *contemporarius*, and the late Latin *contemporalis*, the English 'contemporary' dates from around the mid-seventeenth century. It was only after the Second World War, however, that it began to acquire its current historical and critical connotations through its use, first as a specification of, and then in contrast to, periodizing uses of 'modern'. Perhaps it was the collective sense of survival in the aftermath of a war that had opened up social experience beyond national frontiers that produced in Europe the association of a new historical period with the temporal quality of the shared present itself. The immediate postwar years saw new uses of 'contemporary' in English to denote both a specific style of design ('contemporary design') and the artistic present more generally ('contemporary arts'), in their differences from the preceding period. This is the source of that sense of up-to-dateness with which the term remains predominantly identified in popular usage.

When the Institute of Contemporary Arts (ICA) was founded in London in 1946, for example, it was very up to date indeed. Doubly and paradoxically so, in fact, in so far as it both fed off the residual energies of the pre-war avant-garde, acting out a weakened version of its temporal logic of futurity, and took a step back from that avant-garde's ruptural historical futurity into the more expansive present of a new beginning. In the years immediately following the Second World War, the future was imaged as much by the desire to throw off the restrictions of wartime life and achieve some kind of 'normality' as by the fundamental social changes that the end of the war was to bring about.[1] In the UK, unlike France and Italy, no break with capitalism was envisaged, but rather a different capitalism, of peace and social democratic reconstruction (although 'Cold War' would soon become the new name for peace in Europe). The transformation of 'advanced' art's identification with a radically different future – associated in Britain largely with surrealism – into an identification with a more extended present exchanged the anticipation of an 'end of art' (the famous avant-garde dissolution of art into life) for a focus on interactions between the arts, and popular and technologically advanced arts, like cinema, architecture and advertising in particular. This was characteristic of the work of the Independent Group at the ICA (1952–55), for example, culminating in the *This Is Tomorrow* exhibition at the Whitechapel in 1956. The future, apparently, had already arrived – a standpoint later ironized in Victor Burgin's 1976 photowork, *This Is the Tomorrow You Were Promised Yesterday*.

However, the separating of 'modern' and 'contemporary' that this notion of contemporary arts involves in no way dominated the historical consciousness of the institutional field of art at that time.[2] Rather, the contemporary acted there mainly as a qualification of (rather than a counter to) 'the modern': the contemporary was the most recent modern, but a modern with a moderated, less ruptural futurity. 'Contemporary' was still not enough of a critical concept in its own right by the 1970s to be included in Raymond Williams's influential *Keywords: A Vocabulary of Culture and Society* (1976). And a decade later, when Matei Calinescu updated his book *Faces of Modernity* (1977) into *Five Faces of Modernity* (1987), it was 'postmodernism' that provided the topic for the new chapter, alongside terms already established by the end of the 1930s – 'modernism', 'avant-garde', 'decadence' and 'kitsch' – despite the fact that the chapter on 'The Idea of Modernity' (written in the mid-1970s) still ended with the emphatic declaration that 'the *Querelle des anciens et des modernes* has been replaced by a Quarrel between the moderns and the contemporaries.'[3] By the mid-1980s, postmodernism had become the periodizing term of choice to mark the distance from a now-historical modernism, a distance that had previously been registered by the presentness of the contemporary. For some historicists, like Fredric Jameson, this seemed to imply that the postmodern was 'post-contemporary'.[4] Fortunately, the term did not stick. In fact it has only been in the last ten years, with the decisive discrediting of postmodernism as a coherent critical concept, that 'contemporary' has begun to emerge into the critical daylight from beneath its commonplace function as a label denoting what is current or up to date. Hence the recent rush of writing trying to make some minimal theoretical sense of the concept.[5]

This writing reflects the fact that having emerged as a self-designating periodizing term after 1945, of a quasi-epochal kind (much like 'Renaissance' self-designated its present as a new beginning), thereby gradually condemning the established referents of 'modern' to the past, the structure of contemporaneity is itself changing. Indeed, the very idea of contemporaneity as a *condition* is new. At the same time, the widespread diffusion of the term has placed it in danger of being emptied out of its increasingly complex temporal-existential, social and political meanings, by being treated as a simple label or periodizing category. This is of particular concern because what seems distinctive and important about the changing temporal quality of the historical present over the last few decades is best expressed through the distinctive conceptual grammar of con-temporaneity, a coming together not simply 'in' time, but *of* times: we do not just live or exist together 'in time' with our contemporaries – as if time itself is indifferent to this existing together – but rather the present is increasingly characterized by a coming together of *different but equally 'present'* temporalities or 'times', a temporal unity in disjunction, or a *disjunctive unity of present times*.[6] This problematically disjunctive conjunction is covered over by straightforward, historicist use of 'contemporary' as a periodizing term, in the manner in which it is encountered in mainstream art history – for example, in its stabilization of the distinction between modern and contemporary art. Although, within this discourse, as a register of the continual historical movement of the present, we nonetheless find at least three competing periodizations of contemporary art, three overlapping genealogies or historical strata, three differently extended senses of the present, within the wider time-span of a Western modern art. Each is constructed from the standpoint of the rupture of a particular historical event, and each privileges a particular geopolitical terrain.

Three periodizations of contemporary art

The distinction between modern and contemporary was first stabilized after 1945 not in Western art history, but in Eastern Europe, as part of the Soviet reaction against the categories of modernity and modernism.[7] For Georg Lukács, for example, in the 1950s, socialist realism was 'contemporary realism', since the actuality of socialism defined the historical present.[8] The City Gallery of Contemporary Art in Zagreb, founded in 1954, was one of the very few art institutions to use the term before the 1960s (it became the Museum of Contemporary Art, Zagreb, in 1998). In Eastern Europe, 'modernity' was considered an ideological misrepresentation of the historical time of capitalism, covering over its internally antagonistic class forms of historical temporality and representation. Later, in the West, as the distinction between modern and contemporary gradually took hold, it was less of a polemically political one, and more of a straightforward historicist partitioning of chronological time – which is not to say that it was thereby any less ideological in its implicit theoretical structure and its effects. It was not until the 1980s, in fact, that 'art after 1945' was recoded by art institutions and art publishers as 'contemporary art', joining the end of a queue of major historical movements running from the Renaissance through Baroque, Neoclassicism and Romanticism, up to its predecessor, Modern Art.[9] This was an acknowledgement not only that a particular canon of modern art increasingly belonged to the past, but also that the art of the present was no longer to be identified with modernism, in its formalist, medium-specific sense. A wider range of 'art since 1945' could thus be embraced within an extended present, which engulfed and recoded the postwar canon of modernist formalism itself. 'Contemporary' thereby became the art-institutional successor to 'modern' at precisely the same time that, in critical writing, a variety of what had initially been grasped as 'post-formalist' practices were being reconceptualized as 'postmodern'.

1945 represents the beginning of the international hegemony of US art institutions, and thereby of US art itself, of the incorporation of the waste products of pre-war avant-garde practices into the museums, and of the institutional advance of the so-called neo-avant-gardes. Chronologically, this is the broadest periodization of contemporary art currently in use. It is in various respects too broad, while at the same time being, in others, too narrow. Do we really still inhabit the same present, art-historically and art-critically, as Abstract Expressionism, for example? Alternatively, is the Duchamp of the years of the First World War really so distant from us as to fall outside the category of 'contemporary art' altogether, as this chronological periodization is forced to insist? Such problems draw attention to the inadequacy of any merely chronological conception of the time of art history. Nonetheless, even within such crude periodizations, there is always a suppressed qualitative aspect: the moment of the break, in this case, the beginning of the period at issue, the beginning of the postwar. Reflecting on this moment from the standpoint of the present raises a question that is familiar from Japanese debates but is rarely asked in Europe or the US: namely, when will the postwar end? Has it not, in fact, already ended?[10] It is those offering an explicitly affirmative answer to this latter question who have the sharpest, most critically delineated sense of the contemporary, represented by the third periodization (below). On the broad definition, however, we are still essentially living, art-critically, in an extended postwar.

The geographical terrain of this periodization is formally worldwide – marked as it is by the end of a 'world' war. Yet it is effectively an art world seen and selected from the standpoint of the USA – that is, one side of the Cold War inaugurated by the postwar. The postwar definition of the contemporary, until very recently, effectively excluded the 'actually existing socialist' states (1945–90) from historical time, recognizing only an externally intelligible artistic 'dissidence' based on the continuation of past modernist legacies or the importation of then-current Western forms. Art-historically, this was made possible by the Museum of Modern Art's institutional appropriation of the work of the pre-war European avant-gardes during the 1930s, which allowed for the subsequent narration of postwar US abstract art as the authentic continuation of this project, and thereby of the 'Western' artistic tradition as a whole. In artistic terms, the dominant version of this periodization thus privileges the heritage of abstraction.[11] It has tended to read later work in these terms, to the detriment of the conceptual and political heritage of Duchamp, Dada and Surrealism – although the canon is now gradually expanding. (Dadaism and Surrealism appear on Alfred H. Barr's famous flowchart only in so far as they feed into 'non-geometrical abstraction' – that is, as essentially painterly traditions.)

If the first periodization is geopolitically epochal in character – registering the weight within Western art history of the broadest political determinations – yet also parochial in both its backward-lookingness and restricted geographical focus, the second periodization focuses more tightly, in its framing terms, on developments immanent to artistic practices and their art-institutional recognition. This is a periodization that conceives contemporary art as beginning some time in the early 1960s, in that ontological break with prevailing object-based and medium-specific neo-avant-garde practices carried out by a range of new types of work, of which performance, minimalism and conceptual art appear, retrospectively, as the most decisive.[12] From this point of view, contemporary art *is* post-conceptual art.[13] The 'event' marking this rupture is not an empirical, punctually datable one, but rather 'the Sixties' itself – that complex conjunction of social, political and cultural radicalisms that swept through not just North America and Western Europe,[14] but whole swathes of the globe – from South America to South-East Asia. Politically, it is often conveniently epitomized in the figure of '1968', although its artistically decisive manifestations were earlier in the decade. This was also the decade of an initial internationalization of contemporary art *within* its largely North American and residually European hegemonic frame. Japanese and South American artists, in particular, were incorporated into an internationalizing US hegemony.

Despite a conceptual focus on the ontology of the work of art, which derives from a predominantly US narrative frame, this periodization is thus, ironically, more geopolitically expansive in its sense of the artistic terrain than the previous one – although it too has incorporated 'Second World' (state socialist) art of the 1960s and 1970s from the Soviet Union, Eastern Europe and China largely only retrospectively (after 1989), as a supplement, rather than as contributing constitutively to art's contemporaneity. One reason for the expansiveness of this standpoint is that the opening of this period coincides with the intensification of anti-imperialist struggles for national liberation, which had decisive domestic political effects within Western states. Another reason, more simply, was the development of commercial air travel and communications technology. Nonetheless, it is the radically dispersed, materially distributed character of the art – associated with its incorporation of non-traditional means, often from the mass media – that is the unifying principle of the periodization, enacting a decisive break with what went before. Here, contemporary art deploys an open infinity of means, and operates with an institutionally- and philosophically-grounded generic conception of 'art' that exceeds the historically received conventions that had previously defined artistic mediums. A significant amount of the institutionally validated art currently produced still fails to attain contemporaneity in this art-critically immanent sense.

The third main periodization of contemporary art one finds in current art-critical discourse is more immediate: 'art after 1989' – symbolically, the breaching of the Berlin Wall. With respect to the Cold War, 1989 is the dialectical counterpart to 1945. After 1989, the Cold War is finally over. But with respect to world politics, 1989 is the dialectical counterpart to 1917 (the Russian Revolution). If 1917–89 is a meaningful 'period' in world history (the epoch of historical communism) the argument goes, then surely 'contemporary art should now be redefined as art after 1989? Politically, '1989' signifies the end of historical communism (or 'actually existing socialism'), the dissolution of independent Left political cultures, and the decisive victory of a neo-liberal globalization of capital – incorporating the current engine of the world economy, capitalism in China.[15]

This corresponds artistically to three convergent features of institutionally validated art since the 1980s: the apparent closure of the historical horizon of the avant-garde; a qualitative deepening of the integration of autonomous art into the culture industry; and a globalization and transnationalization of the biennale as an exhibition form.[16] Of these, it is the first that is most problematic, since the question of the avant-garde is now as much that of the critical construction of historical meanings as it is of any formal, identifiable features of the works themselves. It is further complicated by the existence of two distinct forms of the avant-garde.

Following Peter Bürger's *Theory of the Avant-Garde*,[17] it has become conventional to distinguish the conjointly artistic and political perspective of the classical or 'historical' avant-gardes of the early twentieth century from the purely artistic 'neo'-avant-gardes of the 1940s and 1950s, which attempted to sustain the avant-garde model of art history independently of its relations to socio-economic and political change. It is this neo-avant-garde art-historical consciousness that is most directly challenged by the sheer diversity of forms of internationally exhibited work produced since 1989 – in fact, since the 1960s. On the other hand, the more socially and politically complex perspective of the historical avant-gardes was also *revived* in the 1960s and 1970s by a range of work, which was either directly political in character, had strong anti-art elements, or embodied art-institutional and social critique. Such work continued to derive its historical intelligibility from its claim on the future, albeit, increasingly, an abstractly projected (imaginary) future, or mere horizon, rather than a politically actual one. These kinds of work – suspended between the perspectives of the historical- and neo-avant-gardes – continue into the immediate present. Nonetheless, international art-institutions rarely present contemporary work in terms of the historical consciousness of the avant-garde, other than in a 'retro' mode, borrowed from some of this work itself (by the Russian group *Chto Delat*, for example).

One reason for this is that the increasing integration of autonomous art into the culture industry has imposed a more immediate and pragmatic sense of historical time onto the institutional framing of contemporary work – although this remains a profoundly contradictory process. For this integration is by no means an outright negation of autonomy by commodification and political rationality, so much as a new systemic functionalization of autonomy itself – a new kind of 'affirmative culture'.[18] This new systemic functionalization of autonomy (this new 'use' of art's 'uselessness') corresponds to the global transnationalization of the biennale as an exhibition form, and its integration into the logics of international politics and regional development. From this point of view, art must reflectively incorporate this new context into its procedures if it is to remain 'contemporary'. From the standpoint of this last periodization, then, our three periodizations of contemporary art are not so much self-sufficient and competing alternative definitions as different intensities of contemporaneity, different interpenetrating historical strata. Each may become closest to the surface on particular occasions, but always as mediated by its relations to the other two. It is this differential historical temporality of the present that renders dynamic, in any particular instance, a work's articulation of the structural features that characterize contemporary art ontologically, according to the second definition.

Idea, problem, fiction, task

The root idea of the contemporary as a living, existing, or occurring together 'in' time, then, requires further specification as a *differential* historical temporality of the present: a coming together of different but equally 'present' times, a temporal unity in disjunction, or a disjunctive unity of present times. As a historical concept, the contemporary thus involves a projection of unity onto the differential totality of the times of human lives that are in principle, or potentially, present to each other in some way, at some particular time – paradigmatically, now, since it is the living present that provides the model of contemporaneity. That is to say, the concept of the contemporary projects a *single historical time of the present*, as a living present: a common, albeit internally disjunctive, present historical time of human lives. 'The contemporary', then, is another way of referring to the historical present. Such a notion is inherently problematic but increasingly inevitable.

It is problematic, theoretically, first because it is an 'idea' in Kant's technical sense of the term: its object (the total conjunction of present times) is beyond possible experience. It is thus an object that exists only 'in the idea' and is hence the site of a problem that requires investigation. All ideas, as concepts of the totality or the unconditioned, are problematic for Kant.[19] Such concepts depend upon an 'as if' – Kant also calls them 'heuristic fictions' – which cannot be objectively validated, but which may legitimately be used to 'regulate' experience, so long as they are not contradicted by it. This is the 'hypothetical' employment of pure reason: the idea of the contemporary hypothetically projects an internally differentiated and dynamic spatial-temporal unity of human practices within the present. As such it is a hypothetical presupposition of any possible 'human science'.[20]

However, the concept of the contemporary is problematic theoretically not only because it goes beyond possible experience (in the narrow Kantian sense of experience as the experience of spatio-temporally given objects of knowledge); it is also problematic, in a more fundamental sense, because of its attribution of unity to the temporal mode of the present, however hypothetical, as such. As Heidegger famously argued, 'the present' itself, by itself, in its presentness, cannot be considered some kind of self-contained temporal receptacle for objects of experience, since it only ex-ists as the differentiation or fractured togetherness of the other two temporal modes (past and future), under the priority of its futural dimension.[21] The concept of the contemporary thus projects into presence a temporal unity that is actually, in principle, futural or anticipatory. The concept of the contemporary is thus inherently speculative, not just because it is epistemologically problematic in its application to history, but because it is *structurally anticipatory*, as such. For Heidegger, it is this essential futurity that allows one to be 'for' one's time.[22]

Third, within the terms of these two problematic theoretical aspects, as a historical concept, the contemporary is also empirically problematic. At the level of the empirical investigation of the contemporary as a problematic concept (the possibility of problematic concepts, Kant says, 'has to be investigated'),[23] the relational totality of the currently coeval times of human existence undoubtedly remains fundamentally socially disjunctive. There is no socially actual shared subject-position of, or within, our present from the standpoint of which its relational totality could be *lived* as a whole, in however epistemologically problematic or temporal-existentially fragmented anticipatory form. Nonetheless, the concept of the contemporary functions *as if* there is. That is, it functions as if the speculative horizon of the unity of human history had been reached. In this respect, the contemporary is a utopian idea, with both negative and positive aspects. Negatively, it involves a disavowal; positively, it is both an act of the productive imagination and the establishment of a task.

The concept of the contemporary involves a disawoval – a disavowal of its own futural, anticipatory or speculative basis – to the extent to which it projects into existence an *actual* total conjunction of times. This is a disavowal of the futurity of the present by its very presentness; essentially, it is a disavowal of politics. More positively, it is a productive act of imagination to the extent to which it performatively projects a non-existent unity onto the disjunctive relations between coeval times. In this respect, in rendering present the absent time of a unity of present times, all constructions of the contemporary are *fictional*, in the sense of fiction as a narrative mode. Epistemologically, one might say, the contemporary marks that point of indifference between historical and fictional narrative that has been associated, since the critique of Hegel, with the notion of speculative experience itself.[24] More specifically, the contemporary is an *operative* fiction: it *regulates the division* between the past and the present within the present. And it does so, in part, not simply by recognizing certain contemporaneities, but by projecting contemporaneity – the establishment of connections within the living present – as a task to be achieved. (In Kant, the ideas of reason ground, first, morality, and later, historical politics, as infinite tasks.)

We can see this regulation at work in, for example, the transformation of the effective meaning of 'generation'. Based in the periodicity of the human life span, 'contemporary' is at base a generational term: generations share time. However, in the wake of modernity's subjection of the temporality of generations to the destruction of tradition (the handing down of knowledge and practices between generations), and its consequent subjection of the temporal rhythms of the social transmission of knowledge and experience to those of communications technologies, the social actuality of 'generational' change no longer just corresponds to human generations, but equally, possibly predominantly, to 'generations' of *technologies*,[25] to which all human generations are subjected, albeit unequally. And these generations are of shorter and shorter duration. The fiction of the contemporary is thus becoming, in this respect at least, progressively contracted. The present of the contemporary is becoming shorter and shorter.[26]

It is the fictional 'presentness' of the contemporary that distinguishes it from the more structurally transitory category of modernity, the inherently self-surpassing character of which identifies it with a permanent transitoriness, familiar in the critical literature since Baudelaire. In this respect, the contemporary involves a kind of internal retreat of the modern to the present. As one recent commentator has put it, contemporaneousness is 'the pregnant present of the original meaning of *modern*, but without its subsequent contract with the future.'[27] This fictive co-presentness of a multiplicity of times associates the contemporary – at a deep conceptual level – with the theological culture of the image. In Michael Fried's famous phrase – from which all sense of the imaginary, fictitious character of the experience is absent – 'presentness is grace'.[28]

If modernity projects a present of permanent transition, forever reaching beyond itself, the contemporary fixes or enfolds such transitoriness within the duration of a conjuncture, or at its most extreme, the stasis of a present moment. Such presentness finds its representational form in the annihilation of temporality by the image. It is in the photographic and post-photographic culture of the image that the contemporaneity of the contemporary is most clearly expressed. The image interrupts the temporalities of the modern and nature alike. It is with regard to the disruption of these normative rhythms that the contemporary appears as 'heterochronic' – the temporal dimension of a general heteronomy or multiplicity of determinations – or even as 'untimely' (*unzeitgemässe*), in Nietzsche's sense.[29] The contemporary marks both the moment of disjunction (and hence antagonism) within the disjunctive unity of the historical present and the existential unity of the disjunctiveness of presentness itself.

This disjunctive, antagonistic unity of the contemporary is not just temporal, but equally – indeed, in certain respects primarily – spatial. This is the fourth respect in which the concept of the contemporary is problematic: the problem of the disjunctive unity of times is the problem of the unity and disjunction of social space – that is, in its most extended form, the problem of the *geopolitical*. The idea of the contemporary poses the problem of the disjunctive unity of space-time, or the *geopolitically historical*. The temporal dialectic of the new, which gives qualitative definition to the historical present (as the standpoint from which its unity is constructed), but which the notion of the contemporary cuts off from the future, must be mediated with the complex global dialectic of spaces, if any kind of sense is to be made of the notion of the historically contemporaneous. That is, *the fiction of the contemporary is necessarily a geopolitical fiction*. This considerably complicates the question of periodization: the durational extension of the contemporary 'backwards', into the recent chronological past, at any particular time. This durational extension of the contemporary (as a projected unity of the times of present lives) imposes a constantly shifting periodizing dynamic that insists upon the question of *when the present begins*. But this question has very different answers depending upon *where* you are thinking from, geopolitically.[30]

The historical motto, 'to each present, its own prehistory,' must thus be interpreted to mean: to each geopolitically differentiated construction of the present, its own prehistory. In this respect, we can distinguish *the subject* of the contemporary (the contemporary's 'I') from that of a classical modernity. For as Ricoeur has put it, the 'full and precise formulation' of the concept of modernity is achieved only 'when one says and writes "our" modernity', at the level of the concept of history.[31] And one can only say and write 'our' modernity at the level of history, in the collective singular, by positing, following Hegel, an 'I that is we and we that is I' as its speculative absolute subject.[32] When one says or writes 'our' contemporaneity, on the other hand, one is referring to the temporal conjunction of differential subject positions, differential temporalities, which produces not 'a we that is I', but a we that is a conjunction of a plurality of temporally co-present 'I's. The subject of modernity (and there is ultimately a singular one) has a 'collective' dialectical unity; the equally speculative, but differently unitary, subject of the contemporary has a 'distributive' unity.[33] In this respect, one might suggest, the discourse of nationally or regionally specific 'multiple modernities' can achieve theoretical coherence at the level of the whole (history) only in articulation with the concept of the contemporary – despite the discrete conceptual content of modernity and contemporaneity as temporal ideas. For the idea of an immanently differential *global modernity* presupposes a certain global contemporaneity as the ground of its immanent production of the temporal differential of the new.

For all these theoretical problems of the fictive character of temporal unity and the disjunction of spatial standpoints, however, constructions of the contemporary increasingly appear as inevitable, because growing global social interconnectedness gives meaningful content to these fictions, filling out their speculative projections with empirical material ('facts'), thereby effecting a transition from fictional to historical narrative. This is the domain of the booming genre of global histories of the present (Hobsbawm, Arrighi, Gunder-Frank, et al.).[34] Such histories are as performative as they are empirical (that is, they are constructions), but they aspire to an empirically consistent hypothetical unity of the present, beyond pure heteronomy or multiplicity. In this respect, the concept of the contemporary has indeed acquired, in practice, the regulative necessity of a Kantian 'idea'. Increasingly, 'the contemporary' has the transcendental status of a condition of the historical intelligibility of social experience.

The global transnational, or, the contemporary today

And increasingly, the fiction of the contemporary is primarily a global or a planetary fiction. More specifically, the fiction of a global transnationality has recently displaced the 140-year hegemony of an internationalist imaginary, 1848–1989, which came in a variety of political forms. This is a fiction – a projection of the temporary unity of the present across the planet – grounded in the contradictory penetration of received social forms ('communities', 'cultures', 'nations', 'societies' – all increasingly inadequate formulations) by capital, and their consequent enforced interconnection and dependency. In short, today, the contemporary (the fictive relational unity of the historical present) is transnational because our modernity is that of a tendentially global capital. Transnationality is the putative socio-spatial form of the current temporal unity of historical experience.[35]

As Gayatri Spivak has argued, 'demographic shifts, diasporas, labour migrations, the movements of global capital and media, and processes of cultural circulation and hybridization' have rendered the twin geopolitical imaginary of a culturalist postcolonial nationalism and a metropolitan multiculturalism at best problematic and at worse redundant. Rather,

> What we are witnessing in the postcolonial and globalizing world is a return of the demographic, rather than territorial, frontiers that predate and are larger than capitalism. These demographic frontiers, responding to large-scale migration, are now appropriating the

contemporary version of virtual reality and creating the kind of parastate collectivities that belonged to the shifting multicultural empires that preceded monopoly capitalism.[36]

Territorial frontiers or borders (basically, nation-states) are subject to erosion by 'globalization' in two ways. First, they have an increasing albeit still restricted physical 'permeability'. 'Borders are easily crossed *from* metropolitan countries, whereas attempts to enter from the so-called peripheral countries encounter bureaucratic and policed frontiers, altogether more difficult to permeate.'[37] People mainly cross borders from the so-called periphery to the metaphorical centre only as variable capital – including as art labour. (Art is a kind of passport. In the new transnational spaces, it *figures* a market utopia of free movement, while in actuality it embodies the contradiction of the mediation of this movement by capital.) Second, informational technology makes possible the constitution of new social subjects, and – equally importantly – the reconstruction of the unity of fragmented older ones, across national frontiers, in a new way.

But how is this geopolitically complex contemporaneity to be experienced or represented? And, in particular, how is it to be experienced through or as art? The issue is less 'representation' than 'presentation' (less *Vorstellung* than *Darstellung*): the interpretation of what is, through the construction of new wholes out of its fragments and modalities of existence. This is as much a manifestation of the *will* to contemporaneity – a will to force the multiplicity of coeval social times together – as it is a question of representation. Art is a privileged cultural carrier of contemporaneity, as it was of previous forms of modernity. With the historical expansion, geopolitical differentiation and temporal intensification of contemporaneity, it has become critically incumbent upon any art with a claim on the present to situate itself, reflexively, within this expanded field. The *coming together of different times* that constitutes the contemporary, and the *relations between the social spaces* in which these times are embedded and articulated, are thus the two main axes along which the historical meaning of art is to be plotted. In response to this condition, in recent years, the inter- and transnational characteristics of an art space have become the primary markers of its contemporaneity. In the process, the institutions of contemporary art have attained an unprecedented degree of historical self-consciousness and have created a novel kind of cultural space – with the international biennale as its already tiring emblem – dedicated to the exploration through art of similarities and differences between geopolitically diverse forms of social experience that have only recently begun to be represented within the parameters of a common world.[38]

If art is to function critically within these institutions, as a construction and expression of the contemporary – that is, if it is to appropriate the de-temporalizing power of the image as the basis for new historical temporalizations – it must relate directly to the socio-spatial ontology of its own international and transnational sites and relations. It is at this point that the critical historical significance of the transformation of the ontology of the artwork, effected in the course of the last fifty years (our second periodization of contemporary art, above), from a craft-based ontology of mediums to a postconceptual and transcategorical ontology of materializations, comes into its own.

This leads me to my main thesis, which at this point I can do no more than baldly state: it is the *convergence* and *mutual conditioning* of historical transformations in the ontology of the artwork (Chapters 2 and 4) and the social relations of art space (Chapter 6) – a convergence and mutual conditioning that has its roots in more general economic and communicational processes – that makes contemporary art possible, in the emphatic sense of an art of contemporaneity. These convergent and mutually conditioning transformations take the common negative form of processes of 'de-bordering' (the Germans would say, *Entgrenzung*): on the one hand, the de-bordering of the arts as mediums, and on the other, the de-bordering of the national social spaces of art. More positively, one might say that these de-borderings have opened up distinctive new possibilities for the practices of a generic 'art', on the one hand, and those of an in-principle-infinite exchange, on the other.[39] This has been an extraordinarily complicated and profoundly contradictory historical process, in which artists, art-institutions and markets have negotiated the politics of regionalism, postcolonial nationalism and migration, in order to overwrite the open spatial logic of post-conceptual art with global political-economic dynamics.

But how can 'art' occupy, articulate, critically reflect and transfigure so global a transnational space? Only, I think, if the subject-position of its production is able to reflect – that is, to construct and thereby express – something of the structure of 'the contemporary' itself. The work of The Atlas Group (1999–2005) is emblematic here because it focuses attention on two distinctive and related aspects of this construction of a subject-position of the contemporary: fictionalization and collectivization.

Joseph Bitar

Joseph Bitar, we are told in the opening section of a 2004 video work by The Atlas Group/Walid Raad entitled *We Can Make Rain but No One Came to Ask*, 'lives in Beirut and is the city's only resident explosives expert . . . [He] has been injured several times in his long career and was decorated in 1952 by Guy Mollet. Booby traps, mines and other murderous or incapacitating devices have no secrets for Joseph, who has plenty to do in today's Beirut.'[40] The text is laid over a photograph – we are

THE FICTION OF THE CONTEMPORARY

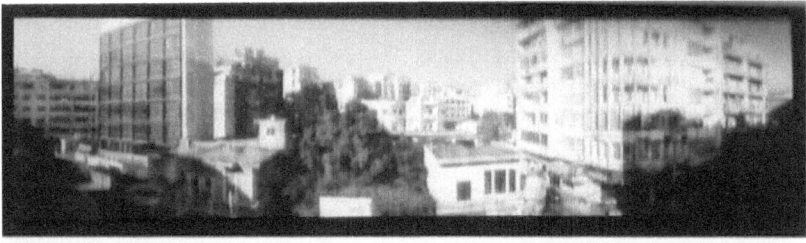
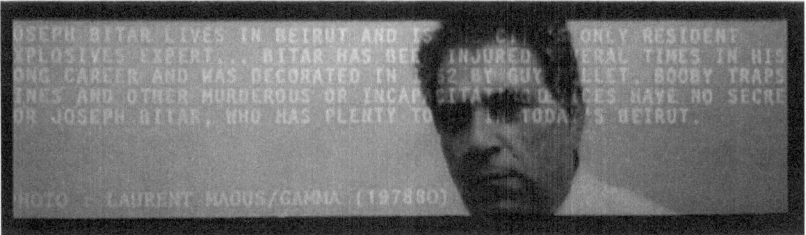

Fig 1: The Atlas Group in collaboration with Walid Raad, Bilal Khbeiz, and Tony Chakar,
We Can Make Rain But No One Came to Ask, 2006

invited to presume of Bitar – credited to Laurent Maous of the Gamma agency, and provided with the classification number, 197880 (Fig. 1).

The figure of Bitar frames and gives narrative meaning to the video that follows, which is largely made up of disjunctive footage from a panoramic camera located at a road junction in the Beirut suburb that is pictured above Bitar in the opening montage. The footage documents the passing of cars and the transformation of the bomb-damaged built environment. Looking out at us as we look onto the suburban panorama, and back at him, a subtle transfer of gazes effects the displacement of Bitar's look from us to the panorama, providing our gaze with his eyes. As a result, the rest of the work appears to us, in large part, through Bitar's eyes – the eyes of someone with expertise in explosives.

This way of presenting contemporary Beirut and, more broadly, the recent history of Lebanon, from the dual standpoint of a fictional character and a documentation of explosions, is familiar from earlier work by The Atlas Group. It dates back to what is labelled 'Volume 38' of the Notebooks in the Fakhouri File in The Atlas Group Archive, *Already Been in a Lake of Fire*: 145 cut-out photographs of cars, allegedly corresponding to the make, model and colour of every car used as a bomb in the twenty-five years of wars in Lebanon between 1975 and 1991.[41] It is probably most familiar from various presentations of material from the Group file, *Thin Neck*; in particular, *My Neck is Thinner Than a Hair: A History of Car Bombs in the Lebanese Wars, Volumes 1–245* (Fig. 2), parts of which were shown at the 2003 Venice Biennale, for example. One hundred four mixed-media works from this document make up the whole of Volume 2 of The Atlas Group's collected works.⁴² In these linked series of works, including the more recent, but rather different, 'A Disclosure' (2007) – about the assassination of the Lebanese Prime Minister Rafik Hariri on Valentine's Day 2005 – the last three decades in the history of Lebanon is condensed into a history of exploding cars. Bitar's surprisingly long life – decorated fifty-five years ago, but still with plenty of work in 'today's Beirut' – encompasses this history, acting as a further condensation: a condensation of the history of the Lebanese car bomb into the figure of Bitar.⁴³

The character of Fakhouri (compiler and annotator of the earlier cut-out photographs of exploded cars) was established at the outset of

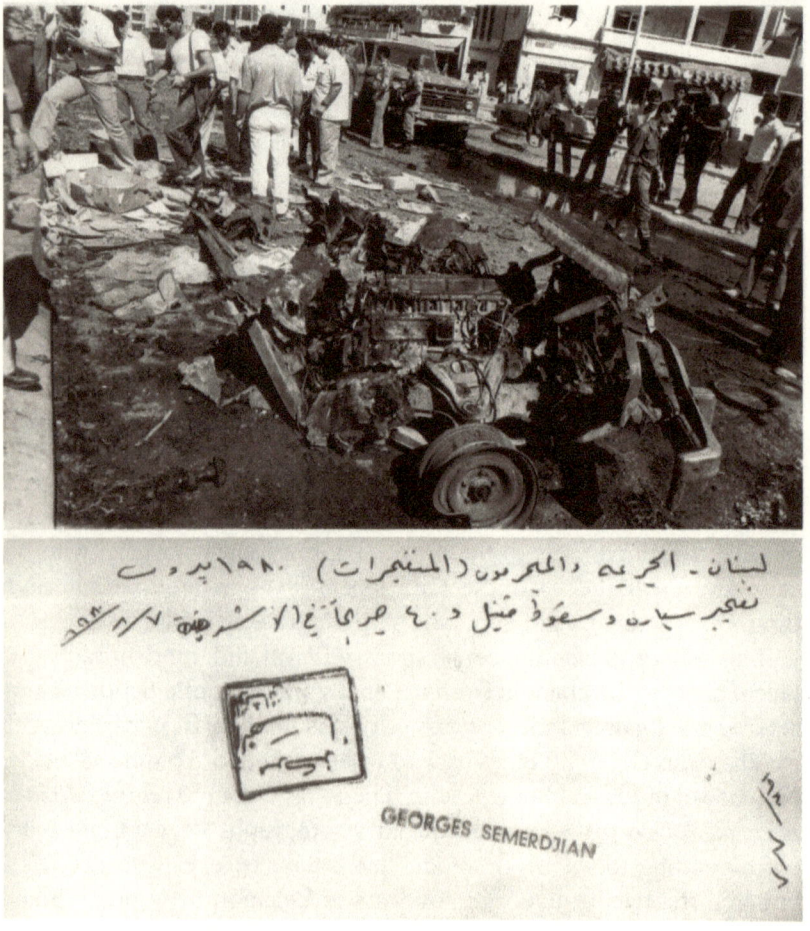

Date: 7 August 1980
Photographer | Original Archive: Georges Semerdjian | An-Nahar Research Center (Beirut, Lebanon)
Subjects and/or Keywords: Lebanon_Crimes_Criminals (Explosions)_1980_Beirut

Fig 2: The Atlas Group in collaboration wiih Walid Raad, *My Neck Is Thinner Than a Hair*. Document attributed to the Atlas Group. Date (attributed): 2001. Date (production): 2003.

The Atlas Group's activities in 1999, in a transitional work that was first attributed to Walid Raad (when it was published as a project in *Public Culture*) and subsequently appeared in the name of the group: *Missing Lebanese Wars* (Fig. 3), a collection of newspaper clippings of the winning horses in weekly races allegedly bet upon by 'the major historians of the Lebanese war'. These are taped into a notebook and embellished by Fakhouri with details of 'the race's distance and duration; the time of the winning horse; calculations of averages; the historians' initials with their respective bets; the time discrepancy predicted by the winning historian' – they were betting not on the winners, but on the timing of the track photographer's photograph of the winner, relative to the winning line – along with 'short descriptions of the winning historian'. Fakhouri had previously appeared in the acknowledgements to an earlier work, *Miraculous Beginnings* (published in 1997), attributed to the Arab Research Institute in collaboration with Fouad Boustani and Walid Raad, in the foreword by Boustani, director of the Beirut Photographic Centre.[44]

In the presentation of *Missing Lebanese Wars*, Fakhouri is claimed to have been 'the most renowned historian of Lebanon', to have died in 1993, and 'to everyone's surprise' to have 'bequeathed hundreds of documents to The Atlas Group for preservation and display'. This surprise was perhaps not least occasioned by the fact that he died some six years prior to the formation of the Group. Systematically aberrant chronologies are a distinctive feature of all of the narratives presented in The Atlas Group's work, and the main sign of their fictional status.

Fakhouri is one of three characters to whom files are attributed in the Group Archive – the other two being Souheil Bachar (a Lebanese man held hostage for ten years between 1983 and 1993, who is said to have spent a brief period with the famous British and American hostages) and Operator #17. Souheil Bachar is heard on the soundtrack of the two videos *Hostage: The Bachar Tapes*, #17 and #31 (two of a purported fifty-three short videos made by Bachar, and the sole items in his file), which narrate a secret erotic dimension of the hostages' relations with their captors. Operator #17 is a Lebanese security agent who regularly turns his surveillance camera from the promenade in Beirut towards the sunset, producing a video document, which The Atlas Group entitled *I Only Wish I Could Have Wept*.

Fakhouri's identity is fixed by a series of twenty-four photographs of him on a trip to Paris and Rome in 1958 and 1959. Yet in 2006, he returned from the dead to collaborate with The Atlas Group, on a project called 'Vituperative Speeches', published in the NYU drama review *TDR*, which also published his correspondence with its editor.[45] As will already be clear, a significant proportion of Atlas

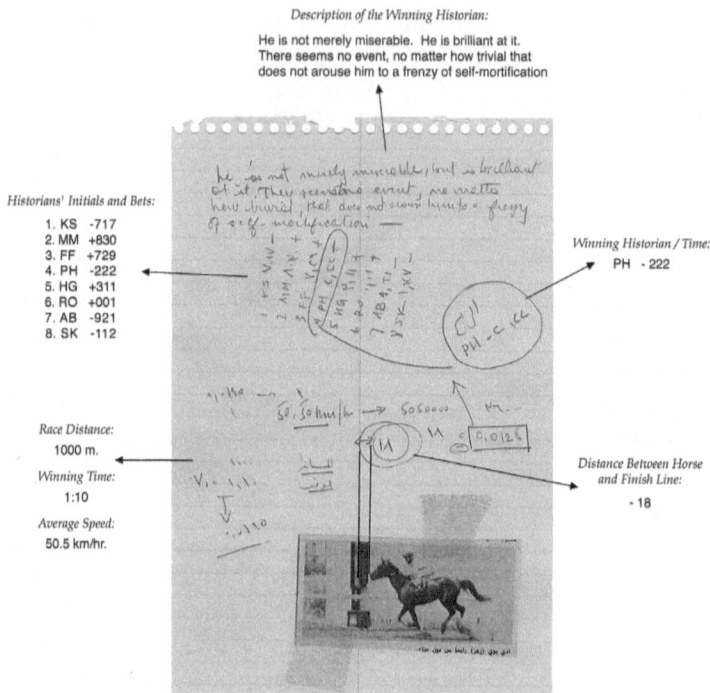

Fig. 3: The Atlas Group in collaboration with Walid Raad, *Notebook Volume 72: Missing Lebanese Wars, Plate 132*. Document attributed to Dr Fadl Fakhouri. Date (attributed): 1989. Date (production): 1998.

Group work has its public origins in intellectual publications, and only thereafter in art spaces.

On brief inspection and reflection, the division of The Atlas Group Archive into the 3 categories of A (for authored), FD (for found documents) and AGP (for Atlas Group Project documents) is thus clearly fictional – since all are actually different types of Atlas Group Project documents. But despite the numerous, albeit at times subtle, markers of the project's overall fictitious character, its documentary apparatus and forms, combined with its significant actual documentary content, continue to persuade viewers of its factual status. This is sometimes true even under extreme provocation, as shown by the audience reaction to Walid Raad's performance at the 2006 Biennale of Sydney, for example, when it seemed that no fictional exaggeration, however extreme, could undermine the presumption of factuality.

Joseph Bitar, then, is the latest of a small cast of fictional characters used by The Atlas Group (to whose own status I shall return) to transfigure documentary material into art by means of fictions, posing, via the documentary form, as facts. There is a double movement here: these are fictional documentaries, but they nonetheless carry important elements of actual documentation within the art. History thus appears here both within and via art, in different ways, as a complex transaction between 'documentation' (as both an indexical and an institutional process) and fiction, in which fiction is the guiding hand.

Fictionalization of artistic authority/collectivization of artistic fictions: A First Transnational

Fictionalization works at two levels here and takes two main forms: the fictionalization of artistic authority or what, adapting Foucault, we may call 'the artist-function', and the fictionalization of the documentary form, in particular, the archive. In the work of The Atlas Group, this dual fictionalization corresponds to and renders visible the fictitiousness of the contemporary itself. It also renders explicit a certain general fictitiousness of the post-conceptual artwork, which is an effect of the counter-factuality inherent in its conceptual dimension, and imparts to it a structurally 'literary' aspect. Each material work, or materialization, can be understood as the performance of a fictive element or idea. In this respect, as we shall see in Chapters 2 and 4, below, the generic post-medium concept of art reincorporates 'literature', returning it to its philosophical origins in early German Romanticism: postconceptual art articulates a post-aesthetic poetics.

Historically, the fictionalization of the artist-function is, of course, not an uncommon authorial strategy. It represents an extension of both the strategy of pseudonymity (prevalent under conditions of censorship and the need for social dissimulation of various kinds) and the 'impersonality' of an Eliotian modernism. Theoretically, it is best conceived in terms of Foucault's analysis of the author-function, which was itself in many ways (like much of post-structuralism) a theoretical generalization of the implications of the practice of the modernist avant-gardes. For Foucault, the replacement of the concept of the author by that of the author-function was 'a matter of depriving the subject (or its substitute) of its role as originator, and of analyzing the subject as a variable and complex function of discourse . . . [by] grasp[ing] the subject's points of insertion, modes of functioning, and system of dependencies'.[46] The construction of an artist-function named 'The Atlas Group' is in many ways a precise application of the terms of this analysis to the production of artistic authority. Its primary characteristic is its dissemblance of a documentary practice.

This dissemblance is dependent upon, first, its creative use of anonymity, within pseudonymity, via the 'Group' form (pseudonymity, one might say, is a condition of *historical* fictionalization); and second, the exploitation of the documentary, simultaneously, as indexical mark and pure cultural form. More deeply, it relies for its productive ambiguity upon a general ambiguity in the relationship between historical and fictional narratives, through which it achieves both its philosophical and political force. On the one hand, this ambiguity is constitutive of a practice that uses fictional historical narratives for critical ends; on the other hand, a rigorous internal demarcation between the indexical and purely formal (that is, fictional) use of documents is marked by systematically aberrant chronologies and narrative contradictions – a procedure that is at times applied to the narration of the formation of The Atlas Group itself, variously specified as 1999, 1977 and 1986–99 (1999 was the actual year). It is through the relation between the anonymous collectivity of the fiction of the Group itself and the national specificity of its fictions ('Lebanon') that the 'contemporary', global, *trans*national character and political meaning of its practice are constructed.

Artist collectives (fictional and actual) are fashionable once again. For over a decade now, they have been proliferating like wildfire through the international art community, whether in purportedly singular form ('Claire Fontaine') or explicitly collective guise (Raqs Media Collective). And there is now a revisionist historiography of such collectives' recent past.[47] There are a variety of reasons for this, mostly to do with the attempts to refashion the modes of effectivity of the relations between politics and art. My thesis is that artistic collectivism has a new function here tied to its fictionalization, at the moment of global transnationalism. The recent spate of collectives (fictional or otherwise) are its generally unconscious manifestation.

The collectivization of the fictionalization of the artist-function works, once again, at two levels: the collectivity of the Group, and the collectivization of authority inherent in the (in this case fictionalized) documentary form – at its limit, the material 'collectivity' of indexicality itself, the signifying power of nature. The link is anonymity. It is through the combination of anonymity and reference inherent in the pseudonym 'The Atlas Group', with its global connotations, that its fictive collectivity comes to figure the *speculative collectivity of the globally transnational* itself.

I claimed earlier that currently it is only capital that immanently projects the utopian horizon of global social interconnectedness, in the ultimately dystopian form of the market: only capital manifests a subject-structure at the level of the global. Yet capitalist sociality (the grounding of societies in relations of exchange) is essentially abstract; it is a matter of *form*, rather than 'collectivity'. Collectivity is produced by the interconnectedness of practices, but the universal interconnectedness and dependencies that capital produces exhibit the structure of a subject (the unity of an activity) only objectively, in their product, separated from individual subjects and particular collectivities of labour, in the self-development of the value-form. Historically, of course, nationalism (the cultural fiction of nations) has filled this lacuna. Nations ('imagined communities') have been the privileged social subjects of competing capitals. But the subject-structure of capital no longer corresponds to the territorially discrete entities of nation-states, and other societies outside the nexus of global capital are being drawn inexorably into it. In this respect, the immanent collectivity of capitalism remains, and will always remain, structurally, 'to come'; hence the abstract and wholly formal character of its recent anticipation as 'multitude'.

The fictional collectivity of *The Atlas Group* and its narrative 'characters' is a stand-in for the missing political collectivity of the globally transnational, which is both posited and negated by capital itself. As such, it corresponds, at a structural level, to the work of such 'authors' as Luther Blissett and Wu Ming in the field of literature.[48] Politically, one might say, such work represents, by virtue of its effective relations to the philosophical history of capital, the continuation of the intellectual tradition of Marxist internationalism by new transnational artistic means. The Atlas Group could be construed as the artistic representative of a kind of 'First Transnational'.

But what then of the specifically *national* focus of the Group's work, its exclusively Lebanese fiction? The transnational is not the non-national, but it changes the status of the national, which was in any case famously only ever an 'imagined community'. Here, the fictionalization of 'Lebanon' – through the fictionalization of the evidence of its existence – effects an emblematic fictionalization of the national itself. Furthermore, this fictionalization of the national acts as the *de*-nationalizing condition of its *trans*nationalization; a transnationalization that is effected via the socio-spatial structure of the artwork/artworld. This is not transnationalism as the abstract other of the nation, but transnationalization as the mediation of the form of the nation-state with its abstractly global other. On the horizon of this movement, we can glimpse something of the radical-democratic aspect of Foucault's projection of a possible replacement of the conventional author-function (tied to relations of ownership) by some form of anonymity. It evokes the rhetorical question that closes Foucault's essay: 'What difference does it make who is speaking?'[49]

2
Art Beyond Aesthetics

In US art writing of the mid-1960s – at the moment of the emergence of what would become 'contemporary art' from the standpoint of its immanently artistic periodization – it mattered very much who was speaking. Whether it was the formalist critic (Clement Greenberg, Michael Fried) or the self-proclaimed conceptual artist (Sol LeWitt, Joseph Kosuth), the authority of the discourse rested heavily on the construction of the author-function. The struggle over art's relationship to aesthetic was a struggle over the institutional authorization of 'the beholder', conducted by a new generation of artist-critics, constructing a new kind of author-function, who refused to offer up objects deemed appropriate to the beholder's gaze.[1] This campaign against a certain 'aesthetic' institution of spectatorship was at once anti-institutional and the bearer of an alternative institutionalization, following the temporal logic of artistic avant-gardes established at least a century before.[2] It so fundamentally transformed the field of practices institutionally recognized as 'art', it will be argued here, as to constitute a change in art's 'ontology' or very mode of being. The new, postconceptual artistic ontology that was established – 'beyond aesthetic' – came to define the field to which the phrase 'contemporary art' most appropriately refers, in its deepest critical sense. The historical ontology of contemporary art, it is argued here, is thus most directly grasped in the proposition: 'Contemporary art is postconceptual art'.[3]

Before I expound this proposition, though, we need to consider the modern concept of art more generally, in its difference from Kant's concept of 'aesthetic art', with which it is still frequently conflated, since this conflation (grounded in a confusion about autonomy) continues to generate confusion about the ontological status of aesthetic aspects of contemporary art. To do this, we need to return to the relationship between Kant's thought and that of Jena Romanticism, to clarify the difference established there between 'aesthetic' and 'metaphysical' conceptions of art. This is the topic of the first section. Next, these terms are returned to the present, in the presentation of early Romantic philosophy of art as the conceptual ground for contemporary art criticism, by virtue of contemporary art's primary historical and metaphysical determination as postconceptual art. The proposition 'contemporary art is postconceptual art', through which this situation is grasped, it is argued, has a philosophical status similar to what Hegel called a 'speculative proposition' – or at least, a speculative proposition reinterpreted romantically. Finally, the early Romantic interpretation of art's conceptuality is emblematically condensed into a reading of Sol LeWitt's *Sentences on Conceptual Art* through Friedrich Schlegel's *Athenaeum Fragments* – a reading that is methodologically grounded in Walter Benjamin's account of the historical meaning of dialectical images. The image in question here is the image of LeWitt's *Sentences* as at once an image of Romanticism and an image of conceptual art.

Art Versus Aesthetic (Jena Romanticism contra Kant)

What is wrong with thinking about art, philosophically, as 'aesthetic'? What is wrong with identifying 'aesthetics' with the philosophy of art? The problem appears in an exemplary formulation in the fortieth of Friedrich Schlegel's *Critical Fragments* (1798):

> In the sense in which it has been defined and used in Germany, aesthetic is a word which notoriously reveals an equally perfect ignorance of the thing and of the language. Why is it still used?[4]

What is this 'equally perfect ignorance' [*gleich vollendete Unkenntnis*] of both the language and the thing? Nothing less, it would seem, than what Kant himself derided in his much-quoted footnote to the Transcendental Aesthetic of his *Critique of Pure Reason* (1781): namely, its use by 'the Germans . . . to designate that which others call the critique of taste'. Schlegel's fragment is an ironic citation or rewriting of this passage. Its reference to 'ignorance of the language' cannot but evoke Kant's advice to 'desist' from the use of the word 'aesthetic' to designate the critique of taste, in order 'to save it for that doctrine which is true science (whereby one would come closer to the language and the sense of the ancients, among whom the division of cognition into *aisthéta* and *noéta* [things of sensibility and things of the mind] was very well known).'[5] The doctrine to which Kant is referring is his own Transcendental Aesthetic, the first part of the Transcendental Doctrine of Elements [of knowledge] in the *Critique of Pure Reason*, within which the passage in question is located. It is dedicated not to taste, but to the exposition of space and time as pure forms of intuition, conditioning the possibility of objects of knowledge in general.

Schlegel's rewriting is ironic, in part because Kant himself equally famously appeared to go against his own advice when, nine years later, in 1790, the first part of his *Critique of Judgement-Power*, 'Critique of Aesthetic Judgement-Power', contained an extensive analysis of aesthetic judgements understood as, precisely, judgements of taste. The idea that 'aesthetics' is a philosophical discourse about art is in large part the fatal legacy of the reception of this text, with its apparent confirmation of the legitimacy of drawing together the three (originally independent) discourses of *beauty*, *sensibility* and *art* into an integral philosophical whole.[6] Schlegel may be read as referring his readers back to Kant's earlier text in the context of Kant's own apparent subsequent concession to Alexander Baumgarten's 'German' usage. He is being sarcastic about the first *Critique*, and hence about Kant's self-understanding; at the very least, he is drawing attention to Kant's apparent inconsistency or change of mind.[7] Schlegel is crowing over the triumph of the 'German' use of 'aesthetic' – a terminological triumph which, in the Romantic philosophy of art, was in the process of being transformed into a philosophical victory of a higher order: a triumph of art over 'philosophy' within metaphysics itself.

However, discursively, the famous Romantic triumph of art within metaphysics (against which Schaeffer rages)[8] is a triumph of philosophical art criticism over systematic philosophy; it is not a triumph of aesthetic, as Kant understood it in *Critique of Judgement-Power*. In the transition within critical metaphysics from systematic philosophy to Romantic art criticism, Kant's transcendental account of aesthetic judgement is a vanishing mediator. In order to understand the disjunction between aesthetics and art criticism that is produced here (prefiguring the development of aesthetics as a discipline, in the course of the nineteenth century), it is necessary to examine the apparent inconsistency between Kant's two meanings of 'aesthetic' in more detail.

The inconsistency in question is that between an insistence upon restricting the term 'aesthetic' to its 'original' meaning, denoting the sensible element in knowledge, and its extended use to refer to judgements of taste. The error of the extension, from the standpoint of Kant's first *Critique*, derives from what Kant describes there as the 'failed hope' of 'bringing the critical estimation of the beautiful under principles of reason, and elevating its rules to a science'; that is, from the aspiration to a *rational doctrine* of the beautiful, an 'aesthetics', in a scientific disciplinary sense. It was this aspiration that led Baumgarten to subsume the philosophical treatment of beauty under the sign of a doctrine of *sensible* knowledge. And it is the 'futility' of this aspiration that led Kant to judge the usage inappropriate, since, he claimed, 'the putative rules or criteria are merely empirical as far as their sources are concerned'. It is not – note – the connection between beauty and sensibility to which Kant objects in the *Critique of Pure Reason*, but the idea that the field of their connection (judgements of taste) might be governed by 'a priori rules'.⁹ For Kant, then, the term 'aesthetic' was from the outset a term of philosophical art, part of the *doctrine* (*Lehre*) of knowledge. And it is for this reason that it should not have been used to refer to taste: not because beauty is not 'sensible', but precisely because of the fact that it *is*, and hence, its judgements are merely empirical. So what led Kant to change his mind?

The fact is that he did not; at least, not on this particular point. For there is a rarely acknowledged underlying consistency to Kant's position, despite the change in usage. When he subsequently himself adopted the supposedly inappropriate, extended usage, Kant never went back upon his initial reason for rejecting Baumgarten's extended use of 'aesthetic'. In *Critique of Judgement-Power*, Kant maintains – in fact he emphasizes – this point: 'There is neither a science [*Wissenschaft*] of the beautiful, only a critique, nor beautiful science'. In fact, he writes it twice: first in section 44, 'On Fine Art', and then again in section 60, the appendix, 'On Methodology Concerning Taste', where it becomes more emphatically, 'there *cannot be* any science of the beautiful'.¹⁰ That is, there neither is, nor can be, a *philosophical* aesthetics. Rather, the change in Kant's position concerns a clarification of the methodological status of 'critique'. Critique appears here no longer in association with doctrine (*Lehre*), but as a conceptually self-sufficient term, distinct from both 'science' (qua doctrine) and 'the empirical'. 'Criticism of taste' is no longer conceived in terms of the application of a priori rules to particular cases, or the judgement of such rules *by* particular cases (Kant's earlier focus), but in terms of the immanent notion of transcendental critique that governed the project of the *Critique of Pure Reason* from the outset. It is a part of 'critique of reason by reason alone': in this instance, critique of aesthetic judgement-*power* (*Urteilskraft*) by transcendental reflection, critique of a particular power of the faculty of judgement, not criticism of particular judgements. Philosophically, where judgements of the beautiful are concerned, there is only critique, transcendental critique, of the structure (but not the content) of what are always *singular* (that is, *radically* empirical) judgements.

This distinctively Kantian idea of philosophy as a critical standpoint beyond positive 'criteria', or positive knowledge, that is nonetheless no longer metaphysically self-sufficient as rational doctrine, but purely reflective, was crucially formative for Romanticism. It is the other side of the more familiar Kantian idea of the 'limits' to reason, which Karl

Ameriks has emphasized as the basis for the construction of a common 'Kantian-Romantic position'.[11] Famously, the method of immanently transcendental critique allowed Kant to stray *beyond* the cognitive limits of reason, legitimately, as a 'standpoint' but never as a doctrine. The critique of aesthetic judgement-power concretizes this standpoint, subjectively, as the feeling of pleasure accompanying reflective awareness of the unity of subjectivity, as the 'harmony' of the faculties. It was precisely this 'straying beyond' that the Romantics seized upon and elaborated further, in a new post-critical metaphysics of art. However, this formal consistency in Kant's position does not appear sufficient to meet his own earlier objection to that use of 'aesthetic' which strays too far from 'the language and sense of the ancients'. For the standpoint of a transcendental critique of the structure of judgement abstracts from all *concretely* sensuous particularity (that is, it *conceptualizes* sensuous particularity in terms of its *logical* singularity). It is thus *not* actually 'aesthetic', in Kant's original sense of 'things of sensibility'. (The pure forms of intuition, on the other hand – space and time – being also 'pure intuitions', are themselves aesthetic.) Transcendental critique of taste – as the critique of a specific type of judgement-power, rather than the critical estimation of sensuous representations – is *not* 'aesthetic' in the sense in which the 'things of sensibility' may be distinguished from the 'things of the mind'. Rather, it is decisively 'of the mind', or, better, it is 'of the mind' and 'of sensibility' at the same time: in pure aesthetic judgements of taste, the ontological distinction between *aisthéta* and *noéta* collapses. The mind feels itself.

This is precisely the point of Kant's transcendental analysis of judgements of taste in terms of the reflective relations between cognitive faculties – linguistic niceties apart, which at this point begin to appear pedantic and (as Hegel later treated them) 'a mere name'.[12] Kant's *Third Critique* transformed the meaning of 'aesthetic' by extending it beyond the sensible (spatial and temporal) apprehension of the objects of 'outer' and 'inner' intuition to include reference to the feelings accompanying the relations of reflection constitutive of the internal cognitive structure of subjectivity itself. What is this but what Novalis would have called a 'romanticization' of aesthetic; its presentation as a self-reflection of the absolute, once, following Johann Gottlieb Fichte, the subject has been absolutized qua self-positing and self-reflective process?[13] The ancient distinction between *aisthéta* and *noéta*, to which Kant initially appealed, is here no more than the linguistic register of a dualistic rationalism that Kant has, finally, managed to move beyond. Human sensibility is irreducibly judgemental and furthermore (contra Aristotle – who thought each sense judged discretely) *internally relationally* so. This is a new philosophical account of the ontological specificity of human subjectivity – the main philosophical source of the early Heidegger's existentialism, in fact. Kant's linguistic innovation – to extend the range of 'aesthetic' to embrace the paradoxical pure '*self*-affection' of the self-relation of human subjectivity[14] – registers this conceptual novelty. Philologically speaking, this is hardly 'ignorance'.

But what of 'the thing', critique of taste, as Kant called it, or more simply 'criticism' as it was known in England at the time, to which the new philosophically extended usage of 'aesthetic' must *also* refer, since aesthetic subjectivity can only feel itself, for Kant, *via* judgements of taste occasioned by objects that 'quicken' it?[15] This is the point at which the satirical charge of 'ignorance' begins to acquire a more literal bite. For, in Kant's later, dialectically ambiguous sense of aesthetic, it is not the extension of sensibility to include the subject's relation to itself – auto-affection – that is the problem, so much as its consequent principled *indifference to the character of the objects* that occasion judgement; in particular, its principled indifference to the cognitive, relational, historical and world-disclosing dimensions of works of *art*, which were such a central part of 'that which *others* call the critique of taste'.

Famously, art judgements (such as 'this is a beautiful painting') – are explicitly excluded by Kant from 'pure' aesthetic judgements of taste. That is, Kant *excludes* from aesthetics precisely those judgements that *constitute* the main part of the critique of taste, historically, as a critical discourse, as an effect of the transcendentalism of his method. These are grasped only by Kant's much neglected and under-elaborated concept of 'logically conditioned' aesthetic judgements – judgements which, operating under the conditions of a determinate concept, such as 'art' or 'painting', are not aesthetically 'pure'. For Kant, artistic beauty can never be what he calls a 'free' or 'purely aesthetic' beauty (at least, not qua artistic beauty), but only an 'accessory' or adherent beauty.[16] This is the conceptual residue of his earlier objection to Baumgarten's use of the term 'aesthetic'. There is thus a conceptual gap between art and aesthetic that cannot be adequately bridged within the terms of Kant's thought. In so far as 'aesthetics' is taken as the name for the philosophical treatment of art, we are confronted with a new and equally ironic 'ignorance of the thing and of the language': aesthetic's principled ignorance of art qua art.[17] For Kant readily acknowledges that 'aesthetic' itself cannot distinguish art from nature: art becomes aesthetically pure only when it appears '*as if* it were a mere product of nature'.[18] Moreover, Kantian aesthetic judgement does not reflect on the conditions of this appearing 'as if' – that is, upon its ontological and epistemological qualities as illusion; it merely takes it as its condition. Kant's restriction of the concept of beautiful or 'fine' art to a type of 'aesthetic art' (his own term) thus excludes most of what has always been and continues to be of most significance about art: the difference from nature marked by its metaphysical, cognitive, and politico-ideological functions, qua art.

In identifying the 'aesthetic' significance of objects with their affect upon the subject in its purely reflective judgement, Kant simultaneously expanded 'aesthetic', giving it a central role in the metaphysics of the subject, and cut it off from any possible metaphysics of the artwork as a self-sufficient or 'autonomous' entity. 'Aesthetic art' is the contradictory result of the negotiation of the impasse.

The nineteenth and twentieth century tradition of 'art as aesthetic' – artistic aestheticism – covertly perpetuated by the very term 'aesthetics', when used to refer to philosophy of art, rests upon a self-contradictory absolutization of Kant's conception of 'aesthetic art'. Contrary to Hegel's acceptance of it as a mere 'name', the term 'aesthetics' functions as much more than a name here: it seals and legitimates the exclusion of art's other aspects from the philosophical concept of art, reducing it to a single plane of significance – namely, its capacity to appear as 'a product of mere nature' and hence as the object of pure judgements of taste. Even Kant's account of genius (otherwise so productive for a post-Kantian, Romantic aesthetic) is subjected to the constraints of this problematic. This ignorance of language – the idea that 'aesthetics' is an appropriate term to designate the philosophical treatment of art – sums up the ignorance of the thing: 'art'. This ignorance persists today in the widespread belief that it is the *logical* autonomy of pure aesthetic judgements of taste from other types of judgement (as theorized by Kant) that is the philosophical basis of the autonomy of art. Even writers as sophisticated in their reading of German idealism as Andrew Bowie and Jay Bernstein, for example, have contributed to the perpetuation of this myth to the level of a philosophical commonplace through their use of the phrase 'aesthetic autonomy' to refer to the autonomy of art.[19] Yet Kant's work cannot, in principle, provide the conceptual ground for an account of the autonomy of the artwork, since it has no account of (nor interest in) the ontological distinctiveness of the work of art. That was the contribution of Jena Romanticism.

Locating the origin of the autonomy claim for art after Kant, in Schiller's reinterpretation of aesthetic appearance in terms of self-determination, in his *Kallias Letters* (1793) – 'a reformulation of Kant's aesthetic theory that reaches its apotheosis in *On the Aesthetic Education of Man*' (1795), the crucial transitional text between Kant and early Romanticism – is more convincing.[20] However, this is so only if one follows through its ontological consequences for the artwork to their Romantic conclusion. Schiller himself remained largely at the epistemological level of aesthetic *appearance*, that is, *illusion* – the illusion of self-determination of the object of aesthetic judgement; at his best, at the level of an aesthetically modified practical reason (thereby founding the notorious problematic of 'aesthetic and politics' to which our intellectual culture compulsively returns).[21] However, there are metaphysical as well as practical implications of the artwork's production of the illusion of its self-determination. The illusion of self-determination appears metaphysically as a distinctive type of productivity. Kant provided the model for this special kind of productivity – call it creativity (as long as you remember it is the creation of an illusion) – in his concept of genius. But he failed to connect genius to self-determination, or to the illusion of self-determination (at least explicitly), let alone to theorize the production of the illusion of self-determination as the self-reflexive structure of the artwork (since he had no ontological concept of the artwork). That was left to Novalis's transposition of the structure of Fichte's absolutization of the subject onto the work of art. Only at this point does art become a distinctive form of presentation of truth: a 'presentation of the unpresentable' (*Darstellung des Undarstellbaren*), as Novalis put it, or 'the infinite finitely displayed', anticipating Jean-François Lyotard's supposedly postmodern sublime by some two hundred years.[22] This is the philosophical ground of the 'autonomy of art' claim – autonomy not of a type of judgement (Kant), nor merely at the level of appearance, the illusion of self-determination (Schiller), but of a certain kind of production of meaning in the object, an autopoiesis, distinct from both *techné* and mimesis (Novalis, Friedrich Schlegel). This is not an 'aesthetic regime of art' but a *supra-aesthetic artistic regime of truth*.

Furthermore, such a regime can only be realized under particular historical and institutional conditions, the social relations of which must thus be considered *constitutive* of a paradoxically ontologically 'autonomous' art. This Hegelian addendum to early Romanticism (art as form of *objective* spirit), or what Adorno called the 'dual character of art as autonomy and social fact' (and which we might be sharpen into 'the *dialectical unity* of art as autonomy and social fact' – the social fact of autonomy), is crucial if philosophical discourse on art is be critically mediated with art-historical, cultural-historical and *social* discourses, and thereby to become capable of engagement with contemporary art in its full social specificity.[23]

This is not the place for an account of the emergence of the Romantic conception of the autonomous artwork out of a displacement of the aporia of Fichte's attempt at a foundational philosophy of the subject into the realm of poetic meaning. Benjamin reconstructed this passage via the concept of reflection in his 1923 dissertation, *The Concept of Art Criticism in German Romanticism*, and others have recently returned to the topic.[24] However, with respect to Kant, three things about the

Romantic theory of art, in particular, should be borne in mind: first, its rejection (or what August Schlegel called its 'denunciation') of the distinction between free and accessory beauty, 'as invalid and as springing from too narrow and too low an assessment of the beautiful';[25] second, its abolition of the categorial separation of the beautiful and the sublime (prefigured in Kant's own notion of aesthetic ideas); third, its elaboration of a metaphysically invested conception of art – as, in Schelling's words, the 'organon of philosophy'[26] – at a concrete-historical level, not as a medium-based system of the arts, but as a *philosophically constructed (negative) theory of genres*, in an ongoing mediation of the categories of the philosophy of art with the history of art. This third feature is the mediating core of the Romantic philosophy of art, through which it acquires its distinctive philosophical shape of being at once *transcendental, metaphysical* and (unlike its later, Heideggerian version) *concretely historical*: an historical-ontological theory of art. This was Friedrich Schlegel's distinctive contribution. In this respect, the early Schelling does not belong to Romanticism proper, but recasts its insights within the tradition of philosophical idealism. In fact, in so far as it retains a concretely historical sense of the present, Hegel's philosophy of art is closer to Schlegel's philosophical Romanticism than is Schelling's early philosophy of art. The difference lies in Hegel's *absolutely* idealist, subject-dissolving presupposition of the possibility of the *purely conceptual* self-reflection of the absolute. With respect to the application of the art-historical problematic of early Romanticism to contemporary art, Schlegel's Romantic categories of poetry and the novel, as absolute genres 'forever becoming', have a similar philosophical status to what Thierry de Duve calls 'generic' art and what I am here calling 'postconceptual' art.[27]

As the product of the displacement of the structure of a seemingly irresolvable metaphysical problem (the infinite reflexivity of a self-positing subject frustrates the project of self-grounding) into a special kind of object (art), the autonomous work of art is as irreducibly conceptual – and metaphysical – in its philosophical structure as it is historical and 'aesthetic' (*felt* by the mind) in its mode of appearance. It is thus a mistake to suppose that because it is conceptual, there is no role for 'aesthetic' within it. Far from it. As the registration of the feeling associated with presentations to the intellect, aesthetic is an ineliminable aspect of the early Romantics' ontological conception of art. It is, however, ontologically both *partial* and *relational*. More generally, the artistic significance of aesthetic must be judged in the context of the historically shifting relations between aesthetic and other – cognitive, semantic, social, political and ideological – aspects of artworks. And the balance and meaning will be different in different kinds of art.

Furthermore, these relations between the aesthetic and other aspects of artworks derive their critical meaning from their relations to the equally historically variable aesthetic dimension of other (non-art) cultural forms – today, predominantly but by no means exclusively: commodity design and display, advertising, mass media and communications technologies – the whole non-art aspects of the apparatus of visual culture. One problem with the philosophical discourse of 'art as aesthetic' is that it militates against recognition of these relations as being *internal* to the critical structure of the artwork, and hence against the understanding of contemporary art in certain of its most significant, historical and *anti*-aesthetic aspects.

Periodization and Historical Ontology: Postconceptual Art

In the light of this brief reconstruction of the philosophical pre-history of the polemical opposition of 'aesthetic' and 'conceptual' art played out in the 1960 and '70s, as a difference between Kant and Jena Romanticism, we can discern two parallel and competing, though to some extent also overlapping traditions in the criticism of art since the end of the eighteenth century, corresponding to the two philosophical discourses of 'art as aesthetic' and 'art as (historical) ontology'. The first runs from Kant through nineteenth-century aestheticism (Baudelaire, Pater, Wilde), via Roger Fry and Clive Bell, to Greenberg's later writings, which mark the aestheticist collapse of his earlier historical self-understanding. It rests upon an aesthetic theory of the arts, with its distant origins in Renaissance naturalism and the new science of optics[28] and its mainstream in an empirical reduction of Kant's transcendentalism to a psychology – at best, a phenomenology – of perception, of which Richard Wollheim was the recent master.[29] The second tradition runs from philosophical Romanticism through Hegel, Duchamp, surrealism and the revolutionary Romanticism of Constructivism, to conceptual art and its consequences in what has been called the 'post-medium condition', but which I prefer to think of as the *trans*media condition of postconceptual art.[30]

The first (aesthetic) tradition finds its concrete critical terms in an aesthetic theory of medium that dates back to Gotthold Lessing. It is currently being revived in both a Friedian variant (by Jeff Wall, amongst others) and a more explicitly Kantian, transcendental variant by Jay Bernstein, as the philosophical basis for a theory of modernism as the cultural representation of nature's resistance to history – a reading which combines Greenberg with Adorno, via an immanent critique of T.J. Clarke's interpretation of Jackson Pollock.[31] The second (historical-ontological) tradition finds its critical terms in a philosophically negative theory of the 'truth of art' which manifests this negativity historically in the concept of 'the new' – a sometimes proto-, sometimes post-avant-gardist constitutive negation that, today, determines artistic meaning as a determination of contemporaneity itself. It derives its content empirically within a *historically open*, but nonetheless *speculatively totalizing*, generic conception of art, within which the historical present is necessarily privileged as the standpoint of an implicit but unactualizable (and therefore negative) totalization. And it comes in a spectrum of relations to the future, from the insistent but increasingly abstract future-orientation of modernism, as the cultural affirmation of the temporality of the new, to the flat presentism of the immediately contemporary. The qualitative historical temporality of art-critical judgement appears here as a consequence of the philosophical dynamics of historical totalization. This second proto-Romantic or generic artistic tradition has developed in active relation to both historical transformations in the institutional conditions of artistic autonomy (which establish the social conditions of possibility of the illusion of autonomous meaning production) and socially progressive political cultures, which have criticised the prevailing social forms of autonomy, and in particular, their misrecognition as 'aesthetic'. Its current representative is the anti-aesthetic*ism* of postconceptual art.

But what exactly is postconceptual art? In what sense does it determine the contemporaneity of 'contemporary art'? And what does this equivalence between 'postconceptual' art and 'contemporary' art tell us about 'the art history that art criticism *is*', or should be? – to return to the terms of Harold Rosenberg's declaration from which we set out in the Introduction.

In the course of the 1980s, it became conventional to periodize the Western art of the previous forty years in terms of a transition from 'modernism' to 'postmodernism' – however vaguely or varyingly the second of these two terms was understood in this context. Greenberg's critical hegemony had tended to fix the art-historical meaning of the first term, in a conceptually and chronologically restrictive manner. It thereby opened up the artistic field of the 'postmodern' as the space of its abstract negation. The problem with this periodization, however, is that it fails to endow the complexly interacting set of what were initially conceived as 'post-formalist', anti-Greenbergian artistic strategies of the 1960s with either sufficient conceptual determinacy and distinctness or adequate historical effectivity. In particular, it fails to register both the *critical* priority of conceptual art within this field and the historical and critical significance of its postconceptual legacy. It thus fails to provide a theoretical basis on which we might specify the ontological distinctiveness of contemporary art. I therefore propose an alternative periodization of 'art after Greenbergian modernism' that privileges the sequence: formalist modernism, conceptual art, postconceptual art – over the modernist–postmodernist couplet, and treats the conceptual–postconceptual trajectory as the standpoint from which to totalize the wide array of other anti-formalist movements. (A broader, philosophically adequate conception of modernism as a temporal logic of cultural forms would embrace the whole sequence; 'postmodernism' being the misrecognition of a particular stage in the dialectic of modernisms.)[32]

By 'postconceptual' art, then, I understand an art premised on the complex historical experience and critical legacy of conceptual art, broadly construed, which registers its fundamental mutation of the ontology of the artwork. Postconceptual art is a critical category that is constituted at the level of the historical ontology of the artwork; it is not a traditional art-historical or art-critical concept at the level of medium, form or style. Rather, as the critical register of the historical destruction of the ontological significance of such categories, it provides new interpretative conditions for analyses of individual works. The critical legacy of conceptual art consists in the combination of six main insights, which collectively make up the condition of possibility of a postconceptual art. These are:

1. Art's necessary conceptuality. (Art is constituted by concepts, their relations and their instantiation in practices of discrimination: art/non-art.)
2. Art's ineliminable – but radically insufficient – aesthetic dimension. (All art requires *some* form of materialization; that is to say, aesthetic – felt, spatio-temporal – presentation.)
3. The critical necessity of an anti-aesthetic*ist* use of aesthetic materials. (This is a critical consequence of art's necessary conceptuality.)
4. An expansion to infinity of the possible material forms of art.
5. A radically distributive – that is, irreducibly relational – unity of the individual artwork across the totality of its multiple material instantiations, at any particular time.
6. A historical malleability of the borders of this unity.

The conjunction of the first two features leads to the third; together they imply the fourth; while the fifth and sixth are expressions of the logical and temporal consequences of the fourth, respectively.

The principle of the ineliminability of the aesthetic dimension of the artwork is the product of the so-called 'failure' of Conceptual Art in its strong, 'pure' or analytical programme; that is, the idea of a 'purely' conceptual art associated for a brief period (1968–72) with Joseph Kosuth in the US and the Art & Language in Britain – although there are important differences between the critical positions of these artists. (The case of Sol LeWitt, the founding father of Conceptual art as a movement, is more complicated, because of his essentially psychological conception of 'ideas'.)[33] What 'failure' means here is the practical demonstration of the incoherence of a particular *self-understanding* of 'conceptual art'. This was not an artistic failure. Indeed, it was a perverse artistic success. It was the ironic historical achievement of the strong programme of 'analytical' or 'pure' conceptual art to have demonstrated the ineliminability of the aesthetic as a *necessary*, though *radically insufficient*, component of the artwork through the failure of its attempt at its elimination: the failure of an absolute anti-aesthetic. In this sense, it staged a certain repetition of the reception of Duchamp: a repetition of the necessary erosion of 'aesthetic indifference'. This experimental programme thereby fulfilled the classically Hegelian function of exceeding a limit in its established form (the aesthetic) in such a way as to render it visible and thereby reinstitute it on new grounds.[34] In this respect, the meaning of 'conceptual art' must be retrospectively critically refigured to incorporate this insight.[35] In its strongest sense, of a 'purely' conceptual or analytical art, conceptual art was an idea that marked the experimental investigation of a particular anti-aesthetic desire.

At the same time, however, in demonstrating the radical insufficiency, or minimal conditionality, of the aesthetic dimension of the artwork to its status as art, conceptual art was able to bring once again to light, in a more decisive way, the necessary conceptuality of the work which had been buried by the aesthetic ideology of formalist modernism – a conceptuality which was always historically central to the allegorical function of art. Conceptual art demonstrated in a whole variety of novel ways, with respect to a whole series of different forms of materiality, the sense in which 'aesthetic' in both its ancient and later Kantian senses (as sensibility and as pure reflective judgement) is *a part of* yet *utterly fails to account for* the ontological specificity of 'art'. The aesthetic concept of art mistakes one of art's many conditions for the whole. It mistakes art's necessary aesthetic appearance for the *ground* of its apparently autonomous, and hence infinite, production of meaning, which is in fact historically relational, rather than 'positive' in an aesthetic sense. Conceptual art demonstrated the radical emptiness or blankness of the aesthetic in itself, as an ontological support, that derives its meaning, in each instance, relationally or contextually, whatever its precise form of materiality – and this includes those instances when it functions as a negation, as well as a carrier, of meaning.

Having exposed the aesthetic misrecognition of the artwork as an ideological fraud, conceptual art thereby established the need for art actively to counter aesthetic misrecognition within the work, through the constructive or strategic aesthetic use of aesthetic materials. The victory of the 'aesthetic remainder' over strong conceptualism (that is, conceptual art's own inevitable pictorialism) was thus ultimately a Pyrrhic one. This Pyrrhic victory – and the transition to a postconceptual art that it represents – accounts for the privileged status of photographic practice within contemporary art, with its strategic or selective pictorialism (see Chapter 5, below). It was reflected upon by Art & Language themselves in their paintings and installations of the 1980s and 1990s, which were increasingly reduced to a historical reflection on their own earlier practice.[36]

The principle of the expansion to infinity of the possible material means of art-making follows from conceptual reflection on the *de facto* expansion of means that destroyed the ontological significance for art of the norms governing the 'mediums' previously constituting art as a system of arts. This is the liberation of the so-called 'post-medium', transmedia condition. It requires a new conception of the unity of the individual work. No longer identifiable with either a physically unique instantiation or a simple set of reproducible tokens (readymades), the unity of the work becomes both distributive and malleable. In its informality, its proliferation of artistic materials and its inclusion of both preparatory and subsequent, documentary materials within its conception of the work, conceptual art demonstrated the radically *distributive* character of the unity of the work. That is to say, each work is distributed across a potentially unlimited, but nonetheless conceptually defined and in practice (at any one time) finite, totality of spatio-temporal sites of instantiation.[37] Furthermore, the material borders of this totality are historically malleable, with regard to the new relations into which the work enters in the course of its 'afterlife'. The role of the afterlife of a work in constituting 'what it is' gives the artwork a *retroactive* ontology.[38]

Methodologically, one might say that the reason for the critical priority of conceptual art, within the field of anti-formalist practices of the 1960s, is that it was the art that raised the retrospective search for the universal determinations of 'art' to the highest theoretical power by its negative totalization of the previous set of practices, to produce a new (negative) artistic absolute, which functions as the enabling condition of a new set of practices: postconceptual art. As Adorno recognized, it is only retrospectively that the concept of art acquires any kind of unity, and this unity is therefore 'not abstract', but 'presupposes concrete analyses, [n]ot as proofs and examples but as its own condition.' The idea of art is given through each work, but no individual work is adequate to this idea. Furthermore, this ongoing retrospective and reflective totalization is necessarily *open, fractured, incomplete* and therefore inherently *speculative*:

> The definition of art is at every point indicated by what art once was, but it is legitimated only by what art became with regard to what it wants to be, and perhaps can, become . . . Because art is what it has become, its concept refers to what it does not contain . . . Art can be understood only by its laws of movement, not according to any set of invariants. It is defined by its relation to what it is not . . . Art acquires its specificity by separating itself from what it developed out of; its law of movement is its law of form.[39]

It is the historical movement of conceptual art from the idea of an absolute anti-aesthetic to the recognition of its own inevitable pictorial dimension that makes it a privileged mediating form – that makes it, in fact, the art in relation to which contestation over the meanings and possibilities of contemporary art is to be fought out. Indeed, if the claim for the critical-historical priority of conceptual art can be sustained, it is *only* in relation to the category of conceptual art, in its inherent problematicity, that a critical historical experience of contemporary art is possible. In this respect, 'postconceptual art' is not the name for a particular type of art so much as the historical-ontological condition for the production of contemporary art in general – art, that is, that can sustain the signifers 'art' and 'contemporary' in their deepest theoretical senses.

A Speculative Proposition

In its most condensed form, then, we may propose: 'Contemporary art is postconceptual art'. However, in its theoretical meaning, this sentence should not be understood as a grammatically 'standard' proposition in which 'postconceptual' is a simple predicate of 'contemporary art', among others. Rather, it is a specifically philosophical proposition. Indeed, I shall propose, one of a very distinctive kind: namely, a 'speculative proposition' in the technical sense in which that phrase is used in Hegel's philosophy (in particular, in paragraphs 60–66 of the Preface to the *Phenomenology of Spirit*). It is the distinctive feature of such a proposition, on Hegel's understanding, that the movement of thinking that establishes the identity of its component parts is understood to 'destroy' the 'general nature of judgement' based on the distinction between subject and predicate, which defines the standard propositional form. As a result of the speculative depth of the identity proposed, the subject is understood to 'disappear' into its predicate, robbing thinking of 'the firm objective basis it had in the subject'. In the process, the predicate (here, 'postconceptual art') thereby itself becomes the subject, inverting the proposition ('Postconceptual art is contemporary art') such that it too consequently, as such, will disappear into its predicate in turn. On Hegel's account, this generates an *infinite movement of thinking* between the two terms, such that the proposition (that is to say, predication) becomes 'immediately a merely empty form'.[40] However, this infinite movement is not experienced as unlimited temporal extension (the endlessness of the 'bad' infinite), but rather as the subjective register of a movement internal to an ultimately atemporal conceptual unity.

For Hegel, a speculative proposition is a specifically philosophical type of proposition because it is its 'philosophical content' (the conceptually fundamental character of its components as mutually determining aspects of the absolute) that destroys the standard propositional form, in such a way that the conceptual difference between the components survives the destruction. This difference is now conceived as that of the internal movement of a certain 'unity' or 'harmony' that emerges out of the infinite process of the adoption and discarding of the grammatical roles of subject and predicate. Briefly put, this is a way of registering linguistically a kind of identity that exceeds the expressive possibilities of predication, but which may nonetheless be experienced through it, in and as its auto-destructive speculative construal. For Hegel, 'speculative experience' – the highest form of philosophical experience, higher than dialectical experience – was the experience of a speculative proposition.[41] Speculative experience refigures dialectical experience from the standpoint of the ultimate oneness of its determinations. This is the moment at which, in a proto-early Romantic, non-propositional mode – infinite self-reflection of the absolute – Hegelian philosophy most closely approaches a certain experience of art. It does so, however, only at *the end* of a very long theoretical process through which the meaning of the elements at issue – in our case here, 'contemporary art' and 'postconceptual art' – have been developed, dialectically. In Hegel's terms, a speculative proposition states, in its immediacy, a 'result' that derives its meaning from its condensation of the totality of the process of which it is the self-reflective result: the philosophical history out of which its elements emerge as higher-level concepts, or in our case, the philosophical history of art that provides the initial determinations of these concepts, which finally come together, *speculatively*, in the guise – and it is a conceptual *disguise* – of the fundamental mutual determinations of the restless movement of the process.

Just as for Hegel, the speculative proposition had a certain constitutive unintelligibility (*Unverstandlichkeit*) – since it is a compromise formation between the propositional structure of language and a philosophical content that exceeds the representational possibilities of language – 'substance is subject', for example, or 'the actual is the rational' – so also for us, the speculative proposition 'contemporary art is postconceptual art' retains a certain productive *opaqueness*. It derives its meaning from the role it plays in the interpretation of the individual works that constitute its referent: contemporary/postconceptual art.

The reason that the idea of postconceptual art may be said to determine the contemporaneity of 'contemporary art' is that it condenses and reflects the critical historical experience of conceptual art in relation to the totality of current art practices. As such, it requires a reflective totality of lower-level critical categories for its more concrete comprehension. The construction of such a reflective totality of categories is the task of criticism. The meaning of these categories, however, ultimately derives from their contribution to the (future-oriented) retrospective totalization of which they are a part. This contribution defines the form of that 'art history that art criticism (ideally) *is*' as an art history of the qualitative historical temporality of the new. From this point of view, 'the art history that art criticism (ideally) is' is thus still, fundamentally, a modernist art history of the qualitative historical novelty of the present, from the multiple standpoints of which the past is to be reconstructed and made legible. Methodologically, however, given the openness of the present onto an indeterminate future – which Hegel's philosophy foreclosed – this cannot involve totalization as a continuous or developmental process of systematic presentation, imagined as approaching a point of completeness, but rather, more Romantically, the placing of emblematic fragments into systematic perspective. In constellating conceptual art with the heritage of philosophical romanticism, in a post-Hegelian historical situation, two sets of Ur-fragments stand out: Friedrich Schlegel's *'Athenaeum' Fragments* and Sol LeWitt's *Sentences on Conceptual Art*. Together, they form an image of Romanticism, a dialectical image of the historico-philosophical meaning of 'art'.

An Image of Romanticism (Benjamin, Schlegel, LeWitt)

What have become known as Schlegel's *'Athenaeum' Fragments* are the bulk of the fragments published anonymously, simply as 'Fragments', in the second issue (Volume 1, Number 2) of the journal *The Athenaeum*, in Jena, Prussia in 1798.[42] LeWitt's *Sentences* were written 170 years later, towards the end of 1968, and published in the fifth issue of Vito Acconci and Bernadette Mayer's journal, *0–9*, in New York in January 1969. They were then reprinted in the first issue of *Art–Language*, the journal of the British conceptual art group Art & Language, in May of the same year.[43] The three contexts of publication are similar in various ways. *The Athenaeum* was the short-lived experimental journal (just six issues, 1798–1800) of a handful of poet-critic-philosophers: in particular, the Schlegel brothers (August and Friedrich), Friedrich Schleiermacher and Novalis – and especially with regard to the concept of art, Friedrich Schlegel. In it, what would become known in the European tradition simply as 'literature' (later, 'writing') achieved its first forms of theoretical and practical self-consciousness. *0–9* and *Art–Language* were, similarly, 'small magazines' – self-published in the manner of the 1960s, printing or mimeographing just 200 or 300 copies of each issue, a print run not so different from those of the 1790s. In these issues, what would soon become known as 'conceptual art' achieved some of its first forms of theoretical and practical self-consciousness.

0–9 was essentially a journal of avant-garde poetry, influenced by John Ashbery. (It is important to remember that in the mid-1960s, figures like Carl Andre and Dan Graham still saw them themselves, in large part, as poets.) Language works in journals like this (such as *Aspen*, which published Graham's important work *Scheme* in 1965) explored the boundaries between concrete poetry, notation, instructions for performances, and criticism, in a fluid experimental manner that helped create the conditions for what would shortly become identified as conceptual art.[44] By 1969, however, the energy of this kind of work, which had its roots in the late 1950s, was becoming dissipated, in part precisely because of the rise of 'conceptual art' as a distinct artistic genre. Number 5 was the penultimate issue of *0–9*; the final issue appeared in July 1969. LeWitt had already published his influential 'Paragraphs on Conceptual Art' in the mainstream *Artforum* in summer 1967, eighteen months previously. It was thus not surprising to see his *Sentences* reproduced, alongside Graham's 1966 *Poem-Schema* and Laurence Weiner's 1968 *Statements*, in the first issue of *Art–Language*, the self-declared 'Journal of Conceptual Art', as a sample of the latest US conceptual art for British readers.

Art–Language was the journal of an intellectual avant-garde too. However, it was moving reflectively from 'art' towards 'philosophy', rather than from 'poetry' to 'art' – each, here, a distinct aspect of what in *The Athenaeum* was a single movement. Furthermore, the philosophy that so fascinated Art & Language was of an analytical, logico-linguistic variety. In the context of *Art–Language*, the poetic dimension of LeWitt's *Sentences* was thus downplayed, to the point of its erasure, in favour of its 'purely' or ideally conceptual content. Placing LeWitt's *Sentences* in the context of *Athenaeum Fragments* allows us to revive something of their formal dimension in a philosophical manner unrelated to the kind of philosophical work that so fascinated Art & Language, but which nonetheless occupies some of the same conceptual space.

Still, this might seem an idiosyncratic and arbitrary conjunction, dreamt up across a gap of 170 years, between two continents, in the spirit of a surrealistic montage. And there is indeed something of surrealist montage about this. However, there is a method in this madness (as there was in surrealism). It is not an arbitrary connection – the method of what Walter Benjamin called the construction of 'an image at the now of recognizability', or what we might call *the experimental method of montage as the means of production of historical intelligibility*. This is the basic method of a post-Hegelian philosophy of history. As Benjamin wrote in one of the notes for his *Arcades Project*:

> It is not that what is past casts its light on what is present, or what is present its light on what is past; rather, an image is that wherein what has been come together in a flash with the now to form a constellation. In other words: image is dialectics at a standstill. For while the relation of the present to the past is purely temporal, the relation of what-has-been to the now is dialectical: not temporal in nature but figural [*bildlich*]. Only dialectical images are genuinely historical... The image that is read... [is] the image in the now of its recognizability [*das Bild im Jetzt der Erkennbarkeit*]...[45]

There is a 'particular recognizability' to the 'now' of LeWitt's *Sentences on Conceptual Art* today (1969 in 2011), through which it 'enters into legibility' with the 'then' of the *Athenaeum Fragments* (1798 in 2011): the recognizability of philosophical romanticism in conceptual art, and thereby, conversely, the retrospective anticipation of conceptual art in philosophical romanticism itself. Or to put it another way, at the level of their critical historical intelligibility, there is a *mutual* constitution of philosophical romanticism and conceptual art, through which they acquire a conjoint contemporaneity. The dialectical image constructed by the relation between the *then* of the *Athenaeum Fragments* and the *now* of *Sentences on Conceptual Art* produces an image of romanticism as a conceptual art, and an image of conceptualism as a romantic art.[46]

I shall proceed by concentrating on two concepts at the heart of philosophical romanticism and contemporary art alike – fragment and project – as lenses through which to focus a reading of LeWitt's

Sentences, which will, I hope, help to give new meaning to these terms in turn. The point is not to *assimilate* LeWitt to philosophical romanticism, or vice versa, but rather to constellate their terms, transforming the historical meaning of each. On the Benjaminian model of historical intelligibility that I am using here: 'Historical "understanding" (*Verstehen*) is to be grasped, in principle, as an afterlife (*Nachleben*) of that which is understood.'[47] In this sense, LeWitt's *Sentences on Conceptual Art* is part of the afterlife of philosophical romanticism; just as this analysis is part of the afterlife of *Sentences* itself.

By philosophical romanticism, I mean something quite precise: namely, that body of thought produced in Jena in the second half of the 1790s, whose main representatives were the authors of *The Athenaeum* along with (among others), most importantly, Friedrich Hölderlin. It is also known as 'early German Romanticism'. This was a moment defined, for Friedrich Schlegel, by the conjunction of a political event, a philosophical event and a literary event: 'the French Revolution, Fichte's philosophy, and Goethe's [*Wilhelm*] *Meister*', which he described as the three 'greatest tendencies of the age' [*AF* 216]. Many of the ideas central to the understanding of modern and contemporary art – indeed, the philosophical concepts of *art* and *criticism* themselves – derive from the writings of this small group in this brief period: *fragment* and *project*, but also the ideas of *the new*, of *collective* (*anonymous or pseudonymous*) *production* (see Chapter 1, above), of the *dissolution of genres* into an artistic process of *infinite becoming* (see Chapters 3 and 4, below) and, finally, *the incomprehensible* (the topic of the final essay/fragment in the last issue of the *Athenaeum*). 'Fragments' is a text that distils much of the art-critical significance of this philosophical romanticism.

But what is it about Sol LeWitt's *Sentences on Conceptual Art* that suggests it be constellated with *this* romanticism? After all, as far as I am aware, there is no philological connection, no 'influence' in an empirical art-historical sense, no 'appearance of continuity' – as Benjamin defined tradition. LeWitt is more commonly associated with the North American reception of Eastern philosophy, than with Romanticism. In fact, the significance of philosophical romanticism for the understanding of the plastic arts was increasingly obscured from the late nineteenth century onwards, by its literary origins, once the generic term 'art' [*Kunst*], whose meaning it articulated, migrated from the field of literature to the plastic arts. In its place came the preoccupation with notions of 'medium' and 'aesthetic', with an emphasis on the specific visuality or opticality of works, which further separated three-dimensional work from the heritage of the early romanticism. It is interesting just how unproblematic the distinction between 'art' and 'literature' remains in

LeWitt's *Sentences*, despite its explicit opposition to the limitations imposed by conventional concepts of medium:

> 8. When words such as painting and sculpture are used, they connote a whole tradition and imply a consequent acceptance of this tradition, thus placing limitations on the artist who would be reluctant to make art that goes beyond the limitations.

Yet, it is claimed:

> 16. If words are used, and they proceed from ideas about art, then they are art and not literature . . .

Sentence 16 depends upon a conventional but nonetheless historically quite odd opposition. When conceptual art broke with these conventions in the 1960s – recovering and extending the alternative modernism of a generic concept of art, and laying the ground for the radical openness of contemporary art – its philosophical self-understanding was largely restricted to the Anglo-American analytical philosophy of its day, unrelated to the philosophical heritage that it was unknowingly recovering.[48] LeWitt was something of an exception in this regard, not because he had other philosophical sources, but because his critical writings offer more direct conceptual reflections on the structure of his practice. This is their strength. Nonetheless, whether they knew it or not, the more or less loosely affiliated groups of artist-critics of the 1960s and 1970s (Donald Judd, Robert Morris, Robert Smithson, Sol LeWitt, Adrian Piper, Mel Bochner, Joseph Kosuth, and more formally, Ian Burn, Roger Cutforth and Mel Ramsden in the Society for Theoretical Art and Analyses, in the US; Terry Atkinson and Michael Baldwin in Art & Language, in the UK; and N.E. Thing Co., in Canada) were following in the footsteps of what Schlegel called the 'poetizing-philosophers, philosophizing poets' of the 1790s [*AF* 249], both in combining the roles of artist and critic and in the collective aspects of their practices.

In the case of LeWitt's *Sentences*, there are more particular connections: both formal and semantic resemblances, which point to deeper affinities – affinities that operate below the level of consciousness and intentionality and hence against any psychological understanding of historical meaning, and which depend upon, precisely, what we might call literary aspects of the work, suppressed by the purely analytical context of reception of *Art–Language*, and the usual comparisons with Kosuth (whose own two-part essay, 'Art and Philosophy', appeared later in autumn 1969, in *Studio International*).[49] The formal resemblance is that between the *fragment* and the *sentence*, and hence between *fragments* and *sentences*, as groups. The similarities of meaning primarily concern *process* and *ideality*. The more fundamental affinities that underlie and give a deeper meaning to these resemblances concern *ideas* and *projects*, and connectedly the artistic role and art-status of a certain kind of *criticism*. For the ultimate question raised by the constellation of LeWitt's *Sentences* with Schlegel's *Fragments* is that of the art-status of *Sentences* itself, and hence the plausibility of its final sentence:

> 35. These sentences comment on art, but are not art.

'These sentences comment on art, but are not art', even though, (Sentence 16) '[i]f words are used, and they proceed from ideas about art, then they are art and not literature . . .' The contradiction is apparent. If we take it literally, Sentence 35 opposes *Sentences* to the self-understanding of both the Society for Theoretical Art and Analyses – alongside whom LeWitt published in *Art Press*, in July 1969[50] – and Art & Language themselves, who were exploring the idea that such sentences could be, precisely, art, *as* a theoretical intervention; hence their publication of *Sentences*. This opposition perhaps explains Sentence 35. But should we take it literally? Or is it rather an invitation to refutation, or at least a way of rendering indeterminate, and *thereby*, ironically, artistic the art-status of the *Sentences*?

Fragment and Sentence

The fragment is the central philosophical concept of early German Romanticism. It appears at first sight to be a narrowly literary or artistic concept, a genre concept (which it is also), but it is crucial to comprehend it in its philosophical meaning. For early Romanticism is characterized, first and foremost, by its crossing and mutual transformation of literary and philosophical discourses, through which a new kind of discourse about art comes into being. In this central case, the concept of the fragment is constituted by the reception into the context of post-Kantian German philosophy of a French and English (and before that, Roman) tradition of brief and occasional moral writings. This context unified what is otherwise a diverse multiplicity of forms – the essay, the *pensée*, the maxim, the aphorism, the opinion, the remark, the anecdote (in Montaigne, Pascal, Shaftsbury, La Rochefoucauld and Chamfort, respectively) – through their mutual 'fragmentariness' or relative incompletion, in order to posit the new form constituted by this unity – that is, the fragment – as an artistic solution to a philosophical problem. The problem was the equal necessity and impossibility of a philosophical system, through which the world might be known as a whole – that is, in its truth.

> It is equally fatal for the mind to have a system and to have none. It will simply have to decide to combine the two. [*AF* 53]

The mode of combination devised by Schlegel was to adopt a systematic *orientation* towards the (potentially infinite) disjunctive ensemble of parts or 'fragments' of knowledge, and thereby to posit what Adorno would later call, in his *Negative Dialectics*, an 'anti-system'.[51] The fragment is the basic unit of intelligibility of the romantic anti-system; the also always-incomplete *collection* of fragments is its higher form. It is important to this philosophical conception of the fragment that, despite their individual independence (and purely negative relation to an absent whole), the genre is plural: fragment*s*.

The occasion for this critically transformative unification of genres into the meta-genre of the fragment was the posthumous publication of Chamfort's *Pensées, Maxims and Anecdotes* in 1795, which was received by Schlegel into the critical debates immediately following the 1794 publication of Fichte's *Theory of Science* [*Wissenschaftslehre*]. Chamfort 'sparked' the fragment, as it were. This is not the occasion to elaborate upon those intense and intricate, often hermetic, philosophical debates. (In 1794 Fichte had taken up the chair in philosophy in Jena, where Schlegel himself arrived, belatedly relative to the 'Jena constellation', in August 1796, attending Fichte's lectures, along with others in the group.) However, a brief summary of Schlegel's argument is necessary. The issue at stake was the possibility of a self-grounding first principle from which a system of philosophy could be deduced. Knowledge of the absolute, in the form of the system (philosophical idealism), appeared dependent upon such a principle. However, the very notion of a first principle from which a system of the absolute could be deduced appeared contradictory, since in order to ground such a system, the principle itself would have to be absolute, thereby dispensing with the need for a system through which to know the absolute. But such *immediate*, intuitive knowledge of the absolute would have no determinate or systematic content, and so would itself lack 'absoluteness'. A philosophical system thus appeared – at this stage in the argument at least – to be both necessary but impossible to ground.

The fragment acquired its philosophical meaning by being posited as the *medium of reflection* of this apparent contradiction between the finite and infinite aspects of an absolute knowledge. On the one hand, it epitomizes self-consciousness of the finitude or partiality of knowledge: it is not only self-enclosed but self-enclos*ing* – a self-*limiting* form, conscious of its incompleteness, yet nonetheless also relatively self-sufficient. On the other hand, constructed from the systematic *standpoint* of its negative relation to the idea of a system (totality or lack of limitation), it carries the *idea* of totality within itself, both negatively, conceptually, and – this is the important bit – positively, in its figural or formal self-sufficiency, its independence from other fragments.

> A fragment, like a miniature work of art, has to be entirely isolated from the surrounding world and be complete in itself like a hedgehog. [*AF* 206]

The hedgehog here is crucial to romantic epistemology: it provides the imagistic 'flash' of understanding associated with insight and wit (*Witz*), without which philosophical knowledge is not possible. The independence of each individual fragment from others *figures* the idea of totality, from which the ensemble or collection of fragments derives both its necessity – as an *externally* imposed or constructed unity of a multiplicity, the unity of a montage – and its own sense of *in*completion. The collection cannot make up for the partiality of the parts; it can only constitute a new partiality at a higher level. There is thus a dialectics of completion–incompletion at work within the philosophy of the fragment at three levels: (i) internal to each fragment, (ii) at the level of each collection of fragments, and finally (iii) at the speculative level of the totality of all possible fragments. In the process of this philosophizing (Novalis would say 'romanticizing') of the fragment, it becomes the basic unit of philosophical intelligibility. Something – anything – becomes a possible object of philosophical interpretation – that is, a possible object of experience of truth, in so far as it is grasped *as* a fragment: namely, a finite form that carries a reference to the infinite, negatively, through the combination of the partiality of its content and the completeness or self-sufficiency of its form. From this point of view, the work of art carries a metaphysical meaning in so far as it is a fragment. In short, philosophically, the fragment *is* the work of art. This is the origin of the modern conception of the *non-organic* work, and the sense in which modern art, contra classicism, is romantic – unless it is reactively neo-classical, that is, but that is another story. In fact, one might say that the developmental structures of both modern art and philosophy after Hegel take the form of *dialectics of romanticizations and reactive neo-classicisms* (returns to order).[52]

That this notion of the fragment is indeed a philosophical concept rather than a merely literary one is attested by Schlegel's reference to its ideality.

... as yet no genre exists that is fragmentary both in form and content, simultaneously completely subjective and individual [this is what separates it off from other fragments – PO], and completely objective and like a necessary part in a system of all the sciences. [*AF* 77]

The fragment is an *ideal* form.

What does this have to do with LeWitt's *Sentences on Conceptual Art*? LeWitt certainly did not write 'fragments' in any self-conscious literary or philosophical sense; or conceive his three-dimensional works and projects in such terms. In terms of his literary production, he wrote, first, 'paragraphs' and then, a year or so later, 'sentences': paragraphs and sentences 'on' conceptual art. In doing so, he was probably more influenced formally by some of Ad Reinhardt's writings from the late 1950s than by anything else; such as the 1957 'Twelve Rules for a New Academy' or the 1958 '25 Lines of Words on Art'.[53] Nonetheless, these literal grammatical designations – paragraphs, sentences – clearly involve a certain literary formalism, quite distinct from the logical and performative uses of grammatical forms by artists like Weiner, Kosuth, early John Baldessari or Mel Ramsden.

Weiner's 1968 'Statements' (reprinted in the same first issue of *Art–Language* as LeWitt's *Sentences*) have an awkward declarative, aphoristic independence and sculptural intent that allowed them to be displayed independently, in a variety of graphical forms, transposed onto walls in a range of public sites, allying them, belatedly, with the Pop-typographic aspect of the early Kosuth, and making them, retrospectively (after Jenny Holzer) into obscure truisms. Early works by Baldessari and Ramsden depend upon context and materials – painting – for the jokey critical effects of their linguistic propositions. While Kosuth's analogical conception of the propositional status of art – 'art as idea as idea' – had a more ambiguous relation to linguistic expression. In Kosuth, language offers a logical model – the analytical proposition; the art need *not* be actually 'made' of language as such.

Indeed, for all the *numerical* formalism of his works, and the subtle *literary* formalism of his main critical statements – and I am suggesting a parallel here between those two formalisms – LeWitt was famously polemically against 'the logical' and the 'rational' forms (words he tended to use as synonyms) seemingly embraced by other practicioners of a conceptual art. LeWitt identified the conceptual with the 'mental', rather than the logical: 'Conceptual, not logical – the mind is used to infer', we read in the 'Notes'.[54] And, of course, he famously wrote in *Sentences*:

1. Conceptual artists are mystics rather than rationalists. They leap to conclusions that logic cannot reach.

Artists are very fond of this sentence. This 'mystical' aspect is one clue to the depth at which one can make a claim for the status of *Sentences* as fragments; to its being, one might say, 'fragmentary both in form and content, simultaneously completely subjective and individual, and completely objective'. But it is philosophically a rather more complicated 'mysticism' than some may care to know (as was that of the early Romantics). The way *Sentences* acquires this fragmentary status is by participating, equally, in the potentially infinite openness but actually finite closure of an exhibited part of a series. The way it does this is by reducing each sentence, formally, to a unit of 'information'.

Information and Series

The historical meaning of the concept of information appears most clearly in Benjamin's 1936 essay 'The Storyteller', which recounts the epochal historical transition from an oral *narrative* tradition, directed towards transmitting the 'epic side of truth' – namely, wisdom' – via the rise of the book form of the novel, to the 'new form of communication' of *information*. Information, associated with the newspaper, is understood to bring about 'a crisis in the novel'. Information has two main features: prompt verifiability and 'understandability in itself', or semantic self-sufficiency. As Benjamin puts it: 'The value of information does not survive the moment in which it was new. It lives only at that moment; it has to surrender to it completely and explain itself to it without losing any time.' This need to 'sound plausible' is understood to be incompatible with the 'spirit' of storytelling. Hence information marks the decline of narrative. However, this is not itself (as it is often taken to be) a narrative of decline:

> ... nothing would be more fatuous than to see in it merely a '"symptom of decay", let alone a "modern" symptom. It is, rather, only a concomitant symptom of the secular productive forces of history, a concomitant that has quite gradually removed narrative from living speech...'[55]

This historical sequence, epic–novel–information (which then gets taken up into montage, in both literary and film forms), was replayed in condensed form at high speed in the curatorial history of conceptual art between spring 1969 and autumn 1970: in the series of exhibitions running from *When Attitudes Become Form* (Bern, spring 1969), subtitled 'Works–Concepts–Processes–Situation–Information' (information is fifth in an informational series), via the seminal show *Information* (Museum of Modern Art, New York, July 1970) – in which information becomes synonymous with the work of art – to *Software: Information Technology – Its New Meaning as Art*, (Jewish Museum, New York, autumn 1970), in which information is itself reduced to its latest technological medium. What is interesting about Sol LeWitt's serialism is that it uses the semantic self-sufficiency of the unit of information – here, the sentence – as its material, but gives it new meaning by reconfiguring the relations between such units, in order to display the pure form of information itself, independently of any particular content, thereby giving the 'major' form a new 'minor' artistic use.[56] As LeWitt himself put it, in his description of his 'Serial Project No. 1', in *Aspen* 5–6 (1967):

> The aim of the artist would not be to instruct the viewer but to give him information. Whether the viewer understands this information is incidental . . . The serial artist does not attempt to produce a beautiful or mysterious object but functions as a clerk cataloguing the results of the premise.[57]

To see how this works at a formal level, we need to turn to the concept of series and what we might call its 'homemade' or minor artistic use. LeWitt's serialism, we might say, in Deleuze and Guattari's terms, is the *becoming-minor* of information.

The concept of the series reveals both the fundamental affinity of Lewitt's *Sentences* to Schlegel's *Fragments* and also some decisive differences, since they involve two very different, albeit crossing, conceptions of series. The thing to bear in mind here is that the 'collection of fragments' is the philosophical model of the work of art; and the series is a form of unity of such a collecting together or assembling. Series is thus a *mode of unity* of the work of art. As such, in both Schlegel and Lewitt the series is associated with the subject, the I – a fractured, or 'fragmented' I, one might say. In the 'Notes' for the *Sentences* we find:

Serial – time
– must be read
Serial – time – paradox
– to be inferred by evidence
– subject's logic

The Romantic Series: From Line to Circle
Series is a central concept of post-Kantian philosophy and philosophical romanticism in particular. Two things define the philosophical specificity of Kantian philosophy: (i) the notion of the *transcendental* as the 'condition of possibility' of some particular form of experience, and (ii) the idea that the *totality* of the series of conditions (the unconditioned or the absolute) cannot be known by sensuous finite beings such as ourselves. Transcendental philosophy is thus ultimately *serial*, in the simple mathematical respect that there is always another condition of possibility to be known – to be added to the series, which cannot be grasped as a whole. Kantianism posits knowledge in the form of an *infinite series*. In practice, this means that the absolute/totality/reason can only be approached through an *infinite approximation* as an *infinite task*, which was also Kant's conception of morality. The early Romantics remained Kantians in both these two basic respects (above). Their philosophical innovation, in the wake of Fichte's philosophy, was to extend this process of infinite approximation, first, to the self-reflective structure of the subject, the I – to produce the concept of infinite reflection – and second, to the internal dynamics of the work of art, as the epistemologically privileged site of such infinite reflection, and hence as a peculiar kind of quasi-subject.[58]

Let us recall the structure of the philosophical problem to which the fragment stood as an aesthetico-philosophical response: the antinomy of principle and system that Schlegel took to characterize the Fichtean project of providing an absolute ground to knowledge. Grounding knowledge of the absolute in a principle is impossible because of the self-contradictory claim to absoluteness of the principle. The more specific form that this antinomy took in Fichte's work was an *infinite regress* in the subject's (the I's) attempt to know itself, since it was the I that Fichte attempted to make into the principle of his system. The specific contradiction inherent to the principle of the I as a first principle of philosophical knowledge is that each time the I posits itself as the object of its own knowledge it separates itself qua object from itself qua subject of that knowledge, thereby knowing itself only incompletely. In then attempting to heal this rift within itself by knowing itself as both subject and object of knowledge, it once again separates itself, qua subject of this second knowledge, from itself as both subject and object of the previous act of knowing, etc, to infinity.

The differences between the various philosophical positions at Jena in the late 1790s were defined by their responses to this infinite regress. The Romantic position, held by both Novalis in his *Fichte Studies* and Friedrich Schlegel was, first, that this contradictory infinite regress of self-reflection simply *is* the structure of the subject. In other words, the problem of grounding cannot be resolved, except in the sense that the very recognition of its irresolvability is a resolution of sorts. (This is an origin of the modern notion of philosophy as a kind of therapeutic dissolution of problems.) This displaces the problem of knowing the world as a whole from a problem of grounding to a problem immanent to the structure of infinite reflection, a structure that is taken to be exemplified in the experience of the work of art, qua fragment. In this respect, the famous 'infinite task' of Kantian ethics (becoming moral) becomes the infinite task of the I's self-understanding. This is objectified or resolved into the infinite task of the self-completion of the (fragmentary) work of art. But while the infinite regress of the I's self-understanding takes the form of the straight line, or what Hegel called the 'bad' or mathematical infinite (to which one can always add one), the infinite self-reflection of the work of art is an infinite reflection on the relation of the *self-limiting finitude* of form to the absolute infinite of the task of reflection itself. Early Romanticism thereby converted the linear mathematical infinity of the *series* of self-reflections of the subject into the *circle* of the experience of a self-enclosed, because self-limiting, and thereby figuratively totalized, collection of fragments. The circular character of philosophical reasoning, familiar from Schleiermacher and Hegel – the one hermeneutical, the other speculative – finds here a *figurative* form. This is a figure that would later be reworked by Adorno, in the shadow of Hölderlin, in the structure of *Aesthetic Theory*, as 'parataxis'. It is this transformation of a straight line into a circle that redefines the infinite as itself absolute – that is, beyond its own opposition to the finite.

But how does this notion of the work of art as medium for the transformation of a linear into a circular infinity of reflection relate to LeWitt's *Sentences*?

LeWitt's Series: The Idea Behind the Rule
In the first place, similarly to LeWitt's three-dimensional work, the principles of the production of which they reflect upon, *Sentences* is a serial work – as the numbering of its sentences indicate (Schlegel's fragments are not numbered) – albeit numerically an extremely simple series: from 1 to 35. This has the effect of giving each of the sentences equal value, and also of making the actual endpoint appear numerically arbitrary, and hence subjective, since the series of finite natural numbers could be extended to infinity. In LeWitt's work in general, however, the focus is not on the subjective dimension of the *potential* infinity of the series (the circle of infinite reflection), evoked by the specifically fragmentary finitude of their members, which always refer beyond themselves. Rather, LeWitt's focus is on the contrast between the

subjectivity of the *starting point* (the idea, or determination of the rule) and the objectivity or *mechanical necessity* of the process it initiates. In his three-dimensional projects, the use of formal numerical rules (rather than poetic intuition) to establish the relations between the elements of a series means that the determination of a work by an idea involves a *withdrawal* of artistic subjectivity from the production of the actuality of the work, which becomes a combination of formal necessity and chance.

> 7. The will is secondary to the process [the artist] initiates from idea to completion. His wilfulness may only be ego.

> 28. Once the idea is established in the artist's mind and the final form is decided, the process is carried out blindly. There are many side effects that the artist cannot imagine. These may be used as ideas for new works.

> 29. The process is mechanical and should not be tampered with. It should run its course.

Now, this looks like an explicitly *anti*-Romantic conception of artistic production, at least, in the conventional sense of Romanticism as valorization of the creative genius of artistic subjectivity. But this appearance is misleading, since the productive infinity of the subject has merely been withdrawn from the realization of the work back into its *idea* – as befits the historical transition from artisanal to mechanized labour. LeWitt, we might say, is *a romantic in the age of mechanization* – not romantically *against* mechanization, but romantically appropriating, or coming to terms with, mechanization itself, as the *means* for romanticization. Repetition is the formal basis of series.[59] *Sentences* itself, however, unlike LeWitt's three-dimensional projects and wall-drawings, *is* an artisanal, quasi-poetic, philosophical or critical work – a kind of handmade meta-series.

The mechanization of the logic of production, to which *Sentences* refers, but in which it does not itself participate, is not so much opposed to, as is the historical complement to, a certain mysticism of subject and idea. For the rationality of any series is compromised by the arbitrariness of its beginning (its rule) and (if it is in principle infinite) the point at which its pursuit is terminated.[60] This is the eternal irony of philosophical axiomatics. On this model, the work is made up of a particular relation of the subjective (the choice of the rule) to the objective (the mechanical process of developing the series by applying the rule). The so-called 'mysticism' is in the intuitive leap to the rule or idea that defines the series; just as in early Romanticism, it is in the irrational aspect of the imagistic element through which the relation of the finite to the infinite is grasped concretely in a fragment (the hedgehog).

> When reason and unreason touch there's an electric shock. [*AF* 300]

In the *Athenaeum Fragments*, 'reason' is the *idea* of a self-limiting totality; 'unreason' is the *image* of the hedgehog. This is what Schlegel was looking for in Romantic poetry (poetizing-philosophy, philosophizing poetry), what Benjamin sought from the dialectical image, and what LeWitt found in an art of series. It is in the priority of the process over the object or result here, which is the consequence of the ontological priority of the idea of the work – the virtual infinity of possible actualizations – that LeWitt's conception of art in his *Sentences* approaches an early Romantic one most closely. Each involves the *dissolution of genres* into an artistic process of *infinite becoming*, and thereby a change in the fundamental status of works from 'objects' to 'projects'.

Process and Project

The transference of infinity from the structure of the subject to the process of realization of its ideas – marked in LeWitt's *Sentences* by the potential but never actualized infinity of the numerical series – appears in Schlegel as the progressive university or *absolute becoming* of Romantic poetry. Most famously:

> . . . The romantic kind of poetry is still in the state of becoming; that, in fact, is its real essence: that it should forever be becoming and never be perfected . . . The romantic kind of poetry is the only one that is more than a kind, that is, as it were, poetry itself: for in a certain sense all poetry is or should be romantic. [*AF* 116]

In this light, conceptual art appears as a further radicalization of the concept of Romantic poetry, which, in any case, the early Romantics considered the conceptual model of 'art' [*Kunst*] in general. LeWitt:

> 15. Since no form is intrinsically superior to another, the artist may use any form, from an expression of words (written or spoken), to physical reality, equally.
>
> 17. All ideas are art if they are concerned with art and fall within the conventions of art.

19. The conventions of art are altered by works of art.

One may thus rewrite *Athenaeum Fragment* 116 in the manner of the French Situationist Guy Debord, replacing the phrase 'romantic poetry' with 'conceptual art':

> ... The conceptual kind of art is still in the state of becoming; that, in fact, is its real essence: that it should forever be becoming and never be perfected ... The conceptual kind of art is the only one that is more than a kind, that is, as it were, art itself: for in a certain sense all art is or should be conceptual.

One ontological consequence of this state of permanent becoming is a change in the status of individual works from 'objects' to 'projects': that is, articulated combinations of ideas and modes of actualization. In Schlegel's words:

> A project is the subjective embryo of a developing object. A perfect project should be at once completely subjective and completely objective, should be an indivisible and living individual. In its origin: completely subjective and original, only possible in precisely this sense; in its character, completely objective, physically and morally necessary. The feeling for projects – which one might call *fragments of the future* – is distinguishable from the feeling for fragments of the past only by its direction: progressive in the former, regressive in the latter. What is essential is to be able to idealize and realize objects immediately and simultaneously: to complete them and in part carry them out within oneself. Since transcendental is precisely whatever relates to the joining or separating of the ideal and the real, one might very well say that the feeling for fragments and projects is the transcendental element of the historical spirit. [*AF* 22, *emphasis added*]

LeWitt, I think one can say, had such a feeling. And *Sentences on Conceptual Art* was, and is, such a project. If it is the case that, as *Sentence* 16 has it,

> If words are used, and they proceed from ideas about art, then they are art

then *Sentence* 35 –

> These sentences comment on art, but are not art.

– appears, wilfully, to deny the obvious: namely that these sentences comment on art, *and are also art*. As such, like all conceptual art, they are open to an infinity of disparate actualizations, both textual and otherwise, as demonstrated with great ironic power when John Baldessari sang LeWitt's *Sentences* to camera in his 1972 video work *Baldessari Sings LeWitt*.

3
Modernisms and mediations

Aesthetics, I have suggested, has an inherent tendency to reduce art to what Kant called 'aesthetic art', in a way that makes it peculiarly ill-suited to the comprehension of contemporary art. Historically, aesthetics has been associated with 'l'art pour l'art' (in France), aestheticism (in England), formalism (in Germany) and modernism (in the USA) as artistic and critical movements, each of which conceived itself as developing Kant's legacy, in one way or another.[1] The relationships between these movements have been subtle and fluid, but they increasingly appear as part of a single, continuous stream, culminating in a modernism that is now, belatedly, providing a revived philosophical aesthetics with art-historical legitimation. From this point of view, it is with modernism that 'art becomes aesthetics', while aesthetics becomes 'the reflective construction of the concepts necessary for the comprehension of the *stakes and meaning of art* in the light of the history of the dominant art of the second half of the nineteenth century and the first half of the twentieth century: modernism.'[2] In the 1860s, it seems, European (for which, read 'French') art (for which, read 'painting') finally caught up with Kant. Aesthetics defers to this modernism for the historical content of 'art'. Indeed, aesthetics *hallucinates* this modernism as 'art'; hence its melancholia about contemporary art. The art of the second half of the twentieth century and the beginning of the twenty-first functions for aesthetics, primarily, as a means of 'sustaining loss'.[3]

But can modernism be as straightforwardly identified with artistic aestheticism as the proponents of a revived aesthetics presume? Can the aesthetic character of modernism really be taken for granted, so as to provide an art historical justification for aesthetics? Is there only one critically and artistically relevant 'modernism' here? If more than one, what if any conceptual features does this multiplicity of modernisms share? Is there an overarching, metacritical modernism? If there is more than one modernism, what are the critical relations between multiple modernisms? And what are their differing relations to 'aesthetic' and to 'art', respectively? How, finally, does this multiplicity of modernisms relate to the present, the complex global present of 'contemporary art'? Can modernism really be written off as a living critical category? Or does it subsist, alongside and within the contemporary, as the affirmation of a discrete, complexly articulated historical–temporal form?

In approaching these questions, I begin by stepping back – both conceptually and historically – to the basic semantic shape of the concept of modernism. For it is only by retrieving the fundamental *thought* of modernism – from both the restricted meaning given to it by a particular hegemonic critical school and its reification into a mere name (the name for 'the dominant [Western] art of the second half of the nineteenth century and the first half of the twentieth century') – that we can begin to ascertain its conceptual relations to 'art' and to 'aesthetic' and, thereby, the scope of its possible critical productivity within current art-critical debates. For modernism, on my understanding of the term, is far from over. Indeed, it structures the entire field of contemporary art to the extent to which 'art' remains a historically critical practice.[4]

I proceed from the thought of modernism in general to an account of three particular, historically successive, art-critical modernisms (the third of which comes in two main competing variations): general-aesthetic modernism, medium-specific modernism, and generic artistic modernism, or the modernism associated with a generic concept of art. What consideration of this plurality of artistic modernisms reveals is the central role in the production of contemporary art played by a crisis-ridden array of mediating critical forms. The question of the modernism of contemporary art, this chapter argues, primarily concerns the character and the status of these mediating critical forms.

The double heritage of the modern in art

I have written previously about the specific qualities of modernity as a form of historical time.[5] Modernism involves a development and appropriation of this temporal logic. It is thus necessary, very briefly, to summarize that previous genealogical account of the modern, to provide the minimal conceptual background needed to comprehend the specificity of modernism as a cultural-temporal form. The English 'modern' (from the Latin *modernus*) means, most simply, 'of today'. However, this 'today' is inscribed within a philosophically specific temporal form, which emerged in Europe around the time of the collapse of the Roman Empire, when the cyclical opposition of 'old and new' characteristic of antiquity was replaced by a sense of the present as an irreversible break with the past. As such, the idea of the modern involves the application of a present-centred phenomenological temporality of present/past/

future (today/yesterday/tomorrow) to a Christian, linear form of historical time. In its basic phenomenological and historical form, the temporality of the modern is thus to be distinguished from the 'objective' chronological time of a quantifiable succession of homogeneous instants (so-called physical or cosmological time), to which it is in no way reducible. In particular, the idea of the modern involves a sense of the present as *new*. More specifically, it picks out from within the present those things that are new and makes them constitutive of its historical meaning, or what we might call 'the historical present'.

As such, the modern relies upon a certain temporal logic of negation, which, in splitting the present from within, makes 'modern' an inherently subjective, value-laden, *critical* term (whether it be judged favourably, as it still largely is today, or unfavourably, as it was overwhelmingly prior to the nineteenth century). In the modern, the new within the present does not merely demand more attention than what is not new; increasingly, it negates the latter's claim on the definition of the present itself. 'Modern' is both a term of temporal ontology and a critical term. (Historical ontology is critical ontology.) Its negation is an antiquation, a making old of the not-new. The present becomes divided internally into the new and the old. 'Modern' is thus an agonistic, conflict-generating term; hence the opposition between the Ancients and the Moderns through which the term 'modern' first acquired an epochal, periodizing significance in twelfth-century Europe. It was not until much later, however, during the eighteenth century, that an intensifying investment in the temporality of the modern as the new—registered by a break not merely with the old, but with the temporality of tradition itself—gave rise at the end of that century to the term 'modernity'. The English 'modernism' predates the intensified sense of the present as modern associated with the word 'modernity', but its application to art in the latter part of the nineteenth century rests upon it.

In its early eighteenth-century applications, the English 'modernism', denoting a collective belief in and sympathy for the modern (as an 'ism' it is both a collective and an affirmative term) was restricted to linguistic change. 'A modernism' was a peculiarity of usage, expression, or style characteristic of recent times – in much the same way that the verb 'modernize' was at first also used mainly only of spelling, buildings, and dress. What these contexts share is a clear sense of change needing to be justified.[6] They indicate that, from its beginnings, modernism was a discourse of the legitimation of change. In its most general form, then, modernism is a *collective affirmation of the modern, as such*: an affirmation of temporal negation, an affirmation of the time-determination of the new. In its basic sense, modernism in art involves the application of this performative temporal logic of negation to the field of art: the project of the production of the qualitatively new in art or, more precisely, the production of an art appropriate to the qualitative novelty of the historical present itself. In this respect, artistic modernism both leans upon that heightened or intensified sense of the time-consciousness of the modern evoked by the term 'modernity' and distinguishes itself from the more particular future-oriented temporality of the avant-garde. As the modern intensifies, it increasingly incorporates the future's prospective negation of the present into its sense of the present itself, approaching a kind of generalized or abstract avant-gardism. However, the future is here reduced to its function of negating the present, irrespective of any particular historical content. This is the difference from avant-gardes, which always act in the name of particular futures: modernism anticipates the future only at the level of pure temporal form (the new). Relative to 'avant-garde', modernism is abstract.

'Modernity' has a double reference here. It refers first to developments within the periodizing use of the term 'modern' that are marked in German by the distinction between *die Moderne* and *Neuzeit* (literally, 'new time'). 'Modernity' (*Neuzeit*) marks a distinct period within the modern age, not by virtue of any particular social content or historical event, but by virtue of the character of its temporality alone: the self-transcending temporality of an investment in the new that opposes itself to tradition in general. Second, it refers directly to the temporal qualities that define modernity as a period. It is this second, more immediately qualitative usage—originating, emblematically, in Baudelaire—that foregrounds the inherently aesthetic aspects of 'modernity' as a temporal form and, by retrospective effect, the aesthetic characteristics of 'the modern' as well. These characteristics are not, at base, to do with aesthetic in its sense of a criticism of taste, but, first of all, in its 'ancient' sense of matters of sensibility: pure temporal form.

In Baudelaire, the temporal aesthetics of 'modernity' become the basis of both an artistic practice (modern lyric) and an art-critical project (painting as the painting of 'modern life'). It was out of the reflexivity of this dual application—to art and to art criticism—that what subsequently became canonized as the mainstream of artistic modernism was born. However—and this is the crucial point—there is no conceptual connection between the aestheticism of this particular art ('early' modernism, be it literary or visual) and its character *as a modernism* – that is, an affirmation of the application of the temporal logic of modernism (the affirmation of temporal negation) to the field of art. As a temporal quality of experience, 'modernity' *is* an inherently aesthetic category, but this relation need not necessarily be carried over into the content of any particular modernist art. Rather, the aestheticism of late nineteenth-century modernism was contingent upon the use of 'aesthetic' as an autonomizing strategy within the modernist struggle against the received dependencies of artistic tradition.[7] 'Aesthetic' functions there as a *symbol* of the modern qua negation (negation of art's previous social functions); it is not internally related to the concept of 'modern art' as such, since, the autonomy of art is to be distinguished from 'aesthetic autonomy', as argued in Chapter 1, above.

In fact, more generally, in its dynamic sense as a temporal logic of negation, artistic modernism necessarily transcends its own historically inaugural (in this case, 'aesthetic') form. Within the ambit of this temporal logic (the historical embeddedness of which is, of course, extra-artistic), there is thus of necessity a *multiplicity* of artistic modernisms, not merely at the level of aesthetic form but at that of the concept of art itself. In particular, as we shall see, historically, there are a multiplicity of modernisms at the level of the most basic relations between 'art' and 'aesthetic'. The differences between them are determined by which aspects of the artistic field the art in question takes as the objects of its practices of negation. Identifying these aspects, we may schematize this generation of a multiplicity of modernisms out of the conceptual logic or basic *operation* of modernism itself. Such schemas provide us with a philosophical framework for a critical history of modernisms. But, before I do this, let me return for a moment to Baudelaire, in order to elaborate a little further the senses in which modernity may be said to be 'aesthetic' and the way in which the temporal logic of modernism in art nonetheless *disengages* it from its inaugural ('aesthetic') form.

In Baudelaire's famous usage, *modernité* denotes not merely the quality of being modern (being new) but the essential transitoriness that this quality had by then come to involve, as a result of its intensification and generalization as a lived experience of time. In Baudelaire's famous formulation, the qualities of *modernité* are 'the ephemeral, the fugitive, the contingent . . . whose metamorphoses are so rapid.'[8] This form of experience had as its condition not merely an extraordinary acceleration in the rhythm of social change – urbanization, industrialization, revolution – but, more specifically, its condensation into the metropolitan cultural logic of fashion. Indeed, it was the increasing importance of fashion to capitalist production – in stimulating both innovation and consumption – that subsequently led to the identification of modernity as capitalism's paradigmatic cultural form.[9] Baudelaire was concerned with the presence of modernity in art, in distinction from – but not in opposition to – modernity in life: as a representation and heightened form of modernity in life ('the painting of modern life'). His use of the term *modernité* registers both an intensification of temporal experience and an investment in the representation of this temporal intensification as both a philosophical and a cultural *value* in art. 'Modernity' is aesthetic in a triple sense here, while art is 'modern' in two different ways.

First, 'modernity' (like the modern more broadly) is aesthetic in the technical, 'ancient' sense of Kant's *Critique of Pure Reason*, where 'aesthetic' refers to the doctrine of sensibility (transcendentally, space and time), since modernity is at root a purely temporal quality. Modernity is transcendentally aesthetic; it is a historical a priori. Modernity is a *feeling of time* (although, as a historical a priori, it is closer to a schema than a pure intuition).[10] Second, as an aspect of the beauty of modern life (what Baudelaire referred to as 'the special nature of present-day beauty'), 'modernity' is an aesthetic term in the more restricted, famously German sense of belonging to the critique of taste. Modernity is a *beautiful* feeling of time. Third, as an attribute of art ('the half of art whose other half is the eternal and the immutable'), 'modernity' is an aesthetic term in the still more constrained (and in my view confusing) sense in which, at the beginning of the nineteenth century, 'aesthetic' acquired a usage synonymous with '*of art*'. Modernity in art, for Baudelaire, is a 'distillation' or 'purification' of the beautiful feeling of transitoriness, a distillation of the beauty of time from life into art, which thereby, paradoxically, effects its *eternalization*. As Walter Benjamin showed, there is a dialectic of the transitory and the eternal at work in Baudelaire's thought (they turn into each other), which extends significantly beyond Baudelaire's self-understanding.[11]

It is the condensation of these three registers of aesthetic (of *sensibility*, of *taste*, and of *art*) into the single term 'modernity' that makes Baudelaire's text such a pivotal moment in the history of the relationship between aesthetic and art. Baudelaire's is the historically first *immanently* artistic aestheticism. (Kant – or rather, those who followed him – imposed philosophical aesthetic onto art, externally.) Baudelaire's exposition of *modernité* is the first successful historical mediation of aesthetic and art. Furthermore, in its affirmation of transitoriness, it is also the first proper (that is, generalized) modernism. This is the truth of Bernstein's claim, cited above, that 'with modernism art becomes aesthetics': with *Baudelaire's* modernism 'art becomes aesthetics' – the artistic re-presentation of the aesthetics of modernity. But only for a while . . .

Art may be said to be modernist in two different senses here, corresponding to that mobile 'empirico-transcendental doublet' that characterizes not just Kant's thought of the human but all thought of the historical a priori as well.[12] On the one hand, art may be called 'modernist' in the quasi-transcendental sense of gaining its intelligibility from its enactment, within and upon the artistic field, of that performative temporal logic of negation that constitutes the structure of modernism in general. This is modernism as an *operation* or a *generative logic*. On the other hand, art may be called 'modernist' in the specific art historical sense of being the modernism of its day: that is, constituted as a *particular* form of negation of a *particular* historically received artistic field. In the first case, modernism is a metacritical term; in the second case, it is a term of an empirical historical criticism. The terminological (and consequently conceptual) difficulty we inherit lies in the fixing of the term 'modernism' to a single occurrence of the latter sense, as the *name* of a particular modernism ('the dominant [Western] art of the second half of the nineteenth century and the first half of the twentieth century') – assuming that this century of art exhibits sufficient formal unity to constitute one modernism. But whatever its precise and inevitably disputed borders, this reduction of modernism to an art historical concept effaces its more fundamental transcendental operation as an *ongoing* affirmation of a structure of temporal negation.

If we are to escape the conceptual trap laid by this conventional usage, we must ask: what happens to our understanding of modernism in art when the temporality of the qualitatively new continues to be affirmed, either against the 'first' (French) modernism of artistic aestheticism, or in other contexts altogether (for example, in Japan or China or Brazil or Latvia, today)?[13] It is at this point that our inquiry intersects with recent debates about modernism and the ontology of the artwork set in motion by Duve's *Kant After Duchamp*: specifically, the polemical counterposition of a Greenbergian 'specific' modernism to a Duchampian 'generic' and nominalistic one. Consideration of this opposition and its relation to the inaugural 'aesthetic' modernism of the late nineteenth century will help to clarify the relationship between the quasi-transcendental structure of modernism in general and the (in principle, unlimited) empirical (but nonetheless critically construed) multiplicity of 'restricted' historical modernisms.

Artistic modernisms: aesthetic, specific, generic

In its fundamental conceptual form, I have suggested, artistic modernism is the ongoing result of an application of the temporal logic of modernism (determinate negation of the old/affirmation of the new) to the field of art. Differences between art-critical modernisms will thus depend upon which aspects of this field are the objects, or targets, of particular practices of negation and the mode or manner in which they are negated. It thus becomes possible to produce conceptual schema of the differences between the main Euro-American modernisms in the visual arts, from the latter part of the nineteenth century through to the end of the 1960s. These schemas are at the same time schemas of different ontologies of art, since the practices of negation at issue operate at the fundamental level of the concepts of 'art' and 'the arts' themselves. As a first approximation, these ontologies may be compared on the basis of the traditional logical division into genera, species, and individuals. On the basis of recent critical debates, three main modernisms in visual art suggest themselves: *general-aesthetic* modernism, *medium-specific* modernism, and *generically artistic* modernism, or the modernism (which is also a nominalism) of the generic concept of art, which comes in two main critical variants. Each of these modernisms privileges a different level of the logical triad of genus/species/individual. (The privileged level is indicated in the tables below by the use of an asterisk.

Genus*	Art	Aesthetics of *Techné* (as opposed to of nature)
Species	The arts	Historically privileged carriers of aesthetic properties [Meta-genre: modes of representation of 'modern life']
Individuals	Works of art	Sites of experiences of (transcendentally defined) aesthetic singularities

A. Aesthetic modernism (aesthetic ontology): a *negation* of the received social dependencies constitutive of academic art; an *affirmation* of aesthetic qualities as means/media of artistic autonomy.

Aesthetic modernism negated the system of social dependencies constitutive of the academic art of the first half of the nineteenth century on the basis of an affirmation of artistic freedom via the aesthetic concept of art: 'free' or 'autonomous' aesthetic art. The modernism of art for art's sake (*l'art pour l'art*) – the negation of dependency – was the modernism of aesthetic art. 'Aesthetic' was a synecdoche for 'freedom' here. To the extent to which *artistic* autonomy was actually an achievement of the market, this freedom is in part illusory. Artistic aestheticism is an *ideology* of autonomy (it misunderstands the autonomy of art). Nonetheless, at a practical and critical level, the bohemian avant-gardes of the second half of the nineteenth century instituted aesthetic art for the first time.[14]

One might think that the proponents of aesthetic art could propose certain shared aesthetic qualities that make individual works of art 'art'. However, being the object of a particular type of ('pure aesthetic') judgement cannot provide the unification that is sought at the level of the genus, since such judgements also apply – indeed, they apply paradigmatically – to nature. For the aesthetic tradition, what makes a work of art 'art' (*techné*) and what gives it critical value, as art (its aesthetic qualities), remain stubbornly disjunctive. Aesthetic criteria must be supplemented by technical criteria in order to define 'aesthetic art', but in pure aesthetic judgement these technical criteria must then be forgotten, or disavowed, in order that the object appear purely aesthetic. Nonetheless, the aesthetic primacy of 'presence' as transitoriness, in Baudelaire – the temporal aesthetic of the modern itself – does privilege representations of modern life as its meta-genre, across the arts.

Despite its occasional critical utilization of a general concept of aesthetic art, in practice aesthetic modernism – early artistic modernism, artistic aestheticism – was not primarily about 'art' as such, but about modernity in 'the arts'. Early modernism inherited from academic art a plurality of historically established discrete arts. The modernity of the arts may be understood as residing in a new emphasis on their autonomously aesthetic qualities, as a result of an emphasis on their 'presentness'. However, these qualities were nonetheless immanent to the particular, historically received, and developing structures of artistic practice that constituted the arts (painting, sculpture, drawing, etc.). These were not merely contingent instantiations of the properties of a generalized quasi-Kantian aesthetic. In this respect, as Greenberg saw, in practice, early modernism involved a retrieval of the aesthetic dimensions of historically received arts, as well as a new emphasis on their exploration and autonomous development – a construction of continuity – in the context of the depiction of modern life. Indeed, only on this basis can the aestheticism of artistic modernism be distinguished from (and valued over) the aestheticism of everyday life, to which it was so intimated to be related, culturally. It is precisely because aestheticism already contained, in the excess of 'aesthetic' over 'art', the principle of the movement from 'art' to 'life' that the historical avant-garde may be considered, in Benjamin's phrase, the 'secret cargo' of aestheticism itself.[15]

In this respect, Greenberg's *medium-specific modernism* (B, below) represents a clarification of the artistic logic of aesthetic modernism that highlights the fact that its practices of negation were internal to the received system of the arts (that is, that they depended upon historically received concepts of painting and sculpture) while neglecting its transformation of subject matter. (Recognition of the latter was T. J. Clark's correction, in his work on Manet, or—better—*completion* of Greenberg.) From this (by then post-impressionist) standpoint, aesthetic modernism in the arts appeared, critically, as an aesthetic redefinition of artistic mediums. Greenberg's brilliance lay in his mediation of this maintenance of an ontological plurality of arts with the general concept of aesthetic art, through the speculative historical redefinition of 'medium' (derived from Lessing), such that each medium expresses an 'irreducible element' of experience.[16] In its speculative completion, the system of the arts was thus implicitly projected to map the totality of the aesthetic. This is the extraordinary, closed structural logic of Greenberg's historical criticism. Greenberg was essentially a structuralist of mediums. In the process, Baudelaire's 'distillation' or 'purification' of transitoriness was generalized from literature across the varying aesthetic properties of the arts (as Baudelaire himself had done in relation to music in his late essay on Wagner), giving rise to the idea of artistic modernism as the ongoing process of the experimental self-purification of artistic mediums. Transformed into medium-specific modernism, aesthetic modernism thereby acquired a certain historicity: the 'restricted' historicity internal to the clarification of the structure of mediums, the historicity of the purification of mediums.

Genus	Art	1. Common properties of artistic mediums (immediate presentation of an 'irreducible element of experience') 2. Totality of the arts
Species*	The Arts	Mediums (painting, sculpture, film, etc)
Individuals	Works of art	Instances of medium self-definition

B. Medium-specific modernism (ontology of arts as mediums): a *negation* of non-medium-specific properties; an *affirmation* of medium specificity.

Yet, ultimately, Greenberg's medium-specific modernism can no more cope with the question of what unifies the concept of art than a generalized aesthetic approach. In fact, perhaps even less so. For medium-specific modernism *ontologizes* the plurality of arts as mediums in such a way, seemingly, as to block the very possibility of attributing significant *critical* meaning to the concept of art in general. From this point of view, the concept of art appears at best aporetic. Writers from both standpoints (general-aesthetic and medium-specific), trading on a fundamental ambiguity of logical form, often use the term 'art' as shorthand for the totality of arts and artworks in such a way as to imply that there is some common underlying property unifying the concept of art and giving meaning to the art-character of each of its instances. Yet in reality there can be no such thing for either position, for the question of artistic mediums (*technê*) remains historically open – open to the development of *new* mediums – in such a way as to undermine the mapping of the transcendental elements of 'aesthetic' onto a few discrete, historically established arts (painting and sculpture, in particular). This was, of course, the ground for the historical destruction of Greenberg's critical position and the reason for his increasing (and increasingly incoherent) retreat to a generalized discourse of aesthetic value.[17] The current revival of aesthetics, as a sub-discipline of philosophy, may be seen, in one aspect at least, as an attempt to provide a more adequate philosophical basis for a revived Greenbergianism.

The arbitrariness of restricting aesthetic judgements of art to the terms of a few historically contingent mediums became a critical problem early on in the twentieth century, as soon as appeals to a generic concept of art came to be used strategically within art practices themselves. This not only represented a challenge to the ontological significance of established mediums but, still more fundamentally, to the artistic relevance of 'aesthetic' itself. This is the significance of Marcel Duchamp and his criterion of 'aesthetic indifference'. In Duchamp, the challenge to the ontological significance of a relatively fixed (transcendentally delimited) plurality of arts, mediating between art and individual works of art, and the challenge to the aesthetic substance of works of art go hand-in-hand. What appeared to others as a process of 'purification' of mediums appeared to him, more negatively, as a series of *abandonments*. In Duchamp (and others), the serial abandonment of particular aspects of what had been the craft of painting was radicalized into an abandonment of craft (*techné*) in general. This abandonment of craft became the basis of an alternative modernist tradition (an alternative to both general-aesthetic and medium-specific modernisms): the modernism of a generic concept of art or what we might call a 'generic artistic modernism'. From the standpoint of the present (post-1960s art), this so-called alternative tradition is, in fact, now the *main* tradition of artistic modernism in the twentieth century, running from Duchamp, Dada, Surrealism, and the Russian avant-gardes through to Fluxus, conceptual art, a certain minimalism, and the postconceptual and postminimalist movements of the 1960s, 1970s and beyond. While critically dominant in the United States in the decade-and-a-half immediately following the Second World War and currently resurgent in a marginal and modified form, the medium-specific modernism of a plurality of arts is essentially a nineteenth-century tradition.

Critically, what I am calling generic artistic modernism is currently best known through the reconstruction of the generic concept of art as a proper name that emerged in the course of Duve's work on Duchamp.[18] Historically, however, it has a far broader scope than the Duchampian and minimalist genealogies with which Duve is concerned. This raises the question of the adequacy of his theoretically idiosyncratic nominalism to the critical interpretation of the broader tradition.[19] Nonetheless, what Duve has demonstrated beyond a doubt is: first, that there is more than one philosophical problematic associated with modernism in the visual arts; and second, that while the initially critically dominant one (medium-specific modernism) is 'aesthetic' in origin and orientation, the main competing alternative (generic artistic modernism) is not. I shall refer to Duve's interpretation of Duchamp's generic concept of art as *generic artistic modernism 1* (C).

Genus	'Art'	1. A proper name 2. Totality of successful claims on the name 'art'
Species	[Empty set]	[Readymade as the vanishing mediator of destruction of mediums/negative meta-medium]
Individuals*	Works of art	Individual claims on the name 'art'

C. Generic modernism 1 (nominalist critique of ontology of 'art'): a *negation* of historically received (= craft-based) mediums; an *affirmation* of the enunciative logic of individual claims on the name of 'art'.

What is most striking about this schema is its radical elimination of mediating forms and its resolution of the problem of the relations of individual works to the genus 'art', directly, with a nominalism of the proper name 'art'. The negation of medium here is also negation of ontology, a negation of ontology by naming, or a negative ontology *of* naming. Duve presents this historically in the form of a repetition: the repetition of the result of Duchamp's dialectical abandonment of painting by Frank Stella and Donald Judd's absolute purification of painting, leaving only its object-character behind. Critically, however, Duve's nominalism is effectively a sophisticated ('enunciative') form of positivism. The modernism of an individual work is dependent upon its ability successfully to claim the *name* 'art' in some new way. The critical challenge to those unconvinced by the positivism of Duve's metacritical artistic nominalism is to theorize the history of post-Duchampian art as the history of a modernist series of *subsequent* determinate negations of the artistic field that derive their intelligibility from the *critical mediations* thereby produced. That is to say, the challenge is to theorize the unity of the generic concept of art conceptually, as the distributive unity of a historical process of determinate negations. The thinker who has attempted to do this most systematically is Adorno, in *Aesthetic Theory*, in his conception of the critical 'preponderance of art' over the individual artwork, despite the latter's growing ontological weight.[20] It may be schematized as *generic artistic modernism 2, or a dialectic of modernisms* (D).

Genus	'Art'	Critical distributional unity of the historical totality of works of art
Species	Arts	Afterlife of mediums within 'art'; critical 'isms', individual series and new forms, corresponding to structural negations of the received artistic field
Individuals	Works of art	Ontologically distinctive subject-like entities producing the illusion of autonomous meaning-production through the mediation of determinate negations

D. Generic artistic modernism 2/dialectic of modernisms (historical ontology): a *negation* of historically received (craft-based) mediums; an *affirmation* of new determinate negations of varying aspects of the established artistic field.

The critical primacy of the mediations means that no one level in the logical triad is privileged, ontologically. Rather, artistic ontology is distributed across the field of relations between the three levels. This is a negatively Hegelian model, in which the primacy of negation to the structure of the modern has the logical consequence of a primacy of mediations. Within this structure, however, everything depends on the character of the negations, which is a historical matter, in a deep philosophical and social sense. Adorno acknowledges a growing nominalism in the art of the 1960s (albeit in a sense quite different to Duve's) subsequent to the decline in the regulative authority of schools, movements and mediums. But this nominalism is not a decisive event, a one-off act – it is a tendency, a tendency equivalent to the crisis of modernism itself. For if modernism is all about negation, and therefore, dialectically viewed, about mediation, any nominalistic crisis of mediating forms will amount to a crisis of modernism. Contemporary art inhabits the space of this crisis of mediations, which is at the same time that of the production of new, more complicated, negatively mediating forms: mediations of the crisis of mediations.

Mediations after mediums: nominalism and genre, isms and series

In Adorno's *Aesthetic Theory*, 'nominalism' does not primarily refer to a general philosophical position about the status of universals. Rather, it is used, by extension, to denote to a socio-historical claim about the declining artistic significance of 'objective' (meaning, socially actualized) aesthetic norms, and the increasing artistic significance of the individuality of artworks. 'The universal', Adorno writes, 'is no longer granted art through types, and older types are being drawn into the whirlpool.' Individual works are forced to establish new relations to universality – including the universality of 'art' itself, in the generic singular – in new ways. This tendency towards a 'prohibition on predefined forms', Adorno argued, is inherent in the modern conception of art as such, in the 'progressive particularization' out of which the modern conception of the autonomous artwork emerged, via the aesthetic conception of an art of genius as an expression of subjective freedom, the mode of judgement of which is contrasted by Kant to a subsumptive model of determinate judgement. However, Adorno recognized, once the principle of individuation becomes a 'directive' – and hence a new form of abstract universality of its own – it threatens the structure of the individual work with a reduction to its materials (its spatio-temporal 'indiscernability'): 'Unchecked aesthetic nominalism . . . terminates in a literal facticity'. Adorno presents this situation as an impasse, an 'historical aporia' in the situation of modern art.[21]

However, there is more movement in this situation than Adorno's formulation suggests. For if modern art is to be true to its rejection of received universals in the name of subjective freedom, it must *also* reject the auto-destructive universalization of its own inherent nominalism and enter into new kinds of relations with universals – both old and new. If contemporary art has social substance to the extent to which it 'gives shape' to the antinomy of aesthetic nominalism by 'winning form from its negation', as Adorno claimed, this need not be a *merely* negative dialectic, which was – for Adorno, in any case – a general epistemological, not a specifically artistic, form.[22] Rather, it requires new forms of mediation. Indeed, this was the historical significance of *isms* for Adorno: those 'programmatic, self-conscious, and often collective art movements', which, in their day, 'by no means shackle[d] the individual productive forces but rather heighten[ed] them . . . in part through mutual collaboration.' However, despite this crucial mediating function, Adorno maintained a predominantly backward-looking conception of isms as 'the secularization of schools' in an age that had destroyed schools as traditionalistic. For Adorno, an ism was 'an island of a tradition' that had been 'destroyed by the principle of individuation'.[23]

By thinking of isms in terms of 'programmatic, self-conscious, and often collective art movements', Adorno neglected the increasing importance since the 1950s of retrospectively constructed *critical* isms, which nonetheless maintain some effective relations to art practice. Such isms retain the structure of, on the one hand, registering the principle of individuation (by virtue of evolving out of the critical interpretation of individual works), while on the other, avoiding 'the schema of *absolute* individuation' (by virtue of the forms of universality they construct). Absolute individuation destroys meaning. A dialectic of individuality and universality ('norms') thus continues to structure the law of form in individual works of contemporary art *within* the ongoing crisis of modernism that is produced by tendentially increasing artistic nominalism (which *is* so-called 'late', but actually, we might say, 'mature' modernism). It may be summarized, briefly, as follows.

The individuality of the work of art is the ontological marker of its autonomy – autonomous production of meaning (or rather, production of the self-conscious *illusion* of an autonomous production of meaning) – and the basis of its constitution as an *enigma*. This enigma lies in the fact that in their autonomous meaning-production, works of art act like subjects. They are objects that act like subjects – human subjects, individual *bourgeois* subjects – the subjectivity of which remains opaque. As such, works of art draw attention to the objecthood, and hence opacity, of human subjects themselves, and thereby to the illusion constitutive of the philosophical concept of the subject itself (the illusion that the subject is not an object). That dialectical transformation of the object into a subject that *is* the work of the artwork is matched, epistemologically, by a dialectical reversal of the human subject into an object, which renders subjectivity, *in itself*, opaque.

However, meaning is irreducibly collective. The work of art must thus mediate its ontological individuality with the collectivity of its (potential) meanings. This is the function of its self-legislating 'law of form'. Form is the artistic mediation of the social, at a whole range of levels, from artistic materials (including technologies of production) to techniques and productive practices. The question thus arises as to what are the main forms of mediation of the individuality of works of contemporary art with the collective dimension of their potential meanings. This question is initially complicated – and then answered – by the peculiarity of social form in capitalist societies, to which attention was directed in Chapter 1.[24] For in capitalist societies collectivity is itself largely *already formal*: abstract and alienated via exchange relations and the commodity form. Famously, exchange relations break down historically received collective meanings. In this respect, 'the social' in its distinctively capitalistic sense (as opposed to the communal) is not necessarily a 'collective' form in any active practical sense. Capitalistic sociality (the commodity/the value form) produces 'individuals' who are united only in the mutual alienation of their sociability, in a form of what Kant called 'asocial sociability'. Yet such individuality has nonetheless, historically, provided the model of freedom in capitalist societies; hence the political centrality of liberalism and libertarianism – of all stripes – to capitalist societies. This is why, in the structure of contemporary art, there is another, ontologically more basic mediation than the fragile critical *ism*: the *series*.²⁵

In flight from the substantive universalities of genres and mediums, contemporary art distributes its universalities across critical *isms* and individual *series*. One may thus schematize the predominant forms of critical mediation between individual works and the universality of 'art', across the broad historical period of 'modern art', from the mid-eighteenth century onwards, like this:

Periodization	Mediating principle(s)	Logical form
Classicism	hierarchy of genres	subsumption
Romanticism	primacy of the individual work	fragment
Aestheticism/aesthetic modernism	aesthetic intensities of modern life	aesthetic identity
Modernism of avant-gardes	isms of movements	groups
Formalist modernism	mediums	species
Generic modernism 1	['readymade' as negative meta-medium/vanishing mediator of the destruction of mediums]	proper name
'Contemporary art' / generic modernism 2: dialectic of modernisms	critical *isms* and series	distributive unities

E. Periodization of mediating forms

With regard to the final stage of this scenario, what Sartre says in his *Critique of Dialectical Reason* about what he takes to be the ontologically basic form of collectivity of human individuals, the series – whilst arguably mistaken about human individuals – appears true of works of art: the collapse of objective norms subjects works of art to the *rule of series*.

> The structural relation of the individual to other individuals remains in itself completely indeterminate until the ensemble of material circumstances on the basis of which the relation is established has been defined, from the point of view of historical totalization. In this sense, the contrast between the 'reciprocity as a relation of interiority' and 'the isolation of organisms as a relation of exteriority',

which, in the abstract, conditions an unspecified tension within multiplicities, is in fact transcended, and merged in a new type of 'internal-external' relation by the action of the practico-inert field, which transforms contradiction in the milieu of the Other into *seriality*. In order to understand the collective one must understand that this material object [that is, the practico-inert field – PO] realizes the unity of interpenetration of individuals as beings-in-the-world-outside-themselves to the extent that it structures their relations [as practical organisms] in accordance with the new rule of *series* . . . *a series is a mode of being for individuals both in relation to one another and in relation to their common being* and this mode of being transforms all their structures.[26]

In this context, the artist's œuvre appears as a succession of serially mediated individuations, or, increasingly, as a 'series of series'; hence the totemic historical significance of life-series, such as Roman Opalka's *1965 / 1 – ∞* series (painting the process of counting from one to infinity, from 1965 until his death in 2011) and other series sustained over long periods of time that formalize their seriality, often chronologically, such as On Kawara's *TODAY* series of *Date Paintings* (1966 to the present).

Under conditions of tendentially increasing aesthetic nominalism, each work must create the mediating conditions of its own intelligibility. In the absence of new, unalienated social forms of universality, the series is the most common formal mode for the construction of such conditions. It is here that the structural libertarianism of contemporary art resides. As subjects of exchange in capitalist societies, we live 'within and against' the series as a social form of relations between individuals. The work of art reflects and re-presents this form, in the form of a wish. The relationship between seriality and what Sartre called 'the point of view of historical totalization' – world mediation – is perhaps most thematically explicit in the œuvres of two German artists since the early 1960s, Sigmar Polke and Gerhard Richter.

Everything, everywhere? Polke and Richter

I have written about the strategic, postconceptual character of Richter's paintings and their relations to mediums and genres elsewhere.[27] Here, I shall concentrate on the meta-critical moment of Richter's practice, the assemblage of photographs, collages and sketches entitled *Atlas* (1962–97), alongside the selection of Polke's paintings and drawings from 1998–2003 exhibited in 2002–04 as *Sigmar Polke: History of Everything*.[28] Each collection displays an aspiration to the artistic mediation of a comprehensive totality – call it 'world' – in its spatial and temporal aspects, respectively; a quintessentially Romantic displacement of the philosophical desire for the absolute animating the heritage of German idealism. Within the terms of this aspiration, this desire – essentially, the desire that art might continue to perform its archetypically modern metaphysical function of world-mediation, under the changed conditions of the present – three issues stand out: 1. the character of this whole, the world, which this art aspires to mediate; 2. the specific character of the mediation offered by *Atlas*, and why it has become so important – increasingly important, I shall argue – to the critical redemption of Richter's œuvre; 3. the ontological status of *Atlas* in its relations to the postconceptual structure of contemporary art more generally: in particular, the way in which *Atlas* is inscribed within that dialectic of art and non-art that became constitutive of the critical structure of modern art in the wake of the historical avant-gardes.

In asking these questions of world-mediation and post-conceptuality of *Atlas*, in the context of the problem of the critical function of mediating forms, I am concerned to take my distance from an increasingly institutionally consolidated interpretative paradigm governing the reception of Richter's work. This paradigm views Richter's works in terms of three central themes: *epistemological scepticism* (a staging of doubt about 'the real'); *historical remembrance and mourning* (painting 'after the end' of painting); and *'painting' as redemption* (an affirmation of the ontological power of the act and medium of painting, despite, against, and ultimately through its fallen historical condition). Furthermore, it is often implied, by redeeming painting, Richter thereby, more fundamentally, undertakes a redemption of the human subject *through* painting. It is a dialectical redemption, to be sure – redemption via painting's scepticism about redemption – but it is a dialectically *positive* (affirmative) redemption nonetheless.[29] These three themes set the terms within which, ten years ago, Richter was somehow incorporated into the canon of American modernism, in the exhibition *Gerhard Richter: Forty Years of Painting* at the Museum of Modern Art in New York in 2002.[30] Richter's paintings appeared there as the nationally displaced afterlife of an American Painting retrospectively enlivened by the recognition of the underlying affinities – indeed, the ultimate unity – of Abstract Expressionism and Pop Art. This has been a complex ideological operation, of considerable subtlety in its appropriation of an existing critical literature, in which Richter himself has no doubt been deeply complicit. However, I am not concerned here with the legitimating function of Richter's critical self-consciousness; or at least, I am no more concerned with it than with other critical perspectives. (The unreflective privileging of statements by Richter about his work continues to distort the critical literature). Rather, I am interested in the ongoing question of the senses in which Richter's work is, and is not, 'critical'. That is, I am interested in the senses in which it continues – and the senses in which it fails (perhaps, the predominant senses) – to sustain and extend the modern metaphysical, post-Romantic and, today, 'post-conceptual' conception of 'art' into new areas and forms of experience.

The openness of this question is important, since it is only by being radically open to failure that contemporary art succeeds, on the rare occasions that it does. Interpretations that wrap up Richter's work in the garb of a definitively established critical achievement ('the redemption of painting') are thus, ironically, the greatest threat to the afterlife of his work. It is perhaps an intuition of this fact that accounts for both the internal growth of *Atlas* during the 1990s (162 sheets added between 1995 and 1997) and its expanding exhibition history. Having remained unexhibited for thirteen years between 1976 and 1989, while it was in a private collection – the years of Richter's deepening painterly interest in abstraction – it has received numerous outings, in selected and complete form, since the 1995 Dia show in New York. *Atlas*, I shall suggest, acts as a critical element within Richter's œuvre, open to non-art elements, safeguarding it against the increasing closure and 'success' of his paintings. It represents a moment of genuine openness to the world 'outside' art. But what is the world that Richter's art aspires to mediate? And is it the same one mediated in Polke's work? Sigmar Polke: Richter's old comrade of 'capitalist realism'.[31]

The first thing to note here is that the 'world' of world-mediation is not, first and foremost, an empirical one. To use an early Heideggerian distinction, 'world' is not primarily 'the totality of entities which can be present-at-hand within the world' (the everyday, Kantian concept of 'world' as the totality of possible appearances). The title of Polke's show notwithstanding (it was named after a painting; two paintings, in fact), neither 'world' nor 'everything' denotes 'every thing', or 'every possible thing'. Rather, the 'world' of world-mediation is primarily an existential-phenomenological concept denoting, in Heidegger's awkward phrase, 'that "*wherein*" a factical Dasein as such can be said to "live"'.[32] The world of world-mediation is thus, first and foremost, the world of being-in-the-world, in which, in Heideggerian terms, entities appear practically, as *ready*-to-hand. It is only secondarily, and derivatively, the Kantian world of theoretical objectifications, some of which nonetheless present them-selves immediately as 'objects', present-to-hand.

The world ready-to-hand for Polke and Richter in Düsseldorf, in the Federal Republic of Germany, in the early 1960s was, famously, primarily a photographically 'given' world. The visual forms of their being-in-the-world were dominated by the relative novelty of photographically illustrated newspapers and magazines, in which the narration and documentation of events – especially via portraiture – and the advertisement of commodities formed a seamless visual continuum. This was the incipient homogeneous whole of de-realized imagery, yet at a point at which it still remained primarily a world of photographic object-images, in which 'the photograph' still prevailed over the photographic.[33] To rewrite the beginning of Marx's *Capital* yet again, we might say that the visual wealth of their society appeared to them as 'an immense collection of photographs; the individual photograph appeared as its elementary form.'[34] Photographs and their means of production were ready-to-hand: ready-to-hand to be 'remade' as paintings.

Atlas is a highly selective fragment of this 'immense collection of photographs', which, in archetypical philosophically Romantic fashion, uses its title to refer to that figuring of the absent totality that the fragment performs, negatively, via the specific mode of its completion/incompletion – as we saw in Chapter 2, above. If an atlas is an organization of geographical and astronomical knowledge in book form, Richter's *Atlas* maps Richter's world. It is post-Romantic in its necessarily individualistic and fragmentary character – not every place, every thing, every photograph, can appear; yet, on the other hand, there is also something more epistemologically primitive, something 'early modern' about the accumulative and classificatory character of its empiricism, on a scale which is at once grand (thousands of images) and hopelessly, minutely, pathetically partial. (This is a condition that affects all contemporary photography in its relations to the totality of the images readily available at the press of a few keys. Compare, for example, Wolfgang Tillmans's exhibition at Tate Britain, London, *If One Thing Matters, Everything Matters*, 1980–2003 – another reflection on 'the one and the many'. Over 2,000 images: so many, but also so few! A mere drop in the ocean of images.)[35] Epistemologically, this form of accumulation offers an inductive knowledge closer to Bacon's procedures than to Galileo's, closer to the gentleman amateur of colonial fossil-hunting than the professionalized science of hypothesis formation and experimentation. Yet its specimens are more emblems than instances. One might posit a kind of reversal of the anthropological relation of early colonialism here, as, after the move from East to West, Richter becomes a collector of the naturalized image-artefacts of the European capitalist metropolises.

Atlas, one might say – at least to begin with, up to 1972 – offers a kind of domestic, idiosyncratic *natural history* of the photograph. Its temporality is largely a temporality of stasis, a temporality of the preservation of transience, a temporality of the dead, of mere simultaneity (rather than contemporaneity), of the 'non-contemporaneous', and hence an essentially spatial form. It is not a narrative temporality of historical forms. There are no almost 'events' in *Atlas*, in the narrative sense, in which they might be connected to each other via a history of subjects. It is an amnesiac articulation of the temporality of modernity (the eternity of the transient), in which, as Benjamin Buchloh has argued, the peculiar 'banality' of the images marks the anaesthetic function of consumer culture in the repression of historical memory in post-war Germany. However, like Richter's early work as a whole, the early sheets of *Atlas* stage – rather than merely participating in – this 'anomic banality', which is not so much 'affectless' as the carrier of a specific set of affects and, more generally, a certain pervasive existential mood, a kind of psychic deadening.[36]

And they stage this anomic banality in a highly formal manner, through largely pre-established, but also mixed, categories of genre: portrait, cityscape, landscape, seascape . . . are one set of categories (the bulk of the sheets from 24 to 200); photographs from albums, newspapers, books and magazines (the categories of the first twenty-three sheets, classifying by source) are another. Importantly, the latter self-consciously fails to name the images from the concentration camps and pornography that appear alongside each other (sheets 16–23), between some forensically displayed everyday images (sheet 15) and the portrait of Volker Bradke (sheet 24). (The failure of the concentration camp/pornography pairing to function other than as a kind of mutual voyeurism importantly marks a withdrawal from historically and politically explicit content, broken only by the anomalous *October 18, 1977* series from 1988, from which so many of the claims made for Richter's work as remembrance ultimately derive.)

The key to *Atlas* lies, I think, in the character of this 'staging', which is at once a mere staging/re-presentation of artistic materials *and* (via this staging) the production of a highly individual type of artwork, which holds open the boundary between art and non-art in a novel way. I will briefly address this staging in two ways, before returning to the broader issues of world-mediation, criticality and post-conceptuality: first, via the question of the character and cultural form of the object (Is *Atlas* an archive of artistic materials or a work of art?); second, via the spatiality of the display, and its display of spatiality: not simply the mounted sheets (a staple of early conceptual art), but the architectural sketches for installations and rooms, and the presentation of photographs as 'models' (Sheets 289 and 290 – Figs 4 and 5). These are crucial aspects of *Atlas* that register a difference from its simple archival function. They raise the issue of the relational character of the meaning of the elements in Richter's œuvre, and

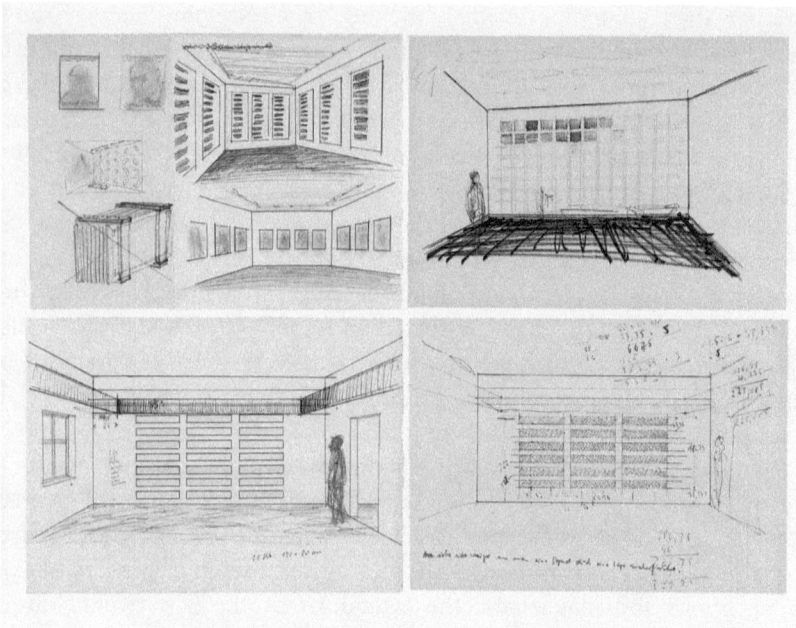

Fig. 4: Gerhard Richter, *Atlas*, 1962–97, Sheet 289

thereby that of the constitutive function of its serialism for the meaning of any particular work.

If one asks the question of precisely what Richter's *Atlas* is, the answer must be, I think, that it is a structurally ambiguous cultural object. At the level of its logic of production, at least, it is at once an archive of sources, a documentation of procedures, and a formal, self-contained result. It is not so much that what is essentially a work of classification is itself unclassifiable 'within the typology and terminology of avant-garde art history'.[37] (This may be so, but the same applies to most important work after 1964). Rather, it is its particular combination of cult-value, exhibition-value and education-value that makes it ambiguous, a combination that is sustained via its connections to Richter's other, more readily classifiable work, the paintings in particular.[38] These connections are of two kinds: external ones, dependent upon the recognition of the images as sources for photo-paintings (this is one of the games the knowing viewer cannot but play in viewing *Atlas*); and internal or immanent ones, where the image is marked in some way to signal its status as a preparatory material: either by being mounted with adhesive tape, within a broader than usual visual field, being marked up in some way; or framed with a sketch for installation, or some other perspective device. In each case, the non-art status of the image as 'artistic material' is secured in contrast to the implied work (whether it came to exist or not).

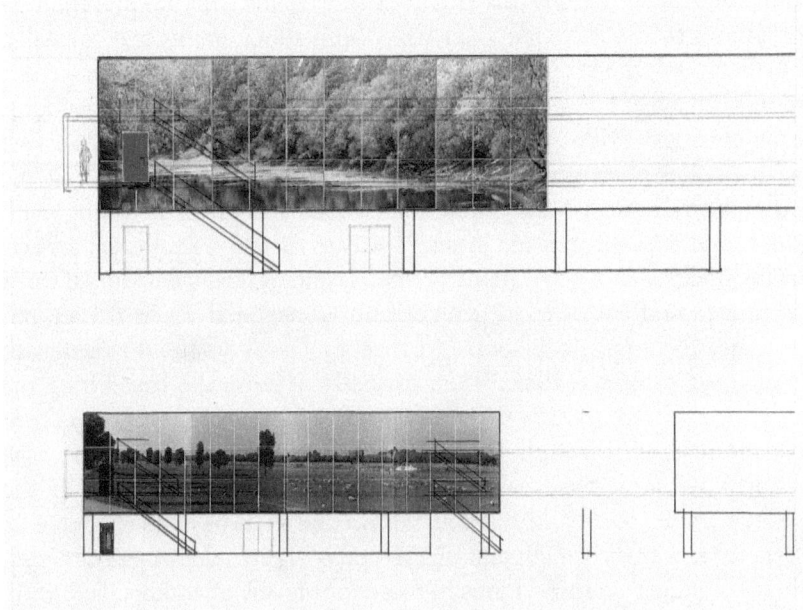

Fig. 5: Gerhard Richter, *Atlas*, 1962–97, Sheet 290

The educational-value predominates over the exhibition-value; or rather, in this case, the exhibition-value *is* its educational-value. Again, this is a staple strategy of early conceptual art: extending the work 'backwards' into its process of conception, as suggested by LeWitt in his 'Paragraphs on Conceptual Art'. However, crucially, these 'marked' photographs are mixed in with others that are displayed without intimation of such relations; or at least, without intimation beyond that conveyed by the contiguous presence of source images. Such images thus present themselves 'for themselves', so to speak, and reciprocally implicate the source images in this aesthetic mode of display. An immanent structural ambiguity thus pervades the whole display. It utilizes, but complicates, the classical avant-garde strategy of displaying 'non-art' as art; and by implication it highlights the 'non-art' aspect of the photo-paintings themselves. This is the respect in which it contributes to their criticality, since, following Adorno, one can associate the (ever-shifting) non-art element of modernist art with that constitutive moment whereby it secures a critical autonomy by breaking with the illusion of autonomy, which it nonetheless also maintains on a new basis. This is one of the deepest dialectical moments in Adorno's account of modernist art.

The structural ambiguity arises out of aspects of the spatiality of the display: the didactic formalization of the mountings on sheets, the architectural sketches for installations and rooms, and the presentation of photographs as 'models' all work both functionally and formally. Furthermore, the references to other works, other practices, make this more than a mere *display* of functionalism. It is quite different from, for example Susan Hiller, *Dedicated to the Unknown Artists* (1972–76): a set of over 200 photographic postcards of seascapes, each bearing the inscription 'Rough Seas', mounted on fourteen boards, along with charts and maps, organized in such a way as to analyze different aspects of the images. As we saw in the previous chapter, this well-known work of mid-period (or 'second generation') Conceptual art in Britain has become, for some, a model of conceptual art's ability to deal with 'Romantic subject matter'.[39] Yet, formally, it lacks the breadth of the system of references, both within itself and outside, whereby *Atlas* constitutes itself through its relations to a series of absent totalities: the totality of *Atlas*, the totality of Richter's œuvre, the totality of the photographic, the totality of the world. This returns us to the issue of seriality and world-mediation. Each totality figures the others and each image signifies via its relations to these four levels of totality.

Each of these totalities is an open totality – open to additions, subtractions and modifications. This is crucial to the critical function of *Atlas* within Richter's œuvre: its openness stands in opposition to the traditional, closed forms of Richter's other individual works – the paintings. Where once it was the negativity of the relationship between painting and photography within Richter's photo-paintings that was the critical, conceptual and 'open' aspect of his works (as paintings of negations),[40] now, since the late 1980s, and since Richter's increasingly affirmative embrace of large-scale abstraction and classically composed photography alike, it is *Atlas* alone that provides the moment of reflection – reflection upon the art/non-art relation – that is essential to the critical claims of the œuvre. Richter's paintings have become increasingly self-sufficient and affirmatively pictorial: 'normal, again' as he has described it.[41]

Polke, on the other hand, has maintained what was once a common strategic approach to the painterly mediation of the visual forms of media culture, while continuing to develop its formal means in new ways. In the works in the exhibition *History of Everything*, this involved a new use of transparent resins (alongside the familiar variety of fabrics) to transform the wooden frames supporting the canvases into an integral grid-like element of the work (Fig. 6). These 'machine-paintings' from the Dallas/Tate show maintain both a technologically based connection to media forms and a polemical relation to the social content of the now-global media. In the first case, pixelizing the images through the massive enlargement of print-processing errors. In the latter case,

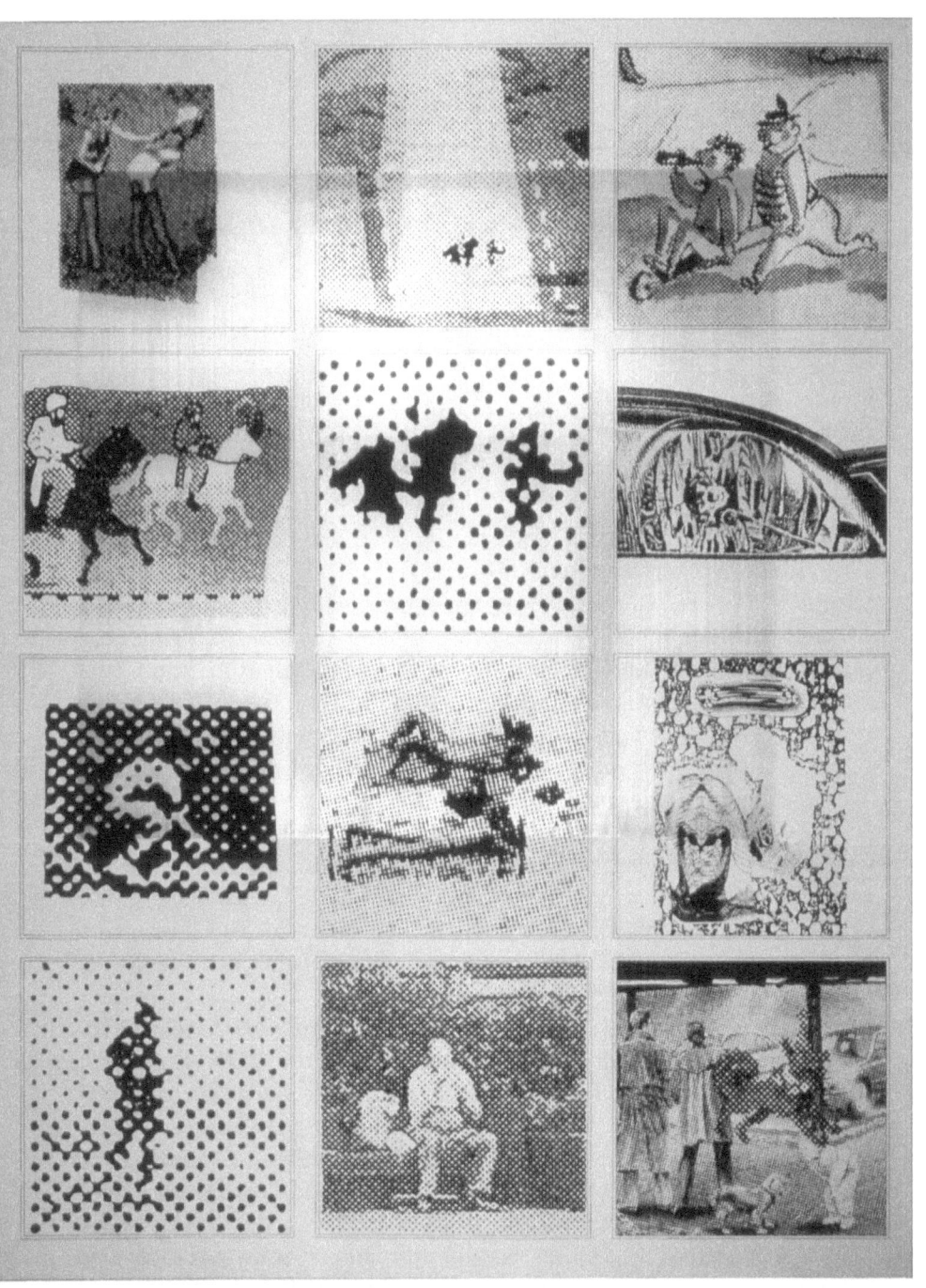

Fig. 6: Sigmar Polke, *History of Everything II*, 2002

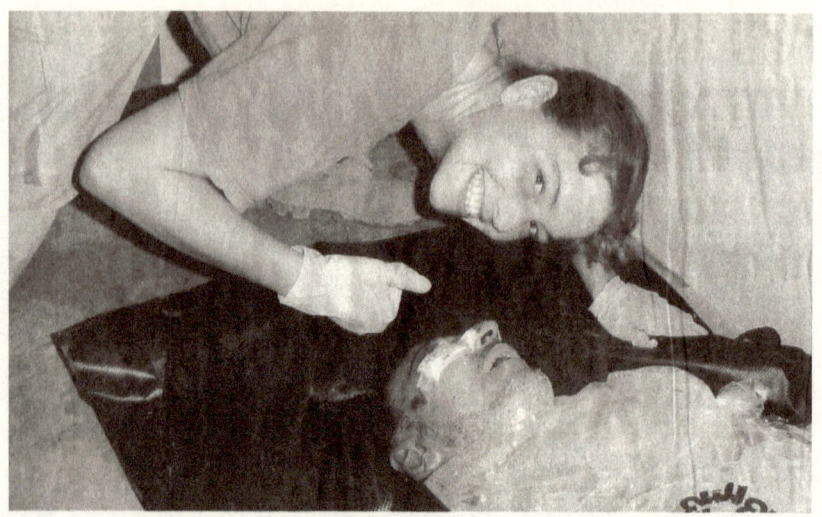

Fig. 7: Sabrina Hardman and Manadel al-Jamadi, Abu Ghraib prison, Iraq, 2004

by a return to photojournalistic source images: *The Hunt for the Taliban and Al Qaeda* (2002), an investigative journalistic diagram, for example, and *Risk Game* (2002), a machine painting on fabric of American marines playing the board game of world domination, Risk, on a ship in the Gulf of Aden.

In fact, the compositional possibilities of digital imaging (enlargement and simplification, in particular) place press photography itself close to photo-painting, since early photo-painting was less about paintings of photographs themselves (it was not photorealism) than about painting *reproductions* of photographs. This continuing reliance on the compositional structure of the source image, in Polke, produces a kind of auto-representation of history, in line with the displacement of professional photographic journalism by participant photography, or 'citizens' journalism'. The paradigmatic example of such participant self-representation is to be found in the images of the abuse of Iraqi prisoners taken by US troops in Abu Ghraib. These are images that, in certain compositional respects, look more like classical conceptual photo-paintings than simple photographs: grotesque versions of John Baldessari's 1969 *Commissioned Paintings*, in which hand gestures at once identify the object of the image (here, the bodies of the prisoners) and celebrate its reduction to an object (Fig. 7).

Richter exited the formal space of media imagery some years ago now, in favour of classically composed photography and resolutely domestic image-making. Even the ongoing land-, sea- and skyscapes are broadly domestic in their articulation of cultural space: the space of reproductions of Romantic paintings. As media has become more global, Richter's images have become more private. In the context of this turn, the inflection of the multiple meanings of the title *Atlas* has begun to turn inwards, becoming medium-based, 'a kind of book', a volume in a private library, away from the outward-looking sense of geographical expansiveness associated with a 'map of the world'. In their essential domesticity, the main theoretical issue raised by Richter's works of the 1990s and immediately beyond – other than *Atlas*, but also in *Atlas* – is that of kitsch. There is a very interesting relationship to kitsch in the baby pictures, in particular. 'Family' has always been one of the main mediations for social and political history in Richter – most famously, *Aunt Marianne* and *Uncle Rudi* (both 1965), the photo-paintings of an aunt killed in the Nazi eugenics programme and an uncle in his Wehrmacht uniform. But where it was previously 'family' as a readymade social form, objectified and ironized, by being viewed at a historical distance through the reproduction of received photographic forms, now the photographer (Richter himself) is implicated in the construction of the forms.

However, just as in 1987, the *October 18, '77* Baader Meinhof series suddenly and stunningly fractured Richter's apparent developmental tendency towards affirmative abstraction, so in 1999, the Reichstag painting sketches fractured the domesticity of *S. mit Kind* – reintroducing concentration camp images into *Atlas*. But the final, flag-based version of that work can hardly be held up besides *October 18, '77* as a piece of historical art. While *September* (2005), Richter's subsequent quiet, domestic painting of the Twin Towers collision on 9/11, appears at first sight as a straightforward acknowledgement of the *inadequacy* of painting to that event[42] – although one might view it more dialectically as an anticipation of the deadening of affect produced by a historical distance to come; or even as a marker of the distance of 'old' Europe from the world for which this was an event on a world-historical scale. The fact that Richter himself was on a flight en route to New York that day, diverted to Canada – cited curatorially to add affect to an effectively affectlessness work – functions in actuality further to highlight the radically disengaged character of the work itself. Just four years on from the event, Richter views 9/11 from a greater cultural and historical distance than he viewed the Nazism of the early 1940s in the mid 1960s.

All of this suggests that the aspiration to world-mediation evoked by the title *Atlas* must be pursued, not in the content of that work, or of the œuvre for which its ambition is metonymic, but rather in the possibilities opened up by the artistic ontology it sustains against Richter's own countervailing tendency to revert to an affirmative return to 'normal' painting: the ontology of a postconceptual art.

4
Transcategoriality: postconceptual art

> Much of the best work being produced today seems to fall between media. This is no accident... We are approaching the dawn of a classless society, to which separation into rigid categories is absolutely irrelevant.
>
> Dick Higgins, 'Intermedia', 1965

> Museums are tombs, and it looks like everything is turning into a museum. Painting, sculpture and architecture are finished, but the art habit continues. Art settles into a stupendous inertia.
>
> Robert Smithson, 'Some Void Thoughts on Museums', 1967

As it turned out, we were not approaching the dawn of a classless society; nor did art settle into a stupendous inertia. Yet, as the 1960s progressed, the classification of artworks into rigid medium-based categories certainly did become increasingly critically irrelevant nonetheless. And the process was not unconnected to the flowering of a certain idea of freedom: the freedom to make art from any of a potential infinity of material and 'immaterial' means. However, this was neither an uncontested process nor a definitive one, critically or institutionally. If the critical destruction of medium as an ontological category was the decisive, collective historical act of the most important art of the 1960s, it is not surprising that it faced a barrage of institutionally reactive and reappropriative criticism and curation from the outset. In this context, the work of Robert Smithson takes on a symptomatic significance. For Smithson was one of a group of US artists who, in the late 1960s and early 1970s, most fully exploited the experimental possibilities of an art freed of the restrictions imposed by conventionally conceived artistic mediums. In this respect, his œuvre in many ways epitomizes the radical *trans*categoriality and 'postconceptuality' of the most important art of the 1960s. At the same time, however, it is the greatest of the many ironies that pervade the reception of this work that, after his early death in 1973, it has taken place primarily within the terms of a debate about the meaning and possibilities of 'sculpture'. Only recently have a younger generation of artists revived a different, definitively post-medium Smithson, on the basis of perceived similarities with aspects of their own situations and practices. Smithson's work thus offers the opportunity for a dual examination: of the tenacity and flexibility of conventional categories of medium in the face of the fundamental challenge to their legitimacy posed by new art practices in the 1960s; and of the categorial consequences of the destruction of the conventional category of medium, which was enacted in those practices.

In this chapter, then, first, I examine the reception of Smithson's work with regard to the restitution of the concept of sculpture, as a case study in critical and institutional conservatism, masquerading as – indeed, constituting, a certain – progressivism. Second, I propose an alternative, transcategorial and postconceptual interpretation of Smithson's significance, in which I draw attention to the decisive importance of a particular conception of abstraction for the conceptual dimension of Smithson's work, and to his aspiration for its termination in an ultimate breakdown of all categorialization in the experience of the work of art, in a state of 'pure perception', modelled on a certain cinematic experience of film.

Smithson and medium (or, against 'sculpture')

According to Robert Hobbs, the foremost and in some respects the best critical interpreter of Smithson's work in the decade immediately following his death, and organizer of the first posthumous retrospective of his work in 1980, symptomatically entitled *Robert Smithson: Sculpture*:[1] 'Smithson's major contribution as an artist was to enlarge the realm of sculptural space . . . [At a time at which] in the United States . . . art was decisively changed when sculpture reasserted itself as a primary framework for reevaluating humanity's relationship to the world.'[2]

This quotation is taken from Hobbs's essay in the catalogue of Smithson's second posthumous retrospective, which he organized for the United States Pavilion at the 40th Venice Biennale in 1982. This was an exhibition that significantly extended the institutional recognition of Smithson's work, especially in Europe, in part precisely by framing it so decisively within the terms of an enlarged notion of sculpture. Hobbs's reading historicized Smithson, confining him to a particular interpretation of the artistic context of his day. In contrast, when the Smithson recent revival began in the mid-1990s, it was on the basis of the resonances of his work in the present. This revival achieved mainstream institutional form only belatedly (most notably in the 2004–05 retrospective that originated at MOCA, Los Angeles) in the wake of academic monographs, such as Ann Reynolds's *Robert Smithson: Learning from New Jersey and Elsewhere* (2003) and Jennifer L. Roberts's *Mirror-Travels: Robert Smithson and History* (2004).[3] And this recognition was fed, in part, by renewed debates about Smithson's earthwork *Spiral Jetty* (1970), which re-emerged in 2002, having been mostly submerged beneath the Great Salt Lake in Utah for the previous thirty-one years. In the meantime, in 1999, it had been acquired from the Smithson estate by the Dia Art Foundation, which subsequently commissioned a handsome volume about the once-again-visible work.[4]

As the cover of the catalogue to Hobbs's first show indicates (Fig. 8), *Spiral Jetty* has long been taken to be emblematic of Smithson's 'enlargement' of the realm of sculptural space, and as such, one of the most important works of the last four decades. In the introduction to the Dia presentation of *Spiral Jetty*, Lynne Cooke noted: 'Excepting possibly Andy Warhol, Robert Smithson may be the most influential artist of the past forty years . . . [and] *Spiral Jetty*, the iconic earthwork . . . is widely regarded as his signature statement.'[5] The equivalent work in Europe, made in the following year, is in Emmen in the Netherlands: *Broken Circle – Spiral Hill* (1971), Smithson's only extant piece involving land reclamation. But it has attracted far less attention.

Claims similar to Hobbs's about Smithson's enlargement of the terms of a specifically sculptural practice can be found in the foremost US theorist of sculpture of the period, Rosalind Krauss. The brief introduction to Krauss's book, *Passages in Modern Sculpture* (1977) – written just prior to her semiotic turn, when she left her position as associate editor at *Artforum* and co-founded *October* in 1977 – contains two images that delimit the scope of its argument: the anonymous sculpture of *Laocoön and His Sons* (first century BC), now at the Vatican Museum, and *Spiral Jetty*. *Laocoön and His Sons* is the central work discussed in Lessing's famous treatise on aesthetics, *Laocoön: An Essay on the Limits of Painting and Poetry* (1766), which served as the main critical source for Clement Greenberg's medium-based formalism.[6] At the time, this was an approach that was being critically extended by Krauss and her colleague Michael Fried, both of whom sought to embrace some of the new artistic developments of the 1960s within its terms. As a new critical history of modern sculpture, *Passages in Modern Sculpture* begins with a chapter on Rodin's *Gates of Hell* (1880–1917) and ends with a discussion of a variety of recent works, grouped together under the idea of a 'new syntax' for sculpture. Pride of place is given to four artists and four sculptural images of passage: Bruce Nauman's *Corridor* (1968–70), Robert Morris's *Labyrinth* (1974), Richard Serra's *Shift* (1970–72), and, once again, Smithson's *Spiral Jetty*. 'With these images of passage', Krauss concludes, 'the transformation of sculpture, from a static, idealized medium to a temporal and material one, that had begun with Rodin is fully achieved.'[7] Sculpture had been radically transformed, but *within* the limits of the received concept of 'medium'.

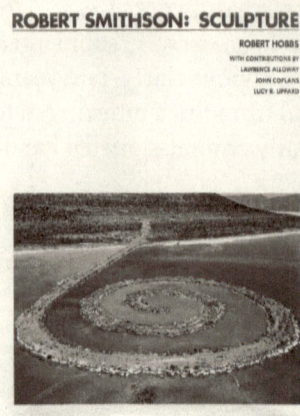

Fig. 8: Cover of Robert Hobbs, *Robert Smithson: Sculpture*

This is a major critical claim – broader than Hobbs's – yet like Hobbs's it flies in the face of Smithson's explicit rejection of the medium-specific formalism that Krauss was extending to embrace the new three-dimensional art of the 1960s and early '70s. As the epigraph at the opening of this chapter indicates, Smithson insisted that sculpture, along with painting and architecture, was *finished*. For example, he wrote about painting: 'The transparency of the ... surface becomes diseased when the artist defines his art by the word "painting" alone. "Painting" is not an *end*, but a *means*, therefore it is a linguistically out-of-date category.'[8]

What are we to make of this disjunction between the terms of the mainstream critical reception of Smithson's work and Smithson's own self-understanding? And how are we to deal with the disjunction critically? If Smithson's works are not 'sculpture', even when they *look* sculptural, then what are they? And wherein does their critical importance lie?

The 'interminable avalanche of categories'

The first thing to be acknowledged with regard to the confusion about medium in the reception of Smithson's work is that the problem of categorization, to which it represents a response, is a very real – that is to say, ongoing, unresolved – critical problem. It is in many ways *the* problem of contemporary art criticism: not simply as the problem of the selection or construction of categories through which to think particular works, but also, more importantly, as that of the status of such categories and their relations to the individuality of the works. Its unresolved status is perhaps the immanently critical reason for the dearth of intellectually serious criticism of contemporary art. Smithson himself, developing his views on museums in a conversation with Allan Kaprow, published in the 1967 *Art Yearbook*, put it like this:

> The categorizing of art into painting, architecture and sculpture seems to be one of the most unfortunate things that took place. Now all these categories are splintering into more and more categories, and it's like an interminable avalanche of categories. You have about forty different kinds of formalism and about a hundred different kinds of expressionism. The museums are being driven into a kind of paralyzed position, and I don't think they want to accept it.[9]

This paralysis was the institutional effect of the intensification of what Adorno described as the increasing nominalism of modern art: the growing critical importance of the individuality of artworks in the face of the erosion of the objectivity of aesthetic norms.[10] Ultimately, the museums could not accept this situation, of course. They were increasingly driven to various, relatively simple, albeit more expansive developments of the system of the arts, conceived as mediums: painting and sculpture were joined by photography, film, video and performance. There was even a medium-based conception of conceptual art, proposed by Henry Flynt – 'an art of which the material is concepts', as he put it.[11] The dynamics of this process of restoration in the face of a proliferating production of increasingly subjective critical categories can be traced in the fate of Krauss's conception of sculpture's 'expanded field'.

In 1979, using her new semiotic resources (principally, Algirdas Greimas's semiotic square), Krauss adjusted her position. In her essay 'Sculpture in the Expanded Field', she relocated Smithson's works within an expanded field of formal possibilities generated by the relations between landscape, architecture, and their negations, within which 'sculpture' was judged to be but one of four main types of work: a three-dimensional commemorative representation of place, formally defined by its location at the point of indifference between negations of landscape and architecture (see overleaf). Different works by Smithson could now be seen to instantiate each of the three other types: axiomatic structures, site construction and marked sites. Within this new framework, *Spiral Jetty* became an exemplar of a 'marked site', while *Partially Buried Woodshed* (1970), for example, became a site construction. An image of the earthwork *Spiral Jetty* was once again reproduced in Krauss's 1979 essay, sustaining its iconic status across this reclassification.[12]

Krauss's 'expanded field' is a theoretical advance on Hobbs's notion of the enlargement of the traditional sculptural paradigm because it offers a determinate multiplicity of new, *non*-sculptural positions, but only relatively so, since it remains restricted to the generative possibilities of the relations of identity and difference between just two categories (landscape and architecture) understood to have generated

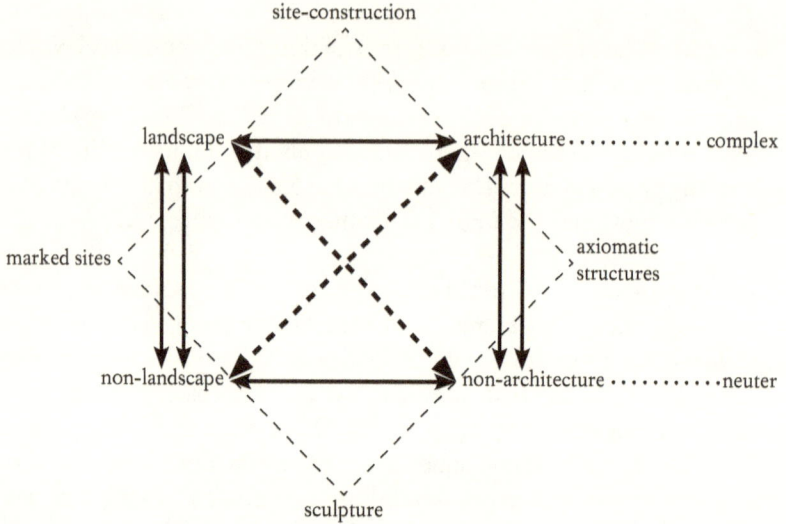

Rosalind Krauss's 'Expanded Field'

the possibility of sculpture in the first place. In this respect, it is a transitional account, between medium-specificity and what Krauss would later acknowledge to be a much more various – and, for her, critically irrecuperable – 'post-medium condition'.[13] Under that condition, the 'expanded field' (within which sculpture was one of four positions) quickly reverted, institutionally, to being treated as an expanded field *of* sculpture – the field of an expanded sculpture, broadly along the lines of Hobbs's interpretation, which it had initially displaced. As the 1980s progressed, Smithson's work was increasingly treated once again as emblematic of a 'new' sculpture, along with works by a whole pantheon of artists from the 1960s who had similarly rejected the sculptural tradition as a whole. By the time of the exhibition Gravity and Grace at the Hayward Gallery in London in 1993, subtitled 'The Changing Condition of Sculpture, 1965–1975', the restoration was complete. And the curatorial mode of presentation of Smithson's works was adjusted accordingly.

Alternative curatorial strategies were developed in ways largely unrelated to the critical artistic meanings of individual works – 'themed' shows of varying kinds producing loosely linked aggregates of works, without specifically artistic unity. These are, in many ways, the 'torn halves' of contemporary exhibition practice: traditional classifications versus curatorial strategies unrelated to the critical categorization of works, reaching out to wider cultural fields. It was from within this latter field – within an *acceptance* of art's post-medium condition, but without a clear art-critical paradigm – that a new generation of artists rediscovered Smithson's works, from the mid-1990s onwards. This generation has embraced Smithson's work less because of its categorical specificity, than out of a growing sense of its seemingly *un*categorizable multiple trajectories – and its associated individualism. For them, Smithson epitomizes freedom from the constraints of medium, or other received norms, while at the same time providing an individualistic political model of the artistic counterculture of the 1960s: at once 'serious' and free. In particular, he offers a model of what, back in 1973, Lawrence Alloway had already described as a post-studio practice – the term used by Cornelia Butler to describe Smithson in her recent catalogue essay for the Museum of Contemporary Art in Los Angeles.[14]

Smithson's emphasis on institutionally negotiated projects and related travel increasingly resonated with the social reality of artists' lives. Smithson became the melancholic phenomenologist of a *professional* condition of dislocation and displacement: the artist not so much as ethnographer as journalist, or cultural worker, on assignment.[15] Here, it is less the iconic sculptural properties of the earthwork *Spiral Jetty* that have been an inspiration than the processes of negotiation involved in its construction, and the eponymous 1971 film which records the construction. But this is less with regard to their complication of the signification of '*Spiral Jetty*', or the ontology of *Spiral Jetty* as a work, than for the portrayal of Smithson himself – especially in the final section of the film where he appears as a wild, 'hunted' figure, in an exuberant parody of the scene in Alfred Hitchcock's 1959 *North By Northwest* in which the character played by Cary Grant is dive-bombed by a crop-dusting airplane. The film has thus served to reinforce the mythologization of Smithson as a Romantic individualist, in a conventional artistic sense, both as its *auteur* and its subject, at the same time as it has served to situate him within a post-medium, 'new media' world.[16]

However, the practical artistic results of what became for some young artists a near infatuation with Smithson have been disappointing and diminishing. The double recovery of Smithson's *Partially Buried Woodshed* on the Kent State University campus in works by Renée Green and Tacita Dean (1997 and 1999, respectively), for example, functions as a metonym for a generational desire to recover something of the 1960s in current art practice, but goes little further than the gesture of recovery. There is a repetition of motifs – and an element of 'recreation' (distinct from re-enactment) – but no real sense of an artistic legacy. So, although Smithson's work has been received enthusiastically by young artists, with a strong intuitive sense of its artistic significance, this reception has thus far in many ways been merely the (blind) other side of the coin of its conventional appropriation as 'sculpture'.

Today, when a new generation of art historians has set about reinterpreting the art of the 1960s from different theoretical perspectives and with new interests – especially in film, video, and performance – the tendency to remain within the conventional category of medium, extended merely empirically, to grasp the specificities of a greater range of practices, continues to dominate. The Dia Art Foundation book on *Spiral Jetty*, for example, sets out to restore the importance of Smithson's film and essay of the same name, previously 'relegated to the status of supplements or proxies'. It does so, however, not by interrogating the ontological significance of the interconnections between the three "components," but rather by recognizing them as 'works in their own right', each in a separate medium: sculpture, film, essay. Indeed, in so far as any categorial slippage is acknowledged here, it serves merely to reinstate the historical-ontological primacy of sculpture. The film appears as an instance of 'film-based sculpture'.[17]

In a second round of citational artistic practices from the last few years, for which the first round has provided models, there is a further attenuation of critical effect. In Nicolas Bourriaud's 'art project' in Murcia, *Estratos* (2008), for example, a range of neo-Smithsonian work was shown, including pieces by Cyprien Gaillard (*The Smithsons*) and Ilana Halperin (*Nomadic Landmass*), which, rather than taking up and developing Smithson's practices, were primarily either simply citational or superficially mimetic in character, functioning as a kind of academic historicism of practice that legitimates the artist in question, by virtue of such references, rather than via any related qualities immanent to the work itself. This is in part because there has been so little serious critical modelling of Smithson's practice.

This intellectual deficit has been compensated by an almost obsessive focus on the composition of Smithson's library. Ever since Lori Cavagnaro catalogued Smithson's library, which Nancy Holt donated to the Archives of American Art in 1987, no account of Smithson has been complete without some reference to the intellectual character and disciplinary range of his books and journals. Yet this fascination with Smithson's library – indicative, no doubt, of a broader twentieth-century interest in libraries in general – primarily functions as a displacement of the desire to understand Smithson's work onto the material remnants of its intellectual conditions of production. This is both a sign of the sanctification of Smithson – the library functions satisfactorily as a collection of relics – and a further avoidance of the question of the current critical status of his work.

We are thus confronted with three disjunctive elements in the current reception of Smithson's work: (1) acknowledgement of a radical experimentalism of practice, combined with, (2) a conventionalism of categorial re-appropriation, and hence as a consequence, (3) a repression of both conceptual content and construction.

Smithson himself bemoaned the original Renaissance distinctions between the arts, in the spirit of an absolute artistic individualism (good American that he was). But as Adorno recognized, the problem is more historical than this. The problematic status of categorization is a consequence of the individualizing logic of the aesthetic definition of the artwork, which is itself the expression of social transformations in the political status of individuals, from which the structural political meaning of post-Romantic art as an expression of freedom derives. We live in societies of still-increasing individualism, of which neo-liberalism is merely the most recent economic-ideological expression. Yet, in art as in life, *absolute* individuation destroys meaning. In Adorno's terms: 'Unchecked aesthetic nominalism ... terminates in a literal facticity.'[18] (This is the historical meaning of Michael Fried's 'literality.')[19] Among other things, it is the rapid appropriation of artistic forms by the culture industry that has led to the declining artistic significance of objective aesthetic norms. Yet works of art continue to require mediating interpretative categories, however negative, to acquire social objectivity – beyond the received conception of medium. There is no escape from the maze of categories – or, to switch metaphors, no option but to try critically to regulate the flow of their avalanche/rundown. In Kant's terms, these are the *logically conditioning* elements of aesthetic judgements of art that make them judgements of *art*, rather than pure aesthetic judgements that could just as well be of nature. This logical conditioning of judgements of individual works of art is a process that remains, oddly, largely theoretically unelaborated, even today; perhaps because it requires a systematic philosophical mediation of the history of art of a kind only Hegel (positively) and Adorno (negatively) have risked. (Duve tried but failed to short-circuit the requirement, in his *Kant After Duchamp*, with the positivism of his Foucauldian version of the institutional theory of art.)[20]

Critical categorization delimits the conceptual space of interpretation; hence the increased importance since the 1950s of critical 'isms' and the competition between critical terms, in the wake of the decline of the hegemony of 'medium'. Idea-art and concept-art, for example, lost out to Conceptual art; Barbara Rose's ABC art and Lucy Lippard's Eccentric Abstraction, lost out to Minimal art (which embraces at least three different, if phenomenonally related kinds of work: by Judd, LeWitt, Morris), etc. Lippard herself came to believe that the works of the late 1960s and early '70s are 'fundamentally uncategorizable', and she consequently now takes either a purely empirical or a pragmatic approach.[21] This is to give up on critical historical discourse altogether. As we have seen, Hobbs and the early Krauss took a conventional medium-based approach; although Hobbs did distinguish 'Earth art' from 'sculpture', adding the rider (or alibi) that 'in Smithson's art... muddled issues are *not to be clarified* because their indeterminate lack of focus is an essential distinguishing characteristic.'[22] It is an interesting remark. However, in the passage referred to, Smithson himself writes not of an 'indeterminate lack of focus' (Hobbs's phrase), but of something both more complicated and more interesting still: namely, the 'indeterminate *certainty*' of the site, and the '*determinate* uncertainty' of the nonsite.[23] Each mirrors the other in a process close to what Hegel referred to in his *Science of Logic* as the mutual constitution of 'determinations of reflection'. Dialectics is at the core of the transition in Smithson's practice to the concept of nonsite. Yet there has been little serious study of the conceptual content of these structures and relations within his practice.

Ontology of materializations: non-site

What is interesting critically about Smithson's work is the extreme tension between, on the one hand, the complex rationality or intellectual logic of its construction – that is, its deliberate, staged *crossing* of categories (its *trans*categorial character) and, on the other, its final staging of determinate breakdowns or *meltdowns* of categorization in various different ways, into a state Smithson described as 'pure perception'.[24] That is to say, the critical importance of Smithson's work lies in its contribution to the constitution (and hence the understanding) of what I am calling 'postconceptual' art. This is not a claim made at the level of style, medium, movement, or periodization. Smithson was the most individual of artists, for all his affinities – and passing pragmatic alliances – with various movements of the 1960s: Minimalism, Conceptual art, and Earthworks or Land art, in particular. Rather, it is a claim made at the level of the historical ontology of the artwork – its mode of being, what it most fundamentally is. This critical claim is thus at the same time a fundamentally historical one. Critical interpretation of Smithson's work lends credence to the claim that, critically speaking, 'contemporary art' *is* postconceptual.

The primary critical significance of Smithson's 'mature' work (from 1964 to 1973, when he was between twenty-six and thirty-five years old) derives from its location at a crucial juncture in the transformation of the ontology of the artwork that marks the fundamental historical significance of the art of the 1960s: the transition from an ontology of mediums (painting, sculpture, architecture, photography, film, video) to a postconceptual ontology of art in general, and, hence a fundamentally *transcategorial* practice – in contrast, for example, to the self-misunderstanding of the main proponents of 'Conceptual art' (through which the category was, historically, critically constituted) of art's ideational ontological purity.[25]

If this is the case – that Smithson's practice is fundamentally transcategorial – then the description of his work as 'sculpture', in however expanded a sense, takes on a conservative, indeed reactionary guise. For in this context, 'sculpture', in word and concept, is a veritable apparatus of capture: capture of the new by the old, in the service of the establishment of a false historical continuity – a continuity of progressive modification – as opposed to the dialectical continuity *of determinate negation* characteristic of the actual history of modernism: that is, the establishment of artistic meaning via specific ('determinate') relations of negation. In this case, specific ways of *not*-painting, *not*-sculpting, *not* producing 'architecture', etc. The main category that Smithson himself developed for his particular version of this kind of negative work was the *non-site*. Nothing reveals the fundamental error of 'sculptural' interpretations of Smithson's work after 1964 so clearly as the concept of *non-site*. Indeed, one may interpret the site/non-site relation as the spatial aspect of that more general dialectic of the aesthetic and conceptual that constitutes postconceptual art, ontologically.[26] There is a homology between the two pairs of oppositional terms:

aesthetic	conceptual
site	non-site

For Smithson, non-sites are sites that represent other sites, and hence, reflectively, that need to represent their own character as such sites as well. 'The investigation of a specific site', Smithson wrote, (i.e. its representation at a non-site) 'is a matter of *extracting concepts*.'[27] This is, I think, perhaps the most important sentence that Smithson wrote. It anticipates institutional critique, for example, as the investigation of specific non-sites (qua sites), at these non-sites themselves – the extraction of the concepts of 'museum', 'gallery', 'biennale' and so on. And it gives the lie to the proliferating aestheticization of 'site specificity', in so far as such an approach represses the constitutive role of the non-site in making the site a site, through an extraction of its concept.

Smithson's *Nonsites* stand at the center of the conceptual radicalization of his practice from 1964 onwards, which may be periodized into four main stages:

1. an immanent critique of the formalist rationality of self-referentiality: *Enantiomorphic Chambers*, 1965; *Alogon*, 1966.

2. the appropriation of "non-art" architectural and photojournalist forms: *A Web of White Gravel Paths Surrounding Storage Tanks* — part of the Dallas–Fort Worth Regional Airport project, 1967; *A Tour of the Monuments of Passaic, New Jersey*, *Artforum*, 1967 [Fig. 9] — which appears in Hobbs's book as a very strange kind of 'sculpture' indeed![28]

3. the 1968 *Non-sites* themselves: for example, Fig. 10.

4. the more expansive site constructions and modifications, 1969–73: *Asphalt Rundown*, Rome, 1969; and its sketch, *1000 Tons of Asphalt*, 1969 — a work that is closely related to *Spiral Jetty* in its full processual form, in its use of the dump truck as artistic material.

All four stages were accompanied by an extensive array of practices that included drawing, writing, film, and photography, the precise art-status of the products of which remains in many ways still ambiguous. They can be regarded simultaneously as preparatory materials, documentation, and constitutive elements of the works themselves. Is the film *Spiral Jetty* a separate, independent work, for example? Is it primarily documentation of the production of another work – a large sculpture or 'Earthwork' also called *Spiral Jetty*? Or is it neither of these two things? Viewed from the standpoint of a postconceptual practice, the film *Spiral Jetty* appears as one element in a complex distribution of artistic materials, across a multiplicity of material forms and practices, the unity of which constitutes a singular, though internally multitudinous work. In this case, *Spiral Jetty* includes both the film and the configuration of mud, precipitated salt crystals and rocks that form a coil, 1,500 feet long and 15 feet wide, jutting out in the water at Rozel Point, in the Great Salt Lake in Utah; as well as the essay of the same name, which includes script from the film; and a variety of related paraphernalia.

From his 1964 'alogical' three-dimensional realizations of perspective onwards, Smithson's is a self-consciously (I would even say systematically orientated) transcategorial practice. All of Smithson's own categories – and for all his talk *against* categorization, he is primarily involved in the production of new kinds of artwork – are transcategorial in origin, the products of highly self-conscious conceptual crossings. For example:

1. *Site-selection* (a variant of the readymade): Pine Flat Dam, Sacramento, in Smithson's 'Towards the Development of an Air

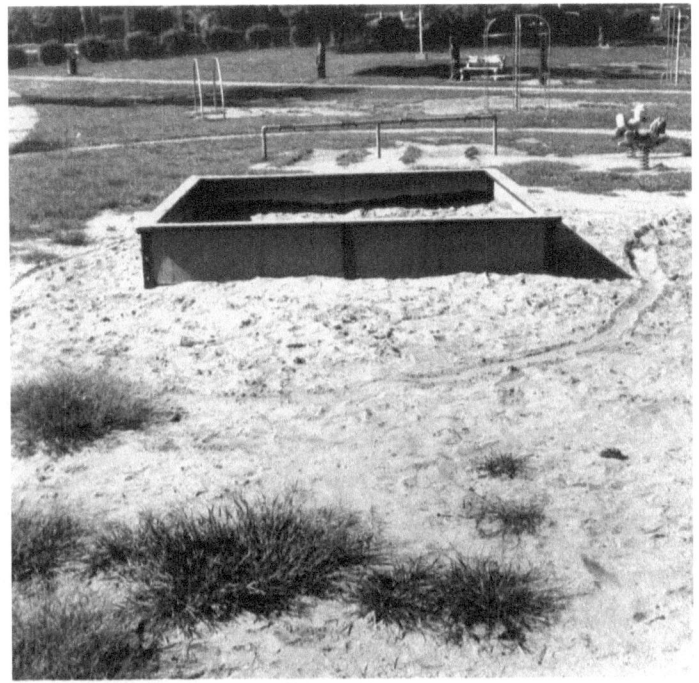

Fig. 9: Robert Smithson, *Monuments of the Passaic,* photographic detail (*The Sandbox Monument*), 1967

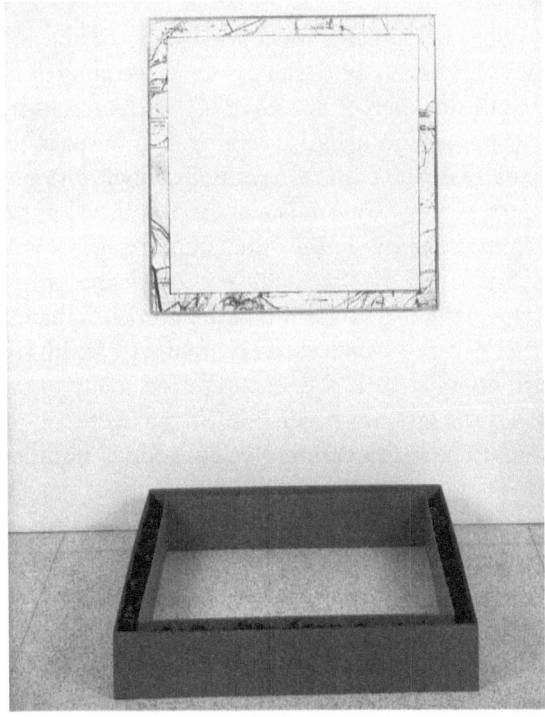

Fig. 10: Robert Smithson, *Mono Lake Nonsite (Cinders Near Black Point)*, 1968

Terminal Site' essay, for instance: 'When it functions as a damn it will cease being a work of art and become a "utility".' Think also of his designation of parked aircraft as temporary buildings.[29]

2. *The magazine work*: a crossing of the art or cultural magazine with the concept of art – a variant on the assisted readymade – mainly taking the form of fictionalized photojournalism, and introducing one of the main conceptual uses of photography, or uses of photography within a conceptual (that is to say, a critically, post-conceptual) art.

3. *The non-site*: which was actually the productive conceptual effect of a pun on Smithson's early anti-formalism: 'non-sight' – recoding the museum/gallery as a *negation* of both 'site' and 'sight': negation of the place outside the gallery via a negation of the sight of it, in the sense of the view of the place.

4. Related to this is Smithson's conception of the artist as *the sight/site-seer*: the artist as tourist – both the one who sees and the wise man – inscribing itinerary into art as an artistic material, in a manner similar to Douglas Huebler. This has been a massively influential model.

5. *The mirror displacements* and *hypothetical islands*: more variants on the dialectical logic of the non-site.

All these practices exhibit the conceptual logic of the non-site. This critical primacy of the non-site derives from its recoding of the museum/gallery space as the location of an *essentially abstract cognitive experience*, a *non-place*. (Hobbs confusingly calls it a 'nonspace'; confusingly because it has a distinctive social *spatiality*, albeit one quite different from the space of places). This non-place is produced by specific combinations of representations of the 'site/sight' itself: samples of earth, descriptions, maps and photographs – unified and contained by an imaginary frame, which is literalized in the non-sites themselves by the actual framework of the samples: steel containers. Smithson sometimes used the word 'non-site' as if the term referred solely to these containers, but this is a transitional restriction of the scope of the term to a passing instantiation, which conceals its conceptual significance.

In Smithson's own words, from his conversations with Dennis Wheeler from 1969, his work is 'a kind of *ensemble of different mediums* that are all discrete', functioning in 'different degrees of abstraction'.[30] (For 'mediums' here, something slightly looser would be better, such as 'sets of artistic materials'.) The painted steel containers, maps, and photographs, then, are all what he called 'different kinds of mental and physical *abstraction*.' Material, that is sensuously significant, signifiers. This is a sense of the materiality of language that is famously epitomized in *A Heap of Language* (1966), Smithson's prefigurative critique of what was about to become the idealistic self-misunderstanding of analytical conceptual art.

Conceptual abstraction and 'pure perception'

As early as 1973, Lawrence Alloway had emphasized the linguistic function of Smithson's nonsites: 'The nonsite . . . acts as the signifier of the absent site, . . . modules . . . have turned into maps.'[31] However, it is not just that, as he later put it, 'the relation of Nonsite to Site is also that of language to the world: [the Nonsite] is a signifier and the Site is that which is signified.'[32] Rather, this is only the first stage. The reflective relation between them (Smithson's 'dialectics') leads to the signification – the showing – of the relation of signification itself. This has the crucial effect of *de*-materializing the site in a moment in the dialectic through which new significations of it are produced, projecting this new status of 'site' beyond the literal site – which is ultimately itself no more than *material* for the site/non-site dialectic of experience. This effect is reinforced, and secured, by the fact that Smithson was interested in changes in sites over time. (This is one reason that isolating the sculptural elements of non-sites is such a mistake.) As Alloway again put it: 'As the sites change . . . nonsites take on increasingly the character of memorials to dead cities (or hypothetical continents).'[33] Utopias. In their abstraction to the status of the hypothetical through change, all sites become mental islands, best represented literally as 'hypothetical islands': continental (*The Hypothetical Continent of Lemuria*, 1969) or domestic (*Floating Island to Travel Around Manhattan*, 1970 – Fig. 11). As such, they acquire an irresistible ideality – some would say a virtuality – which Smithson himself was reluctant to concede; an ideality that makes possible their subsequent actualizations: *The Hypothetical Continent in Shells* (Florida, 2001); *Floating Island to Travel Around Manhattan Island. New York* (2005 – Fig. 12). Such actualizations follow the logic of instruction works – the first genre of conceptual art practice.[34]

From the standpoint of the works' ideality, their material forms appear as *multiple materializations* selected from an infinite set of possible actualizations. These possibilities have the status of *fictions*. Non-sites thus perform a fictionalizing function. It is in the posthumous realization of ideas depicted in several of Smithson's drawings that the conceptual aspect of his art is most visible. To view Smithson's works from the standpoint of the postconceptual means to *activate* this relation to the conceptual in his art, without reducing it to a conceptual result. It is by activating its conceptual aspects that its deepest art-critical and art-historical significance may be disinterred.

In another of his conversations with Wheeler, Smithson described his thought process in a way that recalls his earlier account of the proliferating collapse of categorization in museums, as follows:

> My thoughts are like an *avalanche in the mind*, in the sense that they are breaking apart; there's no information that can't be collapsed or broke down, so that it's not a matter of establishing a perfect system. There is no perfection in this situation. There is no perfection in my range, because my thoughts as well as the material that I'm dealing with are always coming loose, breaking apart and bleeding at the edges.[35]

Smithson's description of his thoughts ('an avalanche in the mind') mirrors quite precisely that of the entropic state of art criticism (the 'interminable avalanche of categories'), which he had earlier identified as the cause of the museum's *paralysis*. Here, however, and shortly afterwards in the 'Spiral Jetty' essay (first published two years after the completion of his marking of the site, the so-called 'earthwork', in 1972) – rather than being paralyzing, this entropic state is refigured productively, even ecstatically, as the *structure of artistic experience* itself.

For all the self-consciously transcategorial construction of the works, Smithson's goal is thus ultimately a kind of meltdown of categorialization, via *trans*categorialization – a kind of determinate negation of its own transcategoriality, in an immediate apprehension of unity that dissolves its own conceptuality – not unlike the structure of the speculative experience of the absolute that concludes Hegel's *Phenomenology of Spirit*. In the words of the 'Spiral Jetty' essay:

> This site was a rotary that enclosed itself in an immense roundness. From that gyrating space emerged the possibility of the *Spiral Jetty*. No ideas, no concepts, no systems, no structures, no abstractions, could hold themselves together in the actuality of that evidence. My dialectics of site and non-site whirled into an indeterminate state, where solid and liquid lost themselves in each other . . . *No sense wondering about classifications and categories, there were none.*[36]

This looks like the ecstatic empiricism of Lucy Lippard's approach to those times. Yet even here, there is no simple elimination of categories, but a *process of internal mutual destruction* or dissolution, leading to a kind of reduction to pure perception of the kind described elsewhere by Smithson in relation to cinema. 'The ultimate film goer', he writes, would watch films constantly 'until the action of each would drown in a vast reservoir of pure perception.'[37] Smithson's imagination of the

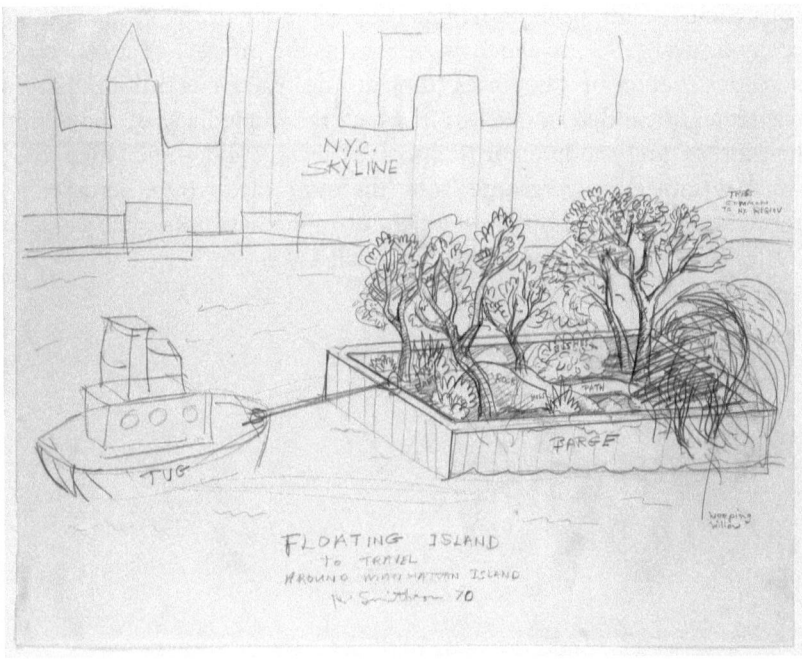

Fig. 11. Robert Smithson, *Floating Island to Travel Around Manhattan*, 1970

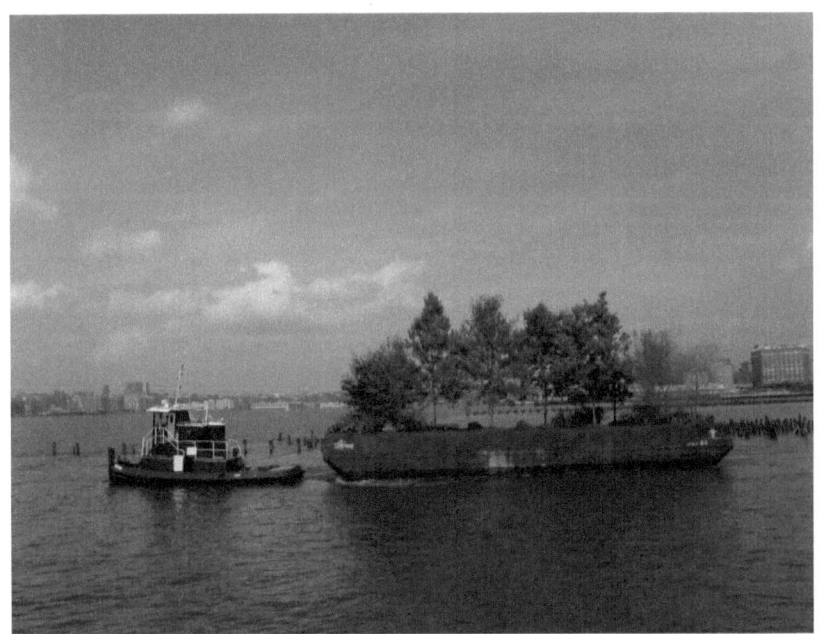

Fig. 12. Robert Smithson, *Floating Island to Travel Around Manhattan Island, New York*, 2005

experience of the site of *Spiral Jetty*, it turns out, is actually the constructed result of his own film. Yet this is not entropy in some grand cosmological sense, so much as entropy as the product of a dialectical auto-destruction of categories (the auto-destructive condition of new transcategorical determinacies) in which the immediacy of the apprehension of unity momentarily dissolves subject and object alike, only for determinacy to reemerge from 'the reservoir of pure perception', reflectively enhanced by this moment of immediate unity, like the jetty itself rising up again out of the Great Salt Lake.

5
Photographic ontology, infinite exchange

Robert Smithson's work is emblematic, as well as unique – emblematic of a fundamental historical shift in art's mode of being – because the relationship between its conceptual dimension (infinite in its possible actualizations) and its multiple actual materializations models the ontological structure of postconceptual art. However, the destruction of the categories of medium, which this art involves, was associated by Smithson with access to a 'vast reservoir' not of ideas, but of 'pure perception' – a kind of transcendental aesthetic immanent within, and accessible via, a cinematic 'atopia'. 'Cinema' stands here for a certain imaginary de-realization of art (dissolution into pure perception, pure image) associated with something like 'absolute' experience. Yet cinema and film (which Smithson did not distinguish in anything more than an inchoate manner) are historical forms. Film, and chemically based photography more broadly, was the dominant artistic form of the twentieth century, in relation to which other art practices derived much of their specific contemporaneities. The migration of Smithson's work from its starting point in painting and sculpture, via a specific series of negations of those categories, towards a generalization of the experience of film, repeated this history *in nuce*. Today, however, in the context of the technological redundancy of the chemically based photographic processes upon which the production of moving images once depended, Smithson's identification of a certain 'absolute' experience with cinematically exhibited film raises the question of whether the 'reservoir of pure perception' – into and out of which, he believed, artistic ideas and their actualizations dissolve and re-emerge – is not better associated with the flow of digital imaging. Is digital imaging, which now pervades all areas of life, a new artistic meta-medium, at once technologically unifying an otherwise disparate artistic field and connecting it to life practices?

This chapter moves from a consideration of the rapidly changing ontology of the photographic image to a construction of the affinities between the infinity of means characteristic of postconceptual art, the infinite reproducibility implicit in digital technology, and the infinity of the exchange relation through which art subsists, economically, as a cultural form.

The development of postconceptual art certainly appears to be connected, historically, to transformations in the ontology of the photographic image. And these transformations are not merely 'technological', but fundamentally social as well. In the sphere of cultural economy, for example, the image-space of the photographic has expanded to global dimensions as a constituent part of what we might call *photo-capitalism*. If print-capitalism was a cultural-economic condition of nationalism,[1] photo-capitalism is a distinctively transnational and translinguistic cultural–economic form. As Régis Debray has argued: 'If you want to make yourself known everywhere and establish dominion over the world, manufacture images instead of writing books . . . This is the moral of the story which all empires have known, from the Byzantine to the American.'[2] The photographic image is, among other things, the dominant visual form of the American empire, through which we are currently experiencing its decline. As such, analysis of changes in the ontology of the photographic image promises to provide insight into not only artistic ontology, but the politics of cultural forms more generally.

Understood historically, the question of the ontology of the photographic image is in large part the question of the *mode of unity of the relational totality* of the variety of different photographic forms coexisting within the present: chemical photography, film, television, video and digital imaging – to name only the five main forms – the spine, if you like, of a still expanding field. (One might also include the remote sensing of microwave, infrared, ultraviolet, and shortwave radio imagery, for example.)[3] This totality is relational, rather than expressive, because as a cultural-historical form there is no single underlying, ontologically fundamental basis to its unity – in a single technology, for example – which would allow for the specification of photography as a 'medium'. Indeed, in the sense in which it has been understood in the visual arts since Greenberg, the question of medium-specificity is precisely the wrong question to ask of the photographic, since it is the peculiar *generality* of the photographic image that laid the ground for the destruction of medium-specificity in the visual arts and the inauguration of a 'post-medium' or 'transmedia' condition, as long ago as the end of the first decade of the twentieth century. The question of the unity of the photographic must thus be separated from the question of medium, in its Greenbergian sense. Rather, the question of the unity of the photographic is the question of the ongoing socio-historical process of unification of the photographic as a *cultural* form. There is a technological basis to this unification – a particular history of technological relations – but it is their meanings-in-*use* that determine the (necessarily 'cultural') unity of these technologies.

It may be, as Debray insists, that the ontology of images must be 'answerable' to productive techniques, in as much as 'one simply does not take the *same kind* of photograph using a photographic plate exposed for two hours during the subject's tedious pose and using a Polaroid camera'. Yet Debray does not dispute (though he does not explain why) both are photographs. It is equally true that: 'The image when formed on a screen by the projection of light behind a photographic frame of film across a darkened room belongs to a *different order of "signs"* from the image electronically induced by a cathodic current on a luminiferous surface.' But it is not clear that the television image does not remain, despite this electronic mediation – indeed, by virtue of the specific character of this electronic mediation – itself 'photographic'.[4]

All such relational unities, being historical, are at once both retrospectively and prospectively constructed (in the sense of depending upon certain projections of the future, as well as certain receptions of the past), but they are nonetheless 'ontological' for that, since, as cultural forms, they partake of the complex historical temporality of existential ontology (in their being-*for* the human), writ large, at the level of social form. Cultural forms articulate specific modes of temporalization of history, photography perhaps more intimately than most. One need look no further than the familiar literature on the existential charge of the photograph in its relationship not only to remembrance, but more fundamentally to death: Bazin's 'embalming' of time; the late Barthes's 'excessive, monstrous mode' of the 'immobilization' of time and hence 'sign of my future death'; even Bourdieu's function of 'solemnization'[5] – although the relationship between the photographic preservation of the past, on the one hand, and historical experience more strictly speaking (and hence politics) on the other, is more theoretically complex and politically contested than this particular French tradition suggests, as earlier and more critical interpretations of the existential ontology of photographic imagery, in the writings of Siegfried Kracauer and Benjamin, attest.[6]

The idea of the photographic posits a certain historical unity to a particular set of technologies of image production. It groups together technically produced indexical images of various sorts, supplemented, more recently, by digital images in which such indexical *effects* are simulated in various ways. This unity derives from connections at the level of both the material form of the technologies (an imprinting of light upon light-sensitive surfaces of different kinds) and their predominant socio-cultural functions and uses (as epistemically privileged representations of the real). All technologies are by definition unstable unities of material form and social use: abstractions of the rationality (*logos*) of specific processes of making (*techné*) in the service of the generalization of their uses – as one can see in the very grammar of the term 'technology'. However, it is meaning – ontologically, one might say 'structures of recognition' – that mediates, or constitutes the unity of, material form and social use: hence the characterization of technology as itself a cultural form, and the necessity for an ontologically based semiotics, or metaphysically grounded existential pragmatics, as the theoretical basis of its comprehension. In so far as there is an adequate concept of the photographic, unifying its various instances, it will be a recovery at the level of theory of an implicit practical unity of forms of signification produced by a discrete set of combinations of material forms and their social uses. Technologies relate to one another on both of these axes.

There is no single thread in the history of a technological form like photography. This is the theoretical difficulty posed by its cultural character. So what is the *conceptual form* and *ontological mode* of such a unity – the unity of 'the photographic' as a practical unity of forms of signification produced by a historically discrete set of combinations of material forms and social uses? I shall approach this question in two ways: first, philosophically, through a reworking of Kant's notion of distributive unity; second, cultural-historically, through the idea of 'the' photograph as an imagistic register of temporal singularity, which functions as a metonym or model providing an *imaginary* ground to the unity of the photographic field. I then proceed, via a brief account of the central role played in the historical articulation of the unity of this field by the notion of dominant form, to reconsider the relationship of the photographic to art, under the conditions of digitalization.

Distributive unity

The unity of the photographic is 'distributive' in form. As such it is implicated, interpretatively, in each individual photographic form. It is also present, more explicitly, in that social distribution of individual images across different material forms – beyond their ostensible boundaries as 'works' – that results from the reproducibility inherent in the photographic. The question of the ontological significance of the latest technological forms is thus less that of their materiality, in itself, than that of their effects upon the still-expanding field of the photographic as a whole. The expansion here is internally technologically and socially generated, continuing and open-ended (rather than being reducible to a discrete, historically received set of binary oppositions in relation to which the signifier 'photography' can be semiotically fixed at the outset).[7]

The notion of distributive unity, as a logically distinct form of unity, derives from Kant's *Critique of Pure Reason*. Kant, however, thinks it there only negatively, as a threat to what he calls the 'collective' unity established by ideas, which, he argues, unites the actions of the understanding in its relations to intuitions and thereby makes a coherent experience of the world possible, over time, at the level of the whole. In Kant's terms:

> Just as the understanding unites the manifold into an object through concepts, so reason on its side unites the manifold of concepts through ideas by positing a certain *collective unity* as the goal of the understanding's actions, which are *otherwise* concerned only with *distributive unity*.[8]

In other words, without 'ideas' (in Kant's particular sense of concepts that posit objects beyond possible experience) there would be a merely 'distributive' unity to the acts of the understanding. The justification of the presumption of collective unity increasingly preoccupied Kant in the aftermath of the *Critique of Pure Reason*, since the need to assert the unity of nature as a teleological system, which collective unity involves, threatened to collapse his critical project back into a form of ontological rationalism. It is the alternative danger, however, that is relevant here: the threat of a merely distributive unity understood as a breakdown of the conceptual unity of experience itself. For, as Kant put it in the First Introduction to the *Critique of Judgement*:

> For although experience constitutes a system in accordance with *transcendental laws*, which contain the condition of possibility of experience in general, there is still possible such an *infinite multiplicity* of empirical laws and such a *great heterogeneity of forms* of nature, which would belong to particular experience, that the concept of a system in accordance with these (empirical) laws must be entirely alien to the understanding, and neither the possibility, let alone the necessity, of such a whole can be conceived. Nevertheless particular experience, thoroughly interconnected in accordance with constant principles, also requires this systematic interconnection of empirical laws . . .[9]

The threat of a merely distributive unity is the threat of a heterogeneity to the forms of nature *beyond* the 'logic of specification' (genus/species/

subspecies) and hence of an *infinite diversity* of empirical laws. It is thus the paradox of Kant's conception of distributive unity that it is *not really a unity at all* at the level of the objects of 'experience', but rather denotes a type of oneness made up of the spatial contiguity and temporal continuity of experience alone. There is no unity to its objects. To put it another way: distributive unity is *aesthetic*, in the primary sense of the term, meaning 'of sensibility'. For Kant, distributive unity is thus, epistemologically, a *negative* construction or limit concept, produced by intellectually abstracting (in the sense of removing) from the empirical content of experience the subjectively necessary presupposition of the 'collective unity' imposed by ideas. If this collective unity cannot be plausibly constructed (and as I have said, Kant himself was progressively pushed back towards rationalist teleology in order to do it) the logic of distribution tends instead to the *multiplication of singularities*. This is the sense in which philosophies of difference are inherently aesthetic. It is, of course, Deleuze who draws this conclusion, and to whom we owe the extraction of the concept of distribution from Kant's work. (The editors of the new Cambridge edition of Kant's *Works* do not consider the term significant enough even to index it.) In the second chapter of *Difference and Repetition*, Deleuze takes Kant's negative conception of distributive unity and turns it into a positive ontological concept of distributive difference. This is in many ways the key concept of Deleuze's philosophy of difference: distributive difference within a univocity of being. This is Deleuze's ontology in a nutshell.[10]

However, if there are to be subjects and objects of knowledge and experience, in whatever secondary or derived form, a 'belonging together' or what Kant called an 'affinity' of multiple singularities must nonetheless occur – and hence be amenable to theoretical construction – in some form. As Deleuze and Guattari put it in *What is Philosophy?*: 'The problem of philosophy is how to acquire a consistency without losing the infinite into which thought plunges.'[11] Despite a certain Deleuzian enthusiasm for pure difference, then, the rhetoric of 'multiple singularities' cannot do away with the philosophical requirement of a construction of unity in or across distribution, at various levels of analysis, in order to render intelligible intelligibility itself. Hence the necessity for the development of Kant's concept of distributive unity beyond both the logical restrictions of Kant's thought and Deleuze's ontological radicalization of distribution into 'difference in itself', which think unity only as subsumption or regulation, on the one hand, and conceptlessness on the other.[12] Such a concept of distributive unity, I want to suggest, would articulate the *logical form of the historical unity of empirical forms* – a way of grasping the insecurely bounded, because constantly shifting, relational totalities of historical forms. The unity of the photographic is a distributive unity in this sense.

The photographic is distributed across a historically (rather than reductively semiotically) determinate, progressive range of technologico-cultural forms – its own 'expanding field' – from early chemical photography, through negative-based prints, film, television and video to digital imaging. This unity is not conceptual in the *Kantian* sense. Rather, I would suggest, it derives from a chain of relations between technologies that is sustained as a distributive unity by their common cultural functions. In this sense, a distributive unity is a pragmatic unity. It is a condition of this commonality of function that the types of images produced share a certain *de*-materialized generality that transcends their technologically particular material forms and acts as a kind of relay between them. It is important, however, to resist the temptation of conceiving of this dematerialized generality as some kind of shared 'essence', since it is ontologically dependent in each instance on a specific technological basis – hence the distributive rather than collective unity of the photographic image-space. Nonetheless, as the founding site of the technological determination of an image, the ontological meaning of which transcends its material form, 'the' photograph (or, more specifically, the 'still' photographic image) has served historically as a kind of metonymic model for the photographic as a whole. It is this metonymic modelling that is thrown into crisis by the potential for 'ontological inversion' inherent in digital technologies: supposedly non-indexical photographs. However – and this is my point – this crisis in a particular *imagined* unity is not necessarily a crisis (although it does correspond to a transformation) in the *actual* distributive unity of the field.

The photograph: metonymic model of an imagined unity

The idea of a founding unity of the photographic (like other ideas of founding unities) is essentially imaginary or mythical: in this case, in its reductive identification of a cultural form with a technology – the ideological fantasy of a 'medium', in Greenberg's sense. Yet it is the social actuality of this mythological identification (its social being qua structure of recognition, as inscribed in the social practices of photography) that gives social reality to photography as a cultural form. There is a constitutive illusion here. Photography, in other words, from this point of view, is a cultural category, the unity of which is based on the imagined and practiced unification of a particular technological process (optical/mechanical/chemical) and a particular set of social functions (the solemnization of festivity/documentation/pornography/advertising/surveillance, etc). This imagined unity is anchored in, or condensed into, the famous *meaning-effect of 'the real'*. This is at once a naturalization of the structure of the theological image – signification via participation in the real, or what André Bazin called the object-image (for photography is without doubt a theological technology) – and an aesthetically novel form of indexical signification, rooted in the technological specificity of the photographic process: that combination of seamless material continuity and tonal differentiation characteristic of its alleged 'analogical perfection'.[13] The identification of the process (photography) with a particular quality of experience (the photographic image) is summed up in the ideal objecthood of the photograph. Yet it is here, on closer inspection, in the very idea of 'the' photograph, that this ontological unity is least secure (or, better, most ideal), since it too is actually distributed, both spatially and temporally, across a number of discrete sites.

This problematizes the whole question of *where* 'the photograph' is, which turns out to be as difficult to answer under the conditions of chemical-based analogue images as it is under those of digitalization. Is it, for example, as ordinary language suggests, to be identified with the photographic print? Hardly, for this is (at least potentially) a multiple – although a print is one place it might be found. Is it the negative? But this is a negative or tonally inverted image (and anyway a film might remain undeveloped). Is it, then, the image captured on the photographic plate or film? After all, photographs are what one 'takes' – one each instance, however many prints. Yet this is, perversely, unviewable, until developed. It soon becomes clear that to ask, 'Where is the photograph?' is the wrong question. Put simply: there is no single site of the photograph. The photograph is not the kind of thing, ontologically, that can be strictly identified in spatial terms. There is a distributive unity to 'the' photograph itself, as well as to the broader field of the photographic. In so far as the question can be meaningfully addressed, the photograph is distributed *across* the sites of its process, which it permeates as an image, de-realized (spectral), albeit in a peculiar ontological state of dependency upon the processes that it transcends, in each of its different technological forms. Hence its peculiar combination of generality and specificity. There is a direct ontological affinity here between photography and the conceptual aspect of art, which is rendered explicit in postconceptual art. For there is no fixed place of either 'the' photograph or the work of art.

The photograph, like the work of art, is an ideal unity. It is held together by the idea of the 'capture' of a moment of time; an idea which is given cultural actuality by the dependence of its social functions upon the meaning-effect of the 'real'. Yet this supposedly fixed temporal singularity is fantasmatic, since the temporality of the photographic image is always that of a relation between a (constantly shifting) 'now' and the photograph's 'then' — a relation sustained, *as if* atemporal, by the material continuity of the photographic form in question. *It is the spatial boundedness of the image that secures the illusion of temporal objectivity* — the idea that time itself might become an 'object'. A photograph is an *objective illusion* of temporal objectification. Subsequent photographic forms — film, television, video, digital — derive their meaning from their historical relations to this primary form: in particular, from the appropriation and technological extension of both its idea and its cultural functions.

Historically, it would seem that the most technologically advanced cultural form (which also means the form most productive of new cultural functions — since technological 'advance' is always relative to cultural function, rather than an independently identifiable, strictly scientific achievement), in each instance, becomes the 'dominant form': that form in relation to which other cultural forms derive their historical meaning, and to which they progressively 'adapt' themselves in various ways. It also seems that, to begin with, each new form models itself on aspects of the previous form that it will replace as 'dominant', before the relationship becomes inverted. Photography modelled itself on painting; film on photography, television on film; video on film and television; digital on video, etc. In Althusserian terms, one might thus say that, historically, *distributive unity is 'structured in dominance' by dominant forms*.[14] The current 'crisis' in the concept of the photographic — such as it is — marks the transition to a new dominant form. The question of the impact on the concept of the photographic of the 'ontological inversion' represented by digital re-mixing (with its ironic return to painterly modes of composition) is thus the question of what sets of relations will be established, in practice, between the new and the old forms. Despite its ontological character, there can be no answer to this question divorced from practical developments — no theoretical pre-determination — if, as I have argued, the ontological issue is that of the character of the distributive unity of the totality of forms. These practical developments are tied up with photography's relationship to art, in general. For the photographic is not merely a particular art, or a particular kind of art. It is the currently dominant form of the image as such.

Digitalization, art and the real (or, anxiety about abstraction)

It is a familiar feature of the history of the relationship between photography and art that it has at least as much to tell us about art, in general, and the consequences and limitations of particular conceptions of art, as it does about photography and its artistic possibilities and limitations.

Indeed, if there is a single practice in relation to which the development of the concept of art over the last 150 years is most frequently narrated, it is undoubtedly photography, in the full historical array of its various technological forms. Given this historical diversity of technologies, there is no more reason to privilege the chemical basis of traditional photographic image-creation in the delimitation of the parameters of the concept of photography than there would be to constrict the parameters of 'painting' by the chemical composition of pigments used during the Renaissance. Today, developments within photography, along with digitally based image production more generally, are *driving* the historical development of art. This is so not just reactively, as was initially mainly the case in the second half of the nineteenth century and the first half of the twentieth century (in the transformation and internal retreat of other forms of representation), but affirmatively, in the use of photographic technologies to produce 'art' of a variety of kinds.

The question of the relationship of photography to art may thus be posed in two different ways: (1) synchronically or conjuncturally, at some specific time in their related histories (in particular, for us, now), and (2) diachronically, as a narrative question about the relationship between two histories, in terms of some possible narrative unity, which might contribute to the intelligibility of each. Each of these methods presupposes a position on the other. What is not helpful is to seek an answer to the question of the relationship between photography and art *in general*, as if they were not historical concepts, in the manner of an analytical philosophy of art. Nonetheless, the existence of a constitutive historical dimension to these concepts does not mean that we need be positivists about history, and deny an ontological dimension to photography or indeed to art – any more than the existence of art institutions, socially delimiting the field of art, means that we need be positivists about institutional form.

The photographic present is, clearly, digital. It thus poses the question, 'What, if anything, does digitalization tell us about the nature of photography?' and more specifically, 'What does digitalization tell us about the nature of photography in art?' I say '*in* art', rather than 'the nature of photography *as* art', since the latter in no way exhausts the former. Photography plays an important role in contemporary art beyond what we may call photographic art, or what others might still want to call 'art photography' – as an element or component of a wide variety of different kinds of installation work, for example. One of the most important unresolved critical questions concerns the relationship between these different kinds of practice: that is, whether they can be subjected to a single overarching critical problematic; and what the consequences are for the concept of art if they cannot. There is a critical contest here between a conception of photography as a *pictorial medium* (sponsored by Michael Fried and Jeff Wall)[15] and a conception of the photographic as the domain of the *image* in general. The paradox here is that photography only gained generalized institutional recognition as an artistic practice after the *destruction* of the ontological significance of medium in the 1960s – a destruction to which photography itself made a distinctive contribution, primarily via its roles in the documentation of performance and within conceptual art practice, as Wall himself has recounted.[16] Photography thus became a part of 'art' at the moment that 'art' became postconceptual. This is the sense in which one might say – contra Wall's recent writings – that photography is art to the extent to which it is itself a postconceptual practice.

There is an ambiguity in the formulation 'photography after digitalization' which goes to the heart of the complexity of the role of photography in contemporary art. It corresponds to the twofold nature of the traditional photographic process. For the phrase can be understood to refer to (1) the digitalization of the *act of photographic capture*, in the sense of the translation of the distribution of intensities of light on the sensor into the binary code of the data file, within the digital camera, in the 'taking' of a photograph – the photographic 'event'; and (ii) the digital condition of the *production of an image* from a data file, the so-called 'digital image' (although the image itself – qua image – is not digital, of course, since the image is a visually structured abstraction of elements of the physical process). These two processes are disjunctive and hence potentially separable, since the data from which a digital image is produced need not be the result of photographic capture, and so the so-called digital image is therefore not necessarily photographic. It is the disjunction between these two processes that raises the possibility of the manipulation and transformation of 'photographic' data, subsequent to the taking of a picture, prior to its projection as an image – that is, computerized image processing. And it is this possibility that generates ontological concern – anxiety – about the 'no longer indexical' character of digital photographs.

There are a number of things to be said about this. The first is that the former of these two processes (the digitalization of the act of photographic capture) *retains* both the causal and deictic aspects of photographic indexicality – and hence its crucial function of grounding reproducibility – but without the iconic aspect of perceptual resemblance previously associated with them.[17] As Benjamin showed, however, the key to the icon is not perceptual resemblance as such, but reproducibility: the semiotic replicability of the pictorial image is grounded in its means of reproduction – a 'rule of construction' (Pierce) derived from a law of production.[18] The ontological anxiety about the real generated by digital photography is *in this respect* misplaced. It derives, rather, from the disjunction between the two stages of the photographic process. Yet this disjunction is also a feature of traditional chemical photography, in the disjunction between the negative and the print – each of which is, in principle, as open to manipulation as a digital data file. Thus the difference does not concern the possibility of manipulation, per se, but rather its precise character and quality – in particular, the extraordinary 'fine grain' manipulation that becomes possible at the level of the pixel, which can be performed in such a way as to leave no *visible* trace – relative to visual expectations governed by conventions of photographic realism. Nonetheless, artists (and others) have been intervening in the mechanisms of the photographic process since its inception, without generating the ontological anxiety about the loss of the real (loss of indexicality) that has accompanied the advent of digital photography. So, one must think, perhaps something else is going on here?

This anxiety appears irrational – which is, of course, no more than to acknowledge it *as* an anxiety: a free-floating anxiousness about the real that has 'latched on' to digital photography as a cultural site in which to invest, because of the social importance but current epistemological uncertainty about the various documentary functions of photography. The basic source of such anxiety has nothing to do with photography itself. Rather, I would speculate, it has to do with the nature of *the abstraction of social relations* characteristic of societies based on relations of exchange; and, in particular, the relationship between social form and the value form (in Marx's sense) – that peculiar sense in which, in the parlance of journalistic commentary, the most decisive sectors of the capitalist economy, associated with finance capital, are *not 'real'*. In the late autumn of 2008, the media began incessantly to repeat the message that the world financial crisis had started to feed through into the 'real' economy. There was, and is, something ontologically peculiar about this. For it is precisely the *most* 'actual' part of the economy – in the sense of it being the most determinative – finance capital, which is declared 'unreal' here. The troubling thing is that in societies based on generalized exchange, certain kinds of abstraction (money being the most famous example) are in fact real or actual in a manner that does not correspond to the ontology of empirical realism that governs ordinary-language uses of the term 'real'. Hence the disjunction between the actually very 'real' economy of finance capital and everyday individual perceptions of the 'real' economy. This is the famously 'spectral' or inverted ontology of value familiar to readers of Marx's *Capital* for nearly 150 years now. The reason I raise it here is because it is anxiety about the real generated by these peculiar social forms (within which the most real *appears* unreal, and the apparently or empirically real has little determinative significance) that is displaced onto and invested in the problem of the referential significance of digitally produced images. The fact that there is, in principle, *no necessary visible indicator* of the referential value of such an image mimics the structure of the commodity, in which there is no necessary relation between exchange-value and use-value.

Philosophically, then, there is no particular ontological problem posed by digital picture-taking. There is, rather, a set of normative issues about the conventions governing the processing of data in the interval between its 'capture' and its projection or printing, under technological conditions facilitating a generalized manipulation of the components of images. This decoupling of the photographic image from its indexical ground (which is still there at the outset of the process) has a particular significance in the context of art, since art has been understood, philosophically, since early German Romanticism as a form of self-conscious illusion. Might it not be the growing self-consciousness of the *potentially* illusory character of the photographic image, subsequent to its digitalization, that makes it the form of image most appropriate to art as self-conscious illusion? And is there not thus a strange convergence here between the digital image and the commodity form?

The visible, the invisible and the multiplication of visualizations

In so far as there is an ontological peculiarity or novelty at issue here, it attaches to the digital image per se, and not just the 'photographically' generated one – although most digitally produced images are, as a matter of empirical fact, photographically based, in one way or another. It derives from the lack of visual 'resemblance' between digital data and the projected or printed form of the image it generates. In so far as it makes any sense to talk of a digitally produced image as some kind of 'copy' of the data out of which it is made, it is a *visible* copy of an *invisible* original, since it is the digital data that plays the role of the original here, rather than the situation or event that is depicted, which is its more distant, shadowy source. This is quite different from the role of the negative as the mediator between the act of photographic capture and the print. The contiguity of these two processes is ruptured by the ontological peculiarity, or self-sufficiency, of digitalized data. On the other hand, however, we might see this as little more than a variation (albeit also an intensification) of the essentially *theological* character of the traditionally chemical-based photographic image itself.

As Boris Groys has pointed out, in so far as a digital image is a visible copy of an invisible original, 'the digital image is functioning as a Byzantine icon – as a visible copy of invisible God'.[19] Groys, however, appears to take this theological structure to be distinctive of digital imagery. Yet this is something it shares with the traditional photograph in a different form. What is distinctive about the digitally produced image is that it exhibits something like a *de-temporalization* of the theological structure of the photograph, consequent upon its rupture in the continuity between the two stages of the photographic process. Its decisive difference lies in the attention it calls to the *multiplication of varieties* of forms of visualization made possible by that rupture, within the parameters of what are still, essentially, processes of replication.

In Barthes's famous account in *Camera Lucida*, the temporal peculiarity of the photograph (as the literal presence of the past) is understood to effect an 'immobilization' and 'engorgement' of time.[20] This represents a naturalization of the theological structure of the icon, via time, because meaning participates in the real through the becoming 'carnal' of light. In the digital image, on the other hand, time is not immobilized or engorged so much as obliterated, in so far as any ontological significance of the physical contiguity of digital data is negated by the rupture in its visual form: its translation into binary code. It is this rupture that allows Groys to figure digital data as 'invisible' and hence metaphorically God-like. But it is not just *invisibility* that figures divinity in this account of the digital image but, ultimately more importantly, the *creative potential* of digitalized data to generate an in-principle-infinite *multiplicity of forms of visualizations*; although Groys does not quite put it like this, since he is primarily concerned with the mediating role of the curator as 'the performer of the image',[21] rather than the infinite potentiality of the data that underlies this role. (For Groys, it is digitalization that allows the curator to usurp the role of the artist.)

Invisibility and the multiplication of visualizations are thus linked in so far as, following the line of thought of iconoclastic religions, it is precisely the multiplicity of visualizations that sustains the invisibility of the invisible; since, were the invisible to be associated with a single, or even a few stable visible forms, the invisible would become identified with them, and would henceforth be rendered visible after all. It is thus the multiplication of possible forms of visualization/projection (screen, monitor, wall, etc.) deriving from the generic power of digitalization to *free itself from any particular medium* that, ultimately, distinguishes the digital image from its chemically photographic predecessor. And it is this multiplication of possible forms of visualization/projection that allows Groys to claim that, although the digital image remains in some sense a copy (a copy of its data), each 'event of its visualization is an original event'.[22] So here we have the 'event' again: not the event of photographic capture, but *the event of visualization*. Originality thus migrates, or at least, is doubled – moving from *what* it is that is copied (now, the data) to the *form* of the copy. This has significant consequences for art practice, as well as for curation.

With regard to photography, though, we can say that the main function of digitalization is to place photography within the generic field of the digital image. This generically digital-based field is the closest thing there is to a material medium of the generic concept of 'art', characteristic of the postconceptual artistic field. Indeed, one might go as far as to propose that the unity of the field of contemporary art is secured (internally to its institutionality, which sets its ultimate, social parameters) by the possibility of the digitally mediated re-presentation of works. Digital imagery, one might say, plays the role projected for language – but which language could not play – within analytical conceptual art.

This is not a 'dematerialization' of art (or photography), however – which was always a misunderstanding of art's conceptual character – but a materially specific medium of generation of an in-principle-infinite field of visualizations (the data file). If there is a meaningful site of 'dematerialization' at stake here, it does not lie in the data file, or in the conceptual dimension of the work (the originally postulated site of dematerialization) – which is actually always historically tied to specific materializations – but rather in *the image itself*, in so far as the image is the name for the perceptual *abstraction* of a visual structure from its material form. Via the multiplicity of visualizations, digitalization draws attention to the essentially *de*-realized character of the image. It is this de-realized image – supported in each instance by specific material processes – that strangely 'corresponds' to the ontological status of the value-form. The return to medium – medium as a reactive response to an anxiety of its own (anxiety about the end of mediums as 'arts' may be understood as a particular manifestation of anxiety about the real), or, we might say, medium as a mode of passive nihilism in art – is the dialectical counterpart to this de-realization of the image. De- (and therefore potentially re-) realized images can be infinitely exchanged. This is the social meaning of the ontology of the digital image, of which photography is now but one – albeit crucial – kind. In the infinite field of visualizations of the digital image, the infinity of exchange made possible by the abstraction of exchange value from use value finds its equivalent visual form.

The proliferating multiplication of visualizations is not the only way in which digitalization affects art. Digital networks have had profound consequences for the character of social space, and thereby also for what we might call 'art space'.

6
Art space

Contemporary visual art is an urban phenomenon, in both its historical formation and cultural form, in a sense that transcends locality to the extent to which the metropolis transcends the city. If the city-state was the urban form resulting from what Edward Soja calls the 'second Urban Revolution', which occurred over two-and-a-half thousand years ago on the alluvial planes of the Tigris and Euphrates rivers, the urban-industrial capitalism of late eighteenth and early nineteenth-century Europe may be taken to have set in motion a third Urban Revolution characterized by a new, fundamentally abstract, urban form: the metropolis. The metropolis, famously, destroys the social-spatial limits of the *urbs*, destroying place as a space of dwelling, as a result of its tendential replacement of hitherto existing social relations with relations of exchange.[1]

However, the spatiality of the metropolis cannot be reduced to an abstract negation of 'place' or of what is sometimes called 'absolute space'. That is, it cannot be reduced to 'abstract space' in either its Lefebvrean or mathematical-topological senses. For, if the metropolis re-places the absolute space of place with 'non-places' of 'encounter, assembly and simultaneity', rendering particular places equivalent by virtue of the functions they support in a universal process of circulation and exchange,[2] these non-places nonetheless remain dialectically entangled with the space of places, through human embodiment and the embedding of economic transactions, however abstract, in material processes of production and exchange. In fact, contrary to Lefebvre's main use of the distinction between abstract and differential space, the abstract space of the metropolis is itself both dialectically and immanently differential: it is dialectically differential in its constitution through the negation of absolute space or locality, and it is immanently differential, qua abstraction, in its spatial instantiation of the relations of difference driving the process of the accumulation of value.[3] Non-place is thus not only itself a peculiar (a peculiarly meaningless) type of place; there are spatially distinctive *kinds* of non-place as well. Airports, offices, factories and galleries are not merely equivalent *as* non-places. Metropolitan urban form unites and condenses these two types of differential spatial relations in an ongoing process of the destruction and spatial re-instantiation of conditions and relations of exchange.

As a metropolitan urban phenomenon, modern art partakes in this complex, abstract yet differential spatiality. Assuming it is plausible to suppose that there is some such relatively unified thing as 'contemporary art' ('distributively' unified, at least), the question of contemporary art's mode of spatial being thus appears, first and foremost, as the question of the relationship of contemporary art to contemporary urban form. This question may be broken down into three more specific but nonetheless still general questions. First, what is the *spatial specificity* of the historical processes currently constituting urban form? Second, via what main *mediating practices* have new forms of social space imposed themselves upon and manifested themselves within the field of contemporary art, as conditions of its contemporaneity – that is, as conditions of its capacity to articulate, reflect upon and transfigure new forms of social experience? Third, how does this formative spatiality appear, immanently, at the level of the *spatial ontology* of contemporary works of art?

The answers to these questions – elaborated below – are, in brief, as follows. First, the spatial specificity of the urban present derives from its articulating position within a complex *global constellation of spaces of places, non-places and flows*. Second, the main mediating practices through which new forms of social space have imposed themselves on and within the field of contemporary art, as conditions of its contemporaneity, have been, successively, *textualization, architecturalization, post-architectural urbanism* and *transnationalization*. Third, this formative social spatiality manifests itself immanently at the level of the ontology of the work of art as the spatial articulation of its distinctively *postconceptual* structure.

Historically, I have suggested, metropolitan urban form united and condensed two types of differential spatial relation: the dialectical differential through which it is constituted by the negation of absolute space, dwelling or locality; and the immanent differential that it itself constructs, in its spatialization of the relations of difference that drive exchange, and production for exchange (commodity production). These are characteristics of the now-classical metropolitan urban form of the late nineteenth and early twentieth centuries. Today, however, there is a further level of spatial differentiation at play in the construction of urban form: relations between metropolitan centres – and the states within which they are located – constructed by global digital economic networks, with their own distinctive kinds of spatiality. On the one hand, this is an extension and intensification of the same kind of globalization of capitalism already familiar in the late nineteenth century, as a result of the tendency to universalization inherent in the value-form of capital – newly set free by the collapse of historical communism. (From this point of view, 1917–89 increasingly appears as a parenthesis in a universal history of capital.) On the other hand, however, it involves a qualitatively new spatial form, based in electronic, informational and communications technologies: computer networking, the internet and large-scale private intranets, in particular: 'electronic space', 'digital space' or what Manuel Castells has called the 'space of flows'. Whether one conceives of this as a transformation of what is still a basically metropolitan form (as Castells and Saskia Sassen each initially did, for example, in their notions of 'informational' and 'global' cities, respectively), or as something 'postmetropolitan' (as Soja prefers), and hence as an element of a broader and more complex global spatiality (as Castells and Sassen subsequently came to), it is undoubtedly a *qualitative* transformation that has introduced a new type of globally immanent spatial differentiation.[4]

These changes have significant implications for the development of contemporary art as a cultural form, of direct relevance to ongoing debates about the autonomy of art, its institutionalizations, and the practices of avant-gardes. This means that there are currently at least three main types of differential space to be taken into account in a consideration of the urban form that is a spatial condition of contemporary art: the spatial dialectic of place and non-place, the spatialization of economic differences immanent to non-places (exchange and accumulation), and electronic space or the space of flows. Contemporary urban form is constituted at a planetary level through the complex mediation of these forms. The spatial specificity of the historical present (our global capitalist modernity) is thus best characterized as a complex *global constellation of spaces of places, non-places and flows*. Within this constellation, the bounded territory of the nation-state remains the primary social form of 'place'. But it is subject to both erosion and the internal transformation of its spatial structures (in particular, currently, the relationship between 'public' and 'private') through its relations to both non-places and the 'space of flows' alike. This is a complex and contradictory process that Sassen has theorized as the 'denationalization' of the state – a process within which components of the state itself are active participants.[5] Denationalization, transnationalization and both what we might call 'accommodating' and 'reactive' renationalizations are integral parts of a single process.

Non-places and the textualization of art

'Non-places' are a spatial consequence of the temporal form of the modern; specifically, of an intensification of the logic of temporal negation constitutive of the modern as 'the new', to the point of the immanent negation of the significance of place as a source of social meaning. This negation of the historically received meaning of 'place' is not a negation of the social significance of *space*, but only of one particular, restricted historical form of it. In Castell's analysis, space is 'crystallized time' or 'the material support of time sharing social practices'.[6] As time-sharing social practices increasingly come to be materially supported by communications technologies that do not require the sharing of the same physical location, so places increasingly become emptied out of social meaning, becoming 'non-places'.

The idea of non-place derives from the French historian of everyday life, Michel de Certeau.[7] However, it is its use by the French anthropologist Marc Augé, in his book, *Non-Places*[8] – which in certain respects inverts Certeau's usage – which is relevant here. Augé is concerned with redefining the object of anthropological study of 'the contemporary world'. He introduces the concept of non-place as the spatial dimension of a conception of 'supermodernity' as a culture of excess, characterized by an 'overabundance of events', in which the idea of individuated culture, 'localized in time and space', has become redundant. As the spatial consequence of 'changes of scale . . . the proliferation of imaged and imaginary references, and . . . the spectacular acceleration of means of transport', Augé's idea of non-place embraces:

> The installations needed for the accelerated circulation of passengers and goods (high-speed roads and railways, interchanges, airports) . . . just as much . . . as the means of transport themselves . . . transit points and temporary abodes . . . under luxurious or inhuman conditions (hotel chains and squats, holiday clubs and refugee camps, shanty towns threatened with demolition or doomed to festering longevity) . . . the great commercial centres . . . where the habitué of supermarkets, slot machines and credit cards communicates wordlessly, through gestures, with an abstract, unmediated commerce . . . and finally the complex skein of cable and wireless networks that mobilize extraterrestrial space for the purposes of a communication so peculiar that it often puts the individual in contact only with another image of himself.[9]

As its syntax indicates, non-place is conceived negatively, as 'a space which cannot be defined as relational, or historical, or concerned with identity.' As such, it is characterized by abstraction, yet it remains experientially concrete. We could think of it as an updated spatialization of the early Lukács's romantic sense of modernity as 'transcendental homelessness'.[10] Its passing inhabitants orientate themselves within it primarily through relations with *signs*. This 'invasion of space by text', mainly taking the form of signs conveying 'instructions for use', is understood to produce a 'solitary contractuality' as its distinctive mode of social existence. Such instructions – 'Take right-hand lane' or 'You are now entering the Beaujolais region', are two of Augé's examples – may be prescriptive, prohibitive or informative. They may be in ordinary language (what the philosophers call 'natural', as opposed to 'ideal', languages), or, increasingly, in codified ideograms. And they invariably convey the messages not of individuals but of institutional authorities of various sorts, whether explicitly stated or only vaguely discernible.[11]

Augé's non-places are the dialectical residue of the dual negation of place by itinerary and textuality. This is a productive notion, with, as we shall see, interesting resonances with twentieth-century art history. However, Augé's presentation of the concept is both theoretically ambiguous and critically ambivalent. Theoretically, it equivocates between an abstract and a dialectical conception of negation. Critically, it oscillates between a backward-looking romanticization of an anthropological conception of place and a forward-looking 'supermodern' ethnology of solitude. This is the result in part of the restrictions of an anthropological perspective, and in part, of a conflation of the spatialities of travel and new communications technologies, respectively.

'The non-place', Augé writes,

> ... never exists in a pure form: places reconstitute themselves in it; relations are restored and resumed in it ... Place and non-place are rather like opposed polarities: the first is never completely erased, the second never totally completed; they are palimpsests on which the scrambled game of identity and relations is ceaselessly rewritten.[12]

Yet if non-place never exists in a pure form, as an absolute negation or annihilation of place, this is surely not a contingency, but because it can only coherently be construed as itself, intrinsically, a special, paradoxical type of 'place'. A non-place is constituted as a type of place by its *immanent* negation of the anthropological sense of place as a space that generates identity-forming meanings out of the permanence (that is, generational continuity) of the physical contiguity of its boundaries. (On Castells's definition, a place is 'a locale whose form, function and meaning are self-contained within the boundaries of physical contiguity.')[13]

That is, *all non-places are places, qua non-places*, not in addition or palimpsestically, since they derive their meaning, qua negations, internal to boundaries of physical contiguity. They register the manifestation of relations other than those of locale within a locale. This is what makes it possible for Augé to name and to list non-places. However, this dialectical interiority of non-place to place tempers the radicalism of the negation, and inhibits the theorization of the positive content of what is qualitatively new, in terms of the spatial logics of non-places. This is because, for Augé, despite the importance of signs – and their intimation of a *purely* communicationally defined space – it is 'traveller's space' that is the 'archetype' of non-place.[14]

The new forms of social relations determined by digital communications technologies exceed the anthropological conception of place not only at the level of identity-forming meanings, but in a more strictly spatial respect: in their negation of the dependence of spatial relations on physical contiguity. If one thinks about non-places in the context of the final item on Augé's list – 'the complex skein of cable and wireless networks that mobilize extraterrestrial space for the purposes of communication' – they appear not as 'empty' or 'solitary' places, but as new spatializations of place constituted qua places through their relations to another spatiality, the 'space of flows'. On Castells's conception, this is a new spatial logic grounded in 'the transformation of location patterns of core economic activities under the new technological system . . . the rise of the electronic home and the . . . evolution of urban forms'. It governs 'flows of capital, flows of information, flows of technology, flows of organizational interaction, flows of images, sounds and symbols.'[15] It would seem that certain non-places are best conceived, not as a simple negation of the meaningfulness of place, but as the product of a dialectic of the space of places (in general, including non-places) and the space of flows, which is equally as constitutive of flows as it is of the (non-)places through which they flow. As Sassen has emphasized, digital networks are heavily dependent on the 'embeddedness' of material infrastructures at nodal points throughout the network. This points to the mediating role of informational/global cities as 'spaces of contemporaneity' in the literal sense of being places where different times come together, nodal points of connection between multiple temporalities. In this respect, the dialectic of places and flows is the spatial register of our now-global contemporaneity.

The institutional spaces of art partake of the post-metropolitan character of these non-places through the network structure of what is increasingly a globally transnational artworld. This is a historical development of the deep-rooted immanence of metropolitan spatial experience to modern art, both in its formal structure and conditions of reception. As Brian O'Doherty has put it: 'The city provided the materials, models of process, and primitive esthetic of juxtaposition – congruity forced by mixed needs and intentions. On this account, the city is the indispensible context of collage and of the gallery space. Modern art needs the sound of traffic outside to authenticate it.'[16] The mythos of the city is the organizing principle of collage; and collage is at the core of a generic (non-medium-based) modernism. The gallery itself, however, in its classical modern form as the 'white cube', is a self-enclosed, self-insulating space. And it is in its specific character as a self-enclosed, specialized place that the gallery appears as an exemplary non-place, in Augé's sense. It is constituted by a dual negation of place-based social functions by itineracy and textuality: the itinerary of the viewer, passing through, the neutrality of the space, and the textuality of the work. The work is 'textual' here both in the general sense in which modern art is necessarily constituted, in part, by the discourses that surround its works (and never more so than when its claims are purely optical), and in the particular sense of the eruption of text within the visual arts themselves, first in 1912 through the 'polyphonic space' of the collage (with newspaper and tickets, in particular) and later in the language-based Conceptual art of the 1960s.[17]

There is an 'invasion of space by text' here, within art itself, that parallels quite precisely the invasion of space by text that Augé takes to be constitutive of non-places. It can hardly be coincidental in this regard that what I have previously (and separately) argued was the first-ever exhibition of conceptual art, was Yoko Ono's *Instructions for Paintings* exhibition in the lobby of the Sogetsu Art Center in Tokyo, in May–June 1962,[18] which precisely mimics the 'instructions for use' of the signs characteristic of non-places. This exhibition was the culmination of a whole series of pre-Fluxus works by La Monte Young, George Brecht, Ono and others, taking the form of instructions for use. The genre developed in a post-Cagean musical context, where it appears as the 'event score' or 'word piece'.[19] Ono's originality lies in her transposition of it into the context of visual art. Such language-based works extract the urban texuality of signage and re-present it, reflectively, in art spaces as a new art form. This is an artistic appropriation of an anonymous form of social communication that is tied to a specific kind of urban space, and which produces a distinctive kind of spatiality for the artwork. This is a different but closely related form of spatiality from other, more canonically 'Conceptual' language-based works, such as Dan Graham, Robert Smithson and Mel Bochner's magazine works (1966–70), Joseph Kosuth's Pop typography (*Titled (Art as Idea as Idea)*, 1967–8), and Art & Language's aesthetic of administration (*Index 001*, 1972).[20] Each of these textualizations of art articulates a different spatial dimension of the textuality of the metropolis. Only the magazine works, however, in their 'embedded' context within magazines *in circulation* (rather than retrospectively displayed) displace modern art space itself from its primal gallery location back into social space.

However, it would be naïve to believe that this transgression of literal or empirical gallery space constitutes a violation of the ontological character of art-space instituted by the gallery in its classical modern form. As O'Doherty argued, 'the empty gallery ... [is] modernism's greatest invention' because the white cube is 'the single major convention through which art is passed.' However, it is precisely that: a convention that constitutes a particular mode of attention. The 'undifferentiated potency' of its space is the 'sophisticated convention' of a culture 'which has cancelled its values in the name of an abstraction called "freedom".' As a result, space is now 'not just where things happen; things make space happen.'[21] The space that art-things make happen is the art-space that renders them intelligible as art, *wherever it is*. As such, it makes them recognizable as art, and open to institutional validation. There is a set of reciprocal relationships here between the object/act, the space it creates, and the institutional validation associated with that space's recoding in terms of an ontological structure derived from modern art's primal gallery space (what Smithson called the non-site). In this sense, once modern art-space is historically established in its basic structure through what O'Doherty aptly called 'the placelessness and timelessness' of the gallery's 'hysterical cell',[22] art can transform all kinds of place into art-space (that is, art non-place), by bringing it into relation with gallery conventions – in the way in which, for Smithson, 'site' is a dialectical *product* of the non-site. The white cube is thus not only 'a unit of esthetic discourse';[23] it establishes the ontological structure of art-space, which must subsequently be *reinstituted* by each work, in each instance, *wherever* it is located. This is one of the things that is meant by the 'autonomy' of the work of art. Contemporary art produces (or fails to produce) the non-place of art-space as the condition of its autonomy and hence its ability to function as 'art'. Art cannot live, *qua* art, within the everyday *as* the everyday. Rather it necessarily disrupts the everydayness of the everyday from within, since it is, constitutively, both 'autonomous' and a 'social fact'.[24] It is the ongoing search for productive forms of this duality that has driven art beyond the confines of the literal physical space (the place) of the gallery into other social spaces. Textualization was the first significant mediating practice through which this transformation in the spatial ontology of the work of art occurred. What has become known as the 'architecturalization of art' was an accompanying process; it contains the conditions for an extended textualization of art within itself.

Architecturalization: three questions

If 'sculpture' is an ontologically redundant category in contemporary art (despite its perennial curatorial revival as a way of presenting the very works that rendered it redundant), 'architecture' is a term without which contemporary art would be hard-pressed to continue to exist. If, as Duve has argued, in the nineteenth century, 'painting' was the name for art (and thereby the most ontologically privileged of medium-specific categories), in the 1960s something like 'architecture' became, if not the new name for art, then certainly, for many, its model. Similarly, just as it was by appropriating (and notionally reapplying) the name 'painting' to readymades that Duchamp invented a generic art, so it has been by appropriating (and notionally reapplying) the name 'architecture' to various art activities that art since the 1960s has transformed its spatial ontology. These practices have strong conceptual components. Like textualization, architecture was thus a mediating practice that combined an expansion and transformation of art's spatial ontology, with a conceptual turn. Architecture has been a primary bearer of the conceptuality of contemporary art. In this regard, architecturalization appears as one of an accumulative series of art-historical revisions of the art of the 1960s, the most important of which have been those stressing the roles of *performance*, *conceptual photography*, and the *internationalism* of the US-centred artistic community of the 1960s and early 1970s.[25] Each is bound up with the conceptual character of contemporary art. There is a complex multiplicity of interacting lineages of negation at work here in the art of the 1960s that converge into the problematic of postconceptual art, of which these successive historiographical revisionisms represent the four currently most significant aspects.

The relationship of contemporary art to architecture gives rise to three specific questions: What is the function of 'architecture' in the *discourses and practices* of contemporary art? What is the place of architecturalization in the *history of art* since the early 1960s? What does the prism of 'architecture' contribute to the *criticism* of contemporary art?

First and foremost, for Western art since the Second World War – locked in the prison of a restricted understanding of its autonomy – architecture has functioned as a *signifier of the social*, of the functionality or practicality of form: economically, technologically and politically. In this respect, architecture – like design more generally – is an *archive of the social use of form*. As such it functions as a gateway to, and metonym for, the urban in its fullest sense, which is to say, for modernity. In particular, as a signifier of the social, via the urban, architecture offers a 'privileged access' to the contemporary via the technologies of social production. The architectural aspect of contemporary art is thus that of a socio-spatial *effectivity*. It represents art's social being-in-the-world, its aspiration to effect change. Architecture is an emblem of the aspiration to what Jeff Wall has called a 'modernism with social content'.[26] For art, one might even say, architecture in general holds open the original hope of Soviet Constructivism: namely, 'to realize the communist expression of material structures'.[27] In this respect, architectural aspects of contemporary art problematize artistic autonomy in so far as, on Adorno's account at least, powerlessness is the price of autonomy. They raise the possibility of 'post-autonomous' works, or at the least, a post-autonomous functioning of autonomous works: works that would partake in the dialectic of autonomy – that is, is the dialectic of art and anti-art within the work – in such a way as to mediate it reflectively with the contradictory social functions of art space, to determinate practical as well as artistic effect. The difficulty, of course, is to produce such works that are *critical* rather than merely affirmative of the social practices with which contemporary art is increasingly associated: urban and regional development, and tourism and cultural policy more generally.

From the point of view of our concerns here, it is the spatial aspect of this socialization that is most important. In particular, 'architecture' should no longer be understood to refer to one or the other side of the opposition between design/plan and building. It cannot be identified exclusively with the space/place of either the design/plan or the building. Rather its deepening historical ambiguity is crucial. The term 'architecture' is distributed *across* conception and materialization, in the traditional senses. This is a particularly prominent aspect of early, proto-conceptual works by Sol LeWitt and Mel Bochner, for example, which exhibited plans and diagrams as 'sketches' – intermediate forms. More generally, architecture stands for a *material organization of social space in the present* at both conceptual and practical levels. Postminimalist contemporary art (from 'object' to 'field') aspires to a *free formation of social space* in this dual imaginary and actual sense. We can see the consequences of this ambiguous architectural spatial form for the ontology of the artwork when we look at the place of architecturalization in the history of contemporary art.

Recent historiography of the art of the 1960s and 1970s has registered the growing importance of the works of Dan Graham, Robert Smithson and Gordon Matta-Clark in the genealogy of current practices. Indeed, their works are frequently cited within current practices themselves, albeit more often for reasons of legitimation than as material for a historically reflective art.[28] Yet the critical meaning of this new pre-eminence is rarely explored. It is to be found, I think, in the way in which their respective experimental relations to architecture led to a fluid *multiplicity of forms of materializations* of works that produces a form of artistic spatiality beyond, yet nonetheless still tied to, 'objects': a spatiality defined by relations between practices, materials and forms – an 'ideal' space in relation to which the multiplication of materializations of an individual art-idea is in principle unlimited. (This is the fourth feature of postconceptual art, listed in Chapter 2, above – the expansion to infinity of the possible material forms of art, consequent upon the destruction of medium as a category of artistic ontology – condensed here into the individual work itself.) It is the self-consciousness of art's conceptual character, at play in the appropriative relation to 'architecture', that grounds this multiplication of materializations, and thereby, the transformation in the spatial ontology of the work of art that it involves. This multiplication profoundly problematizes precisely 'where' any particular work of art of this kind should be considered to be 'located'; in the same way that photographic technology problematizes the spatial site of the photograph, as we saw in the previous chapter.

For example, if we ask 'Where is Dan Grahams's *Homes for America*?' we can find it, currently, distributed across at least four sites or forms, with numerous, often disjunctive, individual material instantiations: 1. as a slide show, first shown at the Finch College 'Projected Art exhibition' (November 1966), and increasingly again, in various venues, from the late 1990s; 2. as Dan Graham's original paste-up for *Arts Magazine*; 3. as actually published in *Arts Magazine*, with the photographs by Walker Evans; and 4. as a revised paste-up produced for exhibition after 1970. The work itself is distributed *across* these four material forms, as constituted by various exhibition practices and histories of reproduction. (This is the fifth feature of postconceptual art, listed in chapter 2: the distributive character of its unity.) Ironically, given that it was a 'magazine work', but unsurprisingly given the commercial logic of the art market, the art institution has privileged its two most 'individual' forms; the original paste-up for *Arts Magazine* and the revised paste-up produced for exhibition – downgrading the actualization of the 'original' conception (the magazine version) to a reproduction.

If we ask the same question of Robert Smithson's *Floating Island* (discussed in Chapter 4, above), a sketch from 1970 (Fig. 11), we are confronted with the fact that its idea was first 'realized' only thirty-five years later in September 2005, many years after Smithson's death, on the occasion of his retrospective in New York (Fig. 12). The openness of time infinitizes the work's inherently plural spatial possibilities. The borders of the work are historically malleable. (This is the sixth feature of postconceptual art.) This raises the question of how the work's conceptuality unifies it, in relation to both its necessarily limiting *actual* spatializations, and the nonetheless *unlimited* spatial possibilities of *future* realizations. In short, where are the borders of the work?

In conceptualizing this phenomenon, there is a spatial deficit in the established critical discourses of conceptual art as a result of its polemical absolutization of anti-aestheticism. In this respect, architecturalization, or the use of 'architecture' as a model for the work of art, is the antidote to the *spatial deficit* of the self-understanding of Conceptual art (as a movement), which was at the same time a socio-political deficit. (This is Jeff Wall's main claim for the importance of Graham's work: that in relation to other conceptual work, it renders visible the 'defeatism' implicit in this deficit.) On the other hand, there is a conceptual deficit in all conceptions of contemporary art that fails to reflect on its specifically conceptual character. Ironically, it is an undialectical conception of 'site' (the failure to recognize the constitutive role of non-sites in all sites) that is perhaps the greatest culprit here, in producing a simplistic and moralistic conception of 'site-specificity'.[29] It is accompanied in much current art discourse by its temporal twin, a misunderstanding of historical experience embodied in the moralism of so-called memory-work (discussed in the next chapter). 'Art as place' and 'art as memory' are the two main forms of de-conceptualization in contemporary art criticism and practice.

The question of the 'borders' of the work is the question of its unity. So what limits the multiplication of material elements of the work? Nothing immanently material, I would say, but only the character of their representation at a non-site. Increasingly, this representation is primarily photographic. 'Architecturalization' and the mediation of photographic documentation are processes that run in tandem in the constitution of the postconceptual character of contemporary art. In mediating the plan and its actualization, architecture itself draws attention to this unifying role of photography as document, construction, and everyday cultural form – not least, because of the importance of transience (demolition).[30] It is with respect to its role in unifying a diversity of materializations that the documentary function of photography models the ontology of the postconceptual work. Wall has made the case here with respect to photojournalism, in the context of painting in his essay on On Kawara.[31] A similar case can, I think, be made with respect to architectural photography, in the context of the transformation of 'sculpture' into the generic constructions of contemporary 'installations'. We can take as an example here the difference in principle between two bodies of work that have frequently been critically received in similar terms, as interrogations of spaces defined by their 'betweeness': those by Gordon Matta-Clark and Rachel Whiteread. This superficial phenomenological similarity is cut by the difference between the radically *transcategorial*, postconceptual work of Matta-Clark and the restored medium-specificity and essential conservatism of Whiteread's revival of modernist sculpture.[32]

The transcategorial character of Matta-Clark's work is manifest in its articulation of the relations between multiple elements of his practice: performance, documentation and construction. Think, for example, of the relationship between the architectural photograph known as *NYU Checkerboard* (1974) and the subsequent performance/event documented as *Window Blow-Out* (1976); or the way in which his most famous work, *Splitting* (1974), generates multiple materializations as an actualization of an imaginary photomontage (Fig. 13), documentary photography (Fig. 14), and a basis for a form of documentary photomontage (Fig. 15), which soon morphs back into artistic photomontage (Fig. 16). Similarly, *Bingo* (1974) combines building cuts (performance/event), documentary photos, documentary (Super 8) film, and photoworks, in a way that was surely generative for Graham's important work, *Alteration to a Suburban House* (1978) – although the mutual influence of Michael Graves's cutaway Princeton house should also be acknowledged there. The critical point is that it is the *plurality of spatializations* that preserves the conceptuality of the postconceptual work by breaking the identification of the work with any particular material instantiation.

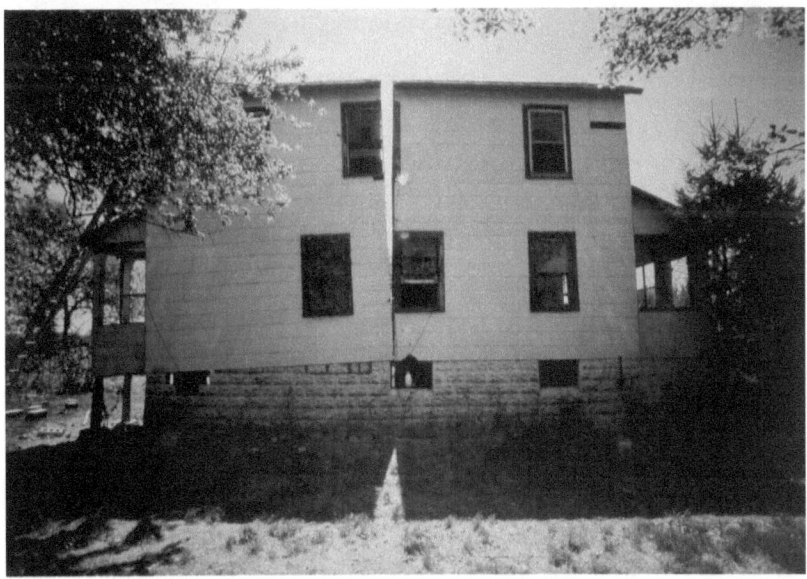

Fig. 13: Gordon Matta-Clark, *Splitting*

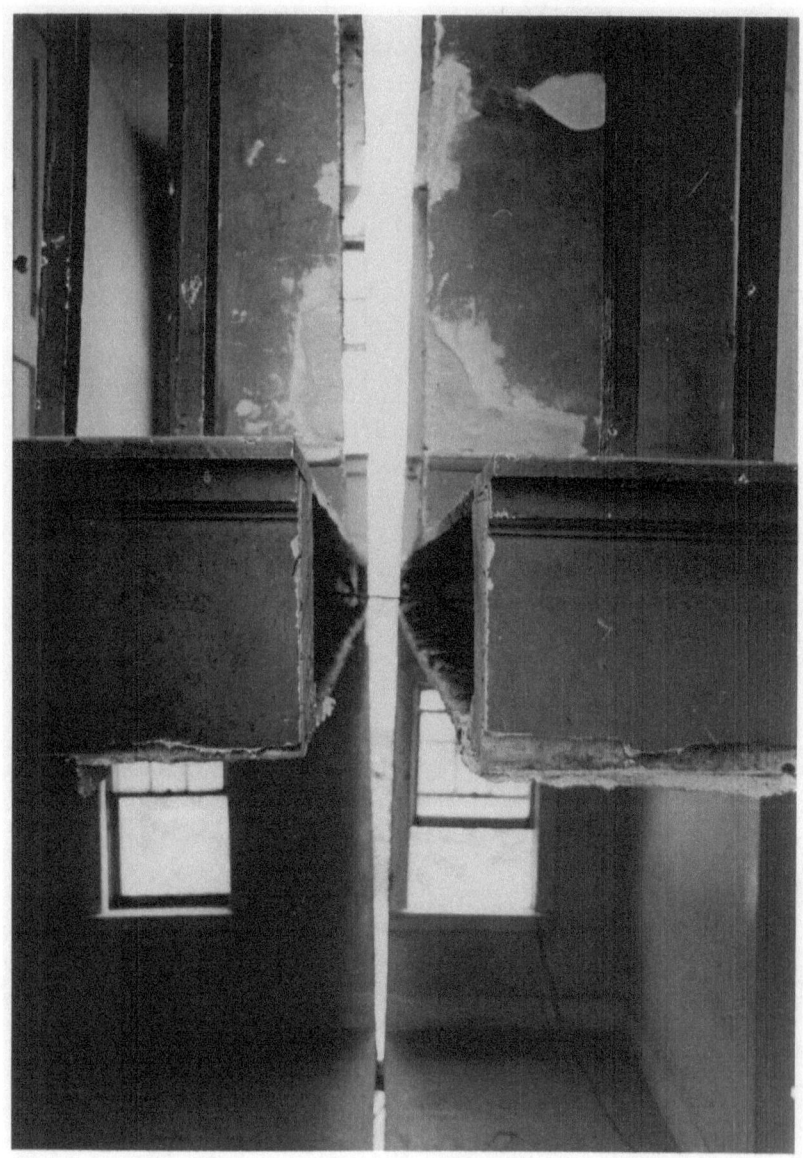

Fig. 14: Gordon Matta-Clark, *Splitting* 6

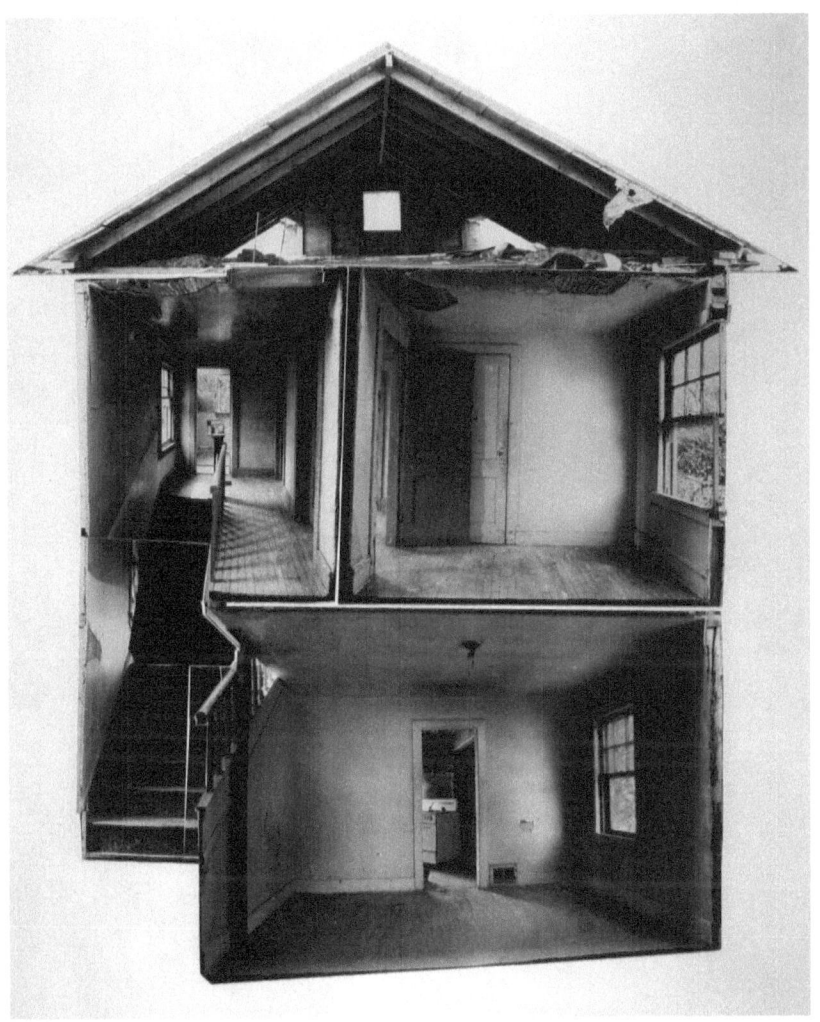

Fig. 15: Gordon Matta-Clark, *Splitting* 32

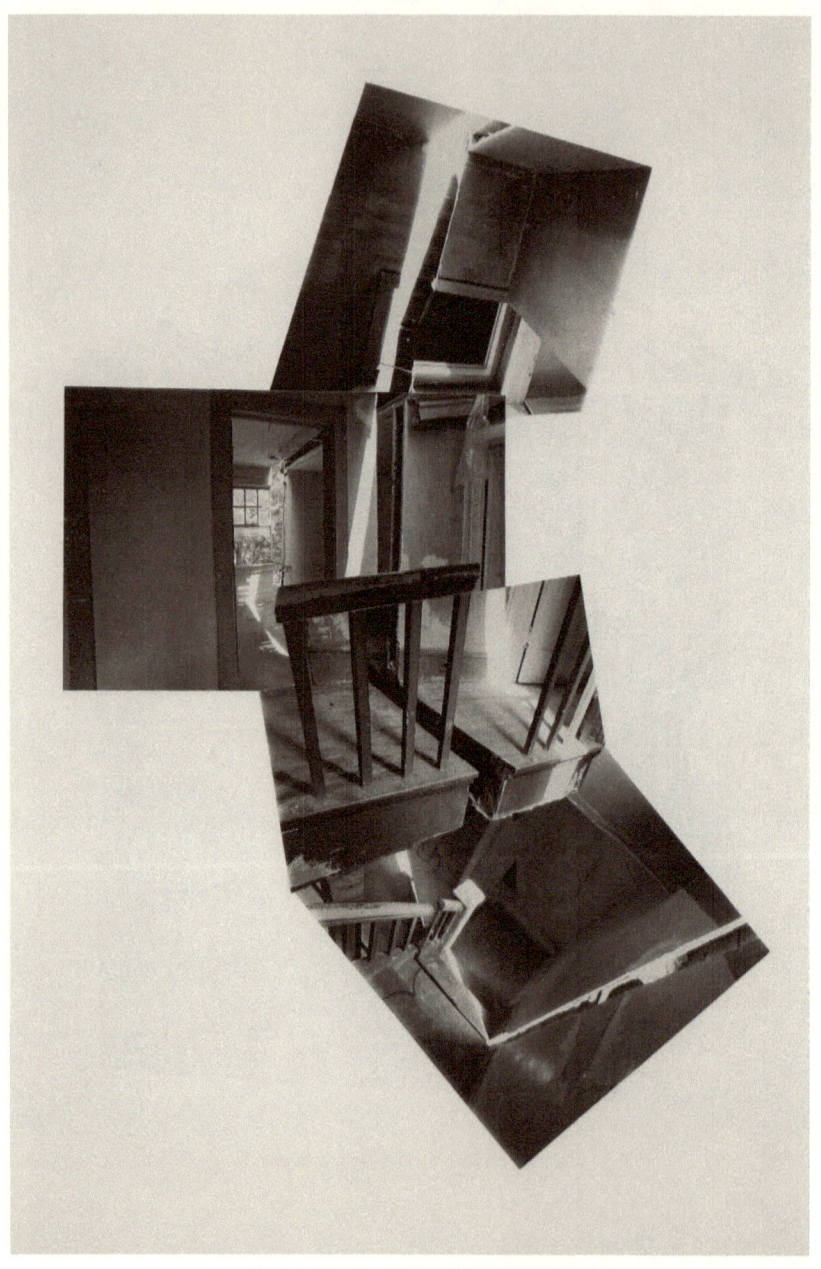

Fig. 16: Gordon Matta-Clark, *Splitting*

Compare these practices of Matta-Clark's with the traditionalism of Whiteread's 'architectural' sculptures. Architecture is rendered immediately sculptural in a peaceful coexistence of received forms, rather than working critically on conventional forms to generate wider possibilities for practice. From the point of view of the art's postconceptual character, Whiteread's most important work, *House* (1993), was only saved as contemporary art by the combination of its function as a relay for public debate, and its ultimate destruction. Demolition appears here as a condition of its critical art status.

With regard to contribution of 'architecture' to the criticism of contemporary art, we may thus say that it lies in its clarification of the spatial dimension of the ontology of postconceptual work and its reorientation of the narrative of critical paradigms away from the modernism/postmodernism dyad to the three-stage movement from (medium-specific) modernism via (architecturally mediated) conceptual and postminimal art to a (generic) postconceptual art. Furthermore, it problematizes the relationship of contemporary art's conceptuality not only to its own aesthetic dimension but also to other social practices. Attention to the architectural mediations of the field of contemporary art teaches us that the network of relations between materializations (and the ultimate indifference in the ontological significance of different types of materialization – 'plan'/'object') *constructs* the 'space' of each work. Hence, we may extend our account of the work's construction of its own art-space, above, with the maxim: *To each work its own spatiality – singular in its temporal instantiations and relations, but social and conceptual in its elements and structures of relations.*

The kind of art space produced by the distributed totality of such works is not that of a simple non-place like any other (although non-place is its condition), but something more akin to what Deleuze called 'any-space-whatever' (*un espace quelconque*).

> Any-space-whatever is not an abstract universal, in all times, in all places. It is a perfectly singular space, which has merely lost its homogeneity, that is, the principle of its metric relations or the connection of its parts, so that the linkages can be made in an infinite number of ways. It is a space of virtual conjunction, grasped as pure locus of the possible. What in fact manifests the instability, the heterogeneity, the absence of link of such space, is a richness in potentials or singularities, which are, as it were, prior conditions of all actualizations, all determinations.[33]

In Deleuze, 'any-space-whatever' is derived as a type of cinematic space: specifically, the space associated with one type of affection-image (which is itself one of three kinds of movement-image). It is 'the genetic element of the affection-image' and itself has two states, 'always implied in each other': 'disconnection and emptiness'. However, Deleuze identifies its 'proliferation' not only with a certain cinematic practices, but also:

> independent of the cinema . . . the postwar situation with its towns demolished or being reconstructed, its waste grounds, its shanty towns, and even in places where the war had not penetrated, its undifferentiated urban tissue, its vast unused places, docks, warehouses, heaps of girders and scrap iron.[34]

These are the historical conditions of Italian neo-realism and the French New Wave as cinemas of the urban everyday, associated in Deleuze's narrative with the crisis of the action-image and the transition from the movement-image to the time-image.[35]

From the standpoint of our interests here, it is less the specifically cinematic articulations of this kind of space that are important (although they are relevant, as we shall see in the next chapter: art time is not unlike the time of the time-image) than the relations between its historical conditions and its philosophical structure: the fact that it is 'a question of undoing space, as well as the story, the plot or the action', as a function of 'an event which exceeds its actualization in all ways.'[36] Any-space-whatever is the *space of presentation* of what Deleuze calls 'a power-quality' or 'potentiality'. Neither concept nor intuition, such a potentiality is 'a set of singularities' which present 'pure powers' or qualities in such a way as to 'combine without abstraction' all possible actualizations of them, without actualizing them.[37] This is a semiotic quality of a particular kind of image (Deleuze's examples are *rain* and the *bridge of Rotterdam* in some of Jorge Iven's films) which carries any-space-whatever with it, as its constructed condition.

We can see in the spatiality of the postconceptual work a similar combination of aesthetic, logical and virtual aspects (albeit one less concerned to disavow the abstraction inherent in this combination) produced by the peculiar nominalism of contemporary art, its radical individualism, to which reference was made in Chapter 3. If Hegelian dialectics was a 'mediation of nominalism and realism' (Adorno),[38] what we have here is the distributive logical form of a new type of *post-Hegelian mediation of singularizations*, whereby the universals at stake are themselves constituted, deconstituted and reconstituted by the process of mediation. This is, in fact, in one respect, *more* singularizing than Deleuze's semiotic conception. For when Deleuze asks himself, 'what maintains an *ensemble* in this world without totality or linkage?', he replies: 'The answer is simple: what forms the *ensemble* are *clichés*, and nothing else. Nothing but *clichés, clichés* everywhere . . .'[39] This may be true of the cinematic language of time-images, in its autonomy and everydayness, but the artwork depends upon a more complex set of social structures (artworld) to maintain it, precisely, in its singularizations – not least, the institution of private property.

To each work its own spatiality – singular in its temporal instantiations and relations, but social and conceptual in its elements and structures of relations. This means that the only answer to the question, asked of a postconceptual work, 'Where is the work of art?' is *'Anywhere or not at all'*. It is in the spatial radicalism of this 'anywhere' that the general structure of postconceptual art provides the ontological condition for more recent, particular developments in the spatial ontology of works of art associated with urban project work and transnationalization.

Thus far, I have treated textualization and architecturalization as the main two practices mediating contemporary art with social space. Yet 'architecture' is a historically limited, and in many ways conservative coding of the social space of the built environment. In fact, in a historical narrative of the expansion of the spatial range and conception of twentieth-century Western art, it would seem to correspond to only the first two of four main phases:

1. the 'environmentalization' of painting and sculpture, from Matisse[40] to Kaprow, via muralism, up to the minimalists' investment of negative space – a movement still grounded in the interior;
2. the expanded significance of architecture for a generic concept of art via the constitutive ambiguity of the design/building (conceptualization/materialization) relation – the moment of Graham, Smithson and Matta-Clark, discussed above;
3. the post-architectural urbanism of various kinds of project work and the functional redefinition of site, based on an awareness of the constitutive role of non-sites (Mark Dion and Andrea Fraser might serve as examples);
4. the transnationalization of art via its production for, and inscription within, a transnational art-space that mediates the global dialectic of places, non-places and flows, via the institutional forms of the *market*, the *large-scale international exhibition* (biennale, triennale, etc.) and the *migrancy of artists*.

It is to the third and fourth of these stages – post-architectural urbanism and transnationalization – that I now turn.

Construction and expression

What does it mean for the art in an exhibition when that exhibition is conceived as an 'instrument of investigation' into its site and a means of cultural and economic 'reinvigoration' of the surrounding area? What does it mean, that is, for our understanding of it as art, rather than the occasion for the pursuit of a set of independently defined social goals? What does it mean not only that this *might* be so (that an exhibition might be so conceived), but that it *is* so, and moreover, as a matter of course? What does it tell us about contemporary art that such a contextualization is a normal part of art's cultural functioning and, furthermore, that it is a central part of art's *critical* functioning as art? What does it tell us about what art is; that is, about what art has become? And what does it tell us about what art is becoming?

One set of answers to these questions revolves around the concept of construction. With the renewed convergence of artistic and architectural practices since the 1960s, and the ongoing subjection of architecture to urbanism, 'construction' has re-emerged as the main term through which art approaches urbanism, via architecture. At the same time, philosophically, where once it was notions of design, foundation and, later, 'ground' (*Grund*) that bound philosophical thought metaphorically to architecture, now, in the wake of various critiques of philosophical 'foundationalism' (be they historicist, pragmatist, contextualist, or deconstructive in form), it is construction that most often plays that role. And construction, it is argued, is a process that is fraught with contingency, with the indeterminacies of dialogue, and the '*mystery* of applicability'.[41] This critique of the original architectural metaphor of philosophy broadly corresponds to changes within architecture itself.

If Western philosophy has been in one of its central impulses but 'another name' for the will to architecture, historically, this took the form of a will to the first principle, an intellectual absolutization or ideation of the *techné* (skill) of the *architectón* (the original or principle craftsman): design. But the techné of the architectón is no longer to be identified with design. Today, with the subjection of architecture to urbanism (planning), and of urbanism to the tripartite logic of capitalist economics (production, circulation, consumption), '[n]othing is less relevant to the reality of architecture than the idea that it is the realization of a design *qua* idea.'[42] Indeed, it never was, outside of an absolutist ideology of architecture, which derived its credibility from its inscription within a particular system of power. In the early twentieth century, for Le Corbusier, the architect became 'an organizer, not a designer of objects'; after the crisis of the modern movement (the crisis of the ideological function of architecture as utopian planning), the architect has become a technician and organizer of building production.⁴³ Thus it is construction in its most general sense that 'architecture' has become.

Out of a growing interplay between the theoretical discourses of philosophy, architecture, art and urbanism, the idea emerges of a 'new constructivism'. In the 1950s it was asked, 'What is existentialism?'; in the 1960s and early 70s, 'What is structuralism?'; in the late 1970s and 80s, 'What is poststructuralism?', 'What is deconstruction?' or 'What is postmodernism?' Now, increasingly, we ask, 'What is constructivism today?'⁴⁴ To answer this question, it is necessary, first, to return briefly to an earlier phase of constructivism: the Russian Constructivism of the 1920s. For it is there that we find the dialectic of constructivism outlined in its elemental form. And just as Russian Constructivism was split at the outset, between a radically political, Soviet social variant and an interpretation that returned it to its art-historical condition (formalism) – with which it remained identified in the West until well into the 1970s⁴⁵ – so the idea of a new constructivism comes in differing theoretical and ideological variants today. In particular, on the one hand, there is a *philosophical* constructivism and libertarian architectonics that follows the thought of Gilles Deleuze, which would place philosophy, art, architecture and urbanism on a single 'plane of immanence', breaking with socio-historical analysis to affirm simultaneously a new philosophy, a new architecture and a new conception of the work of art, at the level of thought alone.⁴⁶ On the other hand, there is that dense network of historical and conceptual ties that links a certain postconceptual *art criticism, practice and exhibition* to the Constructivism of the 1920s, while at the same time registering a definitive distance from it. The former re-enacts the ideology of the avant-garde at its most abstract, as the permanent invention of beginnings, in the 'positive', non-dialectical form of 'an experimental art of singularizing space' – a singularization which, as such, that is, without concept, can ultimately be no more than *aesthetic*.⁴⁷ The latter works through the historical contradictions of Constructivism under the changed conditions of the present. What follows sketches the conceptual shape of this latter working-through as the tentative emergence of a 'post-autonomous' art. This is an art that, if it is to be more than ironic, increasingly depends upon the constructivism of its exhibition context.

The principle of construction refers to the building up of an object through a combination of independently pre-existent parts. Long familiar in architecture, mathematics and philosophy,⁴⁸ it was first applied to artistic production in the early years of the second decade of the twentieth century, in the cubist pictorial compositions, collages, *papiers collés* and reliefs of Georges Braque and Pablo Picasso. However, it only became explicit as a general principle of artistic production – independent of a critical dialogue with traditional forms – on the basis of

Vladimir Tatlin's self-consciously abstract counter-reliefs of 1914–15, which inspired the explicitly designated spatial 'constructions' of Ivan Klyun and Lev Bruni of 1916–17, and laid the formal basis for the constructivism to come. As a formal principle, construction is independent of any particular materials. It is central to a non-visual art such as music, for example. Nonetheless, a certain *kind* of materials is required, since construction presupposes the independent 'givenness' of the elements of the constructive process as self-sufficient objects or units. This type of materials is intrinsic to the technologies and division of labour of machinofacture. This connection is central to the social meaning of construction, which derives from both the formal principle and the historical condition of the constructed materials.

It is for this reason, for example, that it is important to distinguish the 1915–19 'constructions' of the Russian artist Naum Gabo (whose formalist works were long synonymous with constructivism in the West) from even the early work of Tatlin. As one commentator has put it:

> Whereas Tatlin's starting point was an interest in the qualities of the materials and their juxtaposition and interaction in space, Gabo's was a precise analysis of the structure of form and its internal spatial implications. He began with the idea or image which he then executed in a formal material. There was no exploitation of the *objet trouvé* or any chance combinations of materials.[49]

It is this relative indifference to materials that is the basis of the social and political indifference of Gabo's formalist version of constructivism, set out in *The Realistic Manifesto* (1920). It contrasts sharply with the social utilitarianism and polemically anti-art stance of the First Working Group of Constructivists, founded the same year, with which the term is more properly, and richly, associated. For construction is a rational-instrumental process with historically specific social, material and technological conditions. The 'factual rationalization of artistic labour' that it meant for the First Working Group also meant (reflecting on these conditions) integrating artistic labour into the total social labour out of which its principle arose (machine labour), as part of a collective practice of 'social construction'.[50] This is the central, guiding concept of Constructivism: social construction, the realization of 'the communist expression of material structures.'[51] And the materials of those structures were, principally, those of the industrial technologies of the day. Hence the emblematic significance of an early, pre-Constructivist work of Tatlin's such as *Selection of Materials: Iron, Stucco, Glass, Asphalt* (1914), which, while 'non-utilitarian', nonetheless still has more affinities with the laboratory work of Constructivism proper (formal experimentation within the horizon of social use) than with Gabo's self-sufficient interest in pure spatio-temporal forms.

In its broadest historical meaning, construction is a manifestation of that wider process of societal rationalization theorized by Max Weber as means-end or instrumental rationality (*Zweckrationalität*), which was generalized by the Frankfurt School into the dominant principle of modern societies. In fact, Weber himself applied this theoretical framework to the analysis of musical developments as early as 1911 in *The Rational and Social Foundations of Music* (although it was not published until 1921). In this respect, construction embodies a historical structure of social experience that is a condition of significance in modern art in general. However, there are complexities involved in its artistic use that make it a profoundly dialectical affair. These have to do, first, with the contradictory political dynamics and implications of formalism; and second, with the relationship of construction to expression, which lies at the heart of the question of materials, in both formalist ('non-utilitarian') and social utilitarian applications of the principle.

Formal construction was a historical and conceptual condition of social-utilitarian or revolutionary Constructivism. For formalism destroyed the conventional symbolic attributes of traditional artistic media, as a condition for its rearticulation of their material elements on the basis of a complete freedom of relations (aestheticism). This opened up the contrary possibility of a utilitarian deployment of forms (rationalization). Indifference to the traditional uses and significations of materials was thus the condition of *both* formalist-aestheticism *and* anti-aesthetic instrumentalization: the two opposing currents within constructivism itself.[52] This was a politically contradictory process in two ways. First, formalist construction became a metonym for the freedom of experimentation associated with social revolution; but it was 'anti-revolutionary' in its social confinement of such experimentation to the domain of 'art', cut off from the everyday life and needs of the people. Second, the principle of rationalization is itself inherently politically contradictory. In the revolutionary moment of an anti-traditionalist collectivism, it could appear unambiguously progressive – as it did to the First Working Group – as agreement about social ends overshadowed disputes over means. But in the more clearly transitional period of the New Economic Policy and after, its instrumentality could equally denote alienation: alienation from the social process of determining means. 'Revolutionary' constructivism could then appear as a form of unfreedom in comparison with the aesthetically unlimited (albeit socially confined) scope of formalism. This is the Cold War reading of Soviet Constructivism. And, indeed, the experimental character of Constructivism was inevitably compromised by the practicalities of social production, as the distinction between Constructivism and Productivism (constructive artistic labour and production-art) dissolved as the 1920s progressed. The consolidation of new social forms became a constraint upon forms of construction, and experimentation retreated, back to the non-utilitarian domain. This is the familiar dialectic of the historical and the neo-avant-gardes: 'art into life' versus the autonomy of the artwork.[53]

The first contradiction above (between the revolutionary and anti-revolutionary aspects of formalism) was temporarily mediated by the idea of 'laboratory works' – formal exercises undertaken not for their own sake but as research for future instrumental uses. But the second contradiction, internal to the social process of rationalization under conditions of scarcity, was intractable. It led, inevitably, to the restoration of an independent artistic domain. The politics of that domain were, however, henceforth put on a new footing. For it became a political requirement of the good faith of the artwork that it in some way confront the bad faith of its own autonomy (its withdrawal from the social domain), reflectively, within its own structure. Indeed, subsequently, elsewhere, under the conditions of the capitalist cultural industry, this would become a condition of autonomy itself. Hence the centrality of the dialectic of art and anti-art, internal to the modernist work, to its status as art – the critically constitutive role of anti-art within contemporary art. Art had to become 'critical' once it had failed to become universally actual, if it was to continue to be associated with both the freedom and the social possibilities for critically significant expression that it had acquired in the formalist/aestheticist critique of tradition. From that point on, critical artistic meaning became inextricably but problematically tied to the question of the relationship of the individual artwork to the rationality (and irrationality) of social forms. This problematic relationship is manifest internally, within the work, in the dialectic of construction and expression. It appears externally, at the level of cultural form, in the contradictory character of the social space of art.

For all its interest in materials, motivated by their technological potential and everyday uses (including pleasure in technological forms), the utopian presuppositions of revolutionary Constructivism inhibited it from seeing in materials the site of a possible contradiction between construction and expression. For Constructivism, revolutionary-utilitarian construction was *immediately* communist expression. There was an identity of economic function and political meaning. As economic function and political meaning diverge, however, and economic function becomes the site of social conflict, construction enters into opposition to expression. This opposition appears within the (non-utilitarian) artwork in the fact that the very principle of construction seems to negate the materials' immanent capacity for expression. As Adorno put it:

> What distinguishes construction from composition in the encompassing sense of pictorial composition, is the ruthless subordination not only of everything that originated from outside the artwork, but also of all partial elements immanent to the work. To this extent construction is the extension of subjective domination . . . [It] tears the elements of reality out of their primary context and transforms them to the point where they are once again capable of forming a unity, one that is no less imposed on them internally than was the heteronomous unity to which they were subjected externally . . . if the synthesis of construction is to succeed, it must in spite of all aversion be read out of the elements themselves, and they never wholly accede in themselves to what is imposed on them . . . This is the utopia of construction; its fallibility, on the other hand, is that it necessarily has a penchant to destroy what it integrates and to arrest the process in which it has its life.[54]

This contradiction is not contingent but structural. It arises out of the contradictory character – the irrational rationality – of instrumental reason itself. For the concept of rationalization to which Constructivism was, at least initially, bound (prior to Tatlin's late 'organic' constructivism) was that of the domination of nature. It had no consciousness of the dialectic of Enlightenment rationality. This dialectic determines the primary meaning of expression as expression not of communism, but of *suffering* (an increasingly important theme in Adorno's later work).[55]

The subjugation of the elements of the work to the constructive principle expresses the suffering of an inner nature subjected to the domination of the concept, for which the rational side of the subject is itself the agent. Construction is not simply logical in form, but as such, a *mimesis* (imitation) of rationality. Constructivism is a negative expressionism. It is thus *through*, rather than as a 'corrective' to construction that expression occurs – 'construction gains expression through coldness'[56] – but only negatively and individualistically. On the other hand, to the extent to which construction in art is successful (that is, imposes its principle of organization through, as well as against, its elements, in a reflective process of what Adorno calls 'determinate irreconcilibility'), it represents 'the effort to bear up under the suffering of alienation by exceeding it on the horizon of an undiminished and thus no longer violent rationality'. This is its continuing, if fragile, utopian function: its 'anticipation of a reconciled condition'.[57]

Ultimately though, the principle of construction, essential to the ability of modern art to express social form, seems fated to drive that art into an impasse not unlike that of Constructivism itself. Constructivism took for granted the rationality of construction. Adorno takes for granted the irrationality of this rationality. He thus attributes the compromising of the experimental dimension of constructivism (which was the effect of a socio-political restriction on utilitarian form) to the principle of construction itself: 'constructivism no longer grants any role to inspiration (*Einfall*), which is unplanned arbitrariness ... [This is] the fatality inherent to rationalization'.[58] It is the restoration of the recognition of 'unplanned arbitrariness' that is the goal of the new philosophical constructivism of Deleuze. Yet on Adorno's account, construction cannot eradicate the mimetic basis of the artwork (construction in art *imitates* the form of logicality). This regulates the application of the principle of construction in an undetermined, or at least, unconscious or 'free' way. This is precisely the advantage over utilitarian forms of artistic labour of non-utilitarian art's 'functionlessness'. Unplanned arbitrariness is in this respect ineradicable from the work of art. The threat is thus a threat to art itself. The problem becomes how to find new artistic materials and new forms of construction capable of expressing the latest forms of social (ir)rationality, autonomously, yet in a way which is nonetheless at the same time critical of the social limitations imposed by the current institutionalization of autonomy itself. The solution, more often than not, is via *the urban*. This is the critical problematic of that contemporary art – postconceptual art – which is grounded on a continued working through, transformation and development of the contradictions of constructivism; contradictions which are exemplary of those of the historical avant-garde more generally.

Art as displaced urbanism:
capitalist constructivism of the exhibition-form

One way of reading the critical trajectory of the European and North American art of the 1960s and 1970s is as a displaced repetition of a series of relationships between art forms and movements of the 1920s and 1930s. However, this has generally been understood in terms of the repetition of 'artistic paradigms' – grid formation, monochrome, ready-made, collage, assemblage, photomontage – rather than in terms of the contradictory conceptual structure of the artwork itself.[59] There has thus been a tendency in this work to identify a break with the dialectic of historical and neo-avant-gardes at precisely the point at which it reimposed itself most intensely, moving to a new stage of development, in the practice of an art of institutional critique.[60]

From the standpoint of the contradictory structure of the artwork, the movement from Minimalism, via Conceptual art, to Institutional Critique appears as a displaced repetition of the movement from formal construction, via Constructivism, to the functionalism of Productivism. Institutional critique appears as a political functionalism turned inward, against the social relations of autonomy that are responsible for art's lack of 'productivity' and social impotence. But it is also thereby a functionalism which is turned against the institutional conditions of its own functioning as critique – 'critique' being the one function compatible with art's functionlessness: the function of functionlessness itself. Institutional critique can only be an art of direct practicality by restricting itself to a terrain on which critique is the only form of practicality, the only social use-value: autonomous art. However, it thereby implicitly affirms the critical value of the art institution, the political conditions and social impotence of which it simultaneously exposes.[61] Ironically, this helps the institution to survive its own critique. The very existence of this critique within the institution – the institution's acceptance of institutional critique – negates the practical function of that critique, although not its intellectual value. Institutional critique thus strengthens and develops the art institution.

At one level, this appears as failure: the liquidation of its aspiration to be immediately social or directly practical, a deepening of the sense of art's social impotence, even within its own highly restricted domain. At another level, however, as a critical artistic practice, it appears as a *constructed mimesis* of the ability of cultural institutions within developed capitalist societies to sustain and recuperate their own critique. Its so-called 'failure' is an operative dimension of this critical functioning. There is thus an additional irony here (an 'irony of irony', in Schlegel's sense): the irony of the ironic failure of institutional critique as a political practice is that it thereby succeeds critically as art. It succeeds in giving artistic expression to the irrational rationality of the art institution: the basis of its critical rationality in irrational (oppressive) socio-economic forms. Using institutional forms, histories and relations as artistic materials, and developing new forms of construction – establishing new relationships between the elements of its materials – it expresses an existing form of social (ir)rationality, autonomously, yet in a way which is nonetheless at the same time critical of the current institutionalization of autonomy itself. Furthermore, by expanding the range of artistic materials to include the social relations and practices of institutions, it renders explicit the hitherto repressed social side of the ontology of the artwork. However, by restricting its focus to established forms of art-institutionality (principally, the museum and the gallery), institutional critique retains the defensive structure of self-reference characteristic of formalist modernisms. It thus combines aspects of Formalism and Productivism, but it lacks the key element of Constructivism: social construction. It is in this respect that the 'urban turn' within post-conceptual art practice and curation represents a new departure, in so far as it aspires to the broader social canvas of something like a new constructivism of the exhibition-form.

As Wall has argued with regard to Dan Graham's work (but the point is a general one), 'architecture' (understood here as 'the discourse of siting the effects of power generated by publicity, information and bureaucracy in the city') 'emerges as the determining or decisive art form, because it most wholly reflects institutional structure, and influences behaviour through its definition of positionality.' The city thus becomes 'the single grand subject' of art, at the precise point at which it becomes informational/global in form, and art becomes correspondingly postconceptual.[62] The idea of influencing behaviour through 'definitions of positionality' is a difficult one, and the aspect of Wall's account which is perhaps most specific to some of Dan Graham's work. But it is in 'influencing behaviour' that the constructivist aspect appears. A more explicitly constructivist position would construe such influence more directly, in terms of the construction not only of situations, but of social relations and practices as well. These are changes in the social relations of artistic production and the social character of exhibition space that involve taking cultural forms of an evermore extensive character as the objects of a new constructive – that is organizational – intent. We can see the beginnings of such constructions in recent transformations in the social space of art associated with the idea of the 'functional' or 'informational' site.

On James Meyer's account:

> The functional site may or may not incorporate a physical space. It certainly does not *privilege* this place. Instead, it is a process, an operation occurring between sites, a mapping of institutional and textual filiations and the bodies that move between them (the artist's above all). It is an informational site, a palimpsest of text, photographs and video recordings, physical places, and things . . . It is a temporary thing, a movement, a chain of meanings and imbricated histories . . .[63]

In this context, 'the work' is 'not a single entity, the installation of a given artist in a single place', but 'a *function* occurring between . . . locations and points of view, a series of expositions of information and place.' 'Site' becomes 'a network of sites referring to an *elsewhere*.'[64] This is a negative, still-locational description of what is actually a new, distributional spatial form, with its own (relational) positive effects, derived from the *organizational relations* that constitute such work.

Such art is Constructivist – and hence 'post-autonomous' – to the extent that it has an immanently artistic, as well as a functional, institutional logic: that is, to the extent that there is a simultaneous emergence of definitions of social function and new artistic forms. Jeff Wall has described 'functionalist' or 'post-autonomous' art as work that

> achieves its functional purposes by means of being a work of art and taking on the form of a work of art, albeit experimental in form . . . that is, it responds to no external functional or practical command, it is freely chosen and made by the artist. The artist chooses to make his or her work useful in some way, or even just to pretend it might be useful to act 'as if' it could be useful. This pretense invents possible functions, and presents them to the public, which might not otherwise have thought of them. In this light, post-autonomous art is only a liminal type of autonomous art.[65]

There are thus two discrete senses in which we may speak of 'functionalist' art, which come together in recent practice: the conventional constructivist sense of an art *performing* a social function, to which Wall refers, and Meyer's more recent spatial, dis-located sense of art *existing as* a communicational function 'between locations and points of view, a series of expositions of information and place.' The latter is a necessary historical corrective, not to Wall's constructivism, but to his liberalism: his delegation of functional goals to individual artistic decisions. These are more plausibly conceived as being the overdetermined outcome of a range of structural institutional pressures, and curatorial and career decisions, as well as individual artistic choices – especially when we conceive autonomy as a resistant property of the work, rather than an attribute of the artist. The contemporary project-based urban art of international exhibition spaces is largely the outcome of negotiations between artists and curators, museum or exhibition authorities, and corporations, councils and governments (at local, regional, national and international levels). These practices of organization, co-ordination and negotiation – whether they are about 'production' or 'installation', the difference between which is increasingly tenuous – are crucial mediations of art with urban social forms. At their broadest, they articulate a new kind of exhibition space: a capitalist constructivism of the exhibition-form.

If the white cube remains the major *convention* through which contemporary art passes, the *social space* through which it encounters this convention is predominantly that of the international exhibition, as a temporary network of a huge range of works, articulated in thematic clusters across a string of sites. These sets of sites might be geographically stable (like the Venice Biennale), have shifting boundaries, or be nomadic (like Manifesta). In this expanded and distributional spatial context, 'the exhibition has become the basic unit from which it is possible to conceive of relationships between art and ideology ushered in by technologies, to the detriment of the individual work.' And the constructive technologies are no longer just those of machinofacture, but primarily communicational. This is no longer the exhibition as 'store' (the original, oft-revived Constructivist metaphor), but the exhibition as 'set', within a general remodelling of the cinematic in line with digital technologies.[66] The curator functions as director and the works of art function as elements of the constructive process of exhibition building. Such works are intrinsically double-coded: they have their own ('liminally autonomous') significations and modes of experience, and they have the more fully 'post-autonomous' meanings that accrue to them as a result of their place within the overall (often quite chaotic) logic of construction of the exhibition. This is a logic that is itself contradictory: divided between the presentation of the collective exhibition-value of the works and their putative use-values as models within a speculative programme of social construction. Such programmes are uneasy amalgams of art, economics and politics. But then, what is 'culture' but such an amalgam? The use-values of individual works – and the programme itself – may, or may not, survive to be 'consumed' after the exhibition. But it is the horizon of expectation that they might, that the exhibitions depend upon for their constructive force. This horizon of expectation is increasingly a transnational one.

Transnationalization: art industry

The transnationalization of art via its production for, and inscription within, a transnational space mediates the global dialectic of places, non-places and flows, via the institutional forms of the *market*, the *large-scale international exhibition* (biennale, triennale, etc.), and the *migrancy of artists*. This is a profoundly contradictory process whereby art-institutional and market forms must negotiate the politics of regionalism, postcolonial nationalism and migration, overwriting the general spatial logic of postconceptual work with global political-economic dynamics. There has never been so much art as there is today – so much art produced, reproduced, exhibited, documented, shipped, stored, bought, sold and destroyed. And there has never been so many, or so geographically dispersed, regular, large-scale exhibitions of contemporary art.

They form the nodes of the network structure of a now globalized Western artworld.

As argued in Chapter 1, above, in recent years, the globally transnational character of an art space has become the primary marker of its contemporaneity, and it has thus become incumbent upon art with a claim on the present to situate itself, reflexively, within this expanded world. The coming together of different times that constitutes the contemporary, and the movement across social spaces that make up the transnational, are the main axes along which the social meaning of art is to be plotted today. In bringing together geopolitically diverse forms of social experience that have only recently begun to be represented within the parameters of a common world, these institutions have created genuinely novel kinds of cultural space. It is this heightened awareness of the known-but-previously-unrepresented that provides the context of today's biennales, such as the 2006 Sydney Biennale, *Zones of Contact*, which epitomized many of these features. With its title's connotations of anthropology and warfare – the theoretical and practical aspects of colonial expedition, respectively – the exhibition projected the world as a postcolonial network or matrix of 'contact zones'. However, this was no longer the 'classical' postcolonialism of the period following the Second World War – the postcolonialism of anti-imperialism and national liberation, the postcolonialism of the Cold War, which is now better thought in terms of ongoing processes of decolonization. Rather, it is the postcolonialism of 'after 1989' – the postcolonialism of a global neoliberalism. This is a postcolonialism not of the 'elsewhere' of Meyer's still negatively locationally defined functional sites, but of what Okwui Enwezor has called 'the terrible nearness of distant places', a postcolonialism of proximities, both imagined (through 'the spectacular mediation and representation of nearness') and actual (through the presence within metropolitan centres of migrants from the margins).[67] Indeed, especially in relation to China, our conception of it should be extended to include returning migrants, artists in particular. As Ackbar Abbas has argued, 'culture is not just placed elsewhere, but . . . it is everywhere, displaced; it may even be at home . . . It is not a question of homelands *versus* displacement, but homelands *plus* displacement . . . all places, including homelands, are – to coin a neologism – displaces.'[68] This new, post-1989 postcolonial situation involves both a new anthropology and new forms of war.

Structural anthropology provided an ontology for decolonization by maintaining multiple cultures on a single plane of significance.[69] The postcolonial condition requires an anthropology of a more radically transcultural kind: a transnational and translational study of the cultural, focused on the production of new kinds of social subjects, whose actions are distributed across time and space more widely and with greater complexity than ever before. The new biennales both contribute to, and are prime objects for, such studies. They contribute to them by bringing together art from across the world into the same physical space. They are objects for study in so far as they exemplify the conditions (and hence the restrictions) under which practices of such nationally and transnationally diverse origin come to occupy the same cultural space. For the most significant 'zone of contact' here is not represented within or by the artworks; it is that transcribed by the relations between the works and the biennale itself. This is the real 'contact', the place of translation, representation, negotiation and power. In this anthropological sense, contact is a site of risk, at which the stakes and meaning of exchange are uncertain. There is much to be gained, and much also to be lost. But the risk is not equally distributed.

As a consequence, the geopolitical diversity of the art that is assembled in exhibitions like *Zones of Contact* is a complex one. Some of the works may purport (or be purported) to represent the social space of either its own or its maker's origins. But the more successful an artist, the less likely they are to live and work in their country of origin, or indeed in any single place. (Twenty percent of the artists in *Zones of Contact* no longer lived or worked in their country of origin, and their movement was overwhelmingly 'inwards', from the periphery to Europe – especially, Amsterdam and Berlin – and New York.) The transnational postcoloniality represented here is thus of a general cultural kind. It is at least as much associated with displacement as it is with the social conditions within previously colonized territories themselves. Indeed, notoriously, it is precisely displaced postcolonial subjects who can most successfully represent themselves as 'native'.[70] The native itself, on the other hand, (in so far as the term retains a meaningful referent in such an interconnected world) can acquire its status as 'informant' only by being represented as such, by others, within international cultural spaces.

This is one of the main functions of the new biennales: they are cultural representatives of the market idea of a global system of societies. They mediate exchange relations with artists via the latest cultural discourses of 'globalization', in order to put the latest version of the contemporary on show.[71] Furthermore, by virtue of their power of assembly, international biennales are manifestations of the cultural-economic power of the 'centre', *wherever* they crop up and *whatever* they show. In short, they are the Research and Development branch of the transnationalization of the culture industry. For currently, it is only capital that projects the utopian horizon of global social interconnectedness, albeit in the ultimately dystopian form of the market.

This gives the new international biennales an emblematic status. They are emblems of capital's capacity to cross borders, and to accommodate and appropriate cultural differences. Art labour is variable art capital. Furthermore, currently, it is *only* capital that immanently projects the utopian horizon of global social interconnectedness, in the ultimately dystopian form of the market. However, for all these social determinations, it is still the art-character of the works on show – their particular ways of 'showing', their individual lack of self-evidence – that makes all this possible, that raises it above the status of an extended series of world exhibitions. In particular, it is the ultimate *extra*-territoriality of art (which is part and parcel of its illusion of autonomy, and its *socially produced* ideality) that makes this recent art of multiple and complex territorializations possible.

It is a distinctive feature of the new trans- and international art spaces that art appears *within* the culture industry, as part of distinctively capitalist constructivism. There is a new kind of coexistence of art and the culture industry: a transnational *art industry*. Contemporary art is at the forefront of a rapid expansion of this transnational art industry. It is in the term 'art industry' that the contradictory character of the new international spaces of contemporary art is most directly expressed. For, from the standpoint of the critical tradition, the very phrase 'art industry' suggests one or more of three main things: a collapse of autonomous art into commodity-production (one version of the famous 'end of art'); a restriction in the use of the term 'art' to its pre-modern connotation of craft or techné; and an oxymoron, a contradiction in terms. To understand something of the *objective* character of this contradiction, its developmental dynamism and its productivity, it is necessary briefly to recall the salient features of its canonical presentation in the 'Culture Industry' chapter of Max Horkheimer and Theodor W. Adorno's *Dialectic of Enlightenment*, composed in 1942, in the middle of the Second World War.[72]

Horkheimer and Adorno coined the phrase 'the culture industry' as an alternative to 'mass culture', in order to draw attention to the continuity of social form between the products of twentieth-century mass culture and those of industrialized commodity-production more generally. Their purpose was to distinguish mass culture from the 'popular' culture or 'low art' (which was more spontaneously related to the people) that preceded it.[73] As industrialized mass culture, the culture industry was to be equally distinguished from 'art' in its modern, critical, institutionalized sense as 'autonomous' – autonomous, that is, in its production of meaning, from the dictates of church, state, politics and markets alike. This threefold distinction of popular culture, culture industry, and autonomous art has been the subject of considerable debate and no small amount of simplification and misunderstanding – much of it the result of misjudgements of the rhetorical form of Horkheimer and Adorno's original presentation. From the point of view of our concerns here, three things in particular should be emphasized. First, these are not three 'pure' forms: the terms distinguish cultural products and practices on the basis of whichever of the three rationalities dominates within the productive logic of each particular work. Second, 'autonomous' art has always been for sale, as a commodity, in the market. (Historically, the market is the *social basis* of art's autonomy from its previous social functions.) Autonomous works of art are thus always *also* commodities – always already 'post-autonomous', in Wall's sense. Their difference from the products of the culture industry is not commodification as such, but rather the fact that the latter are commodities 'through and through'. The latter are *produced*, rather than just circulated, *as* commodities – that is, in order to be exchanged – in a manner that determines the structure of the product by the anticipation of its market. Third, art's commodification is the source of contradictions within the autonomous artwork, contradictions between its immanent artistic logic and its saleability. These are contradictions that the artwork must mediate and ultimately *incorporate* into what Adorno called 'the law of form', if it is to achieve autonomy. Autonomy is never a 'given'. In so far as it exists, it is the individual achievement of each work: the victory of technique (the principle of internal organization) over social conditions. Autonomy is the achievement, in each instance, of the production of a law of form.

Furthermore, as is clear from Adorno's later *Aesthetic Theory*, this reflective incorporation of social conditions into the immanent logic of works of art should not be conceived merely negatively, as a constraint upon some original artistic freedom. Rather, this very dependence or 'heteronomy' gives both *life* and *social substance* to the work. It gives *life* because it is the struggle of technique with 'extra-aesthetic' materials (including the projection of conditions of circulation and reception) that animates the work. This includes the residual presence within works of unincorporated elements – itself a paradoxical part of the modern work's law of form, by which it avoids falling into the false formal coherence of 'beauty'. It gives *social substance* to the work because the reflective incorporation of the social conditions of reception into the immanent logic of works of art is one of the main determinations of their 'content', alongside the social form of their technologies and techniques of production. Only if art has social content of this kind will its ultimate 'asociality' – the fetish-like, illusory self-sufficiency of its product – function as a '*determinate* negation of a determinate society'.[74] Only thus will art be truly 'critical'.

The incorporation of contemporary art into the cultural industry, via the new inter- and transnational spaces of art, changes the social conditions within which autonomy is to be achieved. It thereby alters the immanent contradictions within works of art, the formal mediation and articulation of which will determine the character of their 'autonomy' (or lack of it), and hence their critical status. In itself, this dictates neither the 'end of (autonomous) art' nor its survival. All it dictates is the changed conditions to which works must respond if they are to wrestle autonomy out of facticity. (One of these changed conditions is that the culture industry itself no longer only makes 'mass' products, but exhibits a highly sophisticated differentiation into market sectors – including, paradoxically, autonomous art, for which it is now the distributive mechanism.) There are grounds for believing that autonomy is becoming ever harder to achieve. The appropriation and standardization of new artistic forms occurs with ever-increasing speed; and the integration of the different aspects of the culture industry – art, fashion, mass culture, advertising, tourism – is far greater than previously. But these are also grounds for believing that this system itself has an increased need for autonomous art, with which to feed its need for 'the new'. Hence the search for new social 'heterogeneities', to transform into artistic materials, that has been characteristic of the expansion of the international artworld over the last two decades, and the means for its gradual de-nationalization. This process has been massively reinforced by the extension of the world market, subsequent to the collapse of the Soviet Union and the take-off of state capitalism in China.

The new international biennales of contemporary art are inscribed within an updated ('transcultural') anthropological problematic of the plurality of cultures and the universality of sense. However, art's universality is not socially structural, like the anthropologist's 'sense', but historical, socio-spatially conditioned, and ultimately individual in kind. If, as we have argued, following Adorno, modern art is characterized by a decline in the binding power of mediating universals (mediums, forms and genres), and the individual work has come increasingly to bear the burden of mediating its relations to the universality of 'art' directly – to produce artistic universality out of its own (individual) law of form – the exhibition-form has to some extent compensated with new mediating social functions, not necessarily directly, but contextually. Rather than the invention of new mediums (Krauss) or the positivist reduction of 'art' to a proper name (Duve),[75] it is increasingly the transnational exhibition-form that fulfils the requirement of providing social meaning. The art market may still be trading in individual works, but it is the exhibition that is the unit of artistic significance, and the object of constructive intent. In the new international biennales, individual works generate meaning and affect relationally, as components of this new kind of art space. It is up to curators, with their power of assembly, to ensure that such spaces retain their lack of self-evidence – that they remain spaces of uncertainty, of not knowing in advance. Increasingly, since the 1960s, the modern art museum has attempted to take account of and to institutionalize such uncertainty through the notion of 'project space'. However, this institutionalization of the project as a unit of art discourse (today, increasingly the transnational project) has generally involved its contradictory appropriation to a *locationally* conceived exhibition-space.

Project space

The growing recognition that contemporary art 'lives' through its opening onto the future has led to the creation within art institutions since the 1960s of specific, demarcated spaces for the exhibition of 'projects'. The notion of project space has generally been approached empirically, within the terms of a history of art institutions.[76] However it can also be approached philosophically, in relation to the histories – converging and diverging – of the concepts of art and project. For as we saw in Chapter 2, above, the philosophical history of the modern concept of art, as the bearer of a distinctive form of metaphysical experience, encompasses that of 'the project' at its source, in the Jena Romanticism of the 1790s, through the idea of art as being, in principle, 'forever becoming, never completed'.[77] Subsequently, in Heidegger's work of the late 1920s, the philosophical concept of project detached itself from an artistic context and became associated with the structure of human being as Being-in-the-world. This existential notion of project (identified in Heidegger's writings with the German term *Entwurf*, rather than *Projekt*)[78] casts a new light back onto the Romantic conception of the artwork, which appears from this standpoint in a more radically temporal-existential (rather than metaphysical or onto-theological) guise. It is just such a temporal and existential conception of art that came to the fore in that process of the destruction of conventional, medium-based conceptions of the 'fine' or beautiful arts, from the late 1950s through to the early 1970s, known as the art of the Sixties. As it had previously come to the fore, contemporaneously with Heidegger's early writings, but at some considerable geopolitical distance from them, in Russian Futurism and Soviet Constructivism.

Each of the terms associated with the institutional history of project space – *new, young, original, experimental, innovative, initiative, difficult, controversial, speculative, risky*[79] – derives its basic cultural significance from its place within the constellation of early Romanticism. A philosophical interpretation of project space must thus start there, with Friedrich Schlegel's characterization of a project as a 'fragment of the future', in the passage with which we concluded Chapter 2:

> A project (*Ein Projekt*) is the subjective embryo of a developing [literally, 'a becoming'] object (*eines werdenden Objekt*). A perfect project must be at once wholly subjective and wholly objective, must be an indivisible and living individual. In its origin, wholly subjective and original, only possible in precisely this spirit; in its character, wholly objective (*objektiv*), physically and morally necessary. The feeling for projects – which one might call fragments of the future – is different from the feeling for fragments of the past only by its direction: progressive in the former, regressive in the latter. What is essential is the ability to idealize and to realize objects (*Geganstände*) immediately and simultaneously: to make them whole (*ergänzen*) and partly carry them out within oneself. Since transcendental is precisely whatever relates to the joining or separating of the ideal and the real, one might very well say that the feeling for fragments and projects is the transcendental element of the historical spirit.[80]

The project, then, for Schlegel, combines (1) a temporal registration of the necessary incompletion, and hence striving towards the future, of the reality of the work of art (what we might call its inherently *processual* character: it is directed towards an end that it has not reached, and cannot reach) with (2) an ideal image of its completion, from which it derives its meaning as the partial realization of something ideal, or a 'becoming object' (*eines werdenden Objekts*). Projects are articulated combinations of ideas and processes of actualization. As such, a project is the temporal equivalent to – and futural dimension of – the spatiality of the fragment. Just as one may say that, for Schlegel, the fragment *is* the work of art; so one may say that for him, a work of art *is* a project. Art *lives* only in its incompletion, as project.

The temporality of the project is thus more pervasive than is suggested by Schlegel's contrast between projects as 'fragments of the future' and what one may surmise to be ruins, 'fragments of the past'; although Schlegel's reduction of this difference to one of mere direction (*Richtung*) hints at a complexity that is not elaborated. It is, however, of direct relevance to the issue of project space, since within the museum of modern or contemporary art, project space is demarcated in contrast to other exhibition spaces, usually for permanent collections and temporary exhibitions of completed works, which we might associate with 'fragments of the past'. We may therefore suppose that this conception of the project might have something to tell us about the artistic status of such 'fragments of the past', as well as the project space from which they are differentiated.

The Romantic concept of the fragment was constructed on the basis of the appropriation, affirmation and generalization of the ruin as a category of modernity (in opposition to the nostalgic neo-classical appropriation of the ruin initially provoked by the excavations at Pompeii and Herculaneum in the mid-eighteenth century). From this point of view, projects are something like – to borrow a phrase of Robert Smithson's – 'ruins in reverse': buildings that '*rise* into ruin before they are built.'[81] Projects embody the futural impulse conveyed by the constitutive incompletion of the fragment, as such, whatever its 'direction' in chronological time. The direction of the feeling for fragments of the past may be 'backwards' (*regressiv*), but the *feeling* is different *only* in this respect. Fragments of the past are thus, structurally, within themselves, *as futural* (as 'projective'), qua fragments, as fragments of the future are (projects). It is just that their futurity must be interpretatively retrieved, constructively, as part of their afterlife, since they are no longer *subjectively inhabited in their process of production* (as projects are, as 'embryos' of developing or 'becoming' objects), but in their reproduction. The real problem for 'fragments of the past' is not that they lack futurity, but that they are not generally received as fragments at all, in the Romantic sense, but rather as *completed* works – whether whole or partial: cultural treasures or 'heritage'.[82] The fragment, we might say, *rescued the ruin from the past*, for the future. In their difference from the spaces of permanent collections and temporary exhibitions alike, project spaces *antiquate* those spaces.[83] And they do this, not simply by virtue of the dynamic opposition between the new and the old (the modern way of producing a difference between 'the living' and 'the dead'), but in terms of their specification of the artistically 'living' as partaking in the structure of a project: processes of immanent, ongoing realizations of the ideal, 'forever becoming, never completed'.

Heidegger's existential concept of project pertains not to art but to '*Dasein*' (literally, 'being-there'), the philosophical term he used to denote his very particular conception of human existence – relegating the standard modern philosophical opposition between 'subject' (or 'I') and 'object' to the history of metaphysics. Unlike a subject, *Dasein* is always already in the world, a Being-in-the-world. However, in so far as the production of art is a human activity, it falls within the purview of Heidegger's analysis of the 'projective' structure of human existence. This allows us to deepen the Romantic conception of a project, existentially, and thereby to radicalize, as well as to generalize, our sense of its temporality; and with this, to modify, or reinflect, its political meaning.

Beyond the teleological structure implicit in the notion of a project as something projected towards an end, 'projection' has a number of specific meanings in different disciplinary contexts: in particular, geometry, neurology, psychophysiology, psychology and psychoanalysis.[84] When he occasionally draws upon this semantic history, Heidegger uses the term *Projektion*. When he is thinking existentially, however, he uses *Entwurf* (or the cognate verb *entwerfen*), which connotes not merely the teleological structure of directedness towards an end, or the movement of displacement of an end, but also something being thrown (*werfen*). It is thus associated with the existential condition Heidegger calls *Geworfenheit* – 'thrownness' – which, alongside projection, is one of what he identifies as four existential structures of *Dasein*'s state of being. In Being-in-the-world, Heidegger argues, *Dasein* is thrown 'into its "there"', and this existential thrownness is a 'movement' of throwing that 'remains in the throw'. As such, *Dasein* is charactereized by Heidegger as 'thrown projection'. And what it projects, in being thrown, is its possibilities. As Heidegger puts it: 'projection, in throwing, throws before itself possibility as possibility, and lets it *be* as such.' Dasein is thus the kind of Being in which 'it *is* its possibilities as possibilities.' As such it is 'constantly "more" than it factually is'. As 'being-possible' we are 'existentially that which, in [our] potentiality-for-being, . . . is *not yet*.' In other words, we are essentially futural beings.[85] Project space recognizes this futurity *as* possibility.

The terminology grates and the prose appears barbarous (in translation at least), but this is an important philosophical redefinition of what we are, in terms of projecting: we *are* projecting.[86] Projecting projects possibilities as possibilities. And the being of possibility is freedom. This has a number of consequences for the way in which we might think about project space.

In the first place, given this temporal-existential deepening and generalization of the concept of project, it appears peculiar that art institutions should have come to designate certain restricted spaces wholly by their appropriateness for the presentation or exhibition of projects. After all, if human existence is a thrown projection, and all critically significant works of art are fragments/projects, what else are art institutions exhibiting? The corpses of dead projects, it would seem. All art-space in critically functioning art institutions should be project spaces of one kind or another, philosophically speaking. To the extent that art *lives*, art-space *is* project space: the space of presentation or exhibition (the Romantic *Darstellung* translates the Latin *exhibitio*) of being as possibility, through individual instances (including collectively individual instances) of projects: ideas suspended in the movement of their realization as 'becoming objects', which thereby exhibit an ambiguous objectivity (semblance). As Adorno put it: 'The fact that artworks exist signals the possibility of the nonexisting. The reality of artworks testifies to the possibility of the possible.'[87]

But what of the character of project space itself, not as a mere receptacle for the exhibition of projects through the presentations of their materials, but as a mode of spatialization? Is there a distinctive spatialization corresponding to the temporalization of the project? The Constructivist metaphor – revived in the 1960s – was the laboratory. The Constructivist laboratory was a space of experimental activity upon forms (projects), 'divorced from life', but undertaken from the perspective of the prospective transition to an experimentation that has 'a basis in reality', that is to say, is internal to a social function.[88] Divorced from the perspective of such a transition, it regresses to a space of merely aesthetic experimentation and display.

Project space in its current institutional sense is no Constructivist laboratory. However, the question of its specific spatialization is raised by the debates about site specificity (both inside and outside the museum and the gallery) since the 1970s. On the one hand, as a reaction within the museum to the external pressure of the new artistic practices of the 1960s, project space is a relatively conservative phenomenon: the setting aside of a physically demarcated space within the existing architecture of the museum, within which the new practices can be 'showcased'. This is a symbolic function. The role of the museum as the 'non-site' is to represent the site. On the other hand, as a space inhabited or possessed by the new practices, project space becomes subject to the new forms of spatialization immanent within those practices: specifically, those of the 'functional' or 'informational' site.[89] The networked space of the functional site erodes the distinction between site and non-site, upon which the dialectic of Smithson's practice, for example, depended.

Apart from being spaces of installation, performance and documentation, in addition to the exhibition of 'objects' in the broadest sense (including film and video work, in particular), project spaces become hubs in informational networks, in which the social relations conditioning artistic practices of various sorts are increasingly laid bare as an inherent part of those practices themselves – in the wake not only of the new communicational technologies, but primarily, the sedimentation of institutional critique into a dimension of contemporary art practices, in general. In this respect, the architectural qualities of the physical space become of decreasing significance for the art function of these spaces, as the distinction between art practices and more general cultural and communicational (media) forms becomes less a matter of material means than of the conceptual and strategic logics of the individual instances of the practices. The contemporary, socio-historical forms of the general existential structure of 'the project' come to the fore, along with its situational conditions, organized by relations between individual and collective praxis,[90] in which the once curatorial but increasingly directive role of the museum is of growing significance. (This is no longer 'the artist as producer', or even 'the curator as producer', so much as 'the museum as producer'.) The existential and social structure of the project itself becomes the carrier of artistic reflection.

The specificity of the practices associated with project space is thus threatened on three sides: by their lack of distinction from contemporary art in general, by their curatorial overdetermination, and by their dissolution into artistically indifferent modes of communication. Some may bemoan the uncertainties of this situation, brought about by the erosion of clearly spatially structured cultural classifications and divisions. Yet it is the ground upon which the possibility of the social (and thereby critical) significance of contemporary art depends. Such is the current direction of 'the transcendental element of the historical spirit'.

7

Art time

To the extent that art *lives*, art space *is* project space, a space of presentation of possibilities within a historically rapidly shifting matrix of places, non-places and flows, their combinatory articulations and effects. But, what of the time of the viewer? What temporal structures articulate the actualization of 'the possibility of the possible' in the viewer, in their relations to the work? How are we to understand the convention of timelessness that constitutes the gallery's hysterical cell? Is art-time a form of 'no-time', in a way similar to that in which art spaces are non-places, for example, or is it an *any-time-whatever*? These questions can be addressed at a number of different levels of analysis. Most broadly, there are the historical times of the *modern*, the *contemporary* and the *avant-garde*: 'the new', 'the now' and 'the tomorrow'. I have addressed some of the complexities of these abstract yet powerfully actual historical-temporal forms above and elsewhere.[1] More concretely, there is the phenomenological time of reception, the time of the art-viewer, which mediates and particularizes these more fundamental structures. Ever since Augustine first conceived the 'time of the soul' as that of a 'threefold present' in which the temporal dimensions of present/past/future are contracted into the subjective orientations of attention/memory/expectation,[2] the subjective meaning of history has been thought in terms of relations between memory and expectation. Indeed, the abstract temporal formalism of the time of modernity – of which avant-garde and the contemporary are specific, transformative articulations – is itself a projection onto history of just such a fundamentally subjective temporality. This is why the modern concept of history is indissociable from those of 'subject' and 'politics' alike. Augustine's tripartite structure is repeated, in different philosophical modes, in Kant, Husserl and Heidegger. Phenomenologically, the question of the temporality of the work of contemporary art thus appears, first and foremost, as the question of what modes of *attention*, *memory* and *expectation* contemporary art produces and requires as conditions of its experience.

This chapter follows this threefold structure, not at the level of a 'pure' phenomenology, but at that of a (necessarily selective) historical phenomenology of the temporality of art as a distinctive cultural form of capitalist modernity. Its argument, broadly speaking, is, first, that the mode of attention appropriate to the conditions of contemporary art is best conceived in terms of a *historical dialectic of boredom and distraction*, rather than the strictly transcendental timelessness of the model of 'contemplative immersion' historically associated with the exhibition-value of modern art. Or, to put it another way: the apparently transcendental timelessness of the artwork, which constitutes it as 'art', is in each instance the product of a specific set of *idealizing* social and historical relations, practices and processes, which produce it as 'timeless'. As such, timeless within time, as a kind of *any-time-whatever*, the artwork harbours the potential for retemporalization, in each instance. The deliberate production of boredom, or what the Fluxus artist Dick Higgins called 'super-boredom', is one among many such practices of temporalization. Second, it is argued, the way in which certain claims to contemporaneity are currently made via, or even as, claims to cultural memory, is both theoretically and politically problematic. The difference between memory and history, constitutive of historiography, needs to be re-established, if the role of memory in contemporary art is to be clarified. Finally, it is suggested, in the wake of the collapse of historical communism and in the midst of a major geopolitical reordering of the world, the concept of expectation – intrinsic to the Enlightenment concept of politics as the practice of actualizing historical expectations, and associated since Husserl with the secularized Christian notion of a 'horizon of expectation' – requires rethinking. Rather than expectation, contemporary art is better thought in terms of *practices of anticipation*. Its experimental aspects, in their specific contemporaneity, make it a privileged form of such practice.

Contemporary art, in the critical sense in which the concept has been constructed in this book, is a geo-politically reflective art of the historical present of a postconceptual kind. But the historical present, no less than the phenomenological present – the structure of which the historical present generalizes and complicates – is always threefold. The prioritization of the 'presentness' of the conjunction of multiple temporalities within the logic of the contemporary rearticulates and subjectively reinvests – but it cannot suppress – this immanent threefold temporal structure.

Attention and distraction: boredom as possibility

The mode of attention appropriate to the reception of modern art has been subject to three main forms of disciplinary analysis: transcendental aesthetics, psychology of the aesthetic attitude, and institutional analysis. In the wake of eighteenth-century British criticism (Shaftesbury, in particular), Kant's transcendental aesthetics established 'disinterest' as a condition of the possibility of pure aesthetic judgements of taste. Proponents of 'aesthetic art' took such art to be an appropriate object of such judgements. Disinterest thus came to define the critically appropriate mode of attention to modern art. Late nineteenth- and early twentieth-century accounts of the 'aesthetic attitude' psychologized and naturalized the production of such disintestedness, or 'critical distance' as it became known.[3] Social histories of art and sociologies and institutional theories of art have theorized its social conditions.[4] These analyses accompanied a growing interest in attention more generally as a psychological and social problem, within the wide-ranging institutional construction of what Jonathan Crary has identified as a new ideal type of subjectivity, appropriate to the forms of labour, education and consumption characteristic of capitalist societies. (Think, for example, of the prominence given to 'attention-deficit disorder' as a diagnostic category in child psychiatry since the 1970s, and to its subsequent variants, attention-deficit hyperactivity disorder, formally established in the fourth edition of the *Diagnostic and Statistical Manual of Mental Disorders* in 1994, in particular.) In fact, it is possible to view modernity itself as, in Crary's words,

> an ongoing crisis of attentiveness, in which the changing configurations of capitalism continually push attention and distraction to new limits and thresholds, with an endless sequence of new products, sources of stimulation, and streams of information, and then respond with new methods of managing and regulating perception.[5]

Art has played a central role in this education and management of modes of attention and their coding by social class.

Within this scenario, attention – the capacity to extend a present through the focus of consciousness on a single object – is a norm produced by the fear of distraction; while distraction itself appears as a side effect of attempts to produce attentiveness – both negatively (as their failure) and positively (as a condition they reactively provoke). All attempts to produce attentiveness thus generate further demands to discipline, rechannel or otherwise deal with the distractions to which they themselves give rise. The double meaning of the German word *Zerstreuung* is exemplary in catching the ambiguity of this process, since it is used to refer to both the psychological phenomenon of the dispersion or scattering of perception and the principal social object of diverted attention, entertainment.[6] Art has played multiple roles in this process, historically: as a form of distraction; as the very opposite of distraction/entertainment; and more recently as the model for a more complicated form of 'distracted attention'.

But if what art must distract its viewers from – in order to function critically as art – is not just the cares and worries of the world but, increasingly, distraction (entertainment) itself, how to distract from distraction without simply reproducing it? How is art to be received in distraction without becoming just another distraction? Alternatively, how is art to distract from distraction without losing touch with distraction, without entering another realm altogether – 'contemplative immersion' in the work – with no relation to other distractions, and thereby becoming the vehicle of a flight from actuality, from the very temporal structure of experience which it must engage if it is to be 'contemporary' and affective? These are issues with which modernist and avant-garde art has grappled since the 1920s. The experience of time most pertinent to this grappling has not been the sheer presentness of attention, associated in art criticism with 'absorption', but boredom. Boredom, not attention, is the true dialectical other of distraction in modernity. This is already clear in the transitional figure of Pascal, for whom, boredom (*ennui*) is the result of the 'nothingness' of a life without God, but diversion (*divertissement*) is an even greater 'misery', distracting us from the 'more solid means of escape', which, Pascal claimed, boredom itself 'would drive us to seek'.[7] It was not until the twentieth century, however, that boredom became associated, philosophically, with the modality of possibility. But when it did, the connection appeared fundamental. Indeed, Heidegger argued in his 1929–30 lecture course, *The Fundamental Concepts of Metaphysics*, that we should understand boredom existentially – a very particular form of boredom, which he called 'profound boredom' – as *the feeling of possibility itself*.[8]

Contra Heidegger, however (whose analysis is purportedly 'strictly' existential, despite its passing acknowledgement of a contemporary ground), boredom has a social history tied up with its philosophical form. Fragments of such a history are to be found in Convolute D of Benjamin's *Arcades Project*, the material for which, from 1928–29, is almost exactly contemporaneous with Heidegger's lectures.[9] France may have experienced an 'epidemic' of boredom in the 1840s, but it was Weimar Germany that was the site of the outbreak of its analysis.[10] For both Heidegger and Benjamin there is a utopian function to boredom in modernity derived from its distinctive relations to possibility. In Benjamin's phrase from 'The Storyteller', boredom is 'the dreambird that hatches the egg of experience'.[11] Filling in the blank space of history in Heidegger's analysis, one might postulate that boredom is a privileged point of entry into the experience of modernity – Callois called it 'the characteristically modern sentiment'[12] – because it is the one of the main temporal forms of the experience of *abstraction* that characterizes the culture of modernity more generally. Boredom is a particular temporal experience of abstraction, or mode of experience of the inherently abstract temporality of modernity itself.[13] As Benjamin saw, it is the other side of fashion, the dialectical counterpart and existential background to the libidinal discharge associated with the object of fashion, an integral part of the complex and paradoxical temporality of the new. Boredom, Benjamin wrote in the *Arcades Project*, is 'the grating before which the courtesan teases death.'[14] As such, it is part of a constellation of terms, including *attention, curiosity, distraction, fascination, indifference, interest, disinterest* and *reverie* or *daydreaming*, that points towards a phenomenology of modernity as utopian longing, made up of a complex network of dialectical relations.[15]

Combined with its utopian function as an existential mood – possibilization – this connection to abstraction suggests that boredom may function politically as the basis for a new mode of *appropriation* within abstraction: a retemporalization or rehistorization of life, within abstraction, consistent with the structure of modernity itself as a temporal-historical form. As such, there is both an art of boredom, as the practice of the production of boredom, and a politics to boredom, as part of the production of possibility as such. Such a politics would be far more dialectically entwined with boredom than the Situationism that declared: 'We have a world of pleasures to win, and nothing to lose but boredom'.[16] In fact, the production of boredom has become ever more important within art since the Second World War, as a defensive reaction against the expansion of the culture industry into its field of operations, leading most recently to the culture industry's incorporation of the artworld itself.

Boredom has been (perjoratively) associated with modern art – especially music – since the 1950s. It was an explicit object of critical discourse in the New York artworld of the early 1960s – especially around Frank Stella's paintings – primarily, but no longer exclusively, negatively.[17] And its deliberate artistic production was associated by Duchamp with Happenings: 'Happenings have introduced into art an element no one had put there: boredom. To do a thing in order to bore people is something I never imagined! And that's too bad, because it's a beautiful idea.'[18] At around the same time, boredom began to be theorized as a positive artistic condition – as 'super-boredom' – within Fluxus, by Dick Higgins.[19] It was central to avant-garde film of the period – Warhol in particular. In film, it has generally been connected, theoretically, to 'the everyday', in which 'nothing happens'.[20] It is this connection that also explains its interest to Heidegger. 'Everydayness' is central to the 'universal phenomenological ontology' of Heidegger's 1927 *Being and Time*, in part for methodological reasons.[21]

It is a mark of the modernity of Heidegger's early philosophical work that, for a period at least, it considered the analysis of boredom a necessary preparatory stage to outlining the fundamental questions of metaphysics, concerning world, individuation, and finitude. In *The Fundamental Concepts of Metaphysics*, what Heidegger calls 'profound boredom' appears as *the* fundamental attunement or mood of 'contemporary Dasein'. The self-temporalizing structure of human existence, which is presented in *Being and Time* as analytically dependent on the anticipation of death (as the constitutive limit of temporalizing), is re-presented here, purely phenomenologically, as revealed in and by boredom.[22]

Heidegger was interested in boredom as the phenomenologico-ontological condition of a particular kind of questioning (and hence of philosophy), rather than in possibility as such. However, it is via possibility that the analysis proceeds – from boredom, via possibility, to 'the essence of time' as the root of metaphysical questioning – and it is this aspect of the analysis to which I shall attend. Heidegger's discussion is long and complex, full of false starts, gaps, leaps, isolated insights, redundancies and etymological shortcuts, as befits a lecture course. Indeed, it leads one to think that Heidegger's notorious etymologism was largely an artefact of his teaching – much like Raymond Williams's. So a brutal reduction is necessary. The analysis develops through three main stages or 'forms' of boredom of increasing existential-ontological depth: 1. becoming bored 'by' something; 2. being bored 'with' something; and 3. profound boredom, or 'it is boring for one'.

Its five most salient features are as follows.

1. An etymological definition of boredom derived from the German word *Langeweile* as a lengthening of time (literally 'long while'). Boredom is a temporal concept that involves a peculiar remaining, enduring or dragging. More specifically, according to Heidegger, 'Becoming bored is a peculiar *being affected ... by time as it drags and by time in general*, a being affected which oppresses us in its own way ... *a peculiar impressing of the power of that time* to which we are bound.'[23]
2. The idea that our immediate relation to boredom is a negative one, in so far as it manifests itself 'ordinarily', in everyday life, only via our attempt to combat boredom by 'passing the time' (*Zeitvertreib* – literally, a 'driving away of time'.) Since boredom is a lengthening of time (too much time! too long a while!), we

drive boredom away by driving time itself away; or at least, by driving away our sense of time as lingering. Boredom thus 'always *shows itself* in such a way that we immediately turn *against* it'. There is 'a peculiar *unity* of a *boredom* and a *passing the time* in which a confrontation with boredom somehow occurs.'[24] This is crucial to its critical function. However, Heidegger expressly rejects the deliberate production of boredom:

> Are we explicitly and intentionally to produce boredom in ourselves? Not at all. We do not need to undertake anything in this respect. On the contrary, we are always already undertaking too much. This boredom becomes essential of its own accord, if only we are not opposed to it, if we do not always immediately react to protect ourselves, if instead we make room for it.[25]

'Awakening' boredom 'does not mean making it awake in the first place, but *letting it be awake, guarding against it falling asleep*'. By not letting boredom fall asleep, we liberate '*the Dasein in man*'.[26] Heidegger is not interested in any particular possibilities, any possible actualities, that might be made possible by the affective intensification of possibility as an existential mode, but only with this existential mode in itself, as the ground of questioning.

3. This passing the time/driving time away, or more extremely, 'killing time' – an important idea in Pauline Kael's account of Andy Warhol's early films as 'timekillers on the way to the grave' – is necessarily a driving of time onwards, into the future: 'Passing the time is *a driving away of boredom that drives time on*'.[27] Reflection on boredom thus reveals the temporalizing power of our intentional relation to things, at the same time as it reveals 'the strange and enigmatic power of time itself'. This is the power, first, to 'hold us in limbo' or to suspend us in time, and second, to 'leave us empty' in such a way that things appear to refuse us something we expect from them: namely, an ability to be present or to engage us in such a way that time passes, *without* our having to force it to pass, to drive it on.[28] It is the indeterminacy of our relation to boredom here, our failure to grasp quite what it is about something that bores us, that leads Heidegger to posit his second main form of boredom: being bored, not 'by' something, but 'with' something. This is the fourth main feature of the analysis.

4. There is a deeper form of boredom than being bored by some particular object, in which what bores us (what lengthens time) is

*in*determinate; it has no specific object. This is because here, it is 'passing the time' or driving time away itself with which we are bored. (Heidegger's example is a dinner party at which he didn't realize he had been bored until he got home.) In this situation *'boredom and passing the time become intertwined* in a peculiar way'.²⁹ It is not just that boredom manifests itself through our confrontation with it in passing the time (the example there was waiting on a deserted railway station for a train), but boredom and passing the time – fighting boredom – become one. We are doing what we are doing not for its own sake, but only in order to pass the time. Hence we are bored with this too. (There is a phenomenological version of the dialectic of boredom and distraction, familiar from analyses of the cultural industries, buried here beneath Heidegger's abstract prose: distraction itself becomes boring.) What bores us in this boredom is, according to Heidegger, 'I know not what' [*ich weiß nicht was*]:³⁰ that very attribute of an object that was held, in eighteenth-century France, to distinguish it as an object of aesthetic appreciation, a work of art: *je ne sais quoi*.

This second phenomenological form or level of boredom would appear to be close to what is understood by the Pascal's *'ennui'*, received into English in the mid-eighteenth century, according to the *Oxford English Dictionary*, to denote a diffuse form of 'mental weariness and dissatisfaction arising from want of occupation or lack of interest'. (Unsurprisingly, Heidegger does not pursue this French connection.) Art and ennui are, of course, bound together in aestheticism, which, one might propose, was in fact an implicit cultural condition of Heidegger's analysis, as it was explicitly of Benjamin's.³¹ All of which suggests that Heidegger's second phenomenological form of boredom secretly draws on a separate, less Alemannic, more modern, and essentially French semantics. For Benjamin, such boredom was central to the emblematic cultural status of Paris as the capital of the nineteenth century (capitalist modernity), and to Baudelaire as the poet of early modernism, alike.

The temporal immanence of being bored 'with' the passing of time – its failure to release us from the hold of time – is Heidegger's cue for a further ontological deepening of his analysis, reaching the culminating position of what he calls 'profound' boredom.

5. Profound boredom, as the structural unity and temporal immanence of the earlier two forms (becoming bored *by* and being bored *with*) is taken to spring from the temporality of human existence itself. Profound boredom, Heidegger argues, 'arises

from a quite determinate way and manner in which our own temporality temporalizes itself.' *'What bores* us in profound boredom... what is solely and properly boring, is *temporality in a particular way of its temporalizing.*'[32] The third and final form of boredom, profound boredom, thus has the more neutral grammatical form of 'it is boring for one', where the 'it' in question is the temporal character of existence itself. Existing, merely existing, as temporalization, the production or lengthening of time, is itself boring. Profound boredom is the feeling of time in its ability to expand itself. It is not just *a* structure of feeling, in Raymond Williams's sense, so much as *the* structure of feeling. Profound boredom is the temporal structure of affectivity itself. For if human existence is a process of self-temporalizing, within which the 'I' is a moment of self-awareness – time as pure self-affection, in Heidegger's reading of Kant – profound boredom is the phenomenological register of temporality's 'stretching' of itself out into 'time', chronological time, its objectified shell. Profound boredom is an 'entrancement' of existence by time, or, more fundamentally, 'the entrancement *of* the temporal horizon': 'the horizon of whiling... *expands itself into the entire temporality of Dasein*', covering over its own shortness.

The experience of time's lengthening turns out to be a peculiar vanishing of its inherent shortness, its constitutive limit: namely, death. Indeed, it is a kind of *disavowal* or *wishing away* of death. In so expanding itself, profound boredom makes what Heidegger calls 'the extremity of the moment of vision' – the moment of action – vanish. It would therefore appear to be the very opposite of a possible ground for politics. However, Heidegger insists, 'only the [particular] possibility vanishes here, whereby the possibility of whatever is possible is precisely intensified.'[33] The ground emerges, as ground, but in such a way as to block the actuality of the very thing that it grounds. This affective intensification of possibility, per se, in profound boredom, which Heidegger remarks upon in passing but never develops – and which has few of the usual connotations of boredom – may be read as the existential basis for what Ernst Bloch called the 'contentlessness' of utopian longing, or the *spirit* of utopia, and what Adorno identified as the testimony of 'the reality of artworks': 'the possibility of the possible'.[34] It may be understood historically – contra Heidegger – as being both based in and a reaction against abstraction in the precise sense in which, in his critique of Hegel in his *1844 Manuscripts*, Marx writes of boredom as 'the *mystical* feeling which drives the philosopher from abstract thinking to intuition... the longing for a content'.[35] (Marx is discussing the impulse behind the transition from logic to nature in Hegel's system, a discussion that parallels Kierkegaard's account of the role of boredom in God's creation of the world: 'The Gods were bored; therefore they created human beings.')[36] For Marx here, boredom is the experience – both affective and productive – of the emptiness of self-sufficient abstraction, a 'being left empty' by abstraction, rather than by some ontological 'refusal of things' (Heidegger). Boredom drives subjectivity forward in the search for social content, much as, in psychoanalytical accounts, boredom is associated with the 'suspended animation of desire', a return to the childhood mood of 'diffuse restlessness which contains that most absurd and paradoxical wish, the wish for a desire'.[37]

We might transpose this analysis into Marx's later thought, where what has changed is not the relation to abstraction, but the ontology of self-sufficient abstraction. There, the illusion of self-sufficiency is no longer exclusively associated with philosophy (and hence subject to epistemological critique), but is identified with the *actual* abstractions or idealities of the value-form (and hence subject to social critique). In this respect, boredom becomes a central part of that form of subjectivity constituted by the dynamics of the commodity form – as Benjamin's path-breaking but fragmentary analyses testify. Boredom in art, we might thus speculate, has something to do with the character of art's engagement with the commodity form, with a new relationship to possibility derived from its very emptiness (negation of use-value). 'It has always been one of the primary tasks of art', Benjmain argued, 'to create a demand whose hour of satisfaction has not yet come.'[38] It is as demand that art functions politically. Boredom intensifies the demand. Benjamin never moved beyond the series of elliptical formulations about boredom, interspersed with materials from its history, in the *Arcades Project*, but he indicated one way forward with the rhetorical question, 'What is the dialectical antithesis to boredom?'[39] The silent answer is 'distraction' – hence Benjamin's parallel interest in developing a (technologically based) theory of reception in distraction.[40] We can see the emergence here of a constellation – boredom, distraction, immersion/absorption – fracturing any simply binary dialectical relations, dependent upon detailed accounts of historically specific technologies and institutions for its articulation. This is a constellation of temporalities of attention the investigation of which produces further temporal forms, in turn.

Distracted reception (duration and rhythm)

Art distracts and art compels attention, art bores and art produces distraction. Today, perhaps more than ever before, art is received in distraction. For Benjamin, in the 1930s, 'reception in distraction' was already 'the sort of reception which is increasingly noticeable in all areas of art and is a symptom of profound changes in apperception.' Indeed, 'the sort of distraction that is provided by art' represented for him 'a covert measure of the extent to which it has become possible to perform new tasks of apperception'; that of a 'distracted examination' in particular, an 'evaluating attitude' that requires 'no attention'. Historically, it has been architecture that offered the prototype of an artwork that is 'received in a state of distraction', but Benjamin took the 'training ground' of distracted reception in his day to be film; or rather cinema, as a particular architectural space and social use of the temporal qualities of film.[41] By the 1960s the cultural training ground of distracted reception had changed location, from cinema to television. Commercial cinema remained a distraction, but as a routinized narrative spectacle that absorbed the viewer, it set few new tasks of apperception, leading to a revival of that 'ancient lament that the masses seek distraction', from which Benjamin (following Kracauer) had so decisively distanced himself.[42] Today, with the digitally based convergence of audio-visual communication technologies, the training ground of distracted reception has moved again, from television to the multiplying sites and social functions of the interactive, liquid crystal computer-display screen: smartphones and tablet computers, in particular. We are experiencing a new, much more spatially diffuse 'cult of distraction' of the internet, the social and economic – but not yet the artistic – significance of which is clear.[43]

This is the context of a renewed – and newly historical – interest in film and video in art spaces, in which 'the sort of distraction provided by art', and 'the new tasks of apperception' to which it attests, are at issue once more. As the economic logic of the cultural industries imposes itself on art institutions, subsuming them into its cycles of reproduction, the question of what modes of experience are specific to art, at any particular historical moment, finds itself enlivened once again by technology. Technologies that were once artistically avant-garde (like video) are now commonplace, while the obsolescent commonplaces of the recent past (such as 16 mm film) are being artistically revived by an avant-garde, looking back to previous avant-gardes, in search of more opaque, less immediately received, artistic materials with which to interrupt the new perceptual habits. It is nearly fifty years since Yoko Ono first used closed-circuit video to introduce a real-time live image into gallery space, in *Sky TV* (1966), in which a camera on the roof transmitted live images of the sky to the TV monitor in the gallery below. Today such CCTV imaging is ubiquitous, to be sampled rather than artistically inhabited. In the meantime, works like Matthew Barney's *Cremaster Cycle* turned to the production techniques and certain of the film forms of 1960s and 1970s commercial film; and younger artists self-consciously mimic the (in)formal techniques characteristic of the use of film by conceptual artists in the 1960s. This has less to do with any 'revolutionary energy of the outmoded', than with a more general experimental rearticulation and refunctioning of technologies of perception and patterns of artistic and social use.

That art distracts, as well as resists distraction and is received in distraction, is as true of art in gallery-space today as it was of early cinema. The ideology of 'contemplative immersion' in, or 'absorption' by, the artwork continues to regulate its reception, but distraction is itself deeply implicated in the demand for this special kind of attention. We go to the gallery, in part, to be distracted from the cares and worries of the world. To be so distracted, we must attend to the artworks on display. Yet, once there, the kind of attention demanded by the works (demanded of you by the institution when in front of the works) – contemplative immersion – can produce an anxiety that generates a need for distractions; either because the work does not seem able to sustain such attention – does not help the viewer maintain such attention – or, perhaps, because of the disciplinary character of the demand itself. This need for distraction is readily fulfilled by the gallery: by the sounds and movements and sight of other viewers, by the beguiling architecture of gallery-space (which so frequently overwhelms the works), the view out the window, the curatorial information cards, the attendants, by the gallery shop, the café – as well as by other works. Perhaps this is the function of grouping works together in the same visual space: they provide a psychic space of distraction which eases the anxiety involved in giving oneself up to a particular work. Other works 'gaze' at the viewer behind his or her back, making their own claims on their time, providing the reassurance of possible distraction.

Certainly, contemporary art is received with an attention invested with an anxiety about distraction: both distraction from the work and the 'distraction from distraction' that is attention to the work. Here, attention *is* distraction (from distraction); distraction *is* attention (to other objects). The dialectic of attention and distraction outlines an embodied, non-perspectival, baroque space of distraction[44] – however much the architecture of conventional gallery space (the 'hysterical cell' of the white cube) may try to contain it and discipline it. Its temporal aspect is a dialectics of duration, of continuity and interruption, of rhythm. As such, it is a particular inflection of the process of temporalization – the production of time – itself. Contemporary art intervenes into this temporal dialectic, syncopating the time of the viewer into new rhythms and forms.

In its most general sense, 'duration' names that form of temporal continuity – the experience of being in time – by which time is distinguished from space. It is generally taken to have achieved its first philosophical elaboration in St Augustine's notion of an expanded, 'threefold' present to which reference was made at the outset of this chapter: the coincident consciousness of the past, the present and the future, in memory, attention and expectation, respectively. As a temporal totality – there is nothing in time outside this present – the expanded present is not point-like (the instant), but endures. It endures dynamically as a constant movement between its constituent parts, as what was present to attention becomes memory, new objects of attention are realized, new expectations arise and so on. Today, it is the French philosopher Henri Bergson with whom the concept of duration is primarily associated. For Bergson sought to render duration absolute, by arguing for the complete separation of time as duration from its conceptual dependence on being represented in spatial terms. (The familiar idea of time as a succession of instants, for example, depends upon representing it spatially, as a line; and the Augustinian notion of an 'expanded' present remains dependent upon this spatial analogy.)

According to Bergson in his *Essay on the Immediate Data of Consciousness* (1889), 'time, conceived under the form of a homogeneous medium, is some spurious concept, due to the trespassing of the idea of space upon the field of pure consciousness.' It is 'nothing but the ghost of space haunting the reflective consciousness.' Pure duration, on the other hand, is 'succession without distinction'. It is pure *qualitative* differentiation, without quantitative measure: 'the form which the succession of our conscious states assumes when our ego lets itself *live*, when it refrains from separating its present state from its former states.' This is a 'continuous or qualitative multiplicity with no resemblance to number.' It has as its image the unity of the notes of a tune, which are not discrete to consciousness but continuous, 'each permeating the other'.[45]

Bergson went on to elaborate this phenomenological metaphysics of time in relation to both matter (*Matter and Memory: Essay on the Relation of Body to Mind*, 1896) and evolution (*Creative Evolution*, 1907). Having pushed the dualism of mind and body (time and space) to an extreme, he claimed there to have transcended it with a new philosophy of life based on a single dynamic impulse, the *élan vital*. Initially conceived as a psychological phenomenon, duration became the metaphysically real sphere of 'virtuality', from which (spatial) actuality is incessantly produced as a world of discrete beings and relations by the creative and transformative processes of life itself: 'duration means invention, the creation of forms, the continual elaboration of the absolutely new ... the organized body ... grows and changes without ceasing.'[46] Concrete durations are thus qualitative times specific to the life of different organisms, 'cut out' of the continuous flow of pure duration by the self-organization of life.

After a period at the beginning of the twentieth century in which this religious naturalism of the élan vital dominated French intellectual life, Bergson's philosophy fell rapidly into obscurity in the 1930s, from which it has been rescued only recently by Deleuze, largely on the basis of its affinity with cinema.[47] This was a connection that Bergson himself made as early as 1907, when he referred to 'The Cinematographical Mechanism of Thought' in the title to chapter four of *Creative Evolution*. Despite its apparent historical distance from current debates, this connection (exploited by Deleuze to other ends) can help to clarify a decisive difference between cinema, on the one hand, and film and video in art spaces, on the other.

Bergson's attempt to establish the metaphysical distinctiveness of time via its absolute independence from, and primacy over, space, is the philosophical correlate of the cinematic ideology of the de-realized image. This is an ideology of visual perception that functions by repressing the spatial conditions of viewing; just as cinema itself progressively 'blanked out' all distractions but the screen, in a populist mimicry of the contemplative immersion demanded of the viewer of art by aestheticism. The marked spatiality of the modes of display of film and video in art spaces, on the other hand, and crucially, the movement of the viewer through gallery space, undercuts the false absolutization of time to which cinema is prone. Furthermore, it highlights the *constructed* – rather than received – character of temporal continuity.

Bergson treated 'pure duration' as an absolute continuity from which the continuity of concrete durations derives. However, this begs the question of how continuities within being (and especially psychic continuity) are possible, since they must be established in the face of – across and against – temporal discontinuity as the level of beings (in space), rather than within the virtuality of pure duration itself. For as Bergson himself insisted, time is continuous only as virtuality, hence as 'nothingness': never in being. Within being, there will therefore always be a *dialectical dependence of continuity upon discontinuity*. In Bachelard's words, 'psychic continuity is not given but made'. And it is made out of the temporal structure of the relations between acts: 'what has most duration is what is best at *starting itself up all over again*'.[48] Duration is a dialectical process of continuity, interruption, and beginning again – always beginning again. The fundamental concept of time is thus not continuity (as Bergson thought), but temporalization as rhythm. And the fundamental concept of a general rythmics is 'the restoration of form'.[49]

Time-based technologies of representation construct their own forms of temporal continuity out of their own technologically specific temporal differentiations (twenty-four frames per second, for example). And the temporality of reception will be a product of this temporality of the work and the other temporalities at play in the field of the viewer (the viewer as field) – temporalities that are embodied articulations of spatial relations. Each work makes its own time, in relation to its space, and hence to other times; but it can only succeed in doing so by taking account of the spatio-temporal conditions – the dialectics of attention, boredom and distraction – characteristic of its prevailing reception. It is through the spatial articulations of temporal relations that time is socialized. The temporal dialectic of distracted reception, into which art film and video intervene, is a socio-spatial as well as a psychological one. Indeed, when Benjamin wrote of reception 'in a state of distraction', he identified it with reception 'through the collective' – that is, with a certain public use.[50] (Distraction, one might say, is the sociality of attention.) This raises the question of the character of the collectivity at work in the distracted reception of contemporary film and video art; and through it, the question of the broader, historical time within which it is inscribed and upon which it draws. There is a complex overlay of rhythms condensed into the casual act of viewing a work of art. One criterion of judgement of a work – one new task of apperception – might be the extent to which it opens up this network of temporal connections (psychic, social, historical) to reflective and transfigurative view.

Large-scale quasi-cinematic video installation, for example, is a staple of contemporary art. The sort of distraction it provides is in some respects not unlike that of early cinema, in that it acknowledges its spatial conditions as part of the viewing experience, albeit usually only negatively, by enclosing itself off from the rest of the gallery, but only for a relatively short while in the viewer's tour. But the form of collectivity here is very far from that of the cinematic masses of Kracauer's picture palaces; it is a privatized, serial, small group affair. The work has only a short time to engage, and immobilize, the sampling viewer, by imposing its image and rhythm – although once captured the cinematic conditions of blackout will help to keep the viewer lingering, before they move off and out to the next distraction. A work displayed on a monitor, perhaps, standing ignored in a gallery corner. What this points to, I think, is a deepening of distracted perception, psychic attention in dispersal, not as a barrier to, but more simply, as a condition of reception. At their best, contemporary galleries reproduce the antagonistic multiplicity of the social image-space in such a way as to impose new reflective rhythms of absorption, distraction and boredom, new articulations of duration, interruption, beginning, ending, repetition and delay. The non-places of informational cities are their context; digital technologies are the basis of their operational techniques; and increasingly, the philosophy of time holds the key to understanding the possibilities inherent in the experience of the works on display.

If attention is the temporal orientation that comes first, phenomenologically, in the reception of art, it is memory that is supposed to bear the burden of historical meaning. In fact, currently, memory is understood to be crucial to contemporary art not merely as a condition of its reception into art history (which is a weakening aspect of critical discourse), but as part of its very contemporaneity, as a mode of relation to broader, 'cultural' pasts. Memory is supposed to function here within the work itself, as the concrete presence of particular pasts within the present. However, its relationship to the more strictly *historical* meaning of works of contemporary art is problematic. In its culturally extended conception, memory has come to stand in for historical consciousness.

Memory or history?

The dominance of cultural memory as an interpretative trope in the anglophone humanities, established during the 1990s, has more recently been extended to contemporary art. Particularly striking – within curatorial discourse, criticism and artistic self-description – is the combination of claims to cultural memory with claims to contemporaneity. Claims to contemporaneity are frequently now made not merely via, but *as* claims to cultural memory, in a way that overwhelms other possibilities both for interpreting such work and for marking its contemporaneity. As a result, the historical present is being artistically defined, more and more, in a primarily backward-looking manner, as a time of memory, of recovery, in the very act of articulating its distance or separation from the past that is being remembered. Contemporary works are being understood and valorised as artefacts of remembrance, while remembrance is reduced to, or identified with, memory or recollection, and linked to testimony.

At the same time, as part of this operation, memory is effectively being identified with historical experience itself. Memory claims have thereby become one of the main tools for *existential authentication* and *political legitimation* in art discourse. In particular, the 'culturalization' of memory functions as a medium for the culturalization of political differences. It naturalizes these differences into a hardening 'second nature'. In this way, memory is in danger of becoming a medium of forgetting – a forgetting of the past as active *within*, as opposed to in its separation from, the present – in a reactive manner.[51]

These issues arise at two main levels of analysis. First, at a general-theoretical level, there is a conventional distinction between memory and history. That distinction is here reasserted, sharpened and applied to the historical present – a present that suggests a radical disjunction between the forms of social subjectivity required for something like 'cultural memory' and the social subjects (or 'speculative collectives') at stake in the historically contemporary art of the new kinds of transnational art space. Second, at an artistic level, there is a requirement for the critical interpretation of particular works. I undertake that here through a brief critical comparison of three recent video works which, whilst each taking particular historical events as their subjects (the Lebanese wars, 1975–2001; the abduction and rape of women over a sixty-year period of Indian history; and the communal riots in the state of Gujarat in India in 2002), represent alternative approaches to the issues at stake.

In considering this work, a strong distinction must be made between the problematic notion of art *as* cultural memory (which attempts to suture art to history through a common social subject) and the use of testimony as an artist material – an element of construction – within the art of a reflective historical experience. One of the main problems with the use of the 'memory model' in contemporary art concerns a recurrent failure to register specifically artistic mediations of spatio-temporal relations; a failure to distinguish the way art works (and hence *is*) in different kinds of art space; and hence a failure to appreciate the kind of work required to engage critically with the new transnational social spaces of art. The issue, then, in part, is what *concepts*, what *narratives*, what *theoretical operations* must be put into play for works to function critically in transnational spaces? A philosophically naïve view of memory is one of the main barriers to the production of a critical art. It is the temporal correlate of certain prevalent, empiricist misunderstanding of the artistic significance of 'site', as an apparent ground of artistic meaning, discussed in the previous chapter.

It is conventional, in histories of the discipline of history, such as Jacques le Goff's *History and Memory*,[52] to narrate the emergence of history as the result of a growing separation of historical representation from memory. To be sure, history has its origin and its ontological basis in the unity of individual and collective memories, as registered in the form of the epic and the structure of tradition, as direct, intersubjective, transgenerational transmission. Nonetheless, historiography, the history of the historians and – most importantly for the current situation – history in its modern, post-eighteenth-century *world-historical* sense, begins with the *fracturing* of this unity of individual and collective memory, the *multiplication* of reminiscences and the consequent need for artificial *constructions* of the collective meaning of the past through the assembly and interpretation of exterior, documentary sources. Hence the primacy of the document and the archive in modern historiography.

Recently, however, there have been powerful attempts, most frequently psychoanalytical in form, to reinstate a metaphorically expanded conception of memory as the medium of historical experience. 'Trauma', 'melancholy' and 'mourning' have been extended from categories of individual psychic life to become privileged terms of collective experience in the discourses of both cultural and political history. And these discourses have, in turn, come to play an increasingly central role in discourse on contemporary art, where they are frequently used to re-valorize artists' biographies, and especially their childhood; often serving as a political alibi for the revival of a badly Romantic artistic individualism, legitimating itself through claims to cultural exemplarity.

The motivation for this return to memory is to counter the existential and political effects of the alienation of historical representation from experience, consequent upon the collapse of secular world-historical political projects (socialism and communism), since the culture of capitalist modernity is characterised by a simultaneous abundance of historical representations and a scarcity of forms of historical consciousness and experience. An expanded conception of, and role for, memory thus holds out the hope (and often makes the promise) of healing this rift, of making history, or rather, particular histories – and it is the 'particular' here which does all the work – available as experience. History is *only* 'real' or 'lived', on this view, *as* memory. This is a reversal of the genealogy of the concept of history.

Art plays an important role here because of its culturally privileged relations to subjectivity and feeling. It is through the aesthetic representation or restaging of processes of 'trauma', 'melancholy' and 'mourning', it is often believed, that these processes can be most effectively communicated collectively as *experience*, and, it is believed, such experiences are experiences of history. Such representations often have the explicit political function of sustaining or shoring-up particular existing, often eroded cultural collectivities. Yet might it not be that, to put the case in its harshest form, in the words of Gayatri Spivak: 'The time for producing historically thin "theory" describing the feeling of migrants in pseudo-psychoanalytical vocabulary is over.'[53] It is over, politically, because it has lost its passing progressive function of drawing attention to the legitimate existence of such communities and their histories, and has become the primary discursive mode of their incorporation into regimes of political management. More importantly, from a theoretical standpoint, it rests on a profoundly misguided conception of the way in which historical meaning is produced, both in contemporary art and more generally, for several related reasons of which I shall cite just three: 1. It misunderstands the constructed character of historical representation. 2. It reduces history to representations of past events. 3. It assumes a set of relations between individual subjectivity, social subjects, collectivity and the process of history, which, while still ideologically dominant, is undergoing a process of fundamental historical erosion and transformation.

Each of these things involves a disavowal of the scope and theoretical significance of the ultimate speculative object of historical representation, the transgenerational unity of the human, which is the transcendental horizon or condition of possibility of experience: the idea of history, in the Kantian sense.[54] History is a construction (in a constructivist sense), in the first place, because it must be pieced together out of elements that have been severed from the subjectivity of individual subjects. In this sense, historical representation (as opposed to memory) is grounded on recognition of the absolute character of death; history presupposes and is constituted by death. This is a historical-ontological condition that runs far deeper than the epistemological problems of representation that are associated with the label 'social constructivism', in disciplines such as psychology and sociology, and which are the sorts of thing that give rise to philosophical worries about relativism and scepticism. Rather, because its elements are elements of the world, historical constructivism is a type of realism (an ontological realism) – it has an indexical base. In fact, in this respect, in one dominant usage, the concept of memory has itself been metaphorically transformed, via an analogical objectivization, to refer to a capacity to repeat which is independent of subjectivity. I refer here to computer memory, for example; or the 'memory of heredity' attributed by biology to genetic codes. This is not memory in its primary and restored sense as the technical practice of a subject, or an art, as described in Frances Yates's famous *The Art of Memory*.[55] It is, however, close to its ontological ground in the body.

The restoration of a memory model for history is epistemologically sophisticated about its own limitations; it recognizes the impossibility of fulfilling the goal of historicism (to reconstruct historical processes and events 'the way they really were', in Ranke's nineteenth-century sense). It uses psychoanalytical concepts to diagnose the fantastic character of the aspiration. Yet it is still wedded to the aspiration as an ideal to be approximated through the comprehension of the necessity of the deviations from it. This is rendered plausible only by the limitation of the object of historical representation to the temporal relationship between the present and the past.

It is the virtue of the memory model that it associates history with the *living*, that is, with the present, and not just the past. Indeed, it is one of the main functions of the concept of memory to 'enliven' the past, to give it life within the present. However, it is still too temporally restricted in its expansion of the historicist past, including as 'living' a relation to the present alone. For history is not just a relationship between the present and the past – it is equally about the future. It is this speculative futural moment that definitively separates the concept of history from memory. History is about the future in at least two ways. On the one hand, it is only from the standpoint of a particular future that the ultimate object of history – the unity of the human – can be thought. In this respect, history (like art) is inherently utopian. This is something that ties art to history. It is beyond the scope of all actually existing social subjects. It projects collectivity beyond all actually existing forms. On the other hand, the genealogical primacy of the present in the construction of the past itself contains particular possible futures within it, in the form of expectations and desires that regulate both selection and construction in historical representation, within the regulative framework of the broader terms of its utopian projection of the human itself. (The human is itself a utopian concept here.) The problem with the reactive use of cultural memory is that, as a passive forgetting, it administers the expectations and desires of the present in such a way as to repress those aspects of the past that are attached to the possible futures that existing powers have an interest in suppressing.

The memory model presumes that historical understanding can be grounded in the recovery of a set of determinate intersubjective relations. Not only is this problematic as a matter of general principle, but it neglects the historical fact that what we might call capitalistic sociality (the grounding of social relations in exchange relations) is essentially abstract, and as such, a matter of *form*, rather than of collectivity. This is the historical specificity of capitalist sociality. As argued in Chapter 1, above, collectivity is produced by the interconnectedness of practices, but the universal interconnectedness and dependencies that are produced exhibit the structure of a subject (the unity of an activity) only objectively – that is, in separation from both individual subjects and all *particular* collectivities of labour – principally, as developments of the value-form. Historically, nationalism (the cultural fiction of nations) has filled this lacuna between particular collectivities and capital. Nations (Benedict Anderson's 'imagined communities') have been the privileged social subjects of 'cultural memory' in capitalist states. But the subject-structure of capital no longer corresponds to the territorially discrete entities of nation-states; and those societies outside the nexus of transnational capital are being drawn inexorably into it. In this respect, the collectivity of capitalism is, structurally, still, and will always be likely to be, 'to-come'. Hence, the abstract and wholly formal anticipation of it in a concept 'multitude', which nonetheless becomes politically identified with actual collectivities, thereby, in fact (although not necessarily in the political imaginations of those affirming it) registering their partiality and incompleteness.

The question of the contemporary in 'contemporary art' is the question of the definition of the qualitative novelty of this historical present – that is, the question of the new – and its constant reforming, reframing and reconfiguration of the political meaning and possibilities of social subjects. In relation to the historical and political meanings of works of international contemporary art, everything thus depends on one's sense of what collectivities are implicitly being represented through the constitutive role in the ontological structure of this art played by the inter- and transnational character of the new art spaces. The critical point here is that the forms of collectivity projected by the model of 'art as memory' (primarily, various forms of either *communal*, *national* or *regional* culture) are in contradiction with the forms of social relation that constitute the space of their representation (namely, the new forms of transnational interconnection). Furthermore, the social relations constitutive of these new spaces are in many ways exemplary of the main economic developments constituting the global post-communist historical present: the contradictory penetration of existing social forms (communities, cultures, nations, societies – *all* increasingly inadequate formulations) by exchange relations and their enforced interconnection and dependency. However, as we argued at the outset, in the emergent historical present, new *speculative collectives* (non-national or 'parastate' collectives) are starting to be glimpsed on the basis of the new technological and geo-economic forms that are affecting a radical re-spatialization of social relations. The most artistically effective (that is, art-critically and historically effective) art of the new inter- and trans-national art spaces projects such speculative collectives as its imagined recipient, and even, in the best cases, as its absent but possible producers. It is only within this context – constructions of the speculative collectivity of the historical present – that the problem of the relationship of memory to history in contemporary art can be adequately posed. We can see what this means more concretely by comparing some recent works in which the question of the relationship of memory to history is explicitly posed, via the presentation of testimonies.

The art of The Atlas Group (1999–2005) is once again emblematic of the critical thrust of the argument here, which might be summed by the title of Volume One of the Group's works: *The Truth Will Be Known*

When the Last Witness Is Dead. This is a profoundly subversive and dialectical phrase. It stages the auto-destruction of the memory model of historical experience, since it takes the identification of historical consciousness with the totality of testimony to its absurd conclusion: the truth will be known only at the completion of testimonies, at which time it will have become wholly uncertain, since by then even 'the last witness' will be dead. One might call this *the antinomy of testimony*. This phrase places The Atlas Group, definitively, *against* the memory model. It recalls Walter Benjamin's famous remark: 'Truth is the death of intention'.[56] It is because truth is at stake in art, that art is itself a death of intention. Yet all three works articulate a critical relationship between memory and history, in one way or another.

Testimonies: Three works

Amar Kanwar's *The Lightning Testimonies* (2007) is a four-wall video documentary video work first shown at Documenta 12 in Kassel, Germany, and subsequently in a rather different, less claustrophobic and less spectacular way, at the Indian Highways show at the Serpentine Gallery in London (December 2008–February 2009). The work presents testimony of the abduction and rape of women at critical moments in Indian history, from the 1947 partition up to the present. In the course of 1947, 75,000 women were abducted. The most recent footage, from 2004, is of a demonstration outside an army barracks by Manipuri women, against the rape and killing of a Manipuri girl by the Indian army. The main intervening events narrated in the work relate to the post-1957 conflict in Kashmir (the footage is from the post-1991 upsurge of the separatist movement) and the ongoing Naga insurgency (for which oral testimony of women's three-week captivity in an army camp accompanies footage of the victims' families and friends in the village where they were attacked). In Benjaminian terms, there is a constellation of specific 'then's, each of which appears as part of a dialectical pairing with the same 'now'. A narrative voice-over represents this 'now', suturing the historically disparate narrative elements into the disjunctive synthesis of a series (Figs 17 and 18).[57]

Kanwar presents documents directly *as* testimony, with a multiplicity and plurality of voices that serve not to question, but to reinforce its evidential value, and hence its unity as truth. However, the focus of the piece, critically and politically, is as much on the consequences of this truth as the presentation of the truth itself: the contradictions and tragedies of a reconciliation that involves the arbitrariness of a governmental 'righting' of wrong, which mirrors the original wrong of enforced displacement. Such at least appears

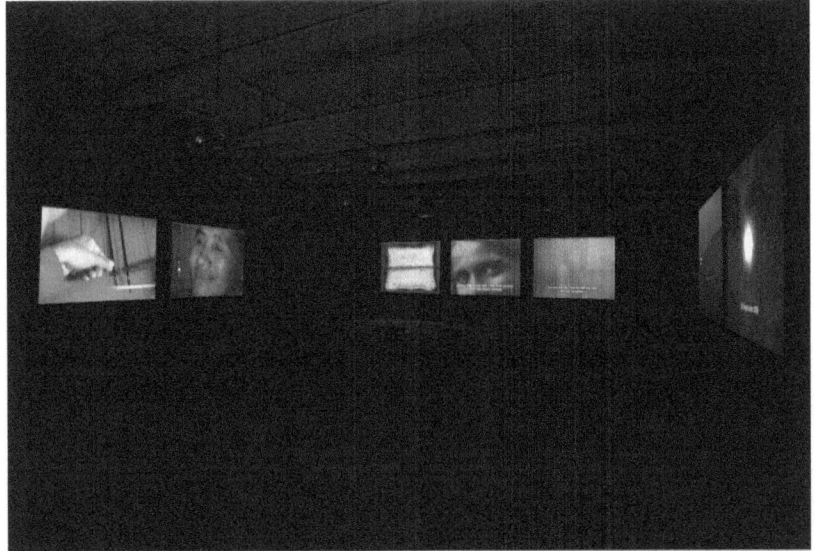

Fig. 17: Amar Kanwar, *The Lightning Testimonies*, 2007

to have been the result of India's 1949 Abducted Persons (Recovery and Restoration) Act.

The Lightning Testimonies is not naïve about memory. It both explicitly problematizes remembrance and uses simple but highly formalized means to present the documentary material. The opening voice-over asks, 'How do *we* remember? What remains and what gets submerged?' And later, in relation to legal testimonies, 'How does *one* remember? How does *one* tell? That you were raped.' The indeterminacies of subject and narrative are cut through by the simplifying power of a factual 'that' (the fact of the rape is not in doubt), allied to the impersonality of legal form. Yet this is itself a narrative *effect*. The main formal means are threefold: a montage of discrete film genres, repetition and a distinctive use of sound. The genres are those of the archival, the documentary and the everyday (trains, washing, rain). Most of the two-screen segments appear six times in five-minute cycles. The sound – of trains, thunder, rain and an atonal dissonant musical score – reinforces the experience of repetition as at once an external imposition and appropriated bodily rhythm. The work is thus highly constructed, but in such a way as to appear as if its truth and affect (force) derives from the factual content of the subjective knowledges of the testimonies themselves; the fragmented character of which evoke a post-traumatic fragmentation of the self. The contradictions of a 'reconciling' relocation appear as exclusively governmental – the result of the very same centralization of violence within a formally federal constitution which perpetrated the

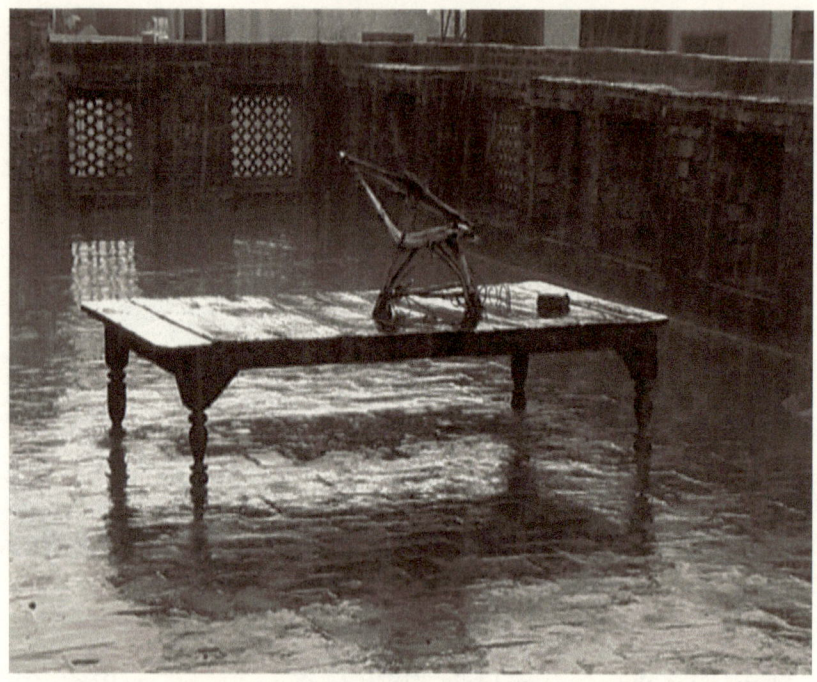

Fig. 18: Amar Kanwar, *The Lightning Testimonies*, 2007

initial violence. The subaltern position appears as a pure outside. This is the ideological function of the quasi-anthropological use of the documentary genre.

Navjot Altaf's *Lacuna in Testimony – Version 2* (2005), shown at the 2006 Sydney Biennale, represents an alternative strategic response to what I take to be the problem motivating Kanwar: namely, the adequacy of testimony to historical events, and the modes of representation through which it is constructed as historical meaning. (An earlier, 2001, installation work by Altaf is entitled *Between Memory and History*.) *Lacuna in Testimony – Version 2* is a nine-and-a-half minute 3-screen video of breaking waves, across which forty-eight windows successively appear, containing both film and still photographic images related to traumatic events in the history of India, and elsewhere; forty-eight corresponding mirrors on the floor completed the installation (Fig. 19).

Lacuna in Testimony is 'about' a single specific event: the communal riots in the state of Gujarat in India in 2002 at the height of the rule of the Bharatiya Janata Party (BJP), the right-wing Hindu nationalist party, which led the national government from 1998 to 2004. The riots were precipitated by events in the Muslim border town of Godhra, following the burning of a bus. The video focuses on the city of Ahmedabad, where transit camps were set up for displaced Muslims. However, it seeks to give a wider historical meaning to these events, analogically, through comparison with other murderous moments, not only in Indian history (again, the 1947 partition, but also the Sikh riots in Delhi and the 1993 Mumbai riots), but within a Westernized twentieth-century world history, and in particular, a sequence of traumatic historical events: European fascism, the Holocaust, Hiroshima and 9/11. This is the function of the windows. Images are progressively overlaid within each window until the frame is 'frozen' by a slab of ice. This is thus a heavily symbolic and allegorical piece, which relies upon certain very well-known historical imagery for an analogical construction of historical meaning. The work is addressed to a Western gaze, within whose pre-established terms a claim is made for the genocidal character of the events in Gujarat. Analogy fills the evidential gap, the 'lacuna in testimony' (figs 20–23).

We may contrast these constructivist, and more lyrical and metaphorical approaches to documentary, respectively, with The Atlas Group's fictionalizing but nonetheless objectivistic approach to Lebanese history – its unitary fictional narration of documentary evidence – in *We Can Make Rain But No One Came to Ask* (2004–06), the piece discussed in Chapter 1, above, in the context of the fictional status of 'the contemporary' itself. The features of that work relevant here, once again, are, first, its use of fictional characters to narrate – and hence to unify – a constructed but nonetheless documentary history; and second, the anonymous fictional collectivity of the artistic persona (The Atlas Group, which is actually a pseudonym of the Lebanese-American artist Walid Raad). This dual fictionalization functions to undercut the claims

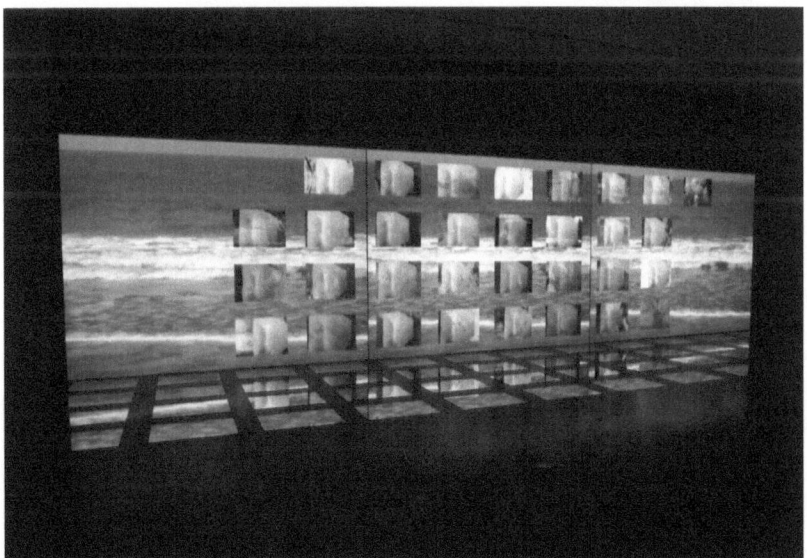

Fig. 19: Navjot Altaf, *Lacuna in Testimony – Version 2*, 2005

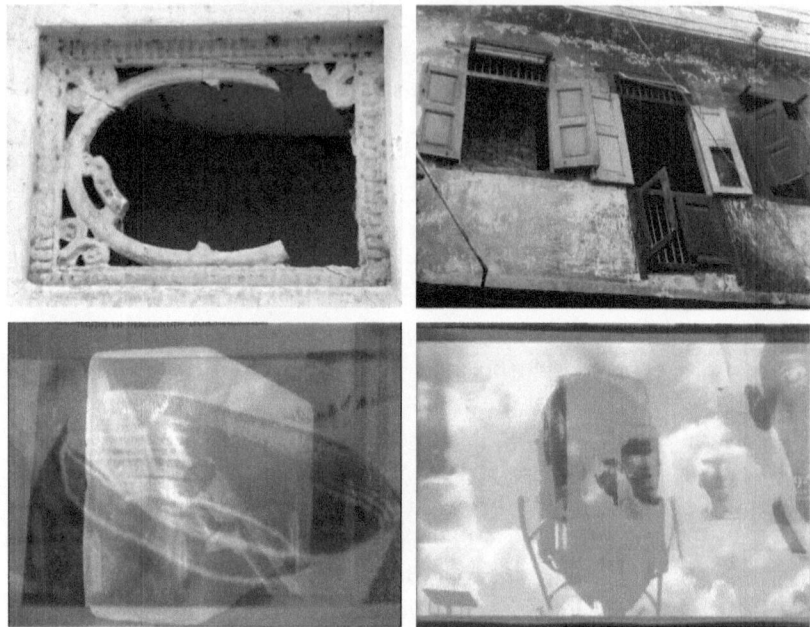

Figs: 20–23. Navjot Altaf, *Lacuna in Testimony – Version 2*, 2005

of witnessing, in favour of a scepticism (much emphasized in the critical literature – overemphasized, in fact) which is nonetheless counterbalanced by the indexical objectivity of the documentary elements of the work, through which meaning is constructed artistically, rather than being reconstructed from the subjective claims of actual witnessing subjects. The work itself thus becomes the subject of the utterance, rather than functioning as the relay, in one way or another, for 'authentic' testimonial voices, although the idea that there are such voices is the *fiction* through which it takes its distance from them.

Each of these three works thus deals with the problem of the 'inadequacy' of testimony in a different way. Kanwar, through the multiplication of documented voices and a post-traumatic fragmentation of narrative; Altaf, through emblematization and historical analogy; The Atlas Group, through philosophical critique and a radically constructivist, fictionalized alternative. Yet they also share certain formal features: they are all video works; they all use multiple tracks or split screens as indexes of narrative 'layering'; and in particular, they all use sound rhythmically to register a more somatic, pre-symbolic level of memory, as a device to ground visual representations in a more embodied perceptual experience – be it traumatic or 'everyday': breaking waves (Altaf), thunder and rain (Kanwar), traffic (Atlas Group). Indeed, Geeta Kapur has suggested that there may be something intrinsic in the very medium of video that 'corresponds' to 'the *already disassembled* nation', which furnishes the geo-political context for each of these works: specifically, its democratic availability, facility and the ease with which it can be used to de- and re-construct images.[58]

Yet each of these three works makes a different strategic use of these formal features. Kanwar's environmental eight-screen surround mimics the 'immersion' of traditional aesthetic appreciation, but in the non-contemplative, engaged mode of a viewer forced actively to construct the relations between different kinds of testimony and representation. Altaf's three-channel, three-screen installation with mirrors and multiple moving video windows both symbolizes (the sea) and allegorizes (the windows) forgetting. The Atlas Group's single-channel but split-screen address figures a unitary narrative projection split from within. *The Lightning Testimonies* is the most powerful in its immediate emotional affect, the most didactic, and the closest to the 'non-art' form of the documentary. *Lacuna in Testimony* is the most ambitious in its range of historical references, and also the most self-consciously poetic, but it is also thereby simultaneously the most academic and rhetorical; the most problematic in its straining for an affect that risks becoming divorced from form. There is a danger in its analogical generalization of a certain historical levelling or indifference – a resigned humanism. *We Can Make Rain But No One Came to Ask* is the most explicitly conceptual and least explicitly 'affective': it gives the greatest amount of reflective determinacy to the fictional aspect of history and the speculative character of collectivity. For all these differences, however, each piece works – in so far as it works – not as an artefact *of* cultural memory, but as a *constructed* history; a staging of the disparity between memory and historical experience through a subjugation of memories to artistic form.

Symptomatically, there is far less contemporary art presented in the temporal mode of expectation than of memory. Western capitalist societies (and their transnational cultural prostheses) have come to expect less and remember more – or at least to surround themselves with representations coded as memories, of one sort or another. However, to insist on the constitutive function of the future (a different future) within the extended present is not necessarily to insist on expectation, in the sense in which it has been understood since Augustine. In fact, a certain conservatism may be detected within the concept of expectation itself, inherited from its Christian pre-history, and reproduced by the phenomenological notion of the 'horizon of expectation'. A critique of expectation as a historico-temporal orientation is thus necessary if the possibilities of a more radically futural aspect to contemporary art are to be grasped.

Expectation as a historical category (critique of Koselleck)

In early twentieth-century European philosophy, Augustine's proto-phenomenological conception of the threefold present was formally freed from its theological presuppositions by the technical rigours of Edmund Husserl's idea of philosophy as 'pure phenomenology'. In the process, the concept of expectation was subjected to Husserl's methodological conception of the 'horizon'. The theologically determined historical framework of the Christian doctrine of the Last Days was thereby replaced by a descriptive idea of the 'horizon of expectation'. A rethinking of the political meaning of expectation thus requires a revisiting of the concept of horizon of expectation and a reconstruction of its conceptual grammar. Should we think of our relationship to the future in terms of new horizons, or, do we need to think beyond the concept of horizon of expectation itself?

The history of the concept of 'horizon of expectation' may be developed in three main stages: from Husserl, via Heidegger, to Reinhart Koselleck. A clue to some of the problems that infect the concept in its later, historical usage may be found in its philosophical source: Husserl's phenomenological description of the 'natural attitude' in the first chapter of Part 2 of the 1913 *First Book* of his *Ideas Pertaining to a Pure Phenomenology and to Phenomenological Philosophy – General Introduction to a Pure Phenomenology* – the chapter entitled 'The Positing That Belongs to the Natural Attitude and Its Exclusion.' It is important to appreciate something of the philosophical specificity of this founding usage. Husserl is discussing the intentional constitution of meaning in perception: 'What is ... perceived and what is more or less clearly co-present and determinate (or at least somewhat determinate)', he writes, 'are penetrated and surrounded by an *obscurely intended to horizon of indeterminate actuality*.' Husserl continues:

> I can send rays of the illuminative regard of attention into this horizon with varying results. Determining presencings [*Vergegenwärtigungen*/ making presents], obscure at first and then becoming alive, haul something out of me; a chain of such quasi-memories is linked together; the sphere of determinateness becomes wider and wider, perhaps so wide that connection is made with the field of actual perception as my *central* surroundings. But generally the result is different: an empty mist of obscure indeterminateness is populated with intuited possibilities or likelihoods; and only the 'form' of the world, precisely as 'the world' is predelineated. Moreover, my indeterminate surroundings are infinite, the misty and never fully determinable horizon is necessarily there.[59]

The misty and never fully determinable horizon is necessarily there . . . As Husserl continues, later on in the same text: 'there always remains a horizon of determinable indeterminateness.'[60]

In the first instance, then, for Husserl, a horizon is part of the 'positing' that belongs to the natural attitude, a pre-reflective immediacy, and it always involves 'a determin*able*, but never *fully* determinable, *inde*terminateness.' Horizon is thus the phenomenological version of what has been known since Kant as a boundary-concept (*Grenzebegriff*): a concept that registers and articulates the bounds of knowledge. However, unlike Kant's rigid conceptualization of transcendental limits (*Schranken*) as borders (*Grenze*) – with its binary classification of concepts that fall on one or other side of it, and are judged as either *legitimate* or *illegitimate* by the transcendental border police of self-reflecting reason – Husserl's conceptualization of limit as horizon (*Horizont*) contains an essential indefiniteness, corresponding to the *movement* of determination. This movement has an ultimate limit, of 'never *fully* determinable indeterminateness,' but – and this is the crucial thing – this limit is *not* conceived as a 'boundary' or 'border', since it does not posit anything on the other side. The horizon is phenomenologically immanent but *infinitely* receding. It remains obscure. A mist.

The concept of horizon thus transforms the spatial imaginary of the Kantian concept of limit, placing the subject of knowledge *within the field* of a moving limit, thereby however, holding it permanently at arm's length. It does so, moreover, in a way that is completely different from the everyday connotation and metaphorical field of the horizon as something that *promises* something *beyond* the limit, and is therefore associated with the idea of *hope* – in its difference from expectation. Hope is a category of the post-Kantian philosophy of religion. More specifically, since Kant, hope has been a category of moral – at best, political – theology. In the chapter on 'The Canon of Pure Reason' in the *Critique of Pure Reason*, Kant claimed that all interest of our reason is united in three questions: 'What can I know?'; 'What should I do?'; and 'What may I hope?' The third question sounds initially as if it is one of historical epistemology. However, in Kant's understanding, it is 'simultaneously practical and theoretical', for it is shorthand for the question '*If I do as I should*, what then may I hope?'[61] As such, hope is part of the Kantian problematic of ideas: concepts of objects beyond possible experience. Horizon, on the other hand, is part of a phenomenological problematic – an alternative approach to Kant's quite different question: 'What may I know?' As a spatial *image*, horizon points towards a beyond, something existent but out of sight, and hence unknown – and yet in principle knowable once you travel there. The horizon will move, but what was beyond the horizon can come to be within it, if you travel; hence the inherent hopefulness of travel. But its phenomenological meaning is not that of possibility so much as a confirmation of finitude and a subjective constitution of meaning that can never, in principle, break through the ultimate *in*determinateness of the horizon as such.

The concept of the horizon of expectation – and metaphorically at least, the notion of horizon seems to be indelibly associated with expectation, even when it refers to the past – derives, firstly, from the simple combination of the phenomenological notion of the 'misty' horizon with the similarly 'naïvely natural' concept of expectation, as *the 'forward-looking' aspect* of what is made present [*Vergegenwärtigung*] to consciousness, one of our three temporal horizons. Secondly, however, in Husserl, it derives methodologically from the 'purification' of this conceptual combination by the reflective method of the phenomenological reduction. This transcendentalizes what was previously the merely descriptive necessity of the horizon within the natural attitude, making it a condition of possibility of experience.

It is this transcendental-phenomenological understanding of horizon that was taken over by Heidegger in *Being and Time* and subjected to the problematic of the question of the meaning of being. And it is within the terms of this ontological problematic that it first acquires a practical dimension. This marks the second stage in the development of the concept. The 'provisional aim' of *Being and Time*, we are told on the first page of the book, prior to the Introduction, is 'the interpretation of *time* as the *possible horizon* for any understanding whatsoever of being'. It is thus within the terms of the transcendental-phenomenological concept of horizon that time comes, in Heidegger's writings, to assert its priority over 'being'. Heidegger's *Being and Time*, as a whole, moves within the conceptual space of horizonality. Horizon is no longer connected to temporality derivatively (as it was in Husserl), but fundamentally, through the notion of the 'horizonal schema'. As Heidegger put it in Part IV of Division 2, 'Temporality and Everydayness':

> The existential-temporal condition for the possibility of the world lies in the fact that temporality, as an ecstatical unity [a unity of the three temporal ecstasies], has something like a horizon. Ecstasies are not simply raptures in which one gets carried away. Rather, there belongs *to each ecstasis* a 'whither' to which one gets carried away. This 'whither' of the ecstasis we call the 'horizonal schema.'

Horizon is immanent to existential temporality. This is Heidegger's ontologized version of Kant's 'schematism' – the transcendental time-determinations as the schema of the pure concepts of the understanding. 'In each of the three ecstasies', Heidegger continues:

> the ecstatical horizon is different . . . The horizon of temporality *as a whole* determines that *whereupon* factically existing entities are essentially *disclosed*. With one's factical being-there, a potentiality-for-being is in each case projected in the horizon of the future . . .[62]

Unlike the phenomenological horizon of expectation, which is part of a subjective constitution of meaning, this *existential* 'horizon of the future' is ontologically fundamental. Earlier in the book, Heidegger prefigures this distinction between horizon of expectation and horizon of the future with a distinction between expectation and anticipation, as different ways of relating to the possible.

To expect something possible is always to understand it and to 'have' it with regard to whether and when and how it will be actually present-at-hand. Expecting is not just an occasional looking-away from the possible to its possible actualization, but is essentially a *waiting for that actualization*. Even in expecting, one leaps *away* from the possible and gets a foothold in the actual. It is for its actuality that what is expected is expected. By the very nature of expecting, the possible is drawn into the actual, arising out of the actual and returning to it.[63] We can feel here the shadow of Augustine's famous definition of expectation, in Book 11 of his *Confessions*, as 'the present time of future things'. In contrast, Heidegger's term for being-towards a possibility *as a possibility* is 'anticipation'. It is because, in being-towards-death, death gives us 'nothing to be "actualized"', but *is* only as a pure possibility, that the ontological distinctiveness of human existence is defined by Heidegger as 'anticipation itself'. For Heidegger, awaiting actualization is a characteristic of the '*inauthentic* future'. 'Expecting' temporalizes itself authentically only as anticipation.[64] And we can also see Heidegger breaking with the theological presuppositions of expectation, which continued to infect Husserl's conception of time-consciousness, in his understanding of more extended forms of expectation, the 'prophetic' aspect of which is explicitly acknowledged in his earlier lectures, *On the Phenomenology of the Consciousness of Internal Time*.[65]

This Heideggerian distinction between expectation and anticipation is helpful in thinking about the political implications of the historical application of the concept of 'horizon of expectation', in the light of the crisis of the Enlightenment philosophy of history. First, though, the narrative of the becoming-historical of the phenomenological concept of horizon of expectation must be completed by turning to Reinhart Koselleck's famous 1976 essay, '"Space of Experience" and "Horizon of

Expectation": Two Historical Categories.'[66] The concept of the horizon of expectation plays no role in Heidegger's 'existential-ontological exposition of the problem of history' (the title of Chapter 72 of *Being and Time*). Rather, it is with the collective and practical aspects of 'anticipatoriness' (*Vorläufigkeit*) – anticipatory resoluteness – that he is concerned. Horizon of expectation acquires its place as a historical category from Koselleck's use of it to specify the distinctiveness of *modernity* (*Neuzeit*) as a structure of historical experience, within the 'generality of history' as a whole. In this respect, Koselleck extends Husserl's concept by placing it into the context of his own work on the semantics of historical time, on the basis of Hans-Georg Gadamer's reiteration of the importance of the concept of horizon to a hermeneutical phenomenology in his 1960 *Truth and Method* (where it is, though, almost exclusively deployed with regard to the 'effective-history' of tradition: the horizon of tradition).[67]

Koselleck's thesis is threefold. First, 'during modernity [*Neuzeit*] the difference between experience and expectation has increasingly expanded; more precisely ... modernity [*Neuzeit*] is first understood as a new time [*neue Zeit*] from the time that expectations have distanced themselves evermore from all previous experience.'[68] Second, this distancing of expectation from experience is constitutive not merely of modernity but of 'history in general' as 'a totality opened towards a progressive future' – indeed, Koselleck claims, the concept of history has 'the same substantive content' as the concept of progress. Both are manifestations of the time-consciousness of modernity. In fact, 'history', in the collective singular, is an *effect* of modernity. Third, such 'expectations have themselves *produced* new possibilities at the cost of passing reality.'

The concept of horizon of expectation is thus used by Koselleck as a way of formally unifying the whole constellation of concepts, the semantic history of which his name is rightly associated with: *modernity, history, progress, revolution, the new*, and *crisis*. In particular, Koselleck is insistent upon the epochal character of the shift from the Christian doctrine of the Last Days, with its apocalyptical mode of historical expectation, to the hazards of an open but 'progressive' future. However, it is not clear that he has reflected sufficiently here either upon the *dialectic of the expected and the unexpected* that is thereby put into play in modernity, or upon the way in which the structure of historical time has been affected by the historical development of capitalism and the experience of historical communism (further complicated now, for us, by the latter's passing). In particular, he seems not to have detected the profound complicity between the phenomenological concept of horizon and *historicism*, as the philosophical form of what Heidegger, Benjamin and Louis Althusser alike conceived as the 'ordinary' or 'vulgar' understanding – we might say, ideological misrepresentation – of history.

Koselleck makes the disjunction between experience and expectation his criterion of modernity as a form of historical time. Yet he also acknowledges that it is the extent to which expectations are *exceeded* (rather than fulfilled) that 'reorders' the relations between experience and expectation: 'Only the unexpected has the power to surprise, and this surprise involves a new experience. The penetration of the horizon of expectation, therefore, is creative of new experiences.'[69] It is the concept of the new as the *un*expected that transforms the relationship between expectation and experience; and it is thus, in the part, the *unexpected* that we come to *expect* and also to value. This renders expectation dialectical, but also abstract, in a way that problematizes Husserl's depiction of it as constrained by a 'horizon' of 'determin*able*, if never *fully* determinable, *in*determinateness' – a 'predelineation' of 'the world'. For expectation of the unexpected paradoxically projects the 'penetration' of its own horizon. As such, it seems closer to what Heidegger called 'anticipatoriness' (*Vorläufigkeit*): a relation to possibility stripped of the determinate shape of a potential actuality, albeit here, nonetheless something 'objective (given by the structure of historical time), rather than grasped as an existential structure of human existence per se. The distinction is important, since the former (the structure of historical time) has definite socio-historical conditions, while the latter (the existential structure of human existence) does not. Or at least, Heidegger's philosophy forbids us to interpret it so; although, as cited above, his philosophy does acknowledge, positivistically, that '[w]ith one's *factical* being-there, a potentiality-for-being is *in each [individual] case* projected in the horizon of the future.' Famously, Heidegger's philosophy achieves a radical possibilization only at the cost of an existential abstraction from its socio-historical conditions – an existential abstraction posing, in Adorno's phrase, as 'pseudo-concreteness'.

Regarding Koselleck, though, the point is that however radically disjunctive the 'horizon of expectation' may be from what he calls the 'space of experience', it can *never* be disjunctive enough, in principle, to produce the unexpected. That comes from outside the phenomenological framework. Yet it is the unexpected that reorders the relations between the space of experience and the horizon of expectation to produce the disjunction that Koselleck takes to *define* modernity, phenomenologically, as a form of historical time. *The concept of horizon of expectation thus obscures the true structure of the problematic that it used to articulate: modernity as the production of the new.* The only phenomenological category adequate to Koselleck's account of the structure of modernity as a form of historical time is the *unexpectedness of the new*. In contrast, the role of the concept of horizon in transcendentally regulating a progressive determination of meaning aligns it with the naturalized temporal continuity of historicism: the projection of future time as chronological continuity with the past, the very opposite of a qualitatively temporalized history.[70] *In the unexpected, meaning is produced (in so far as it is produced) through dialectical negation – not further determination – of the expected.* It is true, of course, that we may come to expect such negations – and 'revolution' did, of course, become established as a horizon of expectation in the 200-year period from 1789 to 1989. However, in so far as expectation is of the genuinely *un*expected, it is not 'horizonal' in either Husserl's or Heidegger's senses. Rather, theoretically, it involves a certain readiness to subject the unexpected to dialectical retrospective interpretation and appropriation (conjunctural analysis). Practically, it involves a certain commitment to *experimental* practices of negation. The political crisis of socialist revolution, on the other hand, stemmed precisely from its becoming part of a horizon of expectation – paradigmatically, in the progressivist form of the Second International – the main object of criticism of Benjamin's 1940 fragments 'On the Concept of History'.[71]

We can see something of what is at stake here in a comparison of what are for many people two recent paradigmatic examples of the unexpectedness of an historical event: the collapse of historical communism in Eastern Europe in 1989–90, and the aerial attack on the Twin Towers of the World Trade Center in New York on 11 September 2001.

Expecting the unexpected: puncturing the horizon

These two events – the collapse of historical communism and the attack on the Twin Towers – have very different temporalities and they are very different kinds of 'event'. But they are both historical events in the same fundamental, if no longer fashionable, sense of being occurrences that move the narrative of 'history' forward. For event is, fundamentally, a narrative category and its meaning has changed as the range and complexity of types of possible narrative have expanded in the wake of literary and other modernisms.

Much has been made of the supposedly unexpected character of the collapse of historical communism. But did the collapse of historical communism really penetrate the horizon of expectation governing the dominant Western political imaginaries, or did it not rather, precisely, *determine* their previously indeterminate but nonetheless determin*able* horizon, fulfilling the long-held expectation of the unviable character of any non-capitalist historical road, thereby simultaneously extending and reinforcing that same existing horizon? *That* particular horizon of expectation was undoubtedly

Fig. 24: Mona Vătămanu and Florin Tudor, *Long Live and Thrive Capitalism!*, 2009

massively reinforced. What is actually meant by the unexpected character of the disintegration of historical communism derives, I think, from the *inability to predict* its occurrence at a particular chronological time – to see when and how it was going to happen – rather than that it was going to happen, which, as I have said, was for many, for a long time, a foregone conclusion. It is thus misleading, I think, to conceive of the post-1989 era as being characterized by a *generalized* 'loss of horizon'. Instead, one might say, it is characterized by the loss of two particular historical horizons and the generalized restitution of a third.

The lost horizons are those of 'communism' and 'revolution', respectively: 'communism' as the horizon of historical communism (an 'empty mist of obscure indeterminateness . . . populated with intuited possibilities or likelihoods' – as Husserl put it – predelineating 'only the "form"' of a world); and 'revolution', similarly, as a horizon of expectation within capitalist and colonial societies ('populated with intuited possibilities' of non-capitalistic social forms) – although the horizon of expectation of revolution had been dissolving in advanced capitalist societies since 1948, and where it persisted, it increasingly functioned as a barrier to the qualitatively historically new – a barrier to revolution, in fact, rather than the framework for it that it understood itself to be, precisely because of the manner in which it 'predelineated' it. The horizon of expectation that has emerged victorious is, of course, that of the renewed development and planetary universalization of capital accumulation as the basis of social development. 'Long Live and Thrive Capitalism!' as artists Mona Vătămanu and Florin Tudor's banner declares (Fig. 24). This inversion of the 1926 Russian revolutionary slogan "Long Live and Thrive Communism!" (that became a staple of Romanian state propaganda in a modified form, as "Long Live and Thrive Socialism!"), nicely reduces the two opposed political imperatives – 'Communism!' and 'Capitalism!' – to a common political-historical form. This has the effect of emphasizing, not only the raw ideological form of capitalism, but also the repetitive and monotonous *stasis* of its dynamic core as an economic ideology and a system for the reproduction of the social relations of commodity exchange. However, this repetitive sameness at the heart of capitalism should not be mistaken for the absence of a horizon: it posits a horizon of endless accumulation (ultimate indeterminateness as infinite progression), politically coded in economic terms as the progressive freedom of ever-greater consumption.

What *was* unexpected about the collapse of historical communism – certainly unexpected to the citizens of the former Eastern European socialist states – was the ferocity of the capitalist revolution that followed, which genuinely punctured the horizon of expectation of those involved in the transformation, who sought a new 'third way', different from either of the existing alternatives. But what of 9/11? It was certainly unexpected in a sense in which the collapse of historical communism was not, and not merely as a punctual event (and there were plenty of unexpected events in the course of the collapse of historical communism, in that sense of event), but as a symbolic harbinger of a new, religiously-coded geopolitical antagonism, and a return to 'civilizational' discourses. In this respect, it both punctured the initial Western horizon of expectation of the post-communist situation, and darkened it, in the sense of rendering it more 'misty and obscure'. As such, that is, by rendering 'the form of the world' *less* determinate, it heightened expectations of the unexpected. One might say that it instituted a certain possibilizing *anticipatoriness* – that it laid bare the political aspect of the historical process. At the level of the determination of that process, however, in its deeper structural respects, 9/11 was (as intended) merely emblematic. In fact, it was emblematic of a geo-politically very particular, secondary antagonism. Within a horizon of expectation internal to future transformations of capitalism, two other far less dramatic events were of far greater significance: China's entry into membership of the World Trade Organization on 11 Dec 2001 (we might call it '12/11') and the Sixteenth Congress of the Communist Party of China, 8–15 November 2002, at which, consequently, a series of decisions were ratified about private property in land and means of production and the regulation of capital, of enormous determinate significance to the future of the world economic system.[72] That congress opened up a new horizon of expectation within capitalism, but the possibilities for the unexpected that it contains are not horizonal, but *counter*-horizonal.

We will not reclaim a future qualitatively different from the present by reinvesting in the idea of horizon. At its best, contemporary art models experimental practices of negation that puncture horizons of expectation.

Acknowledgements

Earlier versions of parts of this book were written for particular occasions and appeared in related publications, with which they sometimes share titles. However, all texts have been significantly revised, rewritten, expanded, contracted or otherwise integrated into a larger argumentative whole. I am grateful to the individuals, institutions and publishers concerned for the opportunities they provided to develop the various different aspects of the project.

Earlier versions of material in Chapter 1 appeared as 'The Fiction of the Contemporary: Speculative Collectivity and Transnationality in The Atlas Group', in *Aesthetics and Contemporary Art*, edited by Armen Avanessian and Luke Skrebowski, Berlin: Sternberg Press, 2011; and 'Look Beneath the Label: Notes on the Contemporary', in *Bloomberg New Contemporaries 2011*, London: Bloomberg, 2011. Chapter 2 includes material previously published in 'Art Beyond Aesthetics: Philosophical Criticism, Art History and Contemporary Art', *Art History*, 27: 4 (September 2004); and 'An Image of Romanticism: Fragment and Project in Friedrich Schlegel's *Athenaeum Fragments* and Sol LeWitt's *Sentences on Conceptual Art*', in *Sol LeWitt's Sentences on Conceptual Art: Manuscript and Draft Materials 1968–69* – the catalogue of the exhibition – Verksted no. 11, Oslo: Office of Contemporary Art, 2009, pp. 5–27. The first parts of Chapter 3 appeared in *Rediscovering Aesthetics: Transdisciplinary Voices from Art History, Philosophy and Art Practice*, edited by Francis Halsall, Julia Jansen and Tony O'Connor, Stanford, CA: Stanford University Press, 2009. Chapter 4 is based on 'An Interminable Avalanche of Categories: Medium, Concept and Abstraction in the Work of Robert Smithson, 1966–1972', in *Cornerstones*, Berlin: Sternberg Press; Rotterdam: Witte de Witt, 2011. Chapter 5 draws upon materials first published in 'Photography in an Expanding Field: Distributive Unity and Dominant Form', in *Where is the Photograph?*, edited by David Green, Brighton: Photoforum, 2003; and 'Infinite Exchange: The Social Ontology of the Photographic Image',

Philosophy of Photography, 1: 1 (2010). Early versions of different parts of Chapter 6 appeared in: 'Non-Places and the Spaces of Art', *The Journal of Architecture*, Vol. 6 (Summer 2001); 'Art as Displaced Urbanism: Notes on a New Constructivism of the Exhibition Form', in . . . *With All Due Intent: Catalogue of Manifesta 5, European Biennial of Contemporary Art*, edited by Marta Kuzma and Massimiliano Gioni, San Sebastian, Spain: Centro Internacional de Cultura Contemporánea, 2004; 'The Power of Assembly: Art, World, Industry', in *Zones of Contact*, catalogue of the 2006 Biennale of Sydney, Sydney, 2006; 'Where is the Work of Art? Contemporary Art, Spatialization and Urban Form', in *Non-Site to Celebration Park: Essays on Art and the Politics of Space*, edited by E. Whittaker and A Landrum, Bath: Bath Spa University, 2007; 'Fragments of the Future: Notes on Project Space', in *Amikejo*, León, Spain: Museo de Arte Contemporáneo de Castilla y León (MUSAC), 2012. Parts of Chapter 7 were previously published in 'Distracted Reception: Time, Art, and Technology', in *Time Zones: Recent Film and Video Art*, edited by Jessica Morgan and Gregor Muir, London: Tate Publishing, 2004; 'The Dreambird of Experience: Utopia, Possibility, Boredom', *Radical Philosophy* 137 (May/June 2006); and as '"The Truth will be Known When the Last Witness is Dead": History not Memory', in *After the Event: New Perspectives on Art History*, edited by Charles Merewether and John Potts, Manchester: Manchester University Press, 2010 and 'Expecting the Unexpected: Beyond the "Horizon of Expectations"', in *The Horizons Reader*, edited by Maria Hlavajova et al., Utrecht: BAK, 2011, pp. 112–128.

I would like to thank Marta Kuzma, Director of the Office for Contemporary Art Norway, whose institutional energies and innovations have provided a rare series of contexts for thinking critically about contemporary art over the past fifteen years; and Yaiza María Hernández Velázquez – previously at CENDEAC, Murcia, and the Museum of Contemporary Art Barcelona (MACBA) – whose translation into Spanish of a number of earlier versions of these and other pieces, for my collection, *El arte más allá de la estética: Ensayos filosóficos sobre arte contemporáneo* (Murcia: CENDEAC, 2010), helped me to think more deeply about the organization of the materials into a structured whole.

I am grateful to John Kraniauskas and Francis Mulhern for their comments on various chapters; to Stella Sandford for reading the manuscript as a whole and offering numerous pertinent suggestions; and to Éric Alliez for his broader, agonistic contribution to my thinking about philosophy and contemporary art, in the context of our common project in the Centre for Research in Modern European Philosophy (CRMEP), Kingston University London.

Thanks to Stella, Ilya and Felix for everything else.

Endnotes

Introduction

1 François Dosse, *Gilles Deleuze & Félix Guattari: Intersecting Lives* (2007), trans. Deborah Glassman, Columbia University Press, New York, 2010, p. 448.
2 Walter Benjamin, 'The Work of Art in the Age of its Technological Reproducibility' (Second Version, 1936), in *Selected Writings, Volume 3, 1936–1938*, Cambridge MA: Harvard University Press, 2002, pp. 104–5; trans. amended to render *Erscheinung* as 'appearance'.
3 Harold Rosenberg, 'Criticism and its Premises', in *Art on the Edge: Creators and Situations*, Chicago: University of Chicago Press, 1975, pp. 135–52, 146.
4 See, for example, James Elkins, *What Happened to Art Criticism?*, Chicago: Prickly Paradigm Press, 2003; James Elkins and Michael Newman, eds, *The State of Art Criticism*, New York: Routledge, 2008; and for the opposite view, Daniel Birnbaum and Isabelle Graw (eds), *Canvases and Careers Today: Criticism and its Markets*, Berlin: Sternberg Press, 2008: 'Criticism never has been as strong as it is today, since it is now part of a knowledge-based economy' (p. 6). The logical gap covered over by the 'since' is indicative of the tenuousness of the latter position. One might equally claim: 'Criticism never has been as weak as it is today, since it is now part of a knowledge-based economy.'
5 Dave Hickey's work remains paradigmatic. See Dave Hickey, *Air Guitar: Essays on Art and Democracy*, Los Angeles: Art issues Press, 1997.
6 Hal Foster, 'The Problem of Pluralism', *Art in America*, January 1982; reprinted as 'Against Pluralism' in Hal Foster, *Recodings: Art, Spectacle, Cultural Politics*, Seattle: Bay Press, 1985.
7 'Round Table: The Present Conditions of Art Criticism', *October* 100 (Spring 2002), pp. 200–28. See also Thomas Crow, 'Art Criticism in the Age of Incommensurate Values: On the Thirtieth Anniversary of *Artforum*', in his *Modern Art in the Common Culture*, New Haven, CT: Yale University Press, 1996.

8 Thierry de Duve, *Kant After Duchamp*, Cambridge, MA: MIT Press, , 1996, pp. 320, 324. This material was largely composed prior to 1989.
9 For the aesthetic deficit of most semiotics, see my 'Sign and Image', in Peter Osborne, *Philosophy in Cultural Theory*, London: Routledge, 2000. For two early reflections on the problem of visual essentialism from within studies in visual culture, see W.J.T. Mitchell, 'Showing Seeing: A Critique of Visual Culture', *Journal of Visual Culture* 1: 2 (August 2002), pp. 165–81; Mieke Bal, 'Visual Essentialism and the Object of Visual Culture', *Journal of Visual Culture* 2: 1 (April 2003), pp. 15–32.
10 See Michael Fried, *Why Photography Matters to Art as Never Before*, New Haven, CT: Yale University Press, 2008. The book might equally be entitled *Why an Opticalist View of Art Matters to Photography as Never Before*.
11 Jeff Wall, 'Depiction, Object, Event', *Afterall* 16 (Autumn/Winter 2007), pp. 5–17; Jeff Wall and Peter Osborne, 'Art After Photography, After Conceptual Art: An Interview with Jeff Wall', *Radical Philosophy* 150 (July/August 2008), pp. 47–50.
12 Michael Fried, *Menzel's Realism: Art and Embodiment in Nineteenth Century Berlin*, New Haven, CT: Yale University Press, 2002; T.J. Clark, *Farewell to an Idea: Episodes from a History of Modernism*, New Haven, CT: Yale University Press, 1999; and *The Sight of Death: An Experiment in Art Writing*, New Haven, CT: Yale University Press, 2006.
13 Rosenberg, 'Criticism and its Premises', p. 148.
14 Jean-Marie Schaeffer, *Art of the Modern Age*, trans. Steven Rendall, Princeton, NJ: Princeton University Press, 2000, p. 3.
15 Ibid., pp. 4–5.
16 Arthur Danto, 'The End of Art', in *The Philosophical Disenfranchisement of Art*, New York: Columbia University Press, 1986, pp. 81–115. Hans Belting offers an alternative version for art historians – namely that the crisis of art history does not lie in a crisis of method or object domain, but in the fact that 'art history can no longer be the guiding image of our historical culture'. Hans Belting, *Art History After Modernism*, Chicago: University of Chicago Press, 2003, p. 6. (This is a revised and expanded edition of Belting's *The End of the History of Art?*, Chicago: University of Chicago Press, 1987.) For a broader range of philosophical interpretations, see Eva Geulen, *The End of Art: Readings in a Rumour After Hegel*, trans. James McFarland, Stanford, CA: Stanford University Press, 2006.
17 Arthur Danto, *Art After the End of Art*, Princeton University Press, Princeton, 1997. Danto's sense of twentieth-century art history is profoundly distorted – indeed, rendered incoherent – by his identification of Andy Warhol's 1964 *Brillo Boxes* as the decisive break with what he thinks of as 'historical' art, rather than Duchamp's readymades, fifty years earlier.
18 Another way has been via a new generation of analytical 'aestheticians' in the UK, dedicated to updated applications of the tenets of Hume's 'Of the

Standard of Taste'. See, for example, Derek Matravers, *Art and Emotion*, Oxford: Oxford University Press, 1998; Matthew Kieran, *Revealing Art*, London: Routledge, 2005; Berys Gaut, *Art, Emotion and Ethics*, Oxford: Oxford University Press, 2007. However, despite their determination to engage recent art, the philosophical terms on which they do so remain at considerable distance from the conditions of its intelligibility.

19 Jacques Rancière, *The Politics of Aesthetics: The Distribution of the Sensible*, trans. Gabriel Rockhill, London: Continuum, 2006; Jacques Rancière, *Aesthetics and its Discontents* (2004), trans. Steve Corcoran, Cambridge: Polity, 2009; Jacques Rancière, *Dissensus: On Politics and Aesthetics*, trans. Steve Corcoran, London: Continuum, 2010; and for the activist Deleuze–Guattarian variant, Gerald Raunig, *Art and Revolution: Transversal Activism in the Long Twentieth Century*, trans. Aileen Derieg, Los Angeles: Semiotext(e), 2007.

20 G.W.F. Hegel, *Hegel's Aesthetics: Lectures on Fine Art*, Vol. 1, trans. T.M. Knox, Oxford: Oxford University Press, 1975, p. 1; Rancière, 'The Aesthetic Revolution and Its Outcomes', in *Dissensus*, pp. 115–33.

21 Alain Badiou, *Handbook of Inaesthetics* (1998), trans. Alberto Toscano, Stanford: Stanford University Press, 2005, p. 1; 'Third Sketch of a Manifesto of Affirmationist Art', in *Polemics*, trans. Steve Corcoran, London: Verso, 2006, p. 144. For Rancière's critique, see 'Alain Badiou's Inaesthetics: The Torsions of Modernism', in *Aesthetics and its Discontents*, pp. 63–87.

22 Martin Heidegger, 'The Origin of the Work of Art' (1936), in *Poetry, Language, Thought*, trans. Albert Hofstadter, New York: Harper and Row, 1971, pp. 15–87. For recent variants, see Gianni Vattimo, *Art's Claim to Truth* (1985), trans. Luca D'Isanto, New York: Columbia University Press, 2008, and Giorgio Agamben, *The Man Without Content* (1994), trans. Georgia Albert, Stanford, CA: Stanford University Press, 1999.

23 For Deleuze's account of the work of art as 'a bloc of sensations – that is to say, a compound of percepts and affects' – see Gilles Deleuze and Félix Guattari, *What is Philosophy?*, trans. Graham Burchell and Hugh Tomlinson, London: Verso, 1994, Ch. 7. For a critique of the cultural conservatism of Deleuze's quasi-neo-aesthetic conception of art, as exemplified in *The Logic of Sensation*, his book on Francis Bacon, see Art & Language and Tom Baldwin, 'Deleuze's Bacon', *Radical Philosophy* 123 (January/February 2004), pp. 29–40. For some reflections on how to apply Deleuze and Guattari's position to contemporary art – after minimalism and conceptual art – see Stephen Zepke, 'Deleuze, Guattari and Contemporary Art', in *Gilles Deleuze: Image and Text*, ed. Eugene Holland, Daniel W. Smith and Charles J. Stivale, London: Continuum, 2009, pp. 176–97. For a more philosophically consistent and insistent Deleuzean position, see Éric Alliez and Jean-Claude Bonne, 'Matisse with Dewey with Deleuze', in *Gilles Deleuze: Image and Text*, ed. Holland et al., pp. 104–123; and Éric Alliez, 'Body

Without Image: Ernesto Neto's Anti-Leviathan', *Radical Philosophy* 156 (July/August 2009), pp. 23–34. In the latter two pieces, the imbrication of Deleuzean categories with the histories of particular works cannot help but mediate them historically, despite themselves. See Éric Alliez and Peter Osborne, 'Philosophy and Contemporary Art, After Adorno and Deleuze: An Exchange', in *Gest: Laboratory of Synthesis*, ed. Robert Garnet and Andrew Hunt, London: Bookworks, 2008, pp. 35–64.

24 Theodor W. Adorno, *Aesthetic Theory* (1970), trans. Robert Hullot-Kentor, London: Athlone Press, 1997.

25 The second English translation of *Aesthetic Theory*, from 1997, is in this respect worse than the first one. The translation there of *Entkunstung* – literally 'de-arting' – as 'de-aestheticization', for example, short-circuits Adorno's entire argument. In the first translation (*Aesthetic Theory*, London: Routledge, 1984), C. Lenhardt offered 'desubstantialization of art', which, whilst clumsy (and introducing a whole new red herring about substance), is less misleading. Generally, although by no means always, Adorno writes of 'artistic experience', *künstleriche Erfahrung*, rather than 'aesthetic experience', *ästhetische Erfahrung*, when it is the experience of the artwork qua artwork that is at issue. Elsewhere in *Aesthetic Theory*, however, 'aesthetic' (*Ästhetik/ästhetisch*) continues to be used to refer to both philosophical discourse on art and experience of art. Theodor W. Adorno, *Ästhetische Theorie*, Vol. 7 of *Gesammelte Schriften*, Frankfurt am Main: Suhrkamp, 1996. This reflects the fact that the metaphysical heritage of romanticism, appropriated by Adorno into the post-Hegelian context of the crisis of modernism, requires further transformation in the wake of the clarifying 'errors' of strong or analytical conceptual art.

26 See, for example, Christoph Menke, *The Sovereignty of Art: Aesthetic Negativity in Adorno and Derrida* (1988), trans. Neil Solomon, Cambridge, MA: MIT Press, 1998; J. M. Bernstein, *Against Voluptuous Bodies: Late Modernism and the Meaning of Painting*, Stanford, CA: Stanford University Press, 2006; J.M. Bernstein et al., *Art and Aesthetics After Adorno*, Berkeley, CA: Townsend Center for the Humanities/University of California Press, 2010.

27 For an Adorno that focuses on this Marxist aspect against a revived Kantian philosophical aesthetics, see John Roberts, 'After Adorno: Art Autonomy, and Critique – A Literature Review', *Historical Materialism* 7 (Winter 2000), pp. 221–39, and Stewart Martin, 'The Absolute Artwork Meets the Absolute Commodity', *Radical Philosophy* 146 (November/December 2007), pp. 15–25. For the debate between the two competing interpretations, see Dave Beech and John Roberts (eds), *The Philistine Controversy*, London: Verso, 2002. Neither, however, grasps the distinctively Benjaminian mediation. In my own initial reading of *Aesthetic Theory* ('Adorno and the Metaphysics of Modernism: The Problem of a "Postmodern" Art', in *The Problem of*

Modernity: Adorno and Benjamin, ed. Andrew Benjamin, London: Routledge, 1989, pp. 23–48), I attempted to balance its Kantian elements with both a principled distinction between Adorno and Greenberg ('Aesthetic Autonomy and the Crisis of Theory: Greenberg, Adorno and the Problem of Postmodernism in the Visual Arts', *New Formations* 9 [Summer 1989], pp. 31–50) and a more dialectical reconstruction of Adorno's dichotomy of 'autonomous' and 'dependent' art ('Torn Halves and Great Divides: The Dialectics of a Cultural Dichotomy', *News From Nowhere* 7 [Winter 1989], pp. 49–63). Nonetheless, at that point, I did not appreciate the significance and philosophical productivity of the Benjaminian mediation, the recovery of which is a condition for the fruitful application of Adornian categories to art since the 1960s.

28 See Peter Osborne, 'Philosophy After Theory: Transdisciplinarity and the New', in *Theory After 'Theory'*, ed. Derek Attridge and Jane Elliott, London: Routledge, 2011, pp. 19–33.

Chapter 1: The fiction of the contemporary

1 See Tony Judt, *Postwar: A History of Europe Since 1945* (2005), London: Vintage, 2010, Part 1.
2 The first art institution to follow the terminological innovation of the ICA in London seems to have been the Boston Museum of Modern Art in the USA, which became the Institute of Contemporary Art, Boston, in 1948. But it was not until the 1960s that the term became more widely used, and even then it was exceptional. Museu de Arte Contemporânea da Universidade de São Paulo (1963), Musée d'art contemporain de Montréal (1964) and the Museum of Contemporary Art, Chicago (1967) are early instances, by which time the contemporary had been around long enough to become an object of museological attention.
3 Matei Calinescu, *Five Faces of Modernity: Modernism, Avant-Garde, Decadence, Kitsch, Postmodernism*, Durham, NC: Duke University Press, 1987, p. 92. Cf. Raymond Williams's 1987 lecture, 'When was Modernism?', in *The Politics of Modernism: Against the New Conformists*, London: Verso, 1989, pp. 31–35, p. 32: 'Very quickly . . . "modern" shifts its reference from "now" to "just now" or even "then", and has for some time been a designation always going into the past with which "contemporary" may be contrasted for its presentness.' Whilst Calinescu was content to treat postmodernism descriptively, for Williams it was a 'new conformism', a 'non-historical fixity' with which we needed to 'break' (p. 35). It is perhaps symptomatic of the only very recent emergence of 'contemporary' as a theoretical term that my own 1995 book, *The Politics of Time: Modernity and Avant-Garde* (London: Verso, 1995 and 2011) which was dedicated to a deepening of the temporal comprehension of the latter two categories, in the

context of an attempt to extend theorization of existential temporalization to historical time – and was critical of the philosophical naïvety of discourses of the postmodern – nonetheless contains no sustained discussion of, or even index entry for, 'contemporary'.

4 Since 1990, Jameson has co-edited a series for Duke University Press entitled 'Post-Contemporary Interventions'.

5 See Terry Smith, 'Contemporary Art and Contemporaneity', *Critical Inquiry* 32 (Summer 2006), pp. 681–707; and Terry Smith, 'Introduction: The Contemporary Question' in *Antinomies of Art and Culture: Modernity, Postmodernity, Contemporaneity*, ed. Terry Smith, Okwui Enwezor and Nancy Condee, Durham, NC: Duke University Press, 2008, pp. 1–19, along with the essays in Part 1 of that collection; Giorgio Agamben, 'What is the Contemporary?', in his *What is an Apparatus? and Other Essays*, Stanford, CA: Stanford University Press, 2009, pp. 39–54; John Rajchman, 'The Contemporary: A New Idea?', in *Aesthetics and Contemporary Art*, ed. Armen Avanessian and Luke Skrebowski, Berlin: Sternberg Press, 2011, pp. 125–44.

6 In this respect, there seems to be something like a social actualization of the insights of Heidegger's critique of the 'ordinary' time consciousness of 'within-timeness' and Fabian's critique of anthropology's denial of the coeval, respectively. Martin Heidegger, *Being and Time* (1927), trans. John Macquarrie and Edward Robinson, Oxford: Blackwell, 1962, pp. 456–72; Johannes Fabian, *Time and the Other: How Anthropology Makes its Object*, New York: Columbia University Press, 1983, pp. 156–65. Cf. Osborne, *The Politics of Time*, pp. 62–8, 17 and 28.

7 Calinescu, *Five Faces of Modernity*, p. 362, note 119.

8 Georg Lukács, *The Meaning of Contemporary Realism* (1957), trans. J and N. Mander, London: Merlin Press, 2006.

9 Previously, the period appeared only through a multiplicity of more particular movements, as in Lucie Edward-Smith's *Movements of Art Since 1945* (London: Thames and Hudson, 1969), for example, which is still periodically updated in this form. It is currently in its fifth edition, 2001.

10 Cf. Peter Osborne, 'Yardsticks: When Will the Postwar End?', in *Jane and Louise Wilson: Tempo Suspendo/Suspending Time*, Galicia, Spain: Centro Galego de Arte Contemporánea, 2011, pp. 33–39.

11 The landmark exhibitions here were the 1936 *Cubism and Abstract Art* show, with Alfred H. Barr's famous stylistic flowchart on the cover of the catalogue, terminating in just two streams ('Geometrical' and 'Non-Geometrical' Abstract Art), and the Bauhaus show of 1938. The claim for the US inheritance of the European tradition (explicit in Clement Greenberg, for example) was, of course, not just a national claim, but a wider ideological one about the USA's leadership of the 'free' world during the Cold War – for which the basic text remains Serge Guilbaut's *How New York Stole the Idea of*

Modern Art: Abstract Expressionism, Freedom, and the Cold War (Chicago: University of Chicago Press, 1983).

12 For an outline of the critical history of the lineages of negation at work here, see the 'Survey' essay in Peter Osborne, *Conceptual Art*, London: Phaidon, 2002, pp. 12–51.

13 See below, pp. 46–53.

14 See Thomas Crow, *The Rise of the Sixties: American and European Art in the Era of Dissent 1955–69*, London: Everyman Art Library, 1996.

15 The origins of this victory date back to a different '9/11', 11 September 1973: the assassination of Salvador Allende, the socialist president of Chile, and the delivery of the Chilean economy to the so-called 'Chicago Boys' – the group of neo-liberal economists gathered around Milton Friedman at the University of Chicago. See David Harvey, *A Brief History of Neo-Liberalism*, Oxford: Oxford University Press, 2005.

16 For the effects in an expanded Europe, see Barbara Vanderlinden and Elena Filipovic (eds), *The Manifesta Decade: Debates on Contemporary Art Exhibitions and Biennals in Post-Wall Europe*, Cambridge, MA: MIT Press, 2005. For a documentation of post-'89 Eastern European art, see IRWIN (ed.), *East Art Map: Contemporary Art and Eastern Europe*, London: Afterall Books, 2006.

17 Peter Bürger, *Theory of the Avant-Garde*, trans. Michael Shaw, Minneapolis: University of Minnesota Press, 1984.

18 See 'Transnationalization: Art Industry', below, pp. 162–8.

19 'I call a concept problematic that contains no contradiction but that is also, as a bounds for given concepts, connected to cognitions, the objective reality of which can in no way be cognized . . . we have an understanding that extends farther than sensibility *problematically* . . .' Immanuel Kant, *Critique of Pure Reason*, trans. Paul Guyer and Allen W. Wood, Cambridge: Cambridge University Press, 1997, A254–55/B310. See also ibid., A310–38/B366–96.

20 Ibid., A681/B709, A771/B800, A646–7/B674–5. Cf. Peter Osborne, 'On Comparability: Kant and the Possibility of Comparative Studies', *boundary 2* 32: 2 (2005), special issue, 'Problems of Comparability/Possibilities of Comparative Study', eds Harry Harootunian and Hyun Ok Park, pp. 1–20.

21 Temporality, Heidegger argued, 'has the unity of a future which makes present in the process of having been.' Martin Heidegger, *Being and Time* (1927), trans. John Macquarrie and Edward Robinson, Oxford: Blackwell, 1962, p. 374.

22 'Only an essentially futural being . . . that is free for its death and can let itself be thrown back upon its factical "there" . . . can, by handing down to itself the possibility it has inherited, take over its own throwness and be in the moment of vision for "its time".' Ibid., p. 437, translation amended.

23 Kant, *Critique of Pure Reason*, A417/B445n.

24 See Paul Ricoeur, *Time and Narrative, Volume 3*, trans. Kathleen Blamey

and David Pellauer, Chicago: University of Chicago Press, 1988, Part IV, Section 2, 'Poetics of Narrative: History, Fiction, Time', pp. 99–240. Interestingly, despite the volume of his writings on time and history, Ricoeur nowhere thematizes the concept of the contemporary. Indeed, it is only very belatedly, in his final major book, that he offers a brief, but important discussion of (necessarily, 'our') modernity. Paul Ricoeur, *History, Memory, Forgetting*, trans. Kathleen Blamey and David Pellauer, Chicago: University of Chicago Press, 2004, pp. 305–14.

25 Cf. Boris Groys, 'The Topology of Contemporary Art', in *Antinomies of Art and Culture*, ed. Smith et al., pp. 71–80, 75.

26 A dystopian vision of the consequences of this acceleration is, of course, the main thing offered by the writings of Paul Virilio. See Steve Redhead, *Paul Virilio: Theorist for an Accelerated Culture*, Edinburgh: Edinburgh University Press, 2004.

27 Smith, 'Contemporary Art and Contemporaneity', p. 703.

28 Michael Fried, 'Art and Objecthood' (1967), in *Art and Objecthood: Essays and Reviews*, Chicago: University of Chicago Press, 1998, p.168. I discuss the theological character of the photographic image in Peter Osborne, *Philosophy in Cultural Theory*, Ch. 2, 'Sign and Image'.

29 Miguel Ángel Hernández-Navarro, 'Presentacíon. Antagonismos Temporales', in *Heterocronías: Tiempo, Arte y Arqueologías del Presente*, ed. Miguel Ángel Hernández-Navarro, Murcia, Spain: CENDEAC, 2008, pp. 9–16. Agamben attributes the proposition 'The contemporary is the untimely' – which he affirms – to Roland Barthes, in his notes to his lectures at the Collège de France. Agamben, 'What is the Contemporary?', p. 40.

30 See, for example, Luis Camnitzer, *Conceptualism in Latin American Art: Didactics of Liberation*, Austin: Texas University Press, 2007, which proposes a new history of conceptual art based on a displacement of its geographical origins. This is not – note – a peripheral supplement to an existing history, but a new history premised on the centrality of a particular 'peripheral' moment. For Camnitzer, 'Latin America' is itself a utopian idea.

31 Ricoeur, *Memory, History, Forgetting*, p. 305.

32 G.W.F. Hegel, *Phenomenology of Spirit*, trans. A.V. Miller, Oxford: Oxford University Press, 1977, p. 110. Cf. Peter Osborne, 'Modernism and Philosophy', in *Oxford Handbook of Modernisms*, ed. Peter Brooker et al., Oxford: Oxford University Press, 2010, pp. 388–409, 397.

33 For the distinction between the 'collective' (or rational) unity of a concept and a 'distributive' (or empirical) unity, see Kant, *Critique of Pure Reason*, A644/B672.

34 Eric Hobsbawn, *The Age of Extremes: The Short Twentieth Century, 1914–1991*, Michael Joesph, London, 1994; Giovanni Arrighi, *The Long Twentieth Century: Money, Power, and the Origins of Our Times*, London: Verso, 1994 (2nd ed., 2009) and *Adam Smith in Beijing: Lineages of the Twenty-First*

Century, London: Verso, 2007; Andre Gunder Frank, *ReOrient: Global Economy in the Asian Age*, Berkeley: University of California Press, 1998.

35 See, for example, William, I. Robinson, *A Theory of Global Capitalism: Production, Class and State in a Transnational World*, Baltimore, MD: Johns Hopkins University Press, 2004; Saskia Sassen, *A Sociology of Globalization*, New York: Norton, 2007; and Saskia Sassen, *Territory, Authority, Rights: From Medieval to Global Assemblages*, Princeton, NJ: Princeton University Press, 2008.

36 Gayatri Chakravorty Spivak, *Death of a Discipline*, New York: Columbia University Press, 2003, pp. 3 and 15; in the first instance, citing Toby Alice Volkman, *Crossing Borders: Revitalizing Area Studies*, Ford Foundation, New York, 1999, p. ix.

37 Ibid., p. 16

38 See pp. 162–8.

39 See pp. 129–31.

40 Initially dated '© 2005', the work was first shown in the Anthony Reynolds Gallery, London, at the end of 2004 – giving the impression of its having arrived from the future. The precise form of individual works, the attribution of dates and the designation of the artist frequently shifts as the fictional Group's oeuvre develops, refusing the fixity conventionally associated with the notion of 'a' work.

41 The Atlas Group and Walid Raad, 'Notebook, Volume 38' in *The Atlas Group, Volume 1, The Truth Will Be Known When the Last Witness Is Dead: Documents from the Fakhouri File in the Atlas Group Archive*, Köln: Walther König; Noisy-le-Sec: La Galerie de Noisy-le-Sec; Aubervilliers: Les Laboratoires d'Aubervilliers, 2004, pp. 57–77. A version of this volume of the Notebooks was first published in the US magazine *Grand Street* in 2003.

42 The Atlas Group and Walid Raad, *The Atlas Group, Volume 2, My Neck Is Thinner Than a Hair: Documents from the Atlas Group Archive*, Köln: Walther König; Toronto: Art Gallery of York University; Liverpool: FACT (Foundation for Art and Creative Technology), 2005. The 'document title' of the mixed media file, *My Neck Is Thinner Than a Hair*, was altered in the presentation of the Archive at the outset of this volume. It no longer appears as *A History of Car Bombs in the Lebanese Wars, Volumes 1–245*, but instead as *Volume 1 (3641) 21 January 1986*. It is accompanied by a reference to an additional file of photographs.

43 For the political significance of the car bomb, more generally, see Mike Davis, *Buda's Wagon: A Brief History of the Car Bomb*, London: Verso, 2007.

44 Walid Raad, *Scratchings on Things I Could Disavow: Some Essays from The Atlas Group Project*, Köln: Walther König; Lisbon: Culturgest, 2007, p. 6.

45 Ibid., p. 126.

46 Michel Foucault, 'What is an Author?' (1969), in *Textual Strategies: Perspectives in Post-Structuralist Criticism*, ed. Josué V. Harari, Ithaca, NY: Cornell University Press, 1979, pp. 141–60, 158.

47 See, for example, Blake Stimson and Gregory Sholette (eds), *Collectivism After Modernism: The Art of Social Imagination After 1945*, Minneapolis: University of Minnesota Press, 2007.
48 Luther Blissett, *Q* (2000), trans. Shaun Whiteside, London: Heinemann, 2003; Wu Ming, *54* (2002), trans. Shaun Whiteside, London: Arrow Books, 2006; and Wu Ming, *Manituana* (2007), trans. Shaun Whiteside, London: Verso, 2009. Luther Blissett and Wu Ming are pseudonyms used by the same group of Italian writers.
49 Foucault, 'What is an Author?', p. 160.

Chapter 2: Art beyond aesthetics

1 See Charles Harrison, 'Conceptual Art and the Suppression of the Beholder', in *Essays on Art and Language*, Oxford: Blackwell, 1991, pp. 29–62; and 'Conceptual Art and its Criticism' and 'Painting and the Death of the Spectator', in *Conceptual Art and Painting: Further Essays on Art and Language*, Cambridge, MA: MIT Press, 2001, pp. 35–48 and 171–91.
2 For two canonical instances of the game, see Griselda Pollock, *Avant-Garde Gambits, 1888–1893: Gender and the Colour of Art History*, London: Thames and Hudson, 1992; and Thierry de Duve, 'Given the Richard Mutt Case', in *Kant After Duchamp*, Cambridge, MA: MIT Press, 1996, pp. 89–143. This avant-garde dialectic of institutional transformation exceeds the simplistic contrast between anti-institutional ('historical') and institutional (neo-) avant-gardes in Peter Bürger's *Theory of the Avant-Garde* (1974), since it involves the transformation of the social-space of the art institution – for more on which, see Chapter 6, below. In the case of the famous 'gang of four' of early conceptual art (Joseph Kosuth, Lawrence Weiner, Robert Barry and Douglas Huebler), it was their gallerist and dealer, Seth Siegelaub, who was the agent of an alternative market-led institutionalization. See, Alexander Alberro, *Conceptual Art and the Politics of Publicity*, Cambridge, MA: MIT Press, 2003.
3 I use the term 'ontology' here quite generally to refer to any discourse about forms and modes of being. That is to say, I do not accept the conceptual restrictions imposed by either classical metaphysical, substance-based ontology or the early Heidegger's use of the term, which would distinguish in principle between Being (*Sein*) as the object of a 'fundamental' ontology and the merely 'ontic' status of beings or entities (*Seiendes*). Rather, as a matter of philosophical principle, I take all ontology to be *historical* ontology, although some things are more historical – more radically subject to time – than others. In this respect, ontology is an ineliminable aspect of philosophical discourse, however critical, dialectical, historical or 'contextual' that discourse purports to be.
4 Friedrich Schlegel, *Philosophical Fragments*, trans. Peter Firchow,

Minneapolis: University of Minnesota Press, 1991, p. 5; '"Athenäums"-Fragmente' (1798), in *'Athenäums'-Fragmente und andere Schriften*, Stuttgart: Reclam, 1978, p. 76–142.

5 Immanuel Kant, *Critique of Pure Reason*, trans. Paul Guyer and Allen W. Wood, Cambridge: Cambridge University Press, 1997, A21; *Kritik der reinen Vernunft*, Vol. 3 of *Werkausgabe*, ed. Wilhelm Weischedel, Frankfurt am Main: Suhrkamp, 1974.

6 Immanuel Kant, *Critique of the Power of Judgment*, trans. Allan Wood and Eric Matthews, Cambridge: Cambridge University Press, 2000; *Kritik der Urteilskraft*, Vol. 10 of *Werkausgabe*, ed. Wilhelm Weischedel, Frankfurt am Main: Suhrkamp, 1974. The precursor of this integration was, of course, Alexander Baumgarten. However, Baumgarten's immediately (intuitively) cognitive version of aesthetic as a discourse on taste failed to resonate beyond the eighteenth century, mainly because of Kant's decisive epistemological critique of the dogmatism of its scientific status.

7 In the second (1787) edition of the *Critique of Pure Reason*, Kant had already begun to concede the struggle over usage. He amended the footnote in question to suggest that 'it is advisable *either . . .* to desist *. . . or else to share the term with speculative philosophy and take aesthetics partly in a transcendental meaning* [his own – PO]; *partly in a psychological meaning*.' A21 / B36. Italics denote the addition in the second (B) edition. However, here, the concession appears merely pragmatic, in the face of the continuing prevalence of the new usage. Note: 'critique of taste' is still at this point associated here with a 'psychological', rather than a 'transcendental', meaning; its transcendental meaning still being restricted to the a priori forms of intuition – namely, space and time. Kant's innovation in the *Critique of Judgement-Power* was to find a new transcendental meaning for 'aesthetic' as the name for a logically new type of judgement: purely 'reflective' or 'indeterminate' judgement.

8 See pp. 6–7.

9 Ibid. In the second edition, Kant qualifies this argument in two ways: he qualifies the claim about the merely empirical sources of the criteria by describing such sources as only the '*most prominent*' (*vornehmsten*) ones; and he qualifies the claim about them never being able to serve as a priori rules, by describing such rules as 'determinate' (*bestimmten*), in an anticipation of the conceptual space of a possible indeterminate judgement, which is the main conceptual innovation of the third *Critique* (*Critique of Pure Reason*, B36).

10 Kant, *Critique of the Power of Judgment*, pp. 184, 228, emphasis added; *Kritik der Urteilskraft*, pp. 239, 299.

11 Karl Ameriks, 'Hegel's Aesthetics: New Responses to Kant and Romanticism', *Bulletin of the Hegel Society of Great Britain* 45/46 (2002), pp. 72–92.

12 *Hegel's Aesthetics*, p. 1.

13 Novalis, *Fichte Studies* (1795–6), trans. Jane Kneller, Cambridge: Cambridge University Press, 2003.
14 Kant, *Critique of Pure Reason*, B152–6. Cf. Martin Heidegger, *Kant and the Problem of Metaphysics* (1929), trans. Richard Taft, Bloomington, IN: University of Indiana Press, 1990, pp. 129–33.
15 This is Kant's materialism – the aesthetic consequence of his 'Refutation of Idealism'. See ibid., B274–9.
16 Kant, *Critique of the Power of Judgment*, $16, pp. 114–7.
17 This is an ironic reversal of Schlegel's rendering ironic of Kant's complaint against Baumgarten's usage: a prime example of 'the irony of irony', in Schlegel's own terms.
18 Kant, *Critique of the Power of Judgment*, p. 185, emphasis added.
19 Andrew Bowie, *Aesthetics and Subjectivity: From Kant to Nietzsche*, Manchester: Manchester: Manchester University Press, 1990; 2003; J.M. Bernstein, *The Fate of Art: Aesthetic Alienation from Kant to Derrida and Adorno*, University Park, PA: Penn State University Press, 1992.
20 'Introduction', in J.M. Bernstein (ed.), *Classical and Romantic German Aesthetics*, Cambridge: Cambridge University Press, 2003, pp. xviii–xxii.
21 See in particular, the 1977 collection *Aesthetics and Politics*, London: Verso, 2010; and more recently, Jacques, Rancière, *Aesthetics and Politics*.
22 Novalis, *Schriften*, Vol. 3, Stuttgart: Kolhammer, 1960, p. 685, number 671; cited in Manfred Frank, *The Philosophical Foundations of Early German Romanticism*, trans. Elizabeth Millán-Zaibert, New York: SUNY Press, 2004, pp. 53, 164. Lyotard seems to derive his notion of the 'presentation of the unpresentable' directly from Kant's notion of the aesthetic Idea as a presentation of the 'undefinable' (*das Unnennbare*). Jean-François Lyotard, *Lessons on the Analytic of the Sublime* (1991), trans. Elizabeth Rottenberg, Stanford, CA: Stanford University Press, 1994, p. 65. It is in the notion of aesthetic art as a presentation of 'aesthetic Ideas' that Kant comes closest to a philosophical concept of the artwork.
23 Adorno, *Aesthetic Theory*, pp. 225–8. For Hegel's interpretation of Romanticism, see *Hegel's Aesthetics: Lectures on Fine Art*, Vol. 1, pp. 517–611. From Hegel's point of view, this is a philosophical *critique*, from the standpoint of the absolute knowing. From our point of view, however, it is more simply a philosophical *depiction* of artistic modernity. The failure of Hegel's standpoint derives from his failure to conceive forms of 'absolute spirit' (religion, art, philosophy – cultural forms of self-consciousness of the whole) as themselves parts of *objective* spirit (world history).
24 Walter Benjamin, 'The Concept of [Art] Criticism in German Romanticism' (1920), in *Selected Writings, Volume 1, 1913–1926*, Cambridge, MA: Harvard University Press, 1996, pp. 116–200; Frank, *The Philosophical Foundations of Early German Romanticism* (1997); Frederick C. Beiser, *The Romantic Imperative: The Concept of Early German Romanticism*,

Cambridge, MA: Harvard University Press, 2003; Elizabeth Millán-Zaibert, *Friedrich Schlegel and the Emergence of Romantic Philosophy*, New York: SUNY Press, 2007. The most important texts from the intervening years are: Maurice Blanchot, 'The Athenaeum', in *The Infinite Conversation* (1969), trans. Susan Hanson, Minneapolis: University of Minnesota Press, 1993, pp. 351–9; Philippe Lacoue-Labarthe and Jean-Luc Nancy, *The Literary Absolute: The Theory of Literature in German Romanticism* (1978), trans. Philip Barnard and Cheryl Lester, New York: State University of New York Press, 1988.

25 August Schlegel, 'Lectures on Aesthetics', in *Theory as Practice: A Critical Anthology of Early German Romantic Writings*, ed. Jochen Schulte-Sasse et al., Minneapolis: University of Minnesota Press, 1997, p. 197.

26 F.W.J. Schelling, *System of Transcendental Idealism* (1800), trans. Peter Heath, Charlottesville: University Press of Virginia, 1978, Part VI, pp. 219–33.

27 Friedrich Schlegel, *Philosophical Fragments*, trans. Peter Firchow, Minneapolis: University of Minnesota Press, 1991, p. 32; de Duve, *Kant After Duchamp*, pp. 51, 194, 205–79.

28 David Summers, *The Judgement of Sense: Renaissance Naturalism and the Rise of Aesthetics*, Cambridge: Cambridge University Press, 1987.

29 Richard Wollheim, *Painting as an Art*, London: Thames and Hudson, 1987. More philosophically, see Maurice Merleau-Ponty, 'Cézanne's Doubt' and 'Eye and Mind' in *The Merleau-Ponty Aesthetics Reader: Philosophy and Painting*, ed. Galen A. Johnson, Evanston, IL: Northwestern University Press, 1993, pp. 3–13 and 59–75, and Mikel Dufrenne, *The Phenomenology of Aesthetic Experience* (1967), trans. Edward S. Casey, Evanston, IL: Northwestern University Press, 1973.

30 'Post-medium' is the category favoured by an increasingly melancholic Rosalind Krauss. See Rosalind Krauss, *'A Voyage on the North Sea': Art in the Age of the Post-Medium Condition*, London: Thames and Hudson, 1999; 'Reinventing the Medium', *Critical Inquiry* 25 (Winter 1999), pp. 289–305; and 'Some Rotten Shoots from the Seeds of Time', in *Antinomies of Art and Culture*, ed. Terry Smith et al., Durham, NC: Duke University Press, 2008, pp. 60–70. 'Transmedia' is a category with its origins in the Fluxus concept of 'intermedia'. See Dick Higgins, 'Intermedia' (1965), in *Horizons, the Poetics and Theory of the Intermedia*, Carbondale: Southern Illinois University Press, 1984. For more on medium, post-medium and transmedia, see the next chapter, below.

31 See Bernstein, *Classical and Romantic German Aesthetics*, pp. xii–xviii, and 'Social Signs and Natural Bodies: On T.J. Clark's *Farewell to an Idea*', *Radical Philosophy* 104 (November/December 2000), pp. 25–38.

32 See Osborne, 'Modernism and Philosophy'.

33 For a comparison of the three positions – LeWitt, Kosuth and Art & Language – see Peter Osborne, 'Conceptual Art as/and Philosophy' in

Rewriting Conceptual Art: Critical and Historical Approaches, ed. Jon Bird and Michael Newman, London: Reaction Books, 1999, pp. 47–65; reprinted in Osborne, *Philosophy in Cultural Theory*, pp. 86–102.

34 Cf. Ibid., p. 65/102.

35 I tried to do this in the 'Survey' essay, in Peter Osborne (ed.), *Conceptual Art*, London: Phaidon, 2002, pp. 13–51.

36 See the section 'The Idea of a "Post-Conceptual" Art', in Charles Harrison, 'The Trouble with Writing', *Conceptual Art and Painting*, pp. 3–34, 27–34. As a member of the Art & Language group, Harrison's conception of 'post-Conceptual art' is restricted to the reinterpretation of the project of presenting artists' writings as art.

37 For more on the concept of distributive unity, see pp. 120–3.

38 This concept of afterlife (*Nachleben*) derives from Benjamin, who used the term ironically, in a scientific sense, analogously to the temporality of the decay of radioactivity, rather than in a religious sense, as an example of the materialistic appropriation of a theological concept; although it also carries the suggestion that there is a relation to something magical or supernatural about the life of objects in all forms of cultural transmission. See, Walter Benjamin, 'Eduard Fuchs, Collector and Historian' (1937), in *Selected Writings, Volume 3, 1935–1938*, Cambridge, MA: Harvard University Press, 1996, pp. 260–302, p. 261: 'For the dialectical historian concerned with works of art, these works integrate their fore-history as well as their after-history; and it is by virtue of their after-history that their fore-history is recognizable as involved in a continuous process of change'; and *The Arcades Project*, trans. Howard Eiland and Kevin McLaughlin, Cambridge MA: Harvard University Press, 1999, p. 460 [N2,3]. 'Historical understanding' is included here in 'the afterlife of that which is understood'.

39 Adorno, *Aesthetic Theory*, pp. 263, 2–3; *Ästhetische Theorie*, pp. 392, 11–12.

40 G.W.F. Hegel, *Phenomenology of Spirit*, pp. 38–40; translation amended.

41 Cf. Gillian Rose, 'From Speculative to Dialectical Thinking: Hegel and Adorno', in *Judaism and Modernity: Philosophical Essays*, Oxford: Blackwell, 1993, pp. 53–64.

42 Friedrich Schlegel, '"Athenäum" Fragmente' (1798), in *'Athenäum' Fragmente und andere Schriften*, Reclam, Stuttgart, 1978, pp. 76–142; 'Athenaeum Fragments', in *Philosophical Fragments*, pp. 18–93. Henceforth all references to this translation of the fragments appear in the main text, as *AF*, followed by the number of the fragment.

43 It is currently available in Osborne, ed., *Conceptual Art*, p. 222 and *Conceptual Art: A Critical Anthology*, ed. Alexander Alberro and Blake Stimson, Cambridge, MA: MIT Press, 1999, pp. 106–8.

44 See Liz Kotz, 'Poetry From Object to Action', in *Words to be Looked At: Language in 1960s Art*, Cambridge, MA: MIT Press, 2007, Ch. 4.

45 Benjamin, *The Arcades Project*, p. 463 [N3,1].
46 It is important to register the depth of this claim, in the (contrasting) light of recent curatorial interest in an adjectival idea of a 'Romantic Conceptualism'. See the special issue of *Frieze Magazine* 71, 'Romantic Conceptualism', November 2002, and Ellen Sefermann, Jorge Haiser et al., *Romanticism Conceptualism*, Bielefeld, Germany: Kerber Verlag, 2007 – the catalogue of an exhibition of the same title, at the Kunsthalle Nürnberg, 10 May–15 July 2007. In the latter, 'Romantic Conceptualism' is conceived as one particular, thematically defined, strand of conceptual art: basically, a conceptual art in which the idea or concept is an emotion. In recent writing, Dutch artist Bas Jan Ader has provided the model for this type of conceptual art. Early work by Susan Hiller has furnished an additional, feminist prototype. However, the term dates back to Boris Groys's 1979 essay, 'Moscow Romantic Conceptualism', which 'used the term "Romantic" precisely to indicate the difference between Anglo-American conceptual art and Moscow art practices'. Boris Groys, 'Introduction', in *History Becomes Form: Moscow Conceptualism*, Cambridge, MA: MIT Press, 2010, p. 7. (The original essay is reprinted there, pp. 35–55.) Groys's use has nothing to do with rejection of 'intellectual coldness', which unifies the recent curatorial category, but is more rigorous in its identification of the Romantic with a particular structure of infinity, associated in this instance with a 'culturally repressed repetition of sameness' (p. 2), staged in such a way that 'things become signs in a poetic sequence' (p. 42). This critical conceptualization of 'Romantic Conceptualism' was never taken up – perhaps because it offered no other examples outside Moscow; while 'Moscow Conceptualism' was quickly adopted as a label for a larger group of artists than the Romantic ones. However, the analysis of the Romantic structure of conceptual art, per se, which is offered here, has more affinities with a generalization of Groys's analysis – to *include* the Anglo-American conceptual art with which it was intended to be contrasted – than the loose usage of 'Romantic' in the 'Romantic Conceptualism' popularized by Haiser. Jan Verwoert approaches the general idea, albeit largely still in a thematic manner, in his 'Impulse Concept Concept Impulse: Conceptual Art and Its Provocative Potential for the Realization of the Romantic Idea', in *Romanticism Conceptualism*, pp. 164–75.
47 See note 38, above.
48 Osborne, 'Conceptual Art and/as Philosophy'.
49 Joseph Kosuth, 'Art and Philosophy' (1969), in *Art and Philosophy and After: Collected Writings, 1966–1990*, Cambridge, MA: MIT Press, 1991, pp. 13–32.
50 See Ann Stephen, 'Soft Talk/Soft-Tape: The Early Collaborations of Ian Burn and Mel Ramsden', in Michael Corris, ed., *Conceptual Art: Theory, Myth, and Practice*, Cambridge: Cambridge University Press, 2004, pp. 80–97, p. 90.

51 Theodor W. Adorno, *Negative Dialectics* (1966), trans H. B. Ashton, London: Routledge, 1973, pp. 20–28.
52 Cf. Peter Osborne, 'Neo-Classic: Alain Badiou's *Being and Event*', *Radical Philosophy* 142 (March/April 2007), pp. 19–29.
53 *Art as Art: The Selected Writings of Ad Reinhardt*, ed. Barbara Rose, Berkeley: University of California Press, 1975, pp. 203–207, 51–52.
54 Sol LeWitt, manuscript notes pertaining to *Sentences on Conceptual Art*, courtesy of Herman Daled, reproduced in *Sol LeWitt's Sentences on Conceptual Art: Manuscript and Draft Materials 1968–69*, Verksted no. 11, Oslo: Office of Contemporary Art, 2009, pp. 38–9.
55 Walter Benjamin, 'The Storyteller: Observations on the Works of Nikolai Leskov', in *Selected Writings*, Vol. 3, pp. 143–166, 147–8.
56 For the concept of minor art, see Gilles Deleuze and Félix Guattari, *Kafka: Towards a Minor Literature* (1975), trans. Dana Polan, Minneapolis: University of Minnesota Press, 1986.
57 Quoted in Kotz, *Words to be Looked At*, p. 229.
58 See Manfred Frank, *The Philosophical Foundations of Early German Romanticism* – a translation of the final volume of a three-volume work on the transition from Kant to Romanticism, entitled *Unendliche Annäherung* [Infinite Approximation], Frankfurt am Main: Suhrkamp, 1997.
59 On the general topic of conceptual art's relationship to the historical process of de-skilling, see John Roberts, *The Intangibilities of Form: Skill and Deskilling in Art After the Readymade*, London: Verso, 2007. For an art-historical approach to seriality in the art of the late 1950s and 1960s, see Briony Fer, *The Infinite Line: Re-Making Art After Modernism*, New Haven, CT: Yale University Press, 2004.
60 In his conversation with Patricia Norvell of 11 June 1969, Lewitt gives the example of one of Hanne Darboven's works, which progresses by adding up the digits representing dates in particular years. Patricia Norvell, 'Interview with Sol LeWitt, 12 June 1969', *Recording Conceptual Art*, ed. Alexander Alberro and Patricia Norvell, Berkeley: University of California Press, 2001, pp. 112–123.

Chapter 3: Modernisms and mediations

1 Benjamin Constant wrote in his *Intimate Journal* in 1804, referring to a contemporary follower of Kant and Schelling, 'Art for art's sake, with no purpose, for any purpose perverts art. But art achieves a purpose which is not its own.' Cited in Andrew McNeillie, 'Bloomsbury', *Cambridge Companion to Virginia Woolf*, ed. Sue Roe and Susan Sellers, Cambridge: Cambridge University Press, 2000, p. 21, note 4. The idea is generally associated with Théophile Gautier, who promoted it in France in the early 1830s. For aestheticism, see William Hamilton, *The Aesthetic Movement in England*

(1882), Whitefish, MT: Kessinger Publishing, 2000; and more recently, Angela Leighton, *On Form: Poetry, Aestheticism and the Legacy of a Word*, Oxford: Oxford University Press, 2007. For Kant and formalism in Germany, see Margaret Iversen and Stephen Melville, 'What the Formalist Knows', in *Writing Art History: Disciplinary Departures*, Chicago: University of Chicago Press, 2010, pp. 60–89. For Kant and modernism, see Gregg M. Horowitz, 'Culture, Necessity and Art: Kant's Discovery of Artistic Modernism', in *Sustaining Loss: Art and Mournful Life*, Stanford: Stanford University Press, 2001, pp. 25–55. Kant's relationship to modernism is a dual one, via both his first and third *Critiques*. In his early work, Clement Greenberg cites Kant as the philosophical source of modernism as a culture of self-criticism (the 'critique of reason by reason alone' of the first *Critique*), but after the mid-1960s he draws increasingly upon (a Humean reading of) Kant's third *Critique*. See Clement Greenberg, 'Modernist Painting', in *The Collected Essays and Criticism, Volume 4: Modernism with a Vengeance, 1957–1969*, Chicago: University of Chicago Press, 1993, pp. 85–93; and *Homemade Esthetics: Observations on Art and Taste*, Oxford: Oxford University Press, 1999, respectively. I contest the former claim – also made, at greater length, by Robert Pippin – in my 'Modernism and Philosophy'.

2   J. M. Bernstein, 'Modernism as Aesthetics and Art History', in *Art History Versus Aesthetics*, ed. James Elkins, New York: Routledge, 2006, pp. 241, 265.

3   Horowitz, 'Culture, Necessity and Art'. The alternative is the later Guattarian 'paradigm', which involves an 'ethico-aesthetic' appropriation of conceptual art. See Félix Guattari, 'On Contemporary Art: An Interview with Oliver Zahm, April 1992' in *The Guattari Effect*, ed. Éric Alliez and Andrew Goffey, London: Continuum, 2011, pp. 40–53. However, this remains unconvincing even to Guattari's supporters. See Stephen Zepke, 'Deleuze, Guattari and Contemporary Art', in *Gilles Deleuze: Image and Text*, ed. Eugene W. Holland and Daniel W. Smith, London: Continuum, 2010, pp. 176–97; and 'From Aesthetic Autonomy to Autonomist Aesthetics: Art and Life in Guattari', in *The Guattari Effect*, pp. 205–19.

4   Cf. Bernstein, 'Modernism as Aesthetics and Art History', p. 266: 'The premise that modernism is over is false.' The difference between us concerns what, precisely, is meant by 'modernism' here; *which* modernism it is that endures. There are many (Arthur Danto, for example) who do not believe that art remains a historically critical practice. For some of them, aesthetics is (re)legitimated on this precise basis, that is, contra modernism. Bernstein defends modernism as aesthetics (and vice versa); Danto defends aesthetics after modernism; I defend the metacritical status of modernism *against* its reduction to aesthetics.

5   Peter Osborne, 'Modernity: A Different Time,' in *The Politics of Time*, Ch. 1.

6 Raymond Williams, *Keywords: A Vocabulary of Culture and Society* (1976), London: Fontana, 1988, pp. 173–74, 208–9.
7 Pierre Bourdieu, *The Rules of Art: Genesis and Structure of the Literary Field* (1992), trans. Susan Emanuel, Stanford, CA: Stanford University Press, 1995, Part I, Ch. 2 and 3, and Part III, Ch. 3. I abstract here from the fundamental and under-researched issue of the transference of the general concept of 'art' from the literary to the visual field, in the course of the nineteenth century.
8 Charles Baudelaire, "The Painter of Modern Life" (1863), in *The Painter of Modern Life and Other Essays*, trans. Jonathan Mayne, London: Phaidon, 1964, p. 13.
9 See Marshall Berman, *All That is Solid Melts into Air: The Experience of Modernity*, London: Verso, 1982.
10 Cf. Peter Osborne, "Modernism as Translation," in *Philosophy in Cultural Theory* London: Routledge, 2000, p. 58.
11 Walter Benjamin, *Charles Baudelaire: A Lyric Poet in the Era of High Capitalism*, trans. Harry Zohn, London: Verso, 1983; David Carrier, *High Art: Baudelaire and the Origins of Modernist Painting*, University Park, PA: Penn State University Press, 1996, Ch. 3.
12 Cf. Michel Foucault, 'Man and his Doubles', *The Order of Things: An Archaeology of the Human Sciences* (1966), London: Tavistock Publications, 1970, Ch. 9. For Foucault, the identification of this doubling constituted a (broadly positivistic) critique of the universal. However, following Balibar, we may alternatively read it as the structure of a complex and paradoxical historical unity of universality and finitude – i.e., a structure characteristic of all genuinely historical concepts. Étienne Balibar, 'Citizen Subject', in *Who Comes After the Subject?*, ed. Eduardo Cadava et al., London: Routledge, 1991, pp. 33–57, 54–5.
13 This is the point at which a meta-critical rethinking of the concept of modernism bears on the urgent but difficult question of a rewriting of art history from the standpoint a more global social inclusion.
14 Autonomous art was conceptually prefigured by Jena Romanticism (against which academic art was itself to some extent a reaction); just as early romanticism also prefigured the modernist concept of the new. See Chapter 2, above. However, neither autonomously aesthetic art nor modernism were actualized in Romanticism, where (subsequent to 1800 and the end of Jena Romanticism) affirmations of autonomy increasingly took the form of the exaltation of the artist's persona and the absolutization of the artist's point of view. Cf. 'The Academic Gaze', in Pierre Bourdieu, 'Manet and the Institutionalization of Anomie', in *The Field of Cultural Production: Essays on Art and Literature*, Cambridge: Polity Press, 1993, pp. 239–50, 239–40.
15 '"Art for art's sake" was scarcely ever to be taken literally; it was almost always a flag under which sailed a cargo that could not be declared because

it still lacked a name.' Walter Benjamin, 'Surrealism: The Last Snapshot of the European Intelligentsia' (1929), in *Selected Writings, Volume 2: 1927–1934*, Cambridge, MA: Harvard University Press, 1999, pp. 211–12.
16 Clement Greenberg, 'Towards a Newer Laocoon' (1940), in *The Collected Essays and Criticism, Volume 1: Perceptions and Judgements, 1939–1944*, Chicago: Chicago University Press, 1986, pp. 23–37; 'Modernist Painting', pp. 85–93.
17 See Greenberg, *Homemade Esthetics* and *Clement Greenberg: Late Writings*, ed. Robert C. Morgan, Minneapolis: University of Minnesota Press, 2003.
18 Thierry de Duve, *Pictorial Nominalism: On Marcel Duchamp's Passage from Painting to the Readymade* (1984), trans. Dana Polan, Minneapolis: University of Minnesota Press, 1991; *Kant After Duchamp*.
19 For criticism of de Duve's peculiar use of Saul Kripke's philosophy of names, for example, see Jason Gaiger, 'Art after Beauty: Retrieving Aesthetic Judgement', *Art History* 20: 4, 1997, pp. 611–16.
20 Adorno, *Aesthetic Theory*, pp. 199–225. See also Theodor W. Adorno, 'Art and the Arts' (1967), in *Can One Live After Auschwitz? A Philosophical Reader*, ed. Rolf Tiedemann, Stanford, CA: Stanford University Press, 2003, Chapter 19.
21 Adorno, *Aesthetic Theory*, pp. 199–201, 219–220.
22 Adorno, *Negative Dialectics*, p. 365. The 'Meditations on Metaphysics' with which *Negative Dialectics* ends – reflections on the possibility of metaphysical experience after 'the course of history' has force[d] materialism on metaphysics' – represents a transition from negative epistemology towards *Aesthetic Theory*, as a contemporary Romantic form of displaced metaphysics.
23 Adorno, *Aesthetic Theory*, pp. 222, 24–25.
24 See pp. 34–5.
25 For the example of Sol Lewitt, see pp. 62–7 above.
26 Jean-Paul Sartre, *Critique of Dialectic Reason, Volume 1: Theory of Practical Ensembles* (1960), trans. Alan Sheridan-Smith, London: Verso, 1976, pp. 255–6, 266. Compare the centrality of 'serialization' to Deleuze's *The Logic of Sense* (itself, formally, a serial text) which one might read as a kind of structuralist appropriation of Sartre's serialism. Gilles Deleuze, *The Logic of Sense* (1969), trans. Mark Lester with Charles Stivale, New York: Columbia University Press, 1990.
27 Peter Osborne, 'Painting Negation: Gerhard Richter's Negatives', *October* 62 (Autumn 1992), pp. 102–13; 'Abstract Images: Sign, Image and Aesthetic in Gerhard Richter's Paintings (1998)', in *Gerhard Richter*, October Files 8, ed. Benjamin H.D. Buchloh, Cambridge, MA: MIT Press, 2009, pp. 95–111.
28 Richter's work is reproduced in Gerhard Richter, *Atlas of the Photographs, Collages and Sketches*, London: Antony d'Offay, 1997. A catalogue for Polke's show appeared as *Sigmar Polke: History of Everything, Paintings and*

Drawings, 1998–2003, ed. John R. Lane and Charles Wylie, Dallas: Dallas Museum of Art, 2003. A selection from *Atlas* was exhibited at the Whitechapel Gallery, London, 6 December 2003–14 March 2004, overlapping with Polke's *History of Everything* at Tate Modern, London, 2 October 2003–4 January 2004. Polke's show started out as *Sigmar Polke: History of Everything, Paintings and Drawings, 1998–2002*, at the Dallas Museum of Art, 15 November 2002–16 April 2003.

29 See for example, Gertrud Koch, 'The Richter Scale of Blur', *October* 62 (Fall 1992), pp. 133–42; and Gregg M. Horowitz, 'The Tomb of Art and the Organon of Life: What Richter Saw', in *Sustaining Loss*, pp. 133–69.
30 Robert Storr, *Gerhard Richter: Forty Years of Painting*, New York: Museum of Modern Art, 2002.
31 'Capitalist realism' – an ironic dialectical inversion of the idea of socialist realism, and a critical German term for Pop art – was inaugurated at the famous 1963 exhibition in a furniture store in Düsseldorf, *Living with Pop – A Demonstration for Capitalist Realism*, which contained works by Richter, Polke, Wolf Vostell and 'Konrad Lueg' (a pseudonym used by Konrad Fischer). It lasted until 1975.
32 *Being and Time*, p. 93.
33 See pp. 118–25.
34 Cf. Karl Marx, *Capital: A Critique of Political Economy, Volume 1: The Process of Production of Capital* (1867; 1873), Harmondsworth: Penguin, 1976, p. 125; Guy Debord, *Society of the Spectacle* (1967), Detroit: Black and Red. Detriot, paragraph 1.
35 Wolfgang Tillman, *If One Thing Matters, Everything Matters*, London: Tate Publishing, 2003.
36 Benjamin H. D. Buchloh, 'Gerhard Richter's Atlas: The Anomic Archive', in B.H.D. Buchloh et al., *Photography and Painting in the Work of Gerhard Richter: Four Essays on Atlas*, Barcelona: Museu d'Art Contemporani de Barcelona, 2000, pp. 11–30; here, 28–30.
37 Ibid., p. 12.
38 For the concepts of cult-value and exhibition-value, see Walter Benjamin, 'The Work of Art in the Age of Its Technological Reproducibility' (Third Version, 1939), in *Selected Writings, Volume 4: 1938–1940*, Cambridge, MA: Harvard University Press, 2003, pp. 251–83, 257–8. For education-value, see Benjamin's remarks on pedagogical function in 'Theatre and Radio' (1932, in *Selected Writings, Volume 2*, pp. 583–6) – a short piece on Brecht's epic theatre, in which education function is opposed to a generic 'entertainment' function. In the second version of the 'Work of Art' essay, the educational function appears in the guise of 'training' and 'teaching' functions of film ('The Work of Art in the Age of its Technological Reproducibility' [Second Version, 1936], in *Selected Writings, Volume 3*, pp. 101–33, 108); in the third version it appears as 'the evaluating attitude'

(*Selected Writings*, *Volume 4*, p. 269). Interestingly, these are the sections in which there is the greatest difference between the two versions.
39 Ellen Seifermann and Christine Kintisch, 'Forward', *Romantic Conceptualism*, p. 7.
40 Osborne, 'Painting Negation'.
41 Quoted in the Foreword to *Gerhard Richter: Panorama. A Retrospective*, eds Mark Godrey et al., London: Tate Publishing, 2011, p. 6. This is an allusion to Cézanne's injunction: 'Paint normally! Even if it's only a stove-pipe.'
42 Dorothée Brill, 'That's as Far as it Goes', in ibid., p. 251.

Chapter 4: Transcategoriality

1 Robert Hobbs, *Robert Smithson: Sculpture*, Ithaca, NY: Cornell University, 1981.
2 Robert Hobbs, 'Robert Smithson: Articulator of Nonspace', in *Robert Smithson: A Retrospective View*, Duisberg: Wilhelm Lehmbruck Museum, 1982, pp. 19, 11.
3 Eugenie Tsai (ed.), *Robert Smithson*, Berkeley: University of California Press, 2004; Ann Reynolds, *Robert Smithson: Learning from New Jersey and Elsewhere*, Cambridge, MA: MIT Press, 2003; Jennifer L. Roberts, *Mirror-Travels: Robert Smithson and History*, New Haven, CT: Yale University Press, 2004.
4 Lynne Cooke and Karen Kelley (eds), *Robert Smithson: Spiral Jetty*, Berkeley: University of California Press, 2005.
5 Lynne Cooke, 'A Position of Elsewhere', in *Robert Smithson: Spiral Jetty*, p. 53.
6 Gotthold Ephraim Lessing, *Laocoön: An Essay on the Limits of Painting and Poetry* (1766), trans. Edward Allen McCormick, Baltimore, MD: Johns Hopkins University Press, 1984; Greenberg, 'Towards a New Laocoön', pp. 23–38.
7 Rosalind Krauss, *Passages in Modern Sculpture*, Cambridge, MA: MIT Press, 1977, pp. 282–83.
8 Robert Smithson, 'Towards the Development of an Air Terminal Site', in *Robert Smithson: The Collected Writings*, ed. Jack Flam, Berkeley: University of California Press, 1996, p. 60.
9 Robert Smithson, 'What is a Museum? A Conversation Between Allan Kaprow and Robert Smithson', in *Robert Smithson: The Collected Writings*, p. 48.
10 Adorno, *Aesthetic Theory*, pp. 199–202. See above p. 83–5.
11 Henry Flynt, 'Concept Art', in *An Anthology of Chance Operations*, ed. La Monte Young, New York: L. Young & J. Mac Low, 1963.
12 Rosalind Krauss, 'Sculpture in the Expanded Field', *October* 8 (1979), reprinted in *The Originality of the Avant-Garde and Other Modernist Myths*, Cambridge, MA: MIT Press, 1985, pp. 276–90 (the diagram appears on p. 283).

13 Krauss, *'A Voyage on the North Sea'*. Like its critical siblings, post-formalism and postmodernism, the post-medium suffers from the indeterminacy of its constitutive negation, rendering it an empty, periodizing term awaiting further determination.
14 Lawrence Alloway, 'Robert Smithson's Development', *Artforum* XI, 3 (1973), reprinted in *Topics in American Art Since 1945*, New York: Norton, 1975, p. 233. Cornelia Butler, 'A Lurid Presence: Smithson's Legacy and Post-Studio Art', in *Robert Smithson*, Los Angeles: Museum of Contemporary Art; Berkeley: University of California Press, 2004, pp. 224–48. See also Claire Doherty (ed.), *Contemporary Art from Studio to Situation*, London: Black Dog Publishing, 2004.
15 Cf. Hal Foster, 'The Artist as Ethnographer', in *The Return of the Real*, Cambridge, MA: MIT Press, 1996, pp. 171–203.
16 This is by no means the only allusion to Hitchcock's film within Smithson's work, but it is certainly the most striking.
17 Cooke, 'A Position of Elsewhere', pp. 53 and 69.
18 Adorno, *Aesthetic Theory*, p. 220.
19 Michael Fried, 'Art and Objecthood', in *Art and Objecthood: Essays and Reviews*, Chicago: Chicago University Press, 1998, pp. 148–72.
20 Immanuel Kant, 'Critique of the Aesthetic Power of Judgment', in *Critique of the Power of Judgment*, section 16, pp. 114–16; Duve, *Kant After Duchamp*. For a comparison of the logical structure of Adorno and Duve's very different nominalisms, see this volume, pp. 82–5.
21 See Lucy Lippard, 'Escape Attempts', in *Reconsidering the Object of Art: 1965–1975*, ed. Anne Goldstein and Anne Rorimer, Los Angeles: Museum of Contemporary Art, 1996, pp. 16–40. Robert Smithson, 'Outline for Yale Symposium: Against Absolute Categories', in *Robert Smithson: The Collected Writings*, pp. 360–1.
22 Robert Hobbs, 'Smithson's Unresolvable Dialectics', in *Robert Smithson: Sculpture*, p. 30.
23 Robert Smithson, 'The Spiral Jetty' (1972), in *Robert Smithson: The Collected Writings*, p. 152, note 1. This opposition of 'indeterminate *certainty*' to '*determinate* uncertainty' is number five of ten that Smithson lists under the heading 'Dialectic of Site and Nonsite'.
24 Robert Smithson, 'A Cinematic Atopia' (1971), in *Robert Smithson: The Collected Writings*, p. 141.
25 See Osborne, 'Conceptual Art and/as Philosophy', pp. 47–65. Smithson considered Conceptual art (in the capitalized sense) a neo-idealist 'escape from physicality'. '"Well, in Nature You Can Fall off Cliffs": Four Conversations Between Dennis Wheeler and Robert Smithson (1969/1970)', in *Robert Smithson Unearthed: Drawings, Collages, Writings*, ed. Eugene Tsai, New York: Columbia University Press, 1991, p. 103.
26 See pp. 46–51.

27 Smithson, 'Towards the Development of an Air Terminal Site', p. 60.
28 Uncomfortable with the 'tour' element, Hobbs goes so far as to reduce the title of the work to 'Monuments of Passaic'. Hobbs, ed., *Robert Smithson: Sculpture*, p. 88, ff.
29 Smithson, 'Towards the Development of an Air Terminal Site', pp. 53 and 58.
30 Smithosn, 'Four Conversations', p. 104.
31 Lawrence Alloway, 'Robert Smithson's Development', in *Topics in American Art Since 1945*, p. 225.
32 Lawrence Alloway, 'Sites/Nonsites', in *Robert Smithson: Sculpture*, p. 42.
33 Alloway, 'Robert Smithson's Development', p. 228.
34 See Peter Osborne, 'Survey', in *Conceptual Art*, ed. Peter Osborne, London: Phaidon, 2002, pp. 19–23.
35 Smithson, 'Four Conversations', p. 99; emphasis added.
36 Robert Smithson, 'The Spiral Jetty', in *Robert Smithson: The Collected Writings*, p. 146.
37 Smithson, 'A Cinematic Atopia', p. 141.

Chapter 5: Photographic ontology, infinite exchange

1 Benedict Anderson, *Imagined Communities: Reflections on the Origin and Spread of Nationalism*, London: Verso, 1983, ch. 2 and 3.
2 Régis Debray, *Media Manifestos: On the Technological Transmission of Cultural Forms*, trans. Eric Rauth, London: Verso, 1996, p. 155.
3 See Sarah Kember, 'New Imaging Technologies in Medicine and Law', in *Virtual Anxiety: Photography, New Technologies and Subjectivity*, Manchester: Manchester University Press, 1998, pp. 17–36.
4 Ibid., pp. 141–2 – emphases added. One might reasonably be sceptical of Debray's claim that television lacks the 'reality effect' possessed by film; especially when, in his discussion of digital remixing, he describes the ontological 'inversion' involved in terms of the replacement of the criterion of 'anteriority' by that of 'actuality'. For what counts visually as 'actuality' here is thoroughly permeated by photographic norms themselves. One need only think of the role of faux-amateur techniques (all that handheld camera) in contemporary televisual and filmic realism alike.
5 André Bazin, 'The Ontology of the Photographic Image' (1945), in his *What Is Cinema?*, Vol. 1, trans. Hugh Gray, Berkeley: University of California Press, 1967, p. 14; Roland Barthes, *Camera Lucida: Reflections on Photography* (1980), trans. Richard Howard, London: Fontana, 1984, pp. 91, 96; Pierre Bourdieu et al., *Photography: A Middle-Brow Art* (1965), trans. Shaun Whiteside, Stanford, CA: Stanford University Press, 1990, Ch. 1.
6 See Osborne, 'Sign and Image', in *Philosophy in Cultural Theory*, pp. 20–52; 35ff.

7 This contrasts with the approach of George Baker in his 'Photography's Expanded Field', *October* 114 (Fall 2005), pp. 118–40, which follows Krauss's 'Sculpture in the Expanded Field' in treating photography (as Krauss treated 'sculpture') as a historically defined artistic 'medium' – thereby designated 'modernist photography' – within a semiotically determinate field that generates three main alternative positions: 'still film' projected images, the digital montage 'talking picture', and the 'film still' cinematic photograph (p. 131).

It might seem that I am taking the opposite position here in relation to the immanent expansion of 'the photographic' to the one I took in the previous chapter in relation to 'sculpture'. However, as we shall see, the technological expansion of the photographic has led to its subjugation to the notion of the digital image, per se, rather than to a re-appropriation of the digital by the pre-digitally photographic – which would be the move analogous to the application of the term 'sculpture' to the minimalist 'object'.

8 Kant, 'Appendix to the Transcendental Dialectic', in *Critique of Pure Reason*, A644/B672 – emphases added.
9 Immanuel Kant, *Critique of the Power of Judgment*, p. 9.
10 Gilles Deleuze, *Difference and Repetition* (1968), trans. Paul Patton, London: Athlone Press, 1994.
11 Deleuze and Guattari, *What Is Philosophy?*, p. 42.
12 Cf. Christian Kerslake, 'The Vertigo of Philosophy: Deleuze and the Problem of Immanence', *Radical Philosophy* 113 (May/June 2002), pp. 10–23. Kerslake emphasizes the constructive character of Deleuze's concept of difference. My suggestion here is that such a construction will, of necessity, yield a concept of absolute difference with a greater distributive unity than Deleuze envisaged. It is the desire to avoid this link between construction and unity that motivates the opposing, purely affirmative reading of Deleuze's 'difference' defended by Peter Hallward. See the exchange between Christian Kerslake and Peter Hallward, 'Justification or Affirmation?', in *Radical Philosophy* 114 (July/August 2002), pp. 29–33. The antinomical character of this opposition is the result of their mutual abstraction from the problem of history.
13 Cf. *Philosophy in Cultural Theory*, pp. 29–41.
14 Louis Althusser, 'Contradiction and Overdetermination: Notes for an Investigation', in *For Marx* (1966), trans. Ben Brewster, London: New Left Books, 1977, pp. 87–128. This is particularly clear in the case of painting, which has had to adapt itself successively to photography, film, television and video – a history that is itself thematized in the shifting uses of abstraction by a postconceptual painter like Richter. See my 'Abstract Images', in Buchloh, ed., *Gerhard Richter*, pp. 95–111.
15 Wall, 'Depiction, Object, Event'; Fried, *Why Photography Matters as Art as Never Before*. See also Osborne and Wall, 'Art After Photography, After Conceptual Art', pp. 47–50.
16 Jeff Wall, '"Marks of Indifference": Aspects of Photography in, or as,

Conceptual Art', in *Reconsidering the Object of Art: 1965–1975*, ed. Anne Goldstein and Anne Rorimer, Los Angeles: Museum of Contemporary Art, 1996, pp. 246–67.
17 I take David Green and Joanna Lowry's point here about the neglected importance of the deictic side of this: the importance of the manner of pointing to the event of inscription – ostension as a constitutive, performative feature of photographic indexicality. David Green and Joanna Lowry, 'From Presence to the Performative: Rethinking Photographic Indexicality', in *Where is the Photograph?*, ed. David Green, Brighton: Photoforum, 2003, pp. 47–62.
18 Osborne, 'Sign and Image', p. 40
19 Boris Groys, 'From Image to Image-File – and Back: Art in the Age of Digitalization', in *Art Power*, Cambridge, MA: MIT Press, 2008, pp. 83–91, 84.
20 Barthes, *Camera Lucida*, p. 91.
21 Groys, p. 85. 'From Image to Image-File', p.85.
22 Ibid., p. 90.

Chapter 6: Art space

1 See David Cunningham, 'The Phenomenology of Non-Dwelling: Massimo Cacciari, Modernism and the Philosophy of the Metropolis', *Crossings* 7 (2004), pp. 137–161, and 'The Concept of Metropolis', *Radical Philosophy* 133 (September/October 2005), pp. 13–25; Edward W. Soja, *Postmetropolis: Critical Studies of Cities and Regions*, Oxford: Blackwell, 2000, pp. 19–49. Cunningham combines a Cacciarian genealogy of the metropolis, as a negation of the restrictions of earlier urban forms, with a Lefebvrean analysis of the urban as a concrete abstraction of pure form (spatialization of the 'quasi-void' of exchange). See Massimo Cacciari, *Architecture and Nihilism: On the Philosophy of Modern Architecture*, trans. Stephen Satarelli, New Haven, CT: Yale University Press, 1993; Henri Lefebvre, *The Urban Revolution* (1970), trans. Robert Bononno, Minneapolis: University of Minnesota Press, 2003, and *The Production of Space* (1974), trans. Donald Nicholson-Smith, Oxford: Blackwell, 1991.
2 Lefebvre, *The Urban Revolution*, pp. 118–9; Cunningham, 'The Concept of Metropolis', p. 20.
3 The theorization of the relationship of 'abstract' to 'differential' space in Lefebvre's *The Production of Space* is famously problematic, since, in so far as it has social actuality, Lefebvre's 'abstract space' is itself necessarily differential. Sometimes Lefebvre appears to recognize this, at other times not. The problem derives from the empiricism of his conception of the 'concrete'. For a critique of such conceptions, which nostalgically code the abstract as necessarily alienated, see Peter Osborne, 'The

Reproach of Abstraction', *Radical Philosophy* 127 (September/October 2004), pp. 21–8.

4   Manuel Castells, *The Informational City: Information Technology, Economic Restructuring, and the Urban-Regional Process*, Oxford: Blackwell, 1989; Saskia Sassen, *The Global City: New York, London, Tokyo*, Princeton, NJ: Princeton University Press, 1991, p. 201; Manuel Castells, *The Information Age: Economy, Society and Culture. Volume 1: The Rise of the Network Society*, Oxford: Blackwell, 1996; Saskia Sassen, 'Electronic Space and Power', in *Globalization and Its Discontents: Essays on the New Mobility of People and Money*, New York: The New Press, 1998, pp. 177–94; Saskia Sassen, *Territory, Authority, Rights: From Medieval to Global Assemblages*, Princeton, NJ: Princeton University Press, 2006; 2008.

The concept of the 'global city', as an infrastructural node and financial centre, is quite different from that of the 'mega-city' – cities with populations exceeding 10 million, generally with the majority living in poverty, without basic amenities – which have new urban spatial dynamics of their own. See Mike Davis, *Planet of Slums*, London: Verso, 2006. Indeed, these two types of city are in many ways, analytically, the obverse of each; although they may in some instances coexist, or at least overlap in the same urban territory: São Paulo, for example.

5   See Sassen, 'Denationalized State Agendas and Privatized Norm-Making', in *Territory, Authority, Rights*, pp. 222–76.
6   *The Rise of the Network Society*, p. 411.
7   Michel de Certeau, *The Practice of Everyday Life* (1974), trans. Stephen Rendall, Berkeley: University of California Press, 1984.
8   Marc Augé, *Non-Places: Introduction to an Anthropology of Supermodernity*, trans. John Howe, London: Verso, 1995.
9   Ibid., pp. 28–32, 78–9.
10 Georg Lukács, *Theory of the Novel: A Historico-Philosophical Essay on the Forms of Great Epic Literature* (1920), trans. Anna Bostock, London: Merlin Press, 1971, pp. 29, 41.
11 Augé, *Non-Places*, pp. 77–8, 83, 99, 94, 101, 96.
12 Ibid., pp. 87, 78–9.
13 Castells, *The Rise of the Network Society*, p. 423.
14 Augé, *Non-Places*, p. 86.
15 Castells, *The Rise of the Network Society*, pp. 377, 412. See also pp. 410–18. For an account of the 'transboundary' structure of digital networks, see Robert Latham, 'Networks, Information, and the Rise of the Global Internet', in *Digital Formations: IT and New Architectures in the Global Realm*, ed. Robert Latham and Saskia Sassen, Princeton, NJ: Princeton University Press, 2005, pp. 146–77.
16 Brian O'Doherty, *Inside the White Cube: The Ideology of Gallery Space* (1976, 1981, 1986), Berkeley: University of California Press, 1999, p. 44.

17 See Rosalind E. Krauss, 'The Circulation of the Sign', in *The Picasso Papers*, London: Thames and Hudson, 1998, pp. 25–85; and Kotz, *Words to Be Looked At*.
18 Osborne, *Conceptual Art*, pp. 21–2.
19 See Kotz, *Words to be Looked At*, Ch. 1 and 2.
20 See, respectively: Osborne, *Conceptual Art*, pp. 35–6, 134–5; Jeff Wall, *Dan Graham's Kammerspiel*, Toronto: Art Metropole, 1991, pp. 101–3; Benjamin Buchloh, 'Conceptual Art, 1962–1969: From the Aesthetic of Administration to the Critique of Institutions', *October* 55 (Winter 1990), pp. 105–43.
21 O'Doherty, *Inside the White Cube*, pp. 38–9.
22 Ibid., p.107.
23 Ibid., p. 80.
24 Adorno, *Aesthetic Theory*, p. 225.
25 See, respectively: Paul Schimmel (ed.), *Out of Actions: Between Performance and the Object, 1949–1979*, Los Angeles: Museum of Contemporary Art, 1998; Jeff Wall, '"Marks of Indifference"'; *The Impossible Document: Photography and Conceptual Art in Britain, 1966–1976*, ed. John Roberts, London: Camerawork, 1977; Luis Camnitzer, Jane Farver and Rachel Weiss (eds), *Global Conceptualism: Points of Origin, 1950s–1980s*, New York: Queens Museum of Art, 1999.
26 Jeff Wall, *Dan Graham's Kammerspiel*, p. 100.
27 'Programme of the First Working Group of Constructivists, Institute of Artistic Culture' (1921), quoted in Christina Lodder, *Russian Constructivism*, New Haven, CT: Yale University Press, 1983, p. 3.
28 I am thinking of such instances as the restaurant-themed pairing of Gordon Matta-Clark and Rirkrit Tiravanija at David Zwirner in New York in March and April 2007. Internal references would include the video works by Renée Green and Tacita Dean documenting their respective searches for the site of Smithson's *Partially Buried Woodshed* (1970) on the campus of Kent State University in Ohio, referred to in Ch. 4. This is all part of that academic historicism that is so prevalent a feature of current work by young (especially US) artists.
29 This derives from a simplistic identification of 'placelessness' with the idea of a 'fixed and transhistorical', ideal meaning; failing to see that the 'no-place' of the ideality of the artwork is *as social* as the 'specific site'. See, for example, Douglas Crimp, *On the Museum's Ruins*, Cambridge, MA: MIT Press, 1993, p. 17.
30 For the beginnings of a project focusing on the neglected architectural importance of demolition, visit www.aesd.nl, the website of the Agency for Economic and Space Development.
31 Jeff Wall, 'Monochrome and Photojournalism in On Karwara's Today Paintings' (1993), in *Robert Lehman Lectures on Contemporary Art*, ed. Lynne Cook and Karen Kelly, New York: Dia Center for the Arts, 1996, pp. 135–156.

32 Compare Michael Tarantino 'The Space Between Things', in *Rachel Whiteread: Shedding Life*, Liverpool: Tate Gallery, 1997, pp. 91–100; and *Gordon Matta-Clark: The Space Between*, ed. James Attlee and Lise Le Feuvre, Tuscon, AZ: Nazraeli Press, 2003; with the section on Matta-Clark in Éric Alliez, 'Undoing the Image (Signposts of a Research Programme)', in *Aesthetics and Contemporary Art*, ed. Armen Avanessian and Luke Skrebowski, Berlin: Sternberg Press, 2011, pp. 65–85; 79–84. The valorization of 'betweenness' is generalized theoretically in Sassen's most recent work into the concept of 'analytical borderlands', which is used to theorize the 'mixing' of different spatial and temporal orders. Sassen, 'Assembling Mixed Spatial and Temporal Orders: Elements for a Theorization', in *Territory, Authority, Rights*, pp. 378–398. However, this merely reproduces the structure of the problem of relations – separation – that it purports to solve.

33 Gilles Deleuze, *Cinema 1: The Movement-Image* (1983), trans. Hugh Tomlinson and Barbara Habberjam, Minneapolis: University of Minnesota Press, 1986, p. 109. The text attributes the term 'espace quelconque' to a Pascal Augé. Commentators' inability to track down the reference has led to a debate as to whether this was not actually a mistakenly cited reference to Marc Augé, and hence a version of his 'non-places' (*non-lieux*). See Charles J. Stivale, 'Duelling Augé's – Pascal and Marc', at www.langlab.wayne.edu/CStivale/D-G/DuellingAuge.html (last updated 17 July 2006). However, this is a red herring, both textually and conceptually. Pascal Augé is a typographical error (in the French original, repeated in the English translation) for Pascal Auger, the source of the term. I owe this clarification to Éric Alliez.

34 Ibid., pp. 110, 120.

35 'The Crisis of the Action-Image', in Deleuze, *Cinema 1*, Ch. 12; Gilles Deleuze, 'Beyond the Movement Image', in *Cinema 2: The Time-Image* (1985), trans. Hugh Tomlinson and Robert Galeta, Minneapolis: University of Minnesota Press, 1989, Ch. 1. Deleuze's periodization of 'the great crisis of the action-image' in Europe is 'something like: around 1948, Italy; about 1958, France; about 1968, Germany.' *Cinema 1*, p. 211.

36 Deleuze, *Cinema 1*, pp. 208, 121.

37 Ibid., pp. 110–111. One can see here Deleuze's characteristic 'neither/nor' response to a Kantian dualism; methodologically, similar in many ways to Adorno's negative dialectics, but ontologically quite different, in its Bergsonism.

38 Theodor W. Adorno, 'An Excursion to Hegel', in *Negative Dialectics*, pp. 300–60.

39 *Cinema 1*, p. 208. I have retained the French *ensemble* where the English translation has used 'set'.

40 Éric Alliez and Jean Claude Bonne, 'Matisse in the Becoming-Architecture

of Painting', in *Painting with Architecture in Mind*, ed. Edward Whittaker and Alex Landrum, Bath: Wunderkammer Press, 2012, pp. 38–70.
41 Kojin Karatani, *Architecture as Metaphor: Language, Number, Money*, Cambridge, MA: MIT Press, 1995, pp. 126–8. Karatani is thinking, in particular, of the late Wittgenstein and deconstruction. For Karatani, 'deconstruction could be realized only by exhaustive construction' and 'if formalized, is tantamount to Gödel's proof.' (pp. xxxiii–iv)
42 Ibid., pp. xxxii, 5, xxxix.
43 Manfredo Tafuri, *Architecture and Utopia: Design and Capitalist Development*, Cambridge, MA: MIT Press, 1976, p. 125, 182.
44 Cf. Gilles Deleuze, 'How Do We Recognize Structuralism?' (1972), in his *Desert Islands and Other Texts 1953–1974*, trans. Michael Taormina, ed. David Lapoujade, Los Angeles: Semiotext(e), 2004, p. 170. This is the point of convergence of the Adornian and Deleuzean problematics.
45 See Christina Lodder, 'Postscript to Russian Constructivism: The Western Dimension', in *Russian Constructivism*, pp. 225–38, and Benjamin H.D. Buchloh, 'Cold War Constructivism', in *Reconstructing Modernism: Art in New York, Paris and Montreal, 1945–1964*, ed. Serge Guilbaut, Cambridge, MA: MIT Press, 1990, pp. 85–112.
46 See, for example, John Rajchman, *Constructions*, Cambridge, MA: MIT Press, 1998; and *The Deleuze Connections*, Cambridge, MA: MIT Press, 2000.
47 Rajchman, *Constructions*, p. 9.
48 In mathematics a construction is a proof of existence of a mathematical entity via its reduction to other demonstrably existing mathematical entities. In philosophy, Schelling used the term for his method of meeting the formal need of a post-Kantian philosophical system to reconcile philosophical principle with recognition of the wealth of contingent particularities, by deriving the latter from the former. It re-emerged later in a radical empiricist form in Rudolf Carnap's *The Logical Construction of the World* (1928). Each of these uses demonstrates that abstraction of the intellectual logic of construction from the practice of building, which is also the theoretical basis of Constructivism.
49 Lodder, *Russian Constructivism*, p. 38.
50 'Statement by the First Working Group of Constructivists' in the catalogue of the 'First Discussional Exhibition of Associations of Active Revolutionary Art' (1924), in *Russian Art of the Avant-Garde: Theory and Criticism, 1902–1934*, ed. John E. Bowlt, London: Thames and Hudson, 1988, pp. 241–3. Gabo and Pevsner's *The Realistic Manifesto* is translated in ibid., pp. 208–14. The reiteration in the former of the 1920 slogan 'We declare implacable war on art' contrasts starkly with the latter's appeal to 'people to whom Art is . . . the source of real exaltation, our word and deed.' The First Working Group was made up of Aleksei Gan (their theorist), Aleksandr Rodchenko,

Varvara Stepanova, Karl Ioganson, Vladimir Stenberg, Georgii Stenberg and Konstantin Medunestsky.

51 See note 27, above.
52 Cf. Tafuri, *Architecture and Utopia*, pp. 153–6. The precursor of Tafuri's analysis is Walter Benjamin's understanding of surrealism as the 'secret cargo' of aestheticism. See Walter Benjamin, 'Surrealism: The Last Snapshot of the European Intelligentsia' (1929), in *Selected Writings, Volume 2*, pp. 207–21.
53 See Bürger, *Theory of the Avant-Garde*. Bürger himself, notoriously, sees this relationship less as a dialectical one than as a historical fall. He thus tends merely to judge, rather than comprehend, the condition of art in capitalist societies after World War II.
54 Adorno, *Aesthetic Theory*, pp. 57–8.
55 See, for example, Theodor W. Adorno, *Lectures on Negative Dialectics: Fragments of a Lecture Course 1965/6*, trans. Rodney Livingstone, Cambridge: Polity Press, 2008, pp. 102–8.
56 Adorno, *Aesthetic Theory*, p. 44.
57 Ibid., pp. 168, 257, 225.
58 Ibid., p. 304. Adorno is writing here about constructivism in music, but the point is a general one.
59 The model of paradigm repetition has its source in Buchloh's critique of Bürger. See Benjamin Buchloh, 'Theorizing the Avant-Garde', *Art in America*, November 1984 and *Neo-Avantgarde and Culture Industry: Essays on European and American Art from 1955 to 1975*, Cambridge, MA: MIT Press, 2000. See also, Hal Foster, 'Who's Afraid of the Neo-Avant-Garde?', in his *The Return of the Real*, Cambridge, MA: MIT Press, 1996, pp. 1–34, where it acquires a psychoanalytical inflection.
60 See Buchloh, *Neo-Avantgarde and Culture Industry*, p. xxiv. For the construction of the category of institutional critique see, Alexander Alberro and Blake Stimson (eds), *Institutional Critique: An Anthology of Artists' Writings*, Cambridge, MA: MIT Press, 2009; and John C. Welchman (ed.), *Institutional Critique and After*, Zürich: JRP/Ringier, 2006.
61 See, for example, Andrea Fraser, 'From the Critique of Institutions to an Institution of Critique', in Welchman, *Institutional Critique and After*, pp. 123–36.
62 Jeff Wall, *Dan Graham's Kammerspiel*, pp. 33, 11, 28.
63 James Meyer, 'The Functional Site; or, The Transformation of Site Specificity', in Erika Suderberg, ed., *Site, Intervention: Situating Installation Art*, Minneapolis: University of Minnesota Press, 2000, pp. 23–37; 25.
64 Ibid., pp. 27, 29. See also, James Meyer, 'The Expanded Site (Beyond Reflexivity)', in *What Happened to the Institutional Critique?*, New York: Paula Cooper Gallery, 1993, pp. 16–18. The idea of institutional functions, derived from Daniel Buren's writings of the early 1970s, is deployed by

Meyer in an immanent critique of the notion of site specificity to which the institutional critique of Buren's generation gave rise, on the basis of (his former teacher) Craig Owens's 'allegorical' reading of Smithson. Craig Owens, 'Earthwords', in *Beyond Recognition: Representation, Power, and Culture*, Berkeley: University of California Press, 1992, pp. 40–51.

65 Jeff Wall, 'Introduction', in Dan Graham, *Two-Way Mirror Power: Selected Writings by Dan Graham on his Art*, ed. Alexander Alberro, Cambridge MA: MIT Press, 1999, pp. x–xvii, xvii.

66 Nicolas Bourriaud, *Relational Aesthetics*, Dijon, France: Les Presses du réel, 2002, pp. 72–3; *Postproduction*, New York: Lukas and Sternberg, 2002. See also, Boris Groys, 'On the Curatorship', in *Art Power*, pp. 43–52. Groys work on Stalinism (Stalin, the great curator) has made him particularly sensitively attuned to the new institutional function of curatorship. See Boris Groys, *The Total Art of Stalin: Avant-Garde, Aesthetic Dictatorship, and Beyond* (1992), London: Verso, 2011.

67 Okwui Enwezor, 'The Black Box', in *Catalogue, Documenta 11_Platform 5: Exhibition*, ed. Okwui Enwezor et al., Ostfildern-Ruit, Germany: Hatje Cantz, 2002, pp. 44–5.

68 Ackbar Abbas, 'Migration as Spatial Fantasy', in *After the Event: New Perspectives on Art History*, ed. Charles Merewether and John Potts, Manchester: Manchester University Press, 2010, pp. 38–42; 42.

69 Emmanuel Levinas, 'Meaning and Sense' (1964), in Emmanuel Levinas, *Basic Philosophical Writings*, ed. Adriaan T. Peperzak, Simon Critchley and Robert Bernasconi, Bloomington, IN: Indiana University Press, 1996, p. 44.

70 Gayatri Chakravorty Spivak, *A Critique of Post-Colonial Reason: Towards a History of the Vanishing Present*, Cambridge, MA: Harvard University Press, 1999, p. ix.

71 See Hans Belting and Andrea Buddenseig (eds), *The Global Art World: Audiences, Markets and Museums*, Ostfildern, Germany: Hatje Cantz, 2009; Elena Filipovic, Marienke Van Hal and Solveig Ovstrbo (eds), *The Biennial Reader*, Ostfildern, Germany: Hatje Cantz, 2010.

72 Max Horkheimer and Theodor W. Adorno, *Dialectic of Enlightenment: Philosophical Fragments* (1944/1947), trans. Edmund Jephcott, Stanford: Stanford University Press, 2002, Ch. 4, 'The Culture Industry: Enlightenment as Mass Deception'. This text is, famously, the product of the confrontation of the German critical philosophical tradition with the experience of the USA. It represents a crucial theoretical shift, within the interpretation of 'mass culture', which subjects it to the Marxian analysis of the commodity form, via Kant's epistemological notion of a schema. See also, Theodor W. Adorno, 'The Schema of Mass Culture', in *The Culture Industry: Selected Essays on Mass Culture*, ed. J.M. Bernstein, London: Routledge, 1991, pp. 53–85.

73 Cf. Theodor W. Adorno, 'Culture Industry Reconsidered' (1963), in *The*

Culture Industry, pp. 85–92, 85. Scott Lash and Celia Lury, in *Global Culture Industry* (Polity Press, Cambridge, 2007), aspires to update the analysis. However, whilst it offers a (somewhat haphazard) mass of materials, it is lacking in any equivalent theoretical apparatus or consistency. While Horkheimer and Adorno 'worked through the logic of the commodity', it argues, 'in global cultural industry we deal with singularities' (p. 12), thereby wishing away the capitalistic character of its object at the outset.

74 Adorno, *Aesthetic Theory*, p. 226.
75 Krauss, *A Voyage on the North Sea* and 'Reinventing the Medium', *Critical Inquiry* 25 (Winter 1999), pp. 289–305; Duve, *Kant After Duchamp*.
76 See, for example, Robert Storr, 'History of Projects', *MoMA Magazine* (Winter/Spring 1996), http://www.moma.org/interactives/exhibitions/projects/ (accessed: 2/12/2011).
77 Friedrich Schlegel, '"Athenäum" Fragmente', no. 116, p. 91; 'Athenaeum Fragments', no.116, p. 32, translation amended. This is part of the famous definition of Romantic poetry as 'progressive, universal poetry'. See pp. 67–8.
78 Martin Heidegger, *Sein und Zeit* (1927), Tübingen: Max Niemeyer, 1993, p.145; *Being and Time*, trans. John Macquarrie and Edward Robinson, Oxford: Blackwell, 1962, p. 185.
79 Storr, 'History of Projects'.
80 Schlegel, '"Athenäums"-Fragmente', no. 22, p. 78; 'Athenaeum Fragments', no. 22, pp. 20–21, translation amended.
81 Robert Smithson, 'A Tour of the Monuments of Passaic', in *Smithson: The Collected Writings*, p. 72. Smithson is writing here about the suburbs of Passaic. Later, he would base a slide work around this idea, *Hotel Palenque* (1969). Smithson himself considered such ruins in reverse to be 'the opposite of the "romantic ruin"' (ibid.). But they are better conceived as its secret meaning. Misunderstandings of Romanticism have plagued the reception of Smithson's work.
82 See Walter Benjamin, 'Eduard Fuchs, Collector and Historian', *Selected Writings, Volume 3*, pp. 260–302.
83 For the essentially modern dynamic of antiquation, see Walter Benjamin, 'Central Park', in *Selected Writings, Volume 4, 1938–1940*, Cambridge, MA: Harvard University Press, 2003, pp. 161–199.
84 See J. Laplanche and J.-B. Pontalis, 'Projection', in *The Language of Psychoanalysis*, trans. Donald Nicholson-Smith, London: Karnac Books, 1988, pp. 349–356.
85 Heidegger, *Sein und Zeit*, pp. 124, 145, 221–2, 135, 179, 145; *Being and Time*, pp. 162, 185, 264, 174, 223, 185.
86 Heidegger, *Sein und Zeit*, p. 145; *Being and Time*, p. 185. In the 1940s, Sartre would make the idea of *choosing* a 'fundamental projection' the basis of his own, distinctively French, brand of existentialism. His subsequent focus on

praxis, in the late 1950s, did not give up this idea of choosing a way of being, but further explored its conditions.
87 Adorno, *Aesthetic Theory*, p. 132.
88 See Maria Gough, 'In the Laboratory of Constructivism: Karl Ioganson's Cold Structures', *October* 84 (Spring 1998), pp. 91–117; and *The Artist as Producer: Russian Constructivism in Revolution*, Berkeley: University of California Press, 2005.
89 James Meyer, 'The Functional Site'.
90 See Jean-Paul Sartre, *Critique of Dialectic Reason*, Volume 1, pp. 79–94 and 539–63, in particular.

Chapter 7: Art time

1 Chapters 1 and 2, above; *The Politics of Time*, Chs 1, 4 and 5; 'The Time of the Artwork', in *Philosophy in Cultural Theory*, Ch. 1; and 'Global Modernity and the Contemporary: Two Categories of the Philosophy of Historical Time', in *Breaking Up Time*, ed. Chris Lorenz and Berber Bevernage, Göttingen: Vandenhoeck and Ruprecht, 2013, pp. 69–84.
2 Augustine, *Confessions* (398), trans. R.F. Pine-Coffin, Harmondsworth: Penguin, 1961, Book XI.
3 The classical formulation is Edward Bullough, '"Psychical Distance" as a Factor in Art and an Aesthetic Principle', *British Journal of Psychology*, Vol. 5 (1912), pp. 87–118. See also, Herbert Sidney Langfeld, *The Aesthetic Attitude*, New York: Harcourt, Brace and Co., 1920; and David Fenner, *The Aesthetic Attitude*, Atlantic Highlands, NJ: Humanities Press, 1996.
4 The most prominent anglophone proponent of an institutional theory of art is also the author of the best-known analytical rebuttal of the concept of the aesthetic attitude. See George Dickie, 'The Myth of the Aesthetic Attitude', *American Philosophical Quarterly*, Vol. 1 (1964), pp. 56–65; *Art and the Aesthetic: An Institutional Analysis*, Ithaca, NY: Cornell University Press, 1974; *The Art Circle: A Theory of Art*, New York: Haven Publications, 1984. For the more sociological French variant, see Pierre Bourdieu, *Distinction: A Social Critique of the Judgement of Taste* (1979), trans. Richard Nice, London: Routledge, 1989.
5 Jonathan Crary, *Suspensions of Perception: Attention, Spectacle, and Modern Culture*, Cambridge, MA: MIT Press, 1999, pp. 13–14; see also pp. 2 and 29.
6 Ibid., pp. 48–9; Howard Eiland, 'Reception in Distraction', *Boundary 2* 30: 1 (Spring 2003), pp. 51–66.
7 Blaise Pascal, *Pensées*, trans. A. J. Krailsheimer, London: Penguin, 1966, p. 148, no. 414.
8 Martin Heidegger, *The Fundamental Concepts of Metaphysics: World, Finitude, Solitude*, trans. William McNeill and Nicholas Walker, Bloomington, IN: Indiana University Press, 1995, pp. 59–167.

9 Benjamin, *The Arcades Project*, 'Convolute D [Boredom, Eternal Return]', pp. 101–119. For an analysis of the contradictory relation to history in Heidegger's account of boredom, and its symptomatic significance for the 'turn' in his thought during the 1930s, see Miguel de Beistegui, 'Boredom: Between Existence and History' (2000), *Thinking with Heidegger: Displacements*, Bloomington, IN: Indiana University Press, 2004, pp. 61–80. Insofar as there is a historical dimension to Heidegger's analysis, in its opening reference to 'our contemporary Dasein' (p. 69), it is part of an epochal history of Being – a subjection of history to Being – rather than anything approaching a history constituted by an interacting multiplicity of socio-temporal forms. The (elite-theoretical) sociology of *Being and Time* was thus displaced by an even less socially differentiated history of epochs of Being.

10 Benjamin, *Arcades Project*, [D3a, 4], p. 108; '1939: "France is bored." (Lamartine)', ibid., [D4a, 3], p. 110. See also, in particular, Siegfried Kracauer, 'Boredom' (1924), *The Mass Ornament: Weimar Essays*, trans. and ed. Thomas Y. Levin, Cambridge, MA: Harvard University Press, 1995, pp. 331–4.

11 Walter Benjamin, 'The Storyteller' (1936), in *Selected Writings, Volume 3*, p. 149. 'If sleep is the apogee of physical relaxation, boredom is the apogee of mental relaxation', ibid.

12 Cited by Benjamin, *Arcades Project*, [D4A, 2], p. 110.

13 See Osborne, 'The Reproach of Abstraction'.

14 Benjamin, *Arcades Project*, [B1, 1], p. 62.

15 There is a characteristic tension in Benjamin's remarks on boredom, distributed across different texts, between the idea that 'the activities that are intimately associated with boredom ... are already extinct in the cities' ('The Storyteller', p. 149) and the suggestion that boredom is an integral part of the experiences of a whole range of figures characteristic of modern metropolitan life, including the courtesan, the gambler, the flaneur, and 'he who waits'. *Arcades Project*, [D3, 4], p. 107. One may view that as ambivalence, as Andrew Benjamin does, for example, in a quasi-Heideggerian, psychoanalytical reading of Benjamin (Andrew Benjamin, 'Boredom and Distraction: The Moods of Modernity', in *Walter Benjamin and History*, ed. Andrew Benjamin, London: Continuum, 2005, pp. 156–170), or more historically, as a sign of the dialectical development of new forms of boredom, as I shall demonstrate here.

16 Raoul Vaneigem, 'Postscript' (1972), in *The Revolution of Everyday Life*, trans. Donald Nicholson-Smith, London: Rebel Press, 1983, p. 216.

17 See the section, 'Boring Art', in Frances Colpitt, *Minimal Art: The Critical Perspective*, Seattle: University of Washington Press, 1990, pp. 116–20.

18 Pierre Cabanne, *Dialogues with Marcel Duchamp* (1967), trans. Ron Padgett, Da Capo Press, New York, 1987, p. 99.

19 Dick Higgins, 'Boredom and Danger' (1966), *Something Else Newsletter*, December 1968; reprinted in *Breaking the Sound Barrier: A Critical Anthology of the New Music*, ed. Gregory Battcock, New York: E.P. Dutton, 1981, pp. 20–7. More generally, see Ina Blom, 'Boredom and Oblivion', in *The Fluxus Reader*, ed. Ken Friedman, Chichester: Academy Editions, 1998, pp. 63–90.

20 Ivone Margulies, *Nothing Happens: Chantal Akerman's Hyperrealist Everyday*, Durham, NC: Duke University Press, 1996, Ch. 1.

21 Martin Heidegger, *Being and Time*, p. 62. A phenomenological analysis begins with the most familiar, culturally given (hence 'everyday') form of an object and attends to the totality of the descriptions of this form in such a way as simultaneously to deepen and to make less certain our sense of it, by revealing contradictions in the descriptions, to the point at which a new sense of it, centred on a new description of it, emerges. This new conception is then subjected to the same process, and so on. In Hegel, this leads inexorably to a phenomenological construction of the absolute, as the only possible endpoint of the process. In the early Heidegger, on the other hand, as a systematic procedure, phenomenology takes the more Kantian form of the elaboration of a *series* of 'equiprimordial' or equally basic conditions of an experience. The formality of this procedure, notoriously, introduces a crucial indeterminacy into the relations between the various conditions. However, it has the advantage of imparting a certain independence or self-sufficiency to each analytical stage. It thus permits a certain recontextualization or philosophical refunctioning of the separate arguments, which is notoriously problematic in a more fully systematic thinker such as Hegel. For the politics of Heidegger's analysis of everydayness, see Osborne, 'The Verso of Modernity: From Everydayness to Historical Life', in *The Politics of Time*, Ch. 5, pp. 185–96.

22 Heidegger, *Fundamental Concepts*, p. 153. Heidegger emphasizes that there is not one, but 'several' fundamental attunements (p. 59). However, boredom is taken to be *the* fundamental attunement of 'the day'; hence the philosophical importance of the (here unacknowledged) problem of the definition of the historical present – which Foucault picked in the late 1970s, in a quasi-existential mode, with his idea of a 'critical ontology of the present'.

Heidegger's brilliant phenomenological analysis of boredom is actually less original than it appears, since it is essentially a philosophical recoding and elaboration of a discussion in Kant's posthumously published lectures, *Anthropology from a Pragmatic Point of View* (1798), trans. Robert B. Louden, Cambridge: Cambridge University Press, 2006, pp. 43, 128–30. Boredom, Kant writes there, 'is preceived as a *void* of sensation by the human being who is *used to* an alteration of sensations in himself, and who is striving to fill up his instinct for life with something or other.' (p. 128) The modernity of this being is explicitly registered here in a marginal note, by way of a colonial opposition (as so often in Kant): 'On the boredom that no Carib feels.' Kant's lectures were the topic of Foucault's 1961 complementary doctoral thesis. Michel Foucault, *Introduction to Kant's Anthropology*, trans. Roberto Nigro and Kate Briggs, Los Angeles: Semiotext(e), 2008.

23 Heidegger, *Fundamental Concepts*, pp. 96, 98.
24 Ibid., p. 95.
25 Ibid., p. 82.
26 Ibid., pp. 79, 171–2.
27 Ibid., p. 93; Cf. Kant, *Anthropology*, p. 43, where he discussed the cause of boredom as 'the natural inclination towards *ease*': 'To deceive it [the natural inclination towards ease – PO] in return (which can be done by playing with the fine arts . . .), is called *passing the time (tempus fallere)*, where the expression already indicates the intention, namely to deceive even the inclination towards idle rest. We are passing time when we keep the mind at play by the fine arts, and even in a game that is aimless in itself within a peaceful rivalry at least the culture of the mind is brought about – otherwise it would be called *killing time*.' The historical difference between Kant and Andy Warhol (a history of alienation of temporal forms) can be measured by the transformation of 'passing the time' *into* killing time'.
28 Ibid., pp. 106, 99, 101.
29 Ibid., p. 113.
30 Ibid., p. 116; *Die Grundbegriffe der Metaphysik*, Klostermann, 1983/2004, p. 176.
31 The *OED* etymology of 'ennui' cites the Latin phrase *in odio* as its source (as in the expression *mihi in odio* – it is hateful to me), thereby connecting it directly to both the English 'annoy' and 'odium', via 'anui', a term common to Middle English and Old French. In fact, the substantive 'annoy' was apparently originally equivalent to 'ennui' in its sense of 'a disturbed or ruffled feeling arising from impressions . . . which one dislikes', before acquiring its current sense of active discomfort. The *OED* cites the expression 'His ennui amounted to annoy' from 1812. The origin of the English word 'bore', on the other hand, is unknown; although it appears as a synonym for the malady of ennui in the 1760s, at more or less the same time that ennui first appears in English, in the phrase 'French bore', connoting 'dullness or lack of interest', but which the *OED* admits it is unable to explain. It certainly lacks both the intensity of aversion associated with 'odium' as a subjective or objective quality and the 'ruffled' element of dislike in 'annoy'.
32 Heidegger, *Fundamental Concepts*, pp. 127, 158.
33 Ibid., pp. 152–3.
34 Ernst Bloch in 'Something's Missing: A Discussion between Ernst Bloch and Theodor W. Adorno on the Contradictions of Utopian Longing' (1964), in Ernst Bloch, *The Utopian Function of Art and Literature: Selected Essays*,

trans. Jack Zipes and Frank Mecklenburg, Cambridge, MA: MIT Press, 1988, p. 5; Adorno, *Aesthetic Theory*, p. 132. See also the two volumes of essays published on the occasion of the exhibition 'Adorno', at Frankfurt Kunstverein, in autumn 2003: Nicholas Schafhuasen et al. (eds), *Adorno: Die Möglichkeit des Unmöglichkeit/Adorno: The Possibility of the Possible*, Frankfurt: Lukacs and Sternberg, 2003.

35 Karl Marx, 'Economic and Philosophical Manuscripts (1844)', in Karl Marx *Early Writings*, trans. Rodney Livingstone and Gregor Benton, Harmondsworth: Penguin, 1975, p. 398. Marx is alluding to Hegel's analysis of Stoicism in the *Phenomenology of Spirit*: 'The True and the good, wisdom and virtue, the general terms beyond which Stoicism cannot get, are therefore in a general way no doubt uplifting, but since they cannot in fact produce any expansion of the content, they soon give rise to boredom [*Langeweile*].' Hegel's *Phenomenology of Spirit*, trans. A.V. Miller, Oxford: Oxford University Press, 1977, p. 122; translation modified. G.W.F. Hegel, *Phänomenologie des Geistes*, Stuttgart: Reclam, 1987, p. 153.

36 Søren Kierkegaard, *Either/Or* (1843), Part 1, trans. Howard V. Hong and Edna H. Hong, Princeton, NJ: Princeton University Press, 1987, p. 286. The source common to Marx and Kierkegaard here, in their boredom-based readings of the moment of externalization in Hegel's system, appears to be Schelling, who first outlined the position in his 1833 lectures, *The Grounding of Positive Philosophy*, and frequently returned to it thereafter. F.W.J. Schelling, *Grundlegung der positiven Philosophie*, ed. Horst Fuhrmanns, Torino: Bottega d'Erasmo, 1972, pp. 225–7; cited in Vijak Haddadi, *Existential Cosmology: The Foundation of Post-Critical Metaphysics in Schelling*, PhD thesis, London: Centre for Research in Modern European Philosophy, Kingston University, 2012, pp. 62–3.

37 Adam Phillips, 'On Being Bored', in *On Kissing, Tickling and Being Bored*, London: Faber and Faber, 1993, pp. 82, 71.

38 Benjamin, 'The Work of Art' (Third Version), *Selected Writings, Vol. 4*, p. 266. In a note, Benjamin quotes Breton: 'The artwork has value only insofar as it is alive to reverberations of the future.' Ibid., p. 280, n. 39.

39 *Arcades Project*, [D2, 7], p. 105.

40 Eiland, 'Reception in Distraction'. The connection was first made by Kracauer in the mid-1920s, in an essay on distraction that followed his essay 'Boredom' (see note 10, above) by two years. Siegfried Kracauer, 'The Cult of Distraction: On Berlin's Picture Palaces" (1926), in *The Mass Ornament*, pp. 323–8. The shows in Berlin cinemas, Kracauer argued, 'raise distraction to the level of culture' (p. 324).

41 Benjamin, 'The Work of Art' *Selected Writings, Vol. 4*, pp. 268–9. The term 'apperception' is used to refer to the immediate self-awareness of the perceiving subject, in distinction from the object-oriented process of perception.

42 Benjamin, 'The Work of Art', p. 268. Cf. Kracauer: 'Self-pitying complaints about the turn to mass taste are belated' ('Cult of Distraction', p. 325).
43 What is clear is that – whatever it turns out to be – its artistic significance will exceed the limited horizons of 'internet art' and involve a generalization of certain formal operations across different media, technically appropriated to each, in the same way that film provided a repertoire of formal techniques for all the arts. See Chapter 5, above.
44 See Anthony Vidler, 'Dead End Street: Walter Benjamin and the Space of Distraction', in his *Warped Space: Art, Architecture, and Anxiety in Modern Culture*, Cambridge, MA: MIT Press, 2000, pp. 81–97.
45 Henri Bergson, *Time and Free Will: An Essay on the Immediate Data of Consciousness* (1889), trans. F.L. Pogson, London: Allen and Unwin, 1910, pp. 98–100, 105.
46 Henri Bergson, *Creative Evolution*, trans. Arthur Mitchell, New York: Henry Holt, 1911, reprinted, New York: Dover, 1998, pp. 11, 14. See also, Keith Ansell-Pearson, *Philosophy and the Adventure of the Virtual: Bergson and the Time of Life*, London: Routledge, 2002.
47 Gilles Deleuze, *Cinema 1: The Movement-Image*; *Cinema 2: The Time-Image*. Deleuze's philosophical understanding of Bergson was essentially complete as early as his 1956 essay, 'Bergson's Conception of Difference', in Gilles Deleuze, *Desert Islands and Other Texts, 1953–1974*, ed. David Lapoujade, trans. Michael Taormina, Los Angeles: Semiotext(e), 2004, pp. 32–51.
48 Gaston Bachelard, *The Dialectic of Duration* (1936), trans. Mary McAllester Jones, Manchester: Clinamen Press, 2000, pp. 44, 19–20; emphasis added. And for an application to art history: Peter Osborne, 'Starting Up All Over Again: Time and Existence in Some Conceptual Art of the 1960s', in *The Quick and the Dead*, ed. Peter Eleey, Minneapolis: Walker Art Center, 2009, pp. 91–106.
49 Bachelard, *Dialectic of Duration*, p. 133.
50 Benjamin, 'The Work of Art', p. 268.
51 For the idea that 'forgetting is essential to action of any kind', see Friedrich Nietzsche, 'The Uses and Disadvantages of History for Life', in *Untimely Meditations*, trans. R.J. Hollingdale, Cambridge: Cambridge University Press, 1997, pp. 57–123: p. 62. For Nietzsche's distinction between active and reactive forces, see Gilles Deleuze, *Nietzsche and Philosophy* (1962), trans. Hugh Tomlinson, London: Athlone Press, 1983, Ch. 2. On this conception, reactive forgetting functions in the service of the reproduction of the status quo, while active forgetting, on the other hand, serves 'life' and is a condition of possibility of its transformation.
52 Jacques Le Goff, *History and Memory*, trans. Steve Rendall and Elizabeth Claman, New York: Columbia University Press, 1992, 'History': pp. 101–216.
53 Gayatri Chakravorty Spivak, *Death of a Discipline*, p. 85.

54 For a discussion of the logical and ontological forms of the unity of history, see Peter Osborne, 'One Time, One History?', in *The Politics of Time*, Chapter 2. History, I argue there (p. 61), extending a formulation of Derrida's from his early critique of Levinas, is best thought as *the movement of the difference between totality and infinity*.

55 Frances Yates, *The Art of Memory* (1966), Chicago: University of Chicago Press, 2001.

56 Walter Benjamin, *The Origin of German Tragic Drama* (1928), trans. John Osborne, London: New Left Books, 1977, p. 36.

57 Walter Benjamin, 'Convolute N [On the Theory of Knowledge, Theory of Progress]', in *The Arcades Project*, pp. 456–88. I take the notion of the disjunctive synthesis of the series from Deleuze, *The Logic of Sense*, pp. 172–6. Deleuze's critique of the dependence of Leibniz's 'negative use of disjunction' on 'the hypothesis of a God who calculates and chooses' (p. 172) parallels Benjamin's famous critique of the 'God's eye point of view' of Ranke's historicism.

58 Geeta Kapur, 'Tracking', in *Indian Highway*, London: Koenig Books, 2008, pp. 185–9, p. 186.

59 Edmund Husserl, *Ideas Pertaining to a Pure Phenomenology and to Phenomenological Philosophy. First Book. General Introduction to a Pure Phenomenology*, trans. F. Kersten, Boston: Kluwer Academic Publishers, 1982, p. 52.

60 Ibid., p. 95.

61 Immanuel Kant, *Critique of Pure Reason*, p. 677.

62 Heidegger, *Being and Time*, p.416, emphasis added.

63 Ibid., p. 306.

64 Ibid., pp. 307, 386–387.

65 Husserl, *Ideas*, p. 175. See also Edmund Husserl, *On the Phenomenology of the Consciousness of Internal Time*, Vol. 4 of *Collected Works*, trans. John Barnett Brough, The Hague: Martinus Nijhoff, 1991.

66 Reinhart Koselleck, '"Space of Experience" and "Horizon of Expectation"': Two Historical Categories', in *Futures Past: On the Semantics of Historical Time*, trans. Keith Tribe, Cambridge, MA: MIT Press, 1985, pp. 267–88.

67 Hans-George Gadamer, *Truth and Method*, London: Sheed and Ward, 1975, pp. 267–274. Gadamer here follows Nietzsche in 'his complaint against historicism that it destroyed the horizon bounded by myth in which culture alone is able to live.'

68 Koselleck, '"Space of Experience" and "Horizon of Expectation"', p. 276.

69 Ibid., p. 275.

70 See Peter Osborne, 'Historicism as Bad Modernity', in *The Politics of Time*, pp. 138–44.

71 Walter Benjamin, 'On the Concept of History,' in *Selected Writings, Volume 4*, pp. 389–400. Benjamin's alternative is famously (negatively) 'messianic'.

The current dilemma of the philosophy of history, one might say, is that it remains trapped in an antinomy of historicism and messianism.

72 Cf. Peter Osborne, 'Interpreting the World: September 11, Cultural Criticism and the Intellectual Left', *Radical Philosophy* 117 (January/February 2003), pp. 2–12.

Bibliography

Abbas, Ackbar, 'Migration as Spatial Fantasy', in *After the Event: New Perspectives on Art History*, ed. Charles Merewether and John Potts, Manchester: Manchester University Press, 2010, pp. 38–42.
Adorno, Theodor W., *Aesthetic Theory*, trans. C. Lenhardt, London: Routledge, 1984.
———, *Aesthetic Theory*, trans. Robert Hullot-Kentor, London: Athlone Press, 1997.
———, *Ästhetische Theorie*, Vol. 7 of *Gesammelte Schriften*, Frankfurt am Main: Suhrkamp, 1996.
———, *Can One Live After Auschwitz? A Philosophical Reader*, ed. Rolf Tiedemann, Stanford, CA: Stanford University Press, 2003.
———, *The Culture Industry: Selected Essays on Mass Culture*, ed. J.M. Bernstein, London: Routledge, 1991.
———, *Lectures on Negative Dialectics: Fragments of a Lecture Course 1965/6*, trans. Rodney Livingstone, Cambridge: Polity Press, 2008.
———, *Negative Dialectics* (1966), trans. H.B. Ashton, London: Routledge, 1973.
Adorno, Theodor W., et al., *Aesthetics and Politics*, London: Verso, 2010.
Agamben, Giorgio, *The Man Without Content*, trans. Georgia Albert, Stanford, CA: Stanford University Press, 1999.
———, 'What is the Contemporary?', in *What is an Apparatus? and Other Essays*, Stanford, CA: Stanford University Press, 2009, pp. 39–54.
Alberro, Alexander, *Conceptual Art and the Politics of Publicity*, Cambridge, MA: MIT Press, 2003.
Alberro, Alexander, and Patricia Norvell (eds), *Recording Conceptual Art*, University of California Press, 2001.
Alberro, Alexander, and Blake Stimson (eds), *Conceptual Art: A Critical Anthology*, Cambridge, MA: MIT Press, 1999, pp. 106–8.
———, *Institutional Critique: An Anthology of Artists' Writings*, Cambridge, MA: MIT Press, 2009.
Alliez, Éric, 'Body Without Image: Ernesto Neto's Anti-Leviathan', *Radical Philosophy* 156 (July/August 2009), pp. 23–34.

———, 'Undoing the Image (Signposts of a Research Programme)', in Avanessian and Skrebowski (eds), *Aesthetics and Contemporary Art*.

Alliez, Éric, and Jean-Claude Bonne, 'Matisse in the Becoming-Architecture of Painting', in *Painting with Architecture in Mind*, ed. Edward Whittaker and Alex Landrum, Bath: Wunderkammer Press, 2012, pp. 38–70.

Alliez, Éric, and Andrew Goffey, eds, *The Guattari Effect*, London: Continuum, 2011.

Alliez, Éric, and Peter Osborne, 'Philosophy and Contemporary Art, After Adorno and Deleuze: An Exchange', in *Gest: Laboratory of Synthesis*, ed. Robert Garnet and Andrew Hunt, London: Bookworks, 2008, pp. 35–64.

Alloway, Lawrence, *Topics in American Art Since 1945*, New York: Norton, 1975.

Althusser, Louis, *For Marx* (1966), trans. Ben Brewster, London: New Left Books, 1977.

Ameriks, Karl, 'Hegel's Aesthetics: New Responses to Kant and Romanticism', *Bulletin of the Hegel Society of Great Britain* 45/46 (2002), pp. 72–92.

Anderson, Benedict, *Imagined Communities: Reflections on the Origin and Spread of Nationalism*, London: Verso, 1983.

Ansell-Pearson, Keith, *Philosophy and the Adventure of the Virtual: Bergson and the Time of Life*, London: Routledge, 2002.

Arrighi, Giovanni, *Adam Smith in Beijing: Lineages of the Twenty-First Century*, London: Verso, 2007.

———, *The Long Twentieth Century: Money, Power, and the Origins of Our Times*, London: Verso, 1994, 2009.

Art & Language and Tom Baldwin, 'Deleuze's Bacon', *Radical Philosophy* 123 (January/February 2004), pp. 29–40.

The Atlas Group and Walid Raad, *The Atlas Group, Volume 1, The Truth Will Be Known When the Last Witness Is Dead: Documents from the Fakhouri File in the Atlas Group Archive*, Köln: Walther König; Noisy-le-Sec: La Galerie de Noisy-le-Sec; Aubervilliers: Les Laboratoires d'Aubervilliers, 2004.

———, *The Atlas Group, Volume 2, My Neck Is Thinner Than a Hair: Documents from the Atlas Group Archive*, Köln: Walther König; Toronto: Art Gallery of York University; Liverpool: FACT (Foundation for Art and Creative Technology), 2005.

Attlee, James, and Lise Le Feuvre (eds), *Gordon Matta-Clark: The Space Between*, Tuscon, AZ: Nazraeli Press, 2003.

Augé, Marc, *Non-Places: Introduction to an Anthropology of Supermodernity*, trans. John Howe, London: Verso, 1995.

Augustine, *Confessions*, trans. R.F. Pine-Coffin, Harmondsworth: Penguin, 1961.

Avanessian, Armen, and Luke Skrebowski (eds), *Aesthetics and Contemporary Art*, Berlin: Sternberg Press, 2011.

Bachelard, Gaston, *The Dialectic of Duration* (1936), trans. Mary McAllester Jones, Manchester: Clinamen Press, 2000.

Badiou, Alain, *Handbook of Inaesthetics*, trans. Alberto Toscano, Stanford, CA: Stanford University Press, 2005.

———, 'Third Sketch of a Manifesto of Affirmationist Art', in *Polemics*, trans. Steve Corcoran, London: Verso, 2006, pp. 133–48.

Baker, George, 'Photography's Expanded Field', *October* 114 (Fall 2005), pp. 118–40.

Bal, Mieke, 'Visual Essentialism and the Object of Visual Culture', *Journal of Visual Culture*, 2: 1 (April 2003), pp. 15–32.

Balibar, Étienne, 'Citizen Subject', in *Who Comes After the Subject?*, ed. Eduardo Cadava et al., London: Routledge, 1991, pp. 33–57.

Barthes, Roland, *Camera Lucida: Reflections on Photography* (1980), trans. Richard Howard, London: Fontana, 1984.

Baudelaire, Charles, *The Painter of Modern Life and Other Essays*, trans. Jonathan Mayne, London: Phaidon, 1964.

Bazin, André, *What is Cinema? Volume One*, tran. Hugh Gray, Berkeley: University of California Press, 1967.

Beech, Dave, et al., *The Philistine Controversy*, London: Verso, 2002.

Beiser, Frederick C., *The Romantic Imperative: The Concept of Early German Romanticism*, Cambridge, MA: Harvard University Press, 2003.

Beistegui, Miguel de, *Thinking with Heidegger: Displacements*, Bloomington: Indiana University Press, 2004.

Belting, Hans, *Art History After Modernism*, Chicago: University of Chicago Press, 2003.

Belting, Hans, and Andrea Buddenseig (eds), *The Global Art World: Audiences, Markets and Museums*, Ostfildern, Germany: Hatje Cantz, 2009.

Benjamin, Andrew, 'Boredom and Distraction: The Moods of Modernity', in *Walter Benjamin and History*, ed. Andrew Benjamin, London: Continuum, 2005, pp. 156–70.

Benjamin, Walter, *The Arcades Project*, trans. Howard Eiland and Kevin McLaughlin, Cambridge, MA: Harvard University Press, 1999.

———, *The Origin of German Tragic Drama*, trans. John Osborne, London: New Left Books, 1977.

———, *Selected Writings, Volumes 1–4*, Cambridge, MA: Harvard University Press, 1996ff.

Bergson, Henri, *Creative Evolution*, trans. Arthur Mitchell, New York: Henry Holt, 1911; reprint, Dover, New York, 1998.

———, *Time and Free Will: An Essay on the Immediate Data of Consciousness*, trans. F.L. Pogson, London: Allen and Unwin, 1910.

Bernstein, J.M., *Against Voluptuous Bodies: Late Modernism and the Meaning of Painting*, Stanford, CA: Stanford University Press, 2006.

———, (ed.), *Classical and Romantic German Aesthetics*, Cambridge: Cambridge University Press, 2003.

———, *The Fate of Art: Aesthetic Alienation from Kant to Derrida and Adorno*, University Park, PA: Penn State University Press, 1992.

———, 'Modernism as Aesthetics and Art History', in *Art History Versus Aesthetics*, ed. James Elkins, New York: Routledge, 2006, pp. 241–68.

———, 'Social Signs and Natural Bodies: On T.J. Clark's *Farewell to an Idea*', *Radical Philosophy* 104 (November/December 2000), pp. 25–38.

Bernstein, J.M., et al., *Art and Aesthetics After Adorno*, Townsend Center for the Humanities/California University Press, Berkeley, 2010.

Birnbaum, Daniel, and Isabelle Graw (eds), *Canvases and Careers Today: Criticism and its Markets*, Berlin: Sternberg Press, 2008.

Blanchot, Maurice, 'The Athenaeum', in *The Infinite Conversation*, trans. Susan Hanson, Minneapolis: University of Minnesota Press, 1993, pp. 351–9.

Blissett, Luther, *Q* (2000), trans. Shaun Whiteside, London: Heinemann, 2003.

Bloch, Ernst, *The Utopian Function of Art and Literature: Selected Essays*, trans. Jack Zipes and Frank Mecklenburg, Cambridge, MA: MIT Press, 1988.

Blom, Ina, 'Boredom and Oblivion', in Friedman, ed, *The Fluxus Reader*.

Bourdieu, Pierre, *Distinction: A Social Critique of the Judgement of Taste* (1979), trans. Richard Nice, London: Routledge, 1989.

———, *The Field of Cultural Production: Essays on Art and Literature*, Polity Press, Cambridge, 1993.

———, *The Rules of Art: Genesis and Structure of the Literary Field*, trans. Susan Emanuel, Stanford, CA: Stanford University Press, 1995.

Bourdieu, Pierre, et al., *Photography: A Middle-Brow Art*, trans. Shaun Whiteside, Stanford: Stanford University Press, 1990.

Bourriaud, Nicolas, *Postproduction*, New York: Lukas and Sternberg, 2002.

———, *Relational Aesthetics*, Dijon, France: Les Presses du réel, 2002.

Bowie, Andrew, *Aesthetics and Subjectivity: From Kant to Nietzsche*, Manchester: Manchester University Press, 1990; 2003.

Bowlt, John E. (ed.), *Russian Art of the Avant-Garde: Theory and Criticism, 1902–1934*, London: Thames and Hudson, 1988.

Buchloh, Benjamin H.D., 'Conceptual Art, 1962–1969: From the Aesthetic of Administration to the Critique of Institutions', *October* 55 (Winter 1990), pp. 105–43.

———, 'Gerhard Richter's Atlas: The Anomic Archive', in *Photography and Painting in the Work of Gerhard Richter: Four Essays on Atlas*, ed. B.H.D. Buchloh et al., Barcelona: Museu d'Art Contemporani de Barcelona, 2000, pp. 11–30.

———, *Neo-Avantgarde and Culture Industry: Essays on European and American Art from 1955 to 1975*, Cambridge, MA: MIT Press, 2000.

Bullough, Edward, '"Psychical Distance" as a Factor in Art and an Aesthetic Principle', *British Journal of Psychology*, Vol. 5 (1912), pp. 87–118.

Bürger, Peter, *Theory of the Avant-Garde*, trans. Michael Shaw, Minneapolis: University of Minnesota Press, 1984.

Butler, Cornelia, 'A Lurid Presence: Smithson's Legacy and Post-Studio Art' in *Robert Smithson*, Los Angeles: Museum of Contemporary Art; Berkeley: University of California Press, 2004, pp. 224–48.

Cabanne, Pierre, *Dialogues with Marcel Duchamp* (1967), trans. Ron Padgett, New York: Da Capo Press, 1987.

Cacciari, Massimo, *Architecture and Nihilism: On the Philosophy of Modern Architecture*, trans. Stephen Satarelli, New Haven, CT: Yale University Press, 1993.

Calinescu, Matei, *Five Faces of Modernity: Modernism, Avant-Garde, Decadence, Kitsch, Postmodernism*, Durham, NC: Duke University Press, 1987.

Camnitzer, Luis, *Conceptualism in Latin American Art: Didactics of Liberation*, Austin: Texas University Press, 2007.

Camnitzer, Luis, Jane Farver et al., *Global Conceptualism: Points of Origin, 1950s–1980s*, New York: Queens Museum of Art, 1999.

Carrier, David, *High Art: Baudelaire and the Origins of Modernist Painting*, Penn State University Press, University Park PA, 1996.

Castells, Manuel, *The Information Age: Economy, Society and Culture. Volume 1: The Rise of the Network Society*, Oxford: Blackwell, 1996.

———, *The Informational City: Information Technology, Economic Restructuring, and the Urban-Regional Process*, Oxford: Blackwell, 1989.

Certeau, Michel de, *The Practice of Everyday Life* (1974), trans. Stephen Rendall, Berkeley: University of California Press, 1984.

Clark, T.J., *Farewell to an Idea: Episodes from a History of Modernism*, New Haven, CT: Yale University Press, 1999.

Colpitt, Frances, *Minimal Art: The Critical Perspective*, Seattle: University of Wshington Press, 1990.

Cooke, Lynne, and Karen Kelley (eds), *Robert Smithson: Spiral Jetty*, Berkeley: University of California Press, 2005.

Corris, Michael (ed.), *Conceptual Art: Theory, Myth, and Practice*, Cambridge: Cambridge University Press, 2004

Crary, Jonathan, *Suspensions of Perception: Attention, Spectacle, and Modern Culture*, Cambridge, MA: MIT Press, 1999.

Crimp, Douglas, *On the Museum's Ruins*, Cambridge, MA: MIT Press, 1993.

Crow, Thomas, *Modern Art in the Common Culture*, New Haven, CT: Yale University Press, 1996.

———, *The Rise of the Sixties: American and European Art in the Era of Dissent 1955–69*, London: Everyman Art Library, 1996.

Cunningham, David, 'The Phenomenology of Non-Dwelling: Massimo Cacciari, Modernism and the Philosophy of the Metropolis', *Crossings* 7 (2004), pp. 137–61.

———, 'The Concept of Metropolis', *Radical Philosophy* 133 (September/October 2005), pp. 13–25.

Danto, Arthur, 'The End of Art', in *The Philosophical Disenfranchisement of Art*, New York: Columbia University Press, 1986.

———, *Art After the End of Art*, Princeton, NJ: Princeton University Press, 1997.

Davis, Mike, *Buda's Wagon: A Brief History of the Car Bomb*, London: Verso, 2007.

Debray, Régis, *Media Manifestos: On the Technological Transmission of Cultural Forms*, trans. Eric Rauth, London: Verso, 1996.
Deleuze, Gilles, *Cinema 1: The Movement-Image*, trans. Hugh Tomlinson and Barbara Habberjam, Minneapolis: University of Minnesota Press, 1986.
———, *Cinema 2: The Time-Image*, trans. Hugh Tomlinson and Robert Galeta, Minneapolis: University of Minnesota Press, 1989.
———, *Desert Islands and Other Texts 1953–1974*, trans. Michael Taormina, ed. David Lapoujade, Los Angeles: Semiotext(e), 2004.
———, *Difference and Repetition*, trans. Paul Patton, London: Athlone Press, 1994.
———, *Francis Bacon: The Logic of Sensation*, trans. Daniel W. Smith, London: Continuum, 2003.
———, *The Logic of Sense*, trans. Mark Lester with Charles Stivale, New York: Columbia University Press, 1990.
———, *Nietzsche and Philosophy*, trans. Hugh Tomlinson, London: Athlone Press, 1983.
Deleuze, Gilles, and Félix Guattari, *Kafka: Towards a Minor Literature*, trans. Dana Polan, Minneapolis: University of Minnesota Press and Oxford, 1986.
———, *What is Philosophy?*, trans. Graham Burchell and Hugh Tomlinson, London: Verso, 1994.
Dickie, George, *Art and the Aesthetic: An Institutional Analysis*, Ithaca, NY: Cornell University Press, 1974.
———, *The Art Circle: A Theory of Art*, New York: Haven Publications, 1984.
———, 'The Myth of the Aesthetic Attitude', *American Philosophical Quarterly* Vol. 1, 1964, pp. 56–65.
Doherty, Claire (ed.), *Contemporary Art From Studio to Situation*, London: Black Dog Publishing, 2004.
Dufrenne, Mikel, *The Phenomenology of Aesthetic Experience* (1967), trans. Edward S. Casey, Evanston, IL: Northwestern University Press, 1973.
Duve, Thierry de, *Pictorial Nominalism: On Marcel Duchamp's Passage from Painting to the Readymade*, trans. Dana Polan, Minneapolis: University of Minnesota Press, 1991.
———, *Kant After Duchamp*, Cambridge, MA: MIT Press, 1996.
Edward-Smith, Lucie, *Movements of Art Since 1945*, London: Thames and Hudson, 1969.
Eiland, Howard, 'Reception in Distraction', *Boundary 2*, 30: 1 (Spring 2003), pp. 51–66.
Elkins, James, *What Happened to Art Criticism?*, Chicago: University of Chicago Press, 2004.
Elkins, James and Michael Newman (eds), *The State of Art Criticism*, New York: Routledge, 2008.
Enwezor, Okwui, et al. (eds), *Catalogue, Documenta 11_Platform 5: Exhibition*, Ostfildern-Ruit, Germany: Hatje Cantz, 2002.

Fabian, Johannes, *Time and the Other: How Anthropology Makes its Object*, New York: Columbia University Press, 1983.

Fenner, David, *The Aesthetic Attitude*, Atlantic Highlands, NJ: Humanities Press, 1996.

Fer, Briony, *The Infinite Line: Re-Making Art After Modernism*, Yale University Press, New Haven, 2004.

Filipovic, Elena et al (eds), *The Biennial Reader*, Ostfildern, Germany: Hatje Cantz, 2010.

Flynt, Henry, 'Concept Art', in *An Anthology of Chance Operations*, ed. La Monte Young, New York: L. Young & J. Mac Low, 1963.

Foster, Hal, *Recodings: Art, Spectacle, Cultural Politics*, Seattle: Bay Press, 1985.

———, *The Return of the Real*, Cambridge, MA: MIT Press, 1996.

Foucault, Michel, *The Order of Things: An Archaeology of the Human Sciences*, London: Tavistock Publications, 1970.

———, 'What is an Author?', in *Textual Strategies: Perspectives in Post-Structuralist Criticism*, ed. Josué V. Harari, Ithaca, NY: Cornell University Press, 1979, pp. 141–60.

———, *Introduction to Kant's Anthropology*, trans. Roberto Nigro and Kate Briggs, Los Angeles: Semiotext(e), 2008.

Frank, Andre Gunder, *ReOrient: Global Economy in the Asian Age*, Berkeley: University of California Press, 1998.

Frank, Manfred, *The Philosophical Foundations of Early German Romanticism*, trans. Elizabeth Millán-Zaibert, New York: SUNY Press, 2004.

Fried, Michael, *Art and Objecthood: Essays and Reviews*, Chicago: University of Chicago Press, 1998.

———, *Menzel's Realism: Art and Embodiment in Nineteenth Century Berlin*, New Haven, CT: Yale University Press, 2002.

———, *Why Photography Matters to Art as Never Before*, New Haven, CT: Yale University Press, 2008.

Friedman, Ken (ed.), *The Fluxus Reader*, Chicehster: Academy Editions, 1998.

Gadamer, Hans-George, *Truth and Method*, London: Sheed and Ward, 1975.

Gaiger, Jason, 'Art After Beauty: Retrieving Aesthetic Judgement', *Art History* 20: 4, 1997, pp. 611–16.

Gaut, Berys, *Art, Emotion and Ethics*, Oxford: Oxford University Press, 2007.

Geulen, Eva, *The End of Art: Readings in a Rumour After Hegel*, trans. James McFarland, Stanford: CA, Stanford University Press, 2006.

Godrey, Mark, et al. (eds), *Gerhard Richter: Panorama. A Retrospective*, London: Tate Publishing, 2011.

Goldstein, Anne, and Anne Rorimer (eds), *Reconsidering the Object of Art: 1965–1975*, Los Angeles: Museum of Contemporary Art, 1996.

Gough, Maria, *The Artist as Producer: Russian Constructivism in Revolution*, Berkeley: University of California Press, 2005.

———, 'In the Laboratory of Constructivism: Karl Ioganson's *Cold Structures*', *October* 84, Spring 1998, pp. 91–117.

Green, David, and Joanna Lowry, 'From Presence to the Performative: Rethinking Photographic Indexicality', in *Where is the Photograph?*, ed. David Green, Brighton: Photoforum, 2003, pp. 47–62.

Greenberg, Clement, *The Collected Essays and Criticism, Volume 1: Perceptions and Judgements, 1939–1944*, Chicago: Chicago University Press, 1986.

———, *The Collected Essays and Criticism, Volume 4: Modernism with a Vengeance, 1957–1969*, Chicago: University of Chicago Press, 1993.

———, *Homemade Esthetics: Observations on Art and Taste*, Oxford: Oxford University Press, 1999.

Groys, Boris, *Art Power*, Cambridge, MA: MIT Press, 2008.

———, *History Becomes Form: Moscow Conceptualism*, Cambridge, MA: MIT Press, 2010.

———, 'The Topology of Contemporary Art', in *Antinomies of Art and Culture*, ed. Smith et al., pp. 71–80.

———, *The Total Art of Stalin: Avant-Garde, Aesthetic Dictatorship, and Beyond* (1992), London: Verso, 2011.

Guattari, Félix, 'On Contemporary Art: An Interview with Oliver Zahm, April 1992' in Alliez and Goffey (eds), *The Guattari Effect*.

Guilbaut, Serge, *How New York Stole the Idea of Modern Art: Abstract Expressionism, Freedom, and the Cold War*, Chicago: University of Chicago Press, 1983.

———, (ed.), *Reconstructing Modernism: Art in New York, Paris and Montreal, 1945–1964*, Cambridge, MA: MIT Press, 1990.

Haiser, Jörge, et al., *Romantischer Konzeptualismus/Romantic Conceptualism*, Bielefeld, Germany: Kerber, 2007.

Hamilton, William *The Aesthetic Movement in England* (1882), Whitefish, MT: Kessinger, 2000.

Harrison, Charles, *Conceptual Art and Painting: Further Essays on Art and Language*, Cambridge, MA: MIT Press, 2001.

———, *Essays on Art and Language*, Oxford: Blackwell, 1991.

Harvey, David, *A Brief History of Neo-Liberalism*, Oxford: Oxford University Press, 2005.

Hegel, G.W.F., *Hegel's Aesthetics: Lectures on Fine Art*, trans. T.M. Knox, Oxford: Oxford University Press, 1975.

———, *Phänomenologie des Geistes*, Stuttgart: Reclam, 1987.

———, *Phenomenology of Spirit*, trans. A.V. Miller, Oxford: Oxford University Press, 1977.

Heidegger, Martin, *Being and Time* (1927), trans. John Macquarrie and Edward Robinson, Oxford: Blackwell, 1962.

———, *The Fundamental Concepts of Metaphysics: World, Finitude, Solitude*, trans. William McNeill and Nicholas Walker, Bloomington: Indiana University Press, 1995.

———, *Kant and the Problem of Metaphysics* (1929), trans. Richard Taft, Bloomington: Indiana University Press, 1990.

———, 'The Origin of the Work of Art' (1936), in *Poetry, Language, Thought*, trans. Albert Hofstadter, New York: Harper and Row, 1971, pp. 15–87.

———, *Sein und Zeit* (1927), Tübingen: Max Niemeyer, 1993.

Heiser, Jörg, 'Emotional Rescue', *Frieze* 71 (November–December 2002), pp. 70–5.

Hernández-Navarro, Miguel Ángel (ed.), *Heterocronías: Tiempo, Arte y Arqueologías del Presente*, Murcia, Spain: CENDEAC, 2008.Hickey, David, *Air Guitar: Essays on Art and Democracy*, Art issues Press, Los Angeles, 1997.

Higgins, Dick, 'Intermedia' (1965), in *Horizons, the Poetics and Theory of the Intermedia*, Carbondale: Southern Illinois University Press, 1984.

———, 'Boredom and Danger' (1966), in *Breaking the Sound Barrier: A Critical Anthology of the New Music*, ed. Gregory Battcock, New York: E.P. Dutton, pp. 20–7.

Hobbs, Robert, *Robert Smithson: Sculpture*, Ithaca, NY: Cornell University, 1981.

——— (ed.), *Robert Smithson: A Retrospective View*, Duisberg: Wilhelm Lehmbruck Museum, 1982.

Hobsbawn, Eric, *The Age of Extremes: The Short Twentieth Century, 1914–1991*, London: Michael Joesph, 1994.

Holland, Eugene, Daniel W. Smith and Charles J. Stivale (eds), *Gilles Deleuze: Image and Text*, London: Continuum, 2009.

Horkheimer, Max and Adorno, Theodor W., *Dialectic of Enlightenment: Philosophical Fragments* (1944/47), trans. Edmund Jephcott, Stanford, CA: Stanford University Press, 2002.

Horowitz, Gregg M., *Sustaining Loss: Art and Mournful Life*, Stanford, CA: Stanford University Press, 2001.

Husserl, Edmund, *Ideas Pertaining to a Pure Phenomenology and to Phenomenological Philosophy. First Book. General Introduction to a Pure Phenomenology*, trans. F. Kersten, Boston: Kluwer Academic Publishers, 1982.

———, *On the Phenomenology of the Consciousness of Internal Time*, Collected Works, Vol. 4, trans. John Barnett Brough, The Hague: Martinus Nijhoff, 1991.

IRWIN (ed.), *East Art Map: Contemporary Art and Eastern Europe*, London: Afterall Books, 2006.

Iversen, Margaret, and Stephen Melville, *Writing Art History: Disciplinary Departures*, Chicago: University of Chicago Press, 2010.

Johnson, Galen A. (ed.), *The Merleau-Ponty Aesthetics Reader: Philosophy and Painting*, Evanston, IL: Northwestern University Press, 1993.

Judt, Tony, *Postwar: A History of Europe Since 1945* (2005), London: Vintage, 2010.

Kant, Immanuel, *Anthropology from a Pragmatic Point of View*, trans. Robert B. Louden, Cambridge: Cambridge University Press, 2006.

———, *Critique of the Power of Judgment*, trans. Allan Wood and Eric Matthews, Cambridge: Cambridge University Press, 2000.

———, *Critique of Pure Reason*, trans. Paul Guyer and Allen W. Wood, Cambridge: Cambridge University Press, 1997.

———, *Kritik der reinen Vernunft*, Vol. 3 of *Werkausgabe*, ed. Wilhelm Weischedel, Frankfurt am Main: Suhrkamp, 1974.

———, *Kritik der Urteilskraft*, Vol. 10 of *Werkausgabe*, ed. Wilhelm Weischedel, Frankfurt am Main: Suhrkamp, 1974.

Kapur, Geeta, 'Tracking', in *Indian Highway*, London: Koenig Books, 2008, pp. 185–9.

Karatani, Kojin, *Architecture as Metaphor: Language, Number, Money*, Cambridge, MA: MIT Press, 1995.

Kember, Sarah, *Virtual Anxiety: Photography, New Technologies and Subjectivity*, Manchester: Manchester University Press, 1998.

Kerslake, Christian, 'The Vertigo of Philosophy: Deleuze and the Problem of Immanence', *Radical Philosophy* 113 (May/June 2002), pp. 10–23.

Kerslake, Christian, and Peter Hallward, 'Justification or Affirmation?', *Radical Philosophy* 114 (July/August 2002), pp. 29–33.

Kieran, Matthew, *Revealing Art*, London: Routledge, 2005.

Kierkegaard, Søren, *Either/Or*, Part One, trans. Howard V. Hong and Edna H. Hong, Princeton, NJ: Princeton University Press, 1987.

Koch, Gertrud, 'The Richter Scale of Blur', *October* 62 (Fall 1992), pp. 133–42.

Koselleck, Reinhart, *Futures Past: On the Semantics of Historical Time*, trans. Keith Tribe, Cambridge, MA: MIT Press, 1985.

Kosuth, Joseph, 'Art and Philosophy' (1969), in *Art and Philosophy and After: Collected Writings, 1966–1990*, Cambridge, MA: MIT Press, 1991.

Kotz, Liz, *Words to be Looked At: Language in 1960s Art*, Cambridge, MA: MIT Press, 2007.

Kracauer, Siegfried, *The Mass Ornament: Weimar Essays*, trans. and ed. Thomas Y. Levin, Cambridge, MA: Harvard University Press, 1995.

Krauss, Rosalind, *Passages in Modern Sculpture*, Cambridge, MA: MIT Press, 1977.

———, *The Picasso Papers*, London: Thames and Hudson, 1998.

———, 'Reinventing the Medium', *Critical Inquiry* 25 (Winter 1999), pp. 289–305.

———, "Sculpture in the Expanded Field," *October* 8 (1979), reprinted in *The Originality of the Avant-Garde and Other Modernist Myths*, Cambridge, MA: MIT Press, 1985, pp. 276–90.

———, 'Some Rotten Shoots from the Seeds of Time', in *Antinomies of Art and Culture*, ed. Terry Smith, Okwui Enwezor and Nancy Condee, Durham, NC: Duke University Press, 2008, pp. 60–70.

———, *A Voyage on the North Sea: Art in the Age of the Post-Medium Condition*, London: Thames and Hudson, 1999.

Lacoue-Labarthe, Philippe, and Jean-Luc Nancy, *The Literary Absolute: The Theory of Literature in German Romanticism* (1978), trans. Philip Barnard and Cheryl Lester, New York: State University of New York Press, 1988.

Lane, John R. and Charles Wylie (eds), *Sigmar Polke: History of Everything, Paintings and Drawings, 1998–2003*, Dallas: Dallas Museum of Art, 2003.

Langfeld, Herbert Sidney, *The Aesthetic Attitude*, New York: Harcourt, Brace and Co., 1920.

Laplanche, J., and J.-B. Pontalis, *The Language of Psychoanalysis*, trans. Donald Nicholson-Smith, London: Karnac Books, 1988.

Lash, Scott and Celia Lury, *Global Culture Industry*, Cambridge: Polity Press, 2007.

Lefebvre, Henri, *The Urban Revolution* (1970), trans. Robert Bononno, Minneapolis: University of Minessota Press, 2003.

———, *The Production of Space* (1974), trans. Donald Nicholson-Smith, Oxford: Blackwell, 1991.

Le Goff, Jacques, *History and Memory*, trans. Steve Rendall and Elizabeth Claman, New York: Columbia University Press, 1992.

Leighton, Angela, *On Form: Poetry, Aestheticism and the Legacy of a Word*, Oxford: Oxford University Press, 2007.

Lessing, Gotthold Ephraim, *Laocoön: An Essay on the Limits of Painting and Poetry* (1766), trans. Edward Allen McCormick, Baltimore, MD: Johns Hopkins University Press, 1984.

Levinas, Emmanuel, *Basic Philosophical Writings*, ed. Adriaan T. Peperzak, Simon Critchley and Robert Bernasconi, Bloomingdon: Indiana University Press, 1996.

Lodder, Christina, *Russian Constructivism*, New Haven, CT: Yale University Press, 1983.

Lukács, Georg, *Theory of the Novel: A Historico-Philosophical Essay on the Forms of Great Epic Literature* (1920), trans. Anna Bostock, London: Merlin Press, 1971.

———, *The Meaning of Contemporary Realism* (1957), trans. J. Mander and N. Mander, London: Merlin Press, 2006.

Lyotard, Jean-François, *Lessons on the Analytic of the Sublime*, trans. Elizabeth Rottenberg, Stanford, CA: Stanford University Press, 1994.

Martin, Stewart, 'The Absolute Artwork Meets the Absolute Commodity', *Radical Philosophy* 146, Nov/Dec 2007, pp. 15–25.

Marx, Karl, *Capital: A Critique of Political Economy, Volume 1: The Process of Production of Capital*, Harmondsworth: Penguin, 1976.

———, *Early Writings*, trans. Rodney Livingstone and Gregor Benton, Harmondsworth: Penguin, 1975.

Matravers, Derek, *Art and Emotion*, Oxford: Oxford University Press, 1998.

Menke, Christoph, *The Sovereignty of Art: Aesthetic Negativity in Adorno and Derrida* (1988), trans. Neil Solomon, Cambridge, MA: MIT Press, 1998.

Meyer, James, 'The Expanded Site (Beyond Reflexivity)', in *What Happened to the Institutional Critique?*, New York: Paula Cooper Gallery, 1993, pp. 16–18.

———, 'The Functional Site; or, The Transformation of Site Specificity', in

Site, Intervention: Situating Installation Art, ed. Erika Suderberg, Minneapolis: University of Minnesota Press, 2000, pp. 23–37.

Millán-Zaibert, Elizabeth, *Friedrich Schlegel and the Emergence of Romantic Philosophy*, New York: SUNY Press, 2007.

Mitchell, W.J.T, 'Showing Seeing: A Critique of Visual Culture', *Journal of Visual Culture* 1: 2 (August 2002), pp. 165–81.

Nietzsche, Friedrich, *Untimely Meditations*, trans. R.J. Hollingdale, Cambridge: Cambridge University Press, 1997.

Novalis, *Fichte Studies*, trans. Jane Kneller, Cambridge: Cambridge University Press, 2003.

October, 'Round Table: The Present Conditions of Art Criticism', *October* 100 (Spring 2002), pp. 200–28.

O'Doherty, Brian, *Inside the White Cube: The Ideology of Gallery Space*, Berkeley: University of California Press, 1999.

Osborne, Peter, 'Abstract Images: Sign, Image and Aesthetic in Gerhard Richter's Paintings (1998)', in *Gerhard Richter*, October Files 8, ed. Benjamin H.D. Buchloh, Cambridge, MA: MIT Press, 2009, pp. 95–111.

———, 'Adorno and the Metaphysics of Modernism: The Problem of a "Postmodern" Art', in Andrew Benjamin (ed.), *The Problem of Modernity: Adorno and Benjamin*, London: Routledge, 1989 pp. 23–48.

———, Aesthetic Autonomy and the Crisis of Theory: Greenberg, Adorno and the Problem of Postmodernism in the Visual Arts', *New Formations* 9, Summer 1989, pp. 31–50.

———, (ed.), *Conceptual Art*, London: Phaidon, 2002.

———, 'Conceptual Art as/and Philosophy' in *Rewriting Conceptual Art: Critical and Historical Approaches*, ed. Jon Bird and Michael Newman, London: Reaction Books, 1999, pp. 47–65.

———, 'Interpreting the World: September 11, Cultural Criticism and the Intellectual Left', *Radical Philosophy* 117 (January/February 2003), pp. 2–12.

———, 'Modernism and Philosophy', in *Oxford Handbook of Modernisms*, ed. Peter Brooker et al., Oxford: Oxford University Press, pp. 388–409.

———, 'Global Modernity and the Contemporary: Two Categories of the Philosophy of Historical Time', in *Breaking Up Time*, ed. Chris Lorenz and Berber Bevernage, Göttingen: Vandenhoeck and Ruprecht, 2013, pp. 69–84.

———, 'Neo-Classic: Alain Badiou's *Being and Event*', *Radical Philosophy* 142 (March/April 2007), pp. 19–29.

———, 'On Comparability: Kant and the Possibility of Comparative Studies', *boundary 2* 32: 2 (2005), special issue, 'Problems of Comparability/Possibilities of Comparative Study', ed. Harry Harootunian and Hyun Ok Park, pp. 1–20.

———, 'Painting Negation: Gerhard Richter's Negatives', *October* 62 (Autumn 1992), pp. 102–13.

———, 'Philosophy After Theory: Transdisciplinarity and the New', in Derek

Attridge and Jane Elliott (eds), *Theory After 'Theory'*, London: Routledge, 2011, pp. 19–33.

———, *Philosophy in Cultural Theory*, London: Routledge, 2000.

———, *The Politics of Time: Modernity and Avant-Garde*, London: Verso, 1995; 2011.

———, 'The Reproach of Abstraction', *Radical Philosophy* 127 (September/October 2004), pp. 21–8.

———, 'Starting Up All Over Again: Time and Existence in Some Conceptual Art of the 1960s', in *The Quick and the Dead*, ed. Peter Eleey, Minneapolis: Walker Art Center, 2009.

———, 'Torn Halves and Great Divides: The Dialectics of a Cultural Dichotomy', *News From Nowhere* 7 (Winter 1989), pp. 49–63.

———, 'Yardsticks: When Will the Postwar End?', in *Jane and Louise Wilson: Tempo Suspendo/Suspending Time*, Galicia, Spain: Centro Galego de Arte Contemporánea, 2011, pp. 33–9.

Owens, Craig, *Beyond Recognition: Representation, Power, and Culture*, Berkeley: University of California Press, 1992.

Pascal, Blaise, *Pensées*, trans. A.J. Krailsheimer, London: Penguin, 1966.

Phillips, Adam, *On Kissing, Tickling and Being Bored*, London: Faber and Faber, 1993.

Pollock, Griselda, *Avant-Garde Gambits, 1888–1893: Gender and the Colour of Art History*, London: Thames and Hudson 1992.

Raad, Walid, *Scratchings on Things I Could Disavow: Some Essays from The Atlas Group Project*, Köln: Walther König; Lisbon: Culturgest, 2007.

Rajchman, John, *Constructions*, Cambridge, MA: MIT Press, 1998.

———, 'The Contemporary: A New Idea?', in *Aesthetics and Contemporary Art*, ed. Armen Avanessian and Luke Skrebowski, Berlin: Sternberg Press, pp. 125–44.

———, *The Deleuze Connections*, Cambridge, MA: MIT Press, 2000.

Rancière, Jacques, *Aesthetics and its Discontents*, trans. Steve Corcoran, Cambridge: Polity, 2009.

———, *Dissensus: On Politics and Aesthetics*, trans. Steve Corcoran, London: Continuum, 2010.

———, *The Politics of Aesthetics: The Distribution of the Sensible*, trans. Gabriel Rockhill, London: Continuum, 2006.

Raunig, Gerald, *Art and Revolution: Transversal Activism in the Long Twentieth Century*, trans. Aileen Derieg, Los Angeles: Semiotext(e), 2007.

Redhead, Steve, *Paul Virilio: Theorist for an Accelerated Culture*, Edinburgh: Edinburgh University Press, 2004.

Reinhardt, Ad, *Art as Art: The Selected Writings of Ad Reinhardt*, ed. Barbara Rose, Berkeley: University of California Press, 1975.

Reynolds, Ann, *Robert Smithson: Learning from New Jersey and Elsewhere*, Cambridge, MA: MIT Press, 2003.

Ricoeur, Paul, *History, Memory, Forgetting*, trans. Kathleen Blamey and David Pellauer, Chicago: University of Chicago Press, 2004.

——, *Time and Narrative, Volume 3*, trans. Kathleen Blamey and David Pellauer, Chicago: University of Chicago Press, 1988.

Roberts, Jennifer L. *Mirror-Travels: Robert Smithson and History*, New Haven, CT: Yale University Press, 2004.

Roberts, John, 'After Adorno: Art Autonomy, and Critique – A Literature Review', *Historical Materialism* 7 (Winter 2000), pp. 221–39.

—— (ed.), *The Impossible Document: Photography and Conceptual Art in Britain, 1966–1976*, London: Camerawork, 1977.

——, *The Intangibilities of Form: Skill and Deskilling in Art After the Readymade*, London: Verso, 2007.

Robinson, William, I., *A Theory of Global Capitalism: Production, Class and State in a Transnational World*, Baltimore: Johns Hopkins University Press, 2004.

Rose, Gillian, 'From Speculative to Dialectical Thinking: Hegel and Adorno', in *Judaism and Modernity: Philosophical Essays*, Oxford: Blackwell, 1993, pp. 53–64.

Rosenberg, Harold, 'Criticism and its Premises', in *Art on the Edge: Creators and Situations*, Chicago: University of Chicago Press, 1975, pp. 135–52.

Sartre, Jean-Paul, *Critique of Dialectic Reason, Volume 1: Theory of Practical Ensembles* (1960), trans. Alan Sheridan-Smith, London: Verso, 1976.

Sassen, Saskia, *Globalization and its Discontents: Essays on the New Mobility of People and Money*, New York: New Press, 1998.

——, *A Sociology of Globalization*, New York: Norton, 2007.

——, *Territory, Authority, Rights: From Medieval to Global Assemblages*, Princeton, NJ: Princeton University Press, 2008.

Schaeffer, Jean-Marie, *Art of the Modern Age*, trans. Steven Rendall, Princeton, NJ: Princeton University Press, 2000.

Schafhuasen, Nicholas et al (eds), *Adorno: Die Möglichkeit des Unmöglichkeit/ Adorno: The Possibility of the Possible*, 2 vols, Frankfurt: Lukacs and Sternberg, 2003.

Schlegel, Friedrich, *'Athenäums'-Fragmente und andere Schriften*, Stuttgart: Reclam, 1978.

——, *Philosophical Fragments*, trans. Peter Firchow, Minneapolis: University of Minnesota Press, 1991.

Schelling, F.W.J., *Grundlegung der positiven Philosophie*, ed. Horst Fuhrmanns, Torino: Bottega d'Erasmo, 1972.

——, *System of Transcendental Idealism* (1800), trans. Peter Heath, Charlottesville: University Press of Virginia, 1978.

Paul Schimmel (ed.), *Out of Actions: Between Performance and the Object, 1949–1979*, Los Angeles: Museum of Contemporary Art, 1998.

Schulte-Sasse, Jochen, et al. (eds), *Theory as Practice: A Critical Anthology of Early German Romantic Writings*, Minneapolis: University of Minnesota Press, 1997.

Smith, Terry, 'Contemporary Art and Contemporaneity', *Critical Inquiry* 32, Summer 2006, pp. 681–707.

——, 'Introduction: The Contemporary Question' in *Antinomies of Art and Culture*, ed. Smith et al.

——, Okwui Enwezor and Nancy Condee (eds), *Antinomies of Art and Culture: Modernity, Postmodernity, Contemporaneity*, Durham, NC: Duke University Press, 2008.

Smithson, Robert, *Robert Smithson: The Collected Writings*, ed. Jack Flam, Berkeley: University of California Press, 1996.

Soja, Edward W., *Postmetropolis: Critical Studies of Cities and Regions*, Oxford: Blackwell, 2000.

Spivak, Gayatri Chakravorty, *A Critique of Post-Colonial Reason: Towards a History of the Vanishing Present*, Cambridge, MA: Harvard University Press, 1999.

——, *Death of a Discipline*, New York: Columbia University Press, 2003.

Stephen, Ann, 'Soft Talk/Soft-tape: The Early Collaborations of Ian Burn and Mel Ramsden', in *Conceptual Art: Theory, Myth, and Practice*, ed. Corris, pp. 80–97.

Stimson, Blake, and Gregory Sholette (eds), *Collectivism After Modernism: The Art of Social Imagination After 1945*, Minneapolis: University of Minnesota Press, 2007.

Storr, Robert, *Gerhard Richter: Forty Years of Painting*, New York: Museum of Modern Art, 2002.

Summers, David, *The Judgement of Sense: Renaissance Naturalism and the Rise of Aesthetics*, Cambridge: Cambridge University Press, 1987.

Tafuri, Manfredo, *Architecture and Utopia: Design and Capitalist Development*, Cambridge, MA: MIT Press, 1976.

Tarantino, Michael, 'The Space Between Things', in *Rachel Whiteread: Shedding Life*, Liverpool: Tate Gallery, 1997, pp. 91–100.

Tillman, Wolfgang, *If One Thing Matters, Everything Matters*, London: Tate Publishing, 2003.

Tsai, Eugenie (ed.), *Robert Smithson Unearthed: Drawings, Collages, Writings*, New York: Columbia University Press, 1991.

—— (ed.), *Robert Smithson*, Berkeley: University of California Press, 2004.

Vattimo, Gianni, *Art's Claim to Truth* (1985), trans. Luca D'Isanto, New York: Columbia University Press, 2008.

Vanderlinden, Barbara and Elena Filipovic, eds., *The Manifesta Decade: Debates on Contemporary Art Exhibitions and Biennals in Post-Wall Europe*, Cambridge, MA: MIT Press, 2005.

Vaneigem, Raoul, *The Revolution of Everyday Life*, trans. Donald Nicholson-Smith, London: Rebel Press, 1983.

Vidler, Anthony, *Warped Space: Art, Architecture, and Anxiety in Modern Culture*, Cambridge, MA: MIT Press, 2000.

Wall, Jeff, *Dan Graham's Kammerspiel*, Toronto: Art Metropole, 1991.

———, 'Monochrome and Photojournalism in On Karwara's Today Paintings', in Lynne Cook and Karen Kelly (eds), *Robert Lehman Lectures on Contemporary Art*, New York: Dia Center for the Arts, 1996, pp. 135–56.

———, '"Marks of Indifference": Aspects of Photography in, or as, Conceptual Art', in *Reconsidering the Object of Art*, ed. Goldstein and Rorimer, pp. 246–67.

———, 'Introduction', in Dan Graham, *Two-Way Mirror Power: Selected Writings by Dan Graham on his Art*, ed. Alexander Alberro, Cambridge, MA: MIT Press, 1999.

———, 'Depiction, Object, Event', *Afterall* 16 (Autumn/Winter 2007), pp. 5–17.

Wall, Jeff, and Peter Osborne, 'Art After Photography, After Conceptual Art: An Interview with Jeff Wall', *Radical Philosophy* 150 (July/August 2008), pp. 36–51.

Welchman, John C. (ed.), *Institutional Critique and After*, Zürich: JRP/Ringier, 2006.

Williams, Raymond, *Keywords: A Vocabulary of Culture and Society* (1976), London: Fontana, 1988.

———, *The Politics of Modernism: Against the New Conformists*, London: Verso, 1989.

Wollheim, Richard, *Painting as an Art*, London: Thames and Hudson, 1987.

Wu Ming, *54*, trans. Shaun Whiteside, London: Arrow Books, 2006.

Zepke, Stephen, 'Deleuze, Guattari and Contemporary Art', in *Gilles Deleuze: Image and Text*, ed. Eugene W. Holland and Daniel W. Smith, London: Continuum, 2009, pp. 176–97.

———, 'From Aesthetic Autonomy to Autonomist Aesthetics: Art and Life in Guattari', in *The Guattari Effect*, ed. Éric Alliez and Andrew Goffey, London: Continuum, pp. 205–19.

Image Credits

Front cover image: The Atlas Group in collaboration with Walid Raad. *Notebook volume 38: Already been in a lake of fire*, plate 58. Documented attributed to Dr. Fadl Fakhouri. Date (Attributed): 1991. Date (Production): 2003. Courtesy of the Paula Cooper Gallery, New York. © Walid Raad.

1. The Atlas Group in collaboration with Walid Raad, Bilal Khbeiz, and Tony Chakar, *We Can Make Rain But No One Came to Ask*, 2006. Single channel video, 18 minutes / color / sound. Courtesy of the Paula Cooper Gallery, New York, USA. © Walid Raad.
2. The Atlas Group in collaboration with Walid Raad, *My Neck Is Thinner Than a Hair*, 7 August 1980. Document attributed to The Atlas Group. Date (attributed): 2001. Date (production): 2003. Courtesy of the Paula Cooper Gallery, New York. © Walid Raad.
3. The Atlas Group in collaboration with Walid Raad, *Notebook Volume 72: Missing Lebanese Wars, Plate 132*. Document attributed to Dr Fadl Fakhouri. Date (attributed): 1989. Date (production): 1998. Courtesy of the Paula Cooper Gallery, New York. © Walid Raad.
4. Gerhard Richter, *A5las*, 1962–1997, Sheet 289. © Gerhard Richter 2012.
5. Gerhard Richter, *Atlas*, 1962–1997, Sheet 290. © Gerhard Richter 2012
6. Sigmar Polke, *History of Everything II*, 2002. Mixed media on fabric (403 x 303 cm). Courtesy of the Michael Werner Gallery, New York. © The Estate of Sigmar Polke, Cologne, DACS 2012.
7. Sabrina Hardman and Manadel al-Jamadi, Abu Ghraib prison, Iraq, 2004. Digital scan.
8. Cover of Robert Hobbs, *Robert Smithson: Sculpture*, Cornell University Press, Ithaca, New York, 1981. Digital Scan.
9. Robert Smithson, *Monuments of the Passaic (The Sandbox Monument)*, 1967, from 'A Tour of the Monuments of the Passaic, New Jersey', *Artforum*, Dec. 1967. Photograph. Image courtesy of the James Cohan Gallery, New York/Shanghai. © Estate of Robert Smithson.

10. Robert Smithson, *Mono Lake Nonsite (Cinders Near Black Point)*, 1968. Image courtesy of the James Cohan Gallery, New York/Shanghai.© Estate of Robert Smithson/DACS, London/VAGA, New York 2012.
11. Robert Smithson, *Floating Island to Travel Around Manhattan*, 1970. Image courtesy of the James Cohan Gallery, New York/Shanghai. © Estate of Robert Smithson/DACS, London/VAGA, New York 2012.
12. Robert Smithson, *Floating Island to Travel Around Manhattan Island, New York*, 2005. Image courtesy of the James Cohan Gallery, New York/Shanghai. © Estate of Robert Smithson/DACS, London/VAGA, New York 2012.
13. Gordon Matta-Clark, *Splitting*, 1974. 322 Humphrey Street, Englewood, NJ. Image courtesy of David Zwirner Gallery. © 2012 Estate of Gordon Matta-Clark / Artists Rights Society (ARS), New York, DACS London.
14. Gordon Matta-Clark, *Splitting* 6. Interior, 1974. Image courtesy of David Zwirner Gallery. © 2012 Estate of Gordon Matta-Clark / Artists Rights Society (ARS), New York, DACS London.
15. Gordon Matta-Clark, *Splitting* 32, 1975. Photo-montage of section. Image courtesy of David Zwirner Gallery. © 2012 Estate of Gordon Matta-Clark / Artists Rights Society (ARS), New York, DACS London.
16. Gordon Matta-Clark, *Splitting*, 1975. Photo-montage. Image courtesy of David Zwirner Gallery. © 2012 Estate of Gordon Matta-Clark / Artists Rights Society (ARS), New York, DACS London.
17. Amar Kanwar, *The Lightning Testimonies*, 2007. Eight-Channel DVD installation. 32:31 minutes. Installation shot. Courtesy of Amar Kanwar and Galerie Marian Goodman, Paris. Photo © Katrin Guntershausen.
18. Amar Kanwar, *The Lightning Testimonies*, 2007. Eight-Channel DVD installation. 32:31 minutes. Still. Courtesy of the artist. ©Amar Kanwar.
19. Navjot Altaf, *Lacuna in Testimony – Version 2*, 2005. Three-channel video installation. 9:30 minutes. Installation shot. Courtesy of the artist. © Navjot Altaf.
20–23. Navjot Altaf, *Lacuna in Testimony – Version 2*, 2005. Three-channel video installation. 9:30 minutes. Stills, details. Courtesy of the artist. © Navjot Altaf.
24. Mona Vătămanu and Florin Tudor, *Long Live and Thrive Capitalism!*, 2009. Banner, variable dimensions. Installation view. Frieze Art Fair, London, 2009. © Mona Vătămanu and Florin Tudor. Photo © Peter Osborne.

Index

0–9, 54
9/11, 199, 208, 210
12/11, 210
Abbas, Ackbar, 163
Abducted Person Act, 197
Absolute, the, 45, 50, 59, 64, 88, 114
Abstract Expressionism, 18, 88
abstraction, 19, 97, 100, 112–13, 125, 128, 131–3, 137, 140, 179, 184, 210
Acconci, Vito, 54
Adorno, T. W., 10–11, 44, 46, 50, 59, 65, 82–4, 93, 103, 107, 142, 150, 157–8, 165–6, 172, 183, 207
   Aesthetic Theory 10, 65, 82–3, 166
   Dialectic of Enlightenment, 10, 165
   Negative Dialectic, 59
advertising, 16, 46, 123, 167
aesthetic(s), 2, 6, 8–12, 37–51, 71, 74, 76, 103, 109, 122, 177, 192
   ideas, 45
   philosophical, 40
   regime, 9, 44
   see also, art, aesthetic; anti-aesthetic; inaesthetics; post-aesthetic
aestheticism/aestheticization, 43, 71, 74–8, 86, 109, 155, 182, 188
affirmation, 9, 73-4, 77–8, 80, 82–3, 88, 94, 97, 170
afterlife, 10, 50, 56
Alliez, Éric, 217–8 n23
Alloway, Lawrence, 105, 113
Althusser, Louis, 125, 207
Altaf, Navjot, 198, 200–201
   Between Memory and History, 198
   Lacuna in Testimony, 198–201
Ameriks, Karl, 41
Anderson, Benedict, 194

Andre, Carl, 54
anonymity, 33–4, 56,
anthropology, 136–7, 163, 198
anti-
   aesthetic-, 9, 46–9, 155
   aestheticism 47, 144
   art, 21, 142
   formalism, 50, 112
   system, 59
anticipation, 176, 205–8, 210
antiquation, 73
anxiety, 125–31, 186
architecture, 11, 16, 99, 102–4, 108–9, 134, 141–2
architecturalization, 140–51
archive, 33, 91, 141, 192, 197
Aristotle, 41
Arrighi, Giovanni, 26
art
   aesthetic, 37, 41–3, 56, 71, 78, 177
   autonomous, 21, 43–5, 78, 84, 159, 165–6
   conceptual, 1–2, 6, 9, 11–12, 19, 33, 38, 48–51, 67–98, 113, 127, 131, 144
   generic concept of, 20, 28, 45, 47, 56–7, 15–41
   historical, 6, 97
   modern, 18
   modernist, 93
   postconceptual, 3, 10–12, 19, 37–8, 45–51, 88–9, 97–100, 108, 110, 113, 117–8, 127, 131, 134, 143–51, 176
   post-historical, 7
   writing, 8
   see also, anti-art, Conceptual art, non-art

INDEX

Art & Langauge, 49–50, 54–5, 57–8, 139
   Index 001, 139
Art-Language, 54, 57, 61
art criticism, 2–8, 11, 39, 46, 52, 102, 114, 141
art history, 3–6, 10, 11, 17–19, 21, 53, 71, 141–2, 168, 177
   avant-garde, 92
   critical, 3
   modernist, 3, 53
   philosophical, 3
   social, 4
Art Press, 58
Art Yearbook, 102
Artforum, 54, 101
artist-function, 33–5, 37
Arts Magazine, 143
Ashbery, John, 54
Aspen, 54, 63
attention, 175–9
Athenaeum, The, 53–4
Atkinson, Terry, 57
Atlas Group, The, 13, 15, 28–35, 195–6, 199–201
   Already Been in a Lake of Fire, 30
   Hostage, 31
   I Only Wish, 31
   Miraculous Beginnings, 31
   Missing Lebanese Wars, 30–31
   My Neck is Thinner than a Hair, 30
   The Truth Will Be Known, 195–6
   We Can Make Rain, 29–30, 199, 201
Augé, Marc, 136–9
   Non-Places, 136
Augustine, St, 175, 187, 210–2, 205
autonomy, 7, 21, 37, 47, 85, 93, 141, 151, 156, 161, 165, 167
   aesthetic, 42–3, 78
   of art, 42–4, 75, 135, 140, 142
   logical, 43
avant-garde, 8, 16–19, 21, 33, 37, 47, 54, 74, 78, 86, 93, 135, 175, 178, 185
   historical, 21, 79, 88, 158
   neo-, 18, 20–21, 156, 158
   Russian, 81
axiomatics, 66

Bachelard, Gaston, 188
Bacon, Francis, 1
Badiou, Alain, 7–9
Baldessari, John, 61, 69, 96
   Baldessari Sings LeWitt, 69
   Commissoned Paintings, 96
Baldwin, Michael, 57
Barney, Matthew, 185
   Cremaster Cycle, 185
Baroque, 18
Barr, Alfred H., 19
Barthes, Roland, 119, 130
   Camera Lucida, 130
Baudelaire, Charles, 24, 46, 74–6, 182
Baumgarten, Alexander, 39–40
Bazin, André, 119, 124
Beirut, 28–9, 31,
Bell, Clive, 46
Benjamin, Walter, 10–11, 38, 44, 55–6, 67, 76, 79, 119, 127, 178–9, 182, 184–5, 189, 196, 206, 208
   Arcades Project, 55, 178–9, 184
   Concept of Art Criticism, 44
   'Concept of History', 208
Bergson, Henri, 187–8
   Creative Evolution, 187–8
   Immediate Data, 187
   Matter and Memory, 187
Bernstein, Jay, 43, 46, 76
Bharatiya Janata Party (BJP), 198
biennale, 21, 27, 109, 151, 162–5, 168
Biennale of Sydney, 31, 163–4, 198
Bitar, Joseph, 28–9, 32,
Blissett, Luther, 35
Bloch, Ernst, 183
Bochner, Mel, 57, 139, 142
boredom, 176–84
Bourdieu, Pierre, 119
Bourriaud, Nicolas, 106
Bowie, Andrew, 43
Braque, George, 153
Brecht, George, 139
Bruni, Lev, 154
Buchloh, Benjamin, 91
Bürger, Peter, 21
   Theory of the Avant-Garde, 21
Burgin, Victor, 16
   This is the Tomorrow, 16
Burn, Ian, 57
Butler, Cornelia, 105

Cage, John, 139
Callois, Roger, 179

INDEX

Calinescu, Matei, 16
   Faces of Modernity, 16
   Five Faces of Modernity, 16
capital, 26, 29, 34–5, 128, 134, 164–5, 194
capitalism, 16, 18, 20, 27, 34, 75, 85, 87, 118, 134, 176–7, 182, 192, 194, 206, 208–11
Castells, Manuel, 135–8
Cavagnaro, Lori, 106
Certeau, Michel de, 136
Chamfort, Nicolas, 58–9
   Pensées, Maxims and Anecdotes, 59
China, 20, 163, 167
Chto Delat, 21
cinema, 16, 114, 117, 149–50, 185, 188
City Gallery, Zagreb, 18
Claire Fontaine, 34
classicism, 60, 86
Clark, T. J., 6, 46, 79
Cold War, 16, 19–20, 155, 163
collectivity/collectivization, 15, 27–8, 33–5, 56, 86, 192–5
commodity/commodification, 10, 21, 85, 90, 165–6, 184, 210
communism, 20, 157, 176, 192, 206, 208–10
Conceptual art, 6, 48, 81, 107–9, 139, 159
   see also art, conceptual
conceptualism, 2, 50
   Romantic, 229 n46
conjuncture, 24
construction, 107, 145–9, 152–8
Constructivism, 11, 46, 153–8, 160–62, 165, 172, 193, 199–200
   laboratory, 11, 172
   philosophical 153
   Russian, 153
   Soviet, 11, 142, 168
contemporaneity/the contemporary, 2, 8, 12, 15–17, 22–8, 47, 53, 91, 134, 163, 175–6, 190, 195
Cooke, Lynne, 101
Corbusier, C-E. J., le, 152
crisis, 4, 6–7, 125, 177, 206
Crary, Jonathan, 177
criticism/critique, 11, 21, 40, 58, 77, 159, 177, 190
   of taste, 38, 41–2
   see also, art criticism; institutional critique

Cultural Studies, 7
culture industry, 21, 107, 164–5, 167, 179, 182
   see also, mass culture
curation, 129–30, 161–2, 168, 173, 190
Cutforth, Roger, 57

Dada, 81
Danto, Arthur, 6–7
Dean, Tacita, 105
death, 180, 183, 193
Debord, Guy, 68
Debray, Régis, 118–9
Deleuze, Gilles, 1, 7–9, 63, 122, 149–50, 153, 158, 188
   Difference and Repetition, 122
   Francis Bacon, 1
   What is Philosophy?, 122
demolition, 149
Derrida, Jacques, 7
Dia Art Foundation, 89, 101, 106
dialectics, 82–3, 108, 113, 138, 176, 179, 208
difference, 122, 165
digitalization, 117, 120, 123, 125–31
   see also, image, digital
Dion, Mark, 151
disciplines, 2–8, 11, 39
   see also, transdisciplinarity
distraction, 176–89
Documenta, 8, 196
document/documentation, 33–4, 110, 123, 127–8, 144–5, 192, 196–200
Dosse, François, 1
Duchamp, Marcel, 5, 19, 46, 77, 81–2, 141, 179
duration, 184–8
Duve, Thierry de, 5, 45, 77, 81–3, 107, 141, 167
   Kant After Duchamp, 77, 107

Earthworks, 101, 105, 108, 110
empiricism, 1, 114
Enlightenment, 176, 205
entropy, 114–16
Enwezor, Okwui, 163
epistemology, 60, 88, 128, 184
essentialism, 5
Evans, Walker, 143

INDEX

event, 127, 130–31, 136, 150, 208–10
everyday, 10, 79, 140, 151, 155–6, 197, 200
exchange, 87, 128, 133–5, 164, 210
   infinite, 28, 117
existentialism, 42, 89, 171–2
expectation, 201–11
experience, 11–12, 15, 22–3, 65, 75, 89, 100, 113–6, 121–2, 124, 134, 175, 178–9, 184, 192, 200
   absolute, 117
   historical, 206
   metaphysical, 168
   philosophical, 1, 52
   speculative, 52, 114
experimentation, 155–6, 172, 176, 186, 208, 211
expression, 151, 155, 1157
expressionism, 103, 157

fascism, 199
fashion, 75, 167, 179
feminism, 4
Fichte, J. G., 41, 44, 56, 59, 64
   Science of Knowledge, 59
fiction/fictionalization, 23, 28, 33–35, 199–200
film, 100, 103, 105–6, 108, 110, 114–7, 123, 125, 172, 185, 188–9
First Working Group of Constructivists, 154–5
form, 34, 60–2, 65, 67, 141
   cultural, 3, 8, 10, 34, 46, 48, 75, 118, 120, 133, 156, 176
   dominant, 120, 125
   exhibition-, 167
   film, 62
   historical, 123
   law of, 51, 85, 166
   legal, 197
   literary, 62
   social, 10, 128, 158
   spatial, 91
   temporal, 72–4
   urban, 12, 134
   see also, value-form
formalism, 3, 62, 71, 101–3, 109, 153, 155, 160
   literary, 61
   numerical, 61
   temporal, 175
formalization, 93
   see also, anti-formalism and post-formalism
Foster, Hal, 4
Foucault, Michel, 33, 35
fragment, 12, 38, 53, 55–6, 58–68, 86, 169–70, 178, 197
Frankfurt School, 155
Fluxus, 81, 139, 176, 179
Fraser, Andrea, 151
freedom, 84, 99, 105, 107, 140, 155, 166, 171, 210
Fried, Michael, 5, 24, 37, 46, 101, 107, 127
Fry, Roger, 46
functionalism, 94, 159–61, 163, 172
Futurism
   Russian, 168
futurity, 8–9, 16, 23–4, 201

Gabo, Naum, 154–5
   Realistic Manifesto, 154
Gadamer, Hans-Georg, 206
   Truth and Method, 206
Gaillard, Cyprien, 106
   The Smithsons, 106
gallery, 109, 112, 139–40, 172, 186
generations, 24
genius, 43–4, 66, 84
genre, 45, 58–9, 67, 86–7, 91, 96–7
geopolitical, 17, 25,
globality/globalization 15, 20–21, 26–7, 34–5, 134–5, 164
Goethe, J. W., 56
   Wilhelm Meister, 56
Goff, Jacques Le, 191
   History and Memory, 191
Graham, Dan, 54, 139, 142–5, 151
   Alteration, 145
   Homes for America, 143
   Poem-Schema, 54
   Scheme, 54
Grant, Cary, 105
Graves, Michael, 145
Green, Renée, 105
Greenberg, Clement, 3, 5, 37, 46–8, 77–81, 101, 118, 123
Greimas, Algirdas, 103
Groys, Boris, 129–30

INDEX

Guattari, Felix, 1, 9, 63, 122
Gunder-Frank, Andre, 26

Halperin, Ilana, 106
  Nomadic Landscapes, 106
Happenings, 179
Haywood Gallery, 104
  'Gravity and Grace', 104
Heidegger, Martin, 7–9, 23, 42, 45, 89, 168, 170–1, 175, 178, 180–4, 202, 204–8
  Being and Time, 180, 204
  Fundamental Concepts, 178, 180
Hegel, G. W. F, 7, 9, 25, 38, 41, 43–6, 49, 51–3, 65, 83, 107–8, 150, 183–4
  Lectures on Fine Art, 9
  Phenomenology, 51, 113
  Science of Logic, 108
Higgins, Dick, 99, 176, 179
  'Intermedia', 99
Hiller, Susan, 94
  Dedicated to the Unknown Artist, 94
Hiroshima, 199
historical a priori, 76
history, 3, 15, 25–6, 33, 62, 96, 119, 175–6, 178, 190–201, 206, 208
  literary, 11
  natural, 90
  philosophical, 35, 52, 168
  see also, art history
Hitchcock, Alfred, 105
  North By Northwest, 105
Hobbs, Robert, 100–104, 107–8
Hobsbawm, Eric, 26
Hölderlin, Friedrich, 56, 65
Holocaust, 199
Holt, Nancy, 106
Holzer, Jenny, 61
horizon – *see* expectation
Horkheimer, Max, 165–6
Huebler, Douglas, 112
humanities, 4
Husserl, Edmund, 176, 202–9
  Ideas, 202
  Consciousness of Internal Time, 205

idealism, 45, 59
  aesthetic, 5
  German, 7, 88
identity, 137

ideology, 6, 49, 78, 186, 188, 193, 198, 207, 210
image, 24, 28, 55, 60, 67, 90, 93–4, 96, 117–19, 123–4, 127–31, 149–50, 169, 199, 201
  dialectical, 38, 53, 67
  digital, 117, 119, 127
  see also, digitalization
imagination, 23
inaesthetics, 9
Independent Group, 16
  This is Tomorrow, 16
indexicality, 123–4, 127–9, 193, 200
indifference, 42, 49,
  aesthetic, 81
individuality (of artworks), 83–7, 102–3, 105, 107, 150
infinity, 64–5, 67, 69, 118, 130
information, 62–3
Information, 63
Information Technology, 63
installation, 126, 136
institutional critique, 109, 158–9, 172
institutional theory of art, 107
Institute of Contemporary Arts (ICA), 16
intermedia, 99
internationalism, 26, 35, 141
isms, 83–4, 107,
Iven, Jorge, 150

Jameson, Fredric, 17
Jewish Museum, 63
Judd, Donald, 57, 82, 107
judgement, 8–10, 40, 51, 78, 189
  aesthetic, 39–43, 177
  art-critical, 47
  historical, 1
  -power, 40–42

Kael, Pauline, 181
Kant, Immanuel, 5, 7, 10, 22–4, 26, 37–44, 46, 49, 64–5, 71, 76, 84, 89, 107, 120–3, 175, 177, 183, 193, 203–4
  Critique of Pure Reason, 38, 40, 76, 121, 203
  Critique of Judgement-Power, 39–41, 121
Kanwar, Amar, 196, 200–201

INDEX

The Lightning Testimonies, 196–7, 200–201
Kaprow, Allan, 102, 151
Kawara, On, 87, 144
   Date Paintings, 87
kitsch, 17, 97
Kierkegaard, Søren, 184
Klyun, Ivan, 154
Koselleck, Reinhard, 202, 205–7
   'Space of Experience', 205–6
Kosuth, Joseph, 37, 49, 57, 61, 139
   'Art and Philosophy', 57
   Titled (Art as Idea . . .), 139
Kracauer, Siegfried, 185, 189
Krauss, Rosalind, 101–4, 108, 167
   Passages in Modern Sculpture, 101
   'Sculpture in the Expanded Field', 103–4

Land art, 108
landscape, 91, 96, 103–4
Laocöon and his Sons, 101
Lebanon, 29–31, 35, 191, 199
Lefebvre, Henri, 133
legitimation, 6–7, 71, 73, 88, 142, 190, 192, 203
Lessing, Gotthold, 46, 80, 101
   Laocöon, 101
LeWitt, Sol, 12, 37–8, 49, 53–8, 61, 63, 65–9, 93, 107, 142
   'Paragraphs on Conceptual Art', 54, 93
   Sentences on Conceptual Art, 38, 53–8, 61–9
   'Serial Project No. 1', 63
liberalism, 85
liberation
   national 20, 163
literature, 33, 54, 56
libertariansm, 87
Lippard, Lucy, 107, 114
   Eccentric Abstraction, 107
Lukàcs, Georg, 18, 137
Lyotard, Jean-François, 7, 44

major/minor, 63
Manet, Eduard, 79
Manifesta, 162
mass culture, 165, 167
Matta-Clark, Gordon, 142, 145–9, 151
   Bingo, 145
   NYU Checkerboard, 145
   Splitting, 145
   Window Blow-Out, 145
Marx, Karl, 90, 128, 183–4
   1844 Manuscripts, 183
   Capital, 90, 128
Matisse, Henri, 151
mechanization, 66
media, 26, 94, 96
   mass, 20, 46
   new, 105
   see also, intermedia and transmedia
medium(s), 3, 5, 11–12, 18–20, 28, 45–6, 48, 50, 56–7, 63, 65, 78–82, 87, 99–108, 117, 123, 127, 130–31, 141, 143, 145, 149, 168, 190, 192, 201
   see also, post-medium and transmedia
memory, 91, 144, 175, 190–201
Merleau-Ponty, Maurice, 7–8
metaphysics, 7, 37, 39, 41, 43–5, 60, 89, 120, 168, 170, 180, 188
metropolis, 133–5, 140
Meyer, James, 160–61, 163
migration, 26, 28, 151, 162–3
Minimal art, 107
minimalism, 19, 81, 108, 159
modernism, 10–12, 16–19, 33, 47, 57, 71–83, 109
   aesthetic, 72, 77–8, 86
   American, 88
   art-critical, 72
   artistic, 77
   formalist, 5, 18, 48-9, 86, 160
   generic, 72, 82–3, 86, 139
   medium-specific, 72, 78–80, 149
modernity, 17–18, 24–7, 73–6, 135, 137, 141, 175–6, 178–9, 182, 206–8
   super-, 136–7
montage, 55, 62, 197
Montaigne, Michel de, 58
Morris, Robert, 57, 101, 107
   Labyrinth, 101
multiculturalism, 26
multiplicity, 12, 24, 27, 71–2, 76–7, 87, 109, 113, 129–31, 143–5, 176, 189, 191, 200
multitude, 35, 195
museums, 99, 103, 109, 114, 169, 172–3

278

INDEX

Museum of Contemporary Art,
   Zagreb, 18
   Los Angeles, 100, 105
Museum of Modern Art, NY, 19, 63, 88
mysticism, 62, 66

nationalism/nationalization, 26, 28, 35,
   118, 162
   de-, 135, 167
   re-, 135
   see also, transnationalization
naturalism, 9
narrative, 62
nature, 8, 24
Nauman, Bruce, 101
   Corridor, 101
Nazism, 97
negation, 47, 49, 73–5, 77–8, 80, 82–3,
   94, 109, 112, 117, 133–4, 136–7, 208,
   211
neo-classical, 18, 60
neo-Kantian, 10
neo-liberalism, 107, 163
N. E. Thing Co., 57
new, 11, 17–18, 25–6, 47, 52, 56, 62,
   72–4, 83, 136, 138, 170, 179, 185,
   195, 206–9
New Economic Policy, 155
Nietzsche, Friedrich, 7, 24
nihilism, 131
no-time, 173
nominalism, 13, 77, 81–4, 103, 150
non-
   art, 10, 13, 46, 48, 88, 91–3, 201
   place, 112, 133–40, 162, 175, 190
   site, 108–113, 140, 144, 151, 172
   space, 112
Novalis, 41, 44, 60, 64
novel, the, 62

October, 4–5, 101,
O'Doherty, Brian, 139–40
Ono, Yoko, 139, 185
   Instructions for Paintings, 139
   Sky TV, 185
ontology, 3, 8–10, 20, 22, 28, 41–51, 68,
   78–86, 88, 97, 99, 105–6, 109, 117–
   31, 134, 140–4, 149, 159, 163, 180,
   184, 191, 193, 195, 224 n 3,
   historical, 10, 12, 37, 45–6, 48, 73, 108

   of materializations, 28, 48, 108–13,
   117
Opalka, Roman, 87
   1965–/1–infinity, 87
opticality/opticalism, 5, 56

painting, 42, 71, 79–80, 87–9, 92, 94,
   96–7, 99, 102–3, 108–9, 117, 126,
   141
   machine-, 94
   modernist, 5, 10
parataxis, 65
Pascal, Blaise, 58, 178, 182
Peter, Walter, 46
Pennsylvannia State University, 3
percept, 10
perception, 10, 100, 108, 114, 116–7, 131,
   177, 188, 200
performance, 20, 103, 127, 141, 145
periodization, 15–22, 25, 28, 37, 46–8,
   108
phenomenology, 72–3, 89, 105, 145,
   175–6, 179–3, 202–7
249–50 (n 21)
philosophy, 3, 6, 10
   analytical, 7, 54, 57, 126
   of art, 10, 38–9, 43, 45, 126
   of difference, 122
   Eastern, 56
   European, 8, 202
   of the fragment, 60
   French, 8
   Hegelian, 52
   of history, 55, 205
   Kantian, 40, 64
   post-Hegelian, 55, 150
   post-Kantian, 5, 7, 43, 58, 64, 203
   of the subject, 44
   of time, 190
   transcendental, 64
   Western, 152
   see also, history, philosophical
photography, 24, 50, 89–91, 93-4, 103,
   108, 110, 112, 117–9, 121–131, 141,
   143, 144
photo-painting, 93–7
Picasso, Pablo, 153
pictorialism, 50, 94
Pierce, C. S., 127
Piper, Adrian, 57

INDEX

place, 133–40, 162, 175
  see also, non-place
pluralism
  liberal, 5
politics, 8, 23, 44, 118–9, 165, 175–6,
Polke, Sigmar, 87, 89, 94–4
  History of Everything, 87, 94
  The Hunt for the Taliban, 96
  Risk Game, 96
Pollock, Jackson, 46
Pop art, 88
pornography, 91, 123
positivism, 126
  analytical-Hegelian, 7
  Foucauldian, 107
  logical, 7
possibility, 171–3, 176–84, 205, 210
post-
  Adornian, 10
  aesthetic, 33
  architectural, 134, 151
  autonomous, 142, 161, 166
  colonial 26, 29, 163–4
  communist, 195
  conceptual – see, art, postconceptual
  conceptuality, 48, 99
  contemporary, 17
  formalist, 18, 47,
  Hegelian, 10
  medium, 11, 33, 46, 50, 100, 104–5, 118, 227 (n 30), 236 (n13)
  minimalist, 142
  modernism, 4, 16–18, 47–8, 149
  photographic, 24
  Romantic, 90, 107
  structuralism, 33
  studio, 105
pragmatics, 120, 123
Productivism, 156, 160
project, 12–13, 55–6, 58, 68, 168–175
proposition
  speculative, 51–3
psychoanalysis, 4, 11, 171, 184, 192
psychology, 171, 177
Public Culture, 31

Raad, Walid, 13, 28, 31–2, 199
radicalism, 7

Ramsden, Michael, 57, 61
Rancière, Jacques, 7–9
Ranke, Leopold von, 193
Raqs Media Collective, 34
rationalism, 41
rationalization, 154–5, 157
readymade, 97, 141
realism, 18, 128, 150, 193
  Capitalist, 89
reception, 184–90
reductionism, 8
regionalism, 28, 162
Reinhardt, Ad, 61
  '25 Lines', 61
  'Twelve Rules', 61
remembrance, 88
Renaissance, 17–18, 46, 107, 126,
repetition, 66, 82, 105, 158, 197
reproducibility, 118, 127
revolution, 76, 206, 208–10
Reynolds, Ann, 100
  Robert Smithson, 100
rhythm, 184, 188
Richter, Gerhard, 87–94, 96–7
  Atlas, 87–92, 94, 97
  Aunt Marianne, 97
  Forty Years of Painting, 88
  October 18, 1977, 91, 97
  S. mit Kind, 97
  September, 97
  Uncle Rudi, 97
Ricoeur, Paul, 25
Roberts, Jennifer L., 100
  Mirror Travels, 100
de la Rochefoucauld, François, 58
Rodin, 101
  Gates of Hell, 101
Roman Empire, 72
romanticization, 41, 60, 66, 137
Romanticism, 7, 9, 11–13, 39–47, 53, 55–6
  Jena/early German, 7, 10–12, 33, 37–8, 43–6, 58, 62, 65–7, 129, 168–71
  Philosophical, 55–6
Rose, Barbara, 107
  ABC Art, 107
Rosenberg, Harold, 3, 6, 47
Russian Revolution, 20

INDEX

Sartre, Jean-Paul, 86–7
  Critique of Dialectical Reason, 86
Sassen, Saskia, 135
Schaeffer, Jean-Marie, 6–7, 39
Schelling, 7, 45
Schiller, 7, 43–4
  Kallias Letters, 43
  Aesthetic Education, 43
Schlegel, August, 45, 54
Schlegel, Friedrich, 38, 44–5, 53–6, 58–60, 63–4, 67–8, 159
  Athenaeum Fragments, 38, 53, 55, 58, 63, 67–8
  Critical Fragments, 38
Schliermacher, Friedrich, 54, 65
Schopenhauer, Arthur, 7
scepticism, 88, 193, 200
science, 10, 38–40, 46, 61
  political, 5
sculpture, 79–80, 99–106, 108, 117, 141, 145, 149
semiotics, 8, 120–1
sensibility/sensation, 9–10, 39, 76
series, 62–7, 86–7, 94
Serpentine Gallery, 196
Serra, Richard, 101
  Shift, 101
Shaftsbury, Lord, 58, 177
signs, 137–8
singularity, 78, 120, 122, 124, 150–51
site, 108–116, 144, 152, 160, 172
  see also, non-site
Smithson, Robert, 12, 57, 97–117, 139–40, 142–3, 151, 170, 172
  1000 Tons of Asphalt, 110
  Alogon, 109
  Asphalt Rundown, 110
  Broken Circle, 101
  Enantiomorphic Chambers, 109
  Floating Island, 143
  A Heap of Language, 113
  Hypothetical Continent of Lemuria, 113
  Hypothetical Continent in Shells, 113
  Non-sites, 109–10
  Partially Buried Woodshed, 103, 105
  'Some Void Thoughts', 99
  Spiral Jetty, 101, 103, 105–6, 110, 116
  'Spiral Jetty', 114
  A Tour of the Monuments, 110
  A Web of White Gravel, 110
socialism, 18–20
Society for Theoretical Art and Analysis, 57–8
sociologism, 8
sociology, 11, 177
Soja, Edward, 133, 135
space
  absolute, 133–4
  abstract, 133
  any-whatsoever, 149
  art, 27–8, 131, 140
  cultural, 27, 96, 163
  differential, 133–4
  digital, 135
  electronic, 135
  exhibition, 168
  of flows, 134–5, 138, 162, 175
  physical, 164
  project, 168–75
  social 25, 28, 112, 131
  transnational, 28
  see also, place; non-place; nonspace
speculation, 7, 23, 38, 51, 193–5
  see also, proposition, speculative
Spivak, G. C., 26, 192
Stella, Frank, 82, 179
Studio International, 57
subject/subjects, 25, 27, 41–4, 63, 85, 170, 175, 197
  absolute, 25
  social, 163, 191, 193, 195
subjectivity, 8, 41–2, 66, 177, 191–3
subject-position, 23
subject-structure, 194
surrealism, 16, 19, 46, 55, 81
system, 13, 60
  see also, anti-system

Tatlin, Vladimir, 153–4, 157
  Selection of Materials, 154
TDR, 31
techné, 78–81, 120, 165,
technology, 12, 20, 24, 27, 46, 117–20, 123–6, 129, 134, 154, 156, 162, 166, 172, 184–6,
television, 119, 123, 125, 185
temporality/temporalization, 9–12, 17, 72–7, 90, 124, 136, 138, 169–70, 175–211

INDEX

historical, 22–4, 28, 47, 53, 91, 119
see also, time
testimony, 190–91, 196–201
textualization, 134, 136–40, 151
theology, 24, 124, 130
theory, 11
   cultural, 8
   photographic, 5
   political, 11
Tillmans, Wolfgang, 90
   If One Thing Matters, 91
time, 130, 204
   cosmological, 73
   historical, 18, 21–2, 72–3, 207–8
   philosophy of, 2–3
   physical, 73
   see also, temporality
timelessness, 140, 175
totality/totalization, 9, 22, 47, 50, 53, 60, 64–5, 80, 91, 94, 118, 123, 187
tradition, 24, 73
transcategoriality, 11–12, 99–100, 105, 108, 110, 114, 145
transcultural, 163, 167
transdisciplinarity, 11–12
translation, 163–4
transmedia, 11, 46, 50, 118
transnationality/transnationalization, 15, 21, 26–8, 33–5, 118, 134–5, 151, 162–8, 191, 194–5
truth, 9, 44, 47

urban studies, 11
urbanism/urbanization, 75, 134, 151
unity, 63, 77, 112, 116, 118, 131, 191
   collective, 121–3
   conceptual, 52
   disjunctive, 22, 25
   distributive, 11–12, 25, 48, 50, 86, 120–25, 143
   historical, 122
utopia, 23, 113, 165, 178–9, 194

value/value-form, 35, 85, 128, 131–4, 184, 194, 234 n 38
   cult-, 92–3
   educational-, 92–3
   exhibition-, 93, 162
   use-, 162
Vatamanu, Mona and Florin Tudor, 209
   Long Live and Thrive Capitalism, 209
Venice Biennale, 30, 100, 162
video, 8, 28–9, 103, 108, 123, 125, 172, 185, 188–9, 196, 198
virtuality, 113
visual culture, 4–5, 46
visualizations, 129–31
Vital, Joachim, 1

Wagner, Richard, 80
Wall, Jeff, 5, 46, 127, 142, 144, 160–61, 166
Warhol, Andy, 179, 181
Weber, Max, 155
Weiner, Lawrence, 54, 61
   Statements, 54, 61
Wheeler, Dennis, 112, 114
When Attitudes Become Form, 763
Whiteread, Rachel, 149
   House, 149
Wilde, Oscar, 46
Williams, Raymond, 16, 180, 183
   Keywords, 16
Wollheim, Richard, 46
world-mediation, 88–91, 94
World Trade Organization, 210
writing, 110
Wu Ming, 35

Yates, Francis, 193
   The Art of Memory, 193
Young, La Monte, 139

www.ingramcontent.com/pod-product-compliance
Lightning Source LLC
Chambersburg PA
CBHW031610210526
45464CB00004B/1516